CREATING RUSSOPHOBIA

CREATING RUSSOPHOBIA

From the Great Religious Schism to Anti-Putin Hysteria

by

GUY METTAN

Clarity Press, Inc

© 2017 Guy Mettan
ISBN: 978-0-9978965-2-7
EBOOK ISBN: 978-0-9978965-5-8

In-house editor: Diana G. Collier
Cover: R. Jordan P. Santos
Cover image: The ex-scarecrow of Europe / J.S. Pughe

ALL RIGHTS RESERVED: Except for purposes of review, this book may not be copied, or stored in any information retrieval system, in whole or in part, without permission in writing from the publishers.

Library of Congress Cataloging-in-Publication Data

Names: Mettan, Guy, author.
Title: Creating Russophobia : from the Great Religious Schism to anti-Putin
   hysteria / by Guy Mettan.
Other titles: Russie-Occident. English
Description: Atlanta, GA : Clarity Press, Inc., 2017. | Includes
   bibliographical references and index.
Identifiers: LCCN 2017006888 (print) | LCCN 2017010567 (ebook) | ISBN
   9780997896558 | ISBN 9780997896527 (alkaline paper)
Subjects: LCSH: Russia--Foreign public opinion, European--History. |
   Russia--Foreign public opinion, American--History. | Soviet Union--Foreign
   public opinion--History. | Russia--Relations--Western countries. | Western
   countries--Relations--Russia. | Soviet Union--Relations--Western
   countries. | Western countries--Relations--Soviet Union. | Fear--Political
   aspects--Western countries--History. | Public opinion--Western
   countries--History.
Classification: LCC D34.R9 (ebook) | LCC D34.R9 M4813 2017 (print) | DDC
   303.48/24701821--dc23

LC record available at https://lccn.loc.gov/2017006888

Printed and bound in Great Britain by Marston Book Services Ltd, Oxfordshire

Clarity Press, Inc.
2625 Piedmont Rd. NE, Ste. 56
Atlanta, GA. 30324 , USA
http://www.claritypress.com

TABLE OF CONTENTS

FOREWORD: Russophobia or Russo-madness? / 11

    Learning from Sarajevo / 13
    Ditching Solzhenitsyn, Defender of Russia / 15
    The Yeltsin Pillage / 16
    Breaching the Wall of Historical Prejudice / 17

PART I
THE POWER OF PREJUDICE

Chapter 1: Understanding Russia / 23

    Neither Same nor Other / 26
    Forgive and Forget for France and Germany; Not for Russia / 29
    Putin-Versteher? Verboten! / 30
    Navigating the Russophiles / 31
    "I love Russia but not Putin" / 32
    Russophobia is a State of Mind / 33
    Congress Kicks In Against Russia / 35
    Self-hating Russians? / 36

Chapter 2: The Pavlovian Russophobic Reflex / 39

    The Überlingen Crash (2002) / 41
    The Beslan Hostage-Taking (2004) / 44
    115 Atlanticists Against Putin / 50
    What Really Happened in Beslan / 53
    The Second Ossetia War (2008) / 58
    The Sochi Olympic Games (2014) / 64

Chapter 3: Media Blinders on Ukraine / 72

    The Anti-Russian Vulgate / 74
    No Questions for Victoria Nuland / 76
    Crimeans Reaffirm Their 1991 Referendum / 80
    Malaysian Flight MH17 / 81
    Alternative Views on NATO Expansion / 82
    One-Track Media Thinking / 86
    Unanswered Questions / 88
    The Unbearable Notion of a Worthy Critical Other / 97

PART II
A SHORT HISTORY OF RUSSOPHOBIA

Chapter 4: A War of Religion since Charlemagne / 100

    Byzantium, City of Light, Beats Rome in Ruins / 104
    Religion as Eighth-Century Soft Power / 106
    Constantinople, Not Rome, Was Ascendant / 107
    The *Filioque* Quarrel Created by Charlemagne / 109
    The Theory of the Two Swords, Papal and Imperial / 111
    The Fraudulent Donation of Constantine and the
        Fight for Papal Supremacy / 113
    Westerners Reappraise the Trinity / 115
    Democratic Easterners versus Absolutist Westerners / 116
    Two Diverted Crusades: 1204 and 2003 / 118
    A Schism Made in the West / 120
    The Invention of Caesaropopery and Byzantinism / 121
    The European Crusades against Russian Orthodoxy / 122
    The Czar and the Roman Germanic Emperor / 124
    The Gothic Churches Divide Europe in Two / 127
    A Thousand-Year Conflict Still Virulent / 131
    Historical Ingratitude towards Byzantium and Russia / 132
    Lies Pervade Western Historiography / 135

Chapter 5: French Russophobia and the Myth of Eastern
        Despotism / 137

  Peter the Great's Forged Testament and the
        Myth of Expansionism / 139
  The First Travelers Launch the Notion of
        Russian Barbarity / 142
  Can There Be a Tyranny with Consenting Subjects? / 145
  Reconceptualizing Despotism / 148
  From the Quarrel of the Ancients and the Moderns
        to the Notion of Progress / 149
  Leibniz and Voltaire as Adepts of Russian Enlightened
        Despotism / 151
  Montesquieu and the Absence of Russian
        Counter-Powers / 153
  French Clichés versus Japanese Objectivity / 155
  The First Liberal Theories and Oriental Despotism / 157
  Tocqueville and the Bible of Russophobia according
        to Custine / 159
  The Rise of Socialism and the Russian Commune / 162
  Individual Freedom versus the Russian Commune / 165
  Final Synthesis: Amendable Russia and Redeemable
        Backwardness / 166
  The Theory of the Cultural Gradient / 171

Chapter 6: English Russophobia: The Obsession with Empire / 176

  Suddenly after 1815, Russia Becomes a Threat / 178
  The Evolution of English Russophobia / 181
  Greek Independence and the Polish Revolt / 184
  The British Press Enflames Public Opinion / 186
  Arming the Circassians / 188
  The Great Game and the Struggle for Asia / 189
  The Orient Issue as Catalyst for the Crimean War / 192
  The Fragility of the British Empire / 193
  Dracula, an Imperialist and Russophobic Novel / 196
  "An Elephant Does Not Fight with a Whale" / 199

FOREWORD

RUSSOPHOBIA OR RUSSO-MADNESS?

> *"Today's enlightened western society (the one that makes the law) is in fact hardly tolerant, especially when it is contested; it is entirely cast in a rigid mold of conventional ideas. Admittedly, to fight contradictors, it does not wield a bludgeon, but uses calumny and, to stifle them, its financial power. Try then to work your way through the tracery of prejudice and tendentious allegations in some bright [American] newspaper with a national audience!"*
> —Aleksandr Solzhenitsyn[1]

This book is at once the fruit of a long professional and personal experience and the consequence of the Ukrainian crisis in 2014.

From the very first weeks of my journalistic internship at *Journal de Genève*, a once prestigious but now defunct liberal newspaper, I learnt the meaning of the double standards western media and western statesmen apply when they pass judgment on countries or political regimes they do not like. I had hardly settled down at my desk when a meeting of the World Anticommunist League was held in Geneva sometime during the spring of 1980. Balmy weather was forecast that weekend and none of the resident pen pushers were eager to go and cover the meeting. So I was sent.

Gathered together there was the darnedest posse of dictators and butchers of the planet: Augusto Pinochet emissaries, Argentinian generals, and Korean, Taiwanese, and other representatives of then proliferating Asian dictatorships. The brows of these dignitaries, ill at ease in their civilian garb, eyes hidden behind dark glasses as in B movies, seemed to me to be still bearing the imprints of their just discarded kepis. I went back to the paper, faithfully summed up what I had seen and what had been said, without any supervision, of course, as it was Sunday.

What a commotion on Monday morning! I was summoned to the office of the editor in chief to face an official warning. I had made the mistake of not knowing that one of the newspaper's main shareholders was the Swiss representative of the League and that discrimination was of the essence. Not all dictatorships were alike. Some were good, those of pro-western generals, and some bad, those in Russia and Eastern Europe. You did not say "these are dictators who imprison their opponents and torture their political prisoners" but "these are defenders of the Free World which they protect against the communist infection." Lesson number one, which I was never to forget.

A few years later, on November 19, 1985, the first Reagan-Gorbachev summit took place in Geneva. It was the first time since the Vietnam War, the intrusion of the Red Army into Afghanistan, the Euro missile crisis, and the launch of Ronald Reagan's Strategic Defense Initiative in March 1983, that the leaders of East and West were meeting. It was also the first time the Kremlin came up with a youngish leader flanked by an attractive spouse who rapidly made the covers of the tabloids and quickly fell for that illusory glory. It was on my 29th birthday and I still remember vividly the huge hope but also the feeling of inconsistency that meeting had fostered in me. Two blocs were clashing and the more rigid of the two was not the obvious one.

The Russian was the more pliant, the more apt to make concessions and adapt his doctrine to achieve an honorable peace, albeit reluctantly, not the American. For him, a treaty was a treaty.

He hadn't understood that for a Westerner, an agreement is but an interim step and that the Rule of Law western jurists boast of is a misuse of language: it is neither an immutable Rule, since it has no static, immutable essence, nor is it a steadfast and straight Law, since it keeps evolving in tortuous, unpredictable ways as interests, lobbies and fleeting intellectual fashions dictate. In accordance with the Anglo-Saxon spirit, Law is less a matter of principles than an evolution of jurisprudence.

For the West, Law thus is a process, valid today but obsolete tomorrow. It is a useful means of making war and conquering new territories in non-military ways, and seldom an end in itself, working rather according to the saying that "everything that is mine is mine and everything that is yours is negotiable." Gorbachev never learned that lesson and in 1991, he repeated the same error when he pulled the Soviet troops out of Eastern Europe in exchange for a verbal agreement that NATO would not enter it. A few years later, all of Eastern Europe had fallen into the arms of NATO, which was intervening even in Georgia and in Afghanistan, thousands of miles away from the North Atlantic. I concluded from all that, that as the saying goes, good intentions never make for good policy. Lesson number two.

Learning from Sarajevo

Four years after the fall of the Berlin Wall, in September 1993, as editor in chief of *Tribune de Genève,* I found myself in Sarajevo with a delegation of international journalists who had come to support the independence of the Bosnian *Oslobodjenje* newspaper threatened by the Serbs. It was a time when the United States and the European Union cited the right of peoples to self-determination with a view to breaking down existing borders and encouraged secession of the various peoples of Yugoslavia without even consulting them. Border inviolability had yet to enter the Western vocabulary and, on the contrary, redrawing the map of Central Europe all over again, from Chechnya to Macedonia, by breaking up a federation of nations that had until then lived under career plans. And once Solzhenitsyn had left the United States to go back to Russia and defend his humiliated, demoralized motherland that was being sold at auction, raising his voice against the Russian "Westernizers" and pluralist liberals who denied the interests of Russia to better revel in the troughs of capitalism, he became a marked man, an outdated, senile writer, even though he himself had not changed in the least, denouncing with the same vigor the defects of market totalitarianism as those of communist totalitarianism.

He was booed, despised, his name was dragged through the mud for his choices, often by the very people who had praised his first fights. Despite that, against all odds, against the most powerful powers that were trying to dissuade him, Solzhenitsyn defended his but one and only cause, that of Russia. He was not forgiven for having turned his pen against that West that had welcomed him and felt it was owed eternal gratitude. A dissident today, a dissident wherever truth compelled, such was his motto. This deserves to be remembered.

The Yeltsin Pillage

Very soon, I was beset by other doubts. At the beginning of the Yeltsin years, the western press applauded, in 1993, at the sight of Russian armored vehicles shooting against the legal parliament of Russia. They expressed no dismay when great physicists had to abandon their laboratories to sell hamburgers at McDonald's because they were no longer able to pay the rent. Western experts began to excuse Islamic terrorists who made war against the Russians in Chechnya and massacred innocent people in Russian theaters and schools, even though they abominated similar terrorist acts against the twin towers in New York and on western interests in the East. Nor when our media considered it a good idea to heap praise on the Russian oligarchs who, as soon as they had plundered the riches of their country, sold them to their foreign competitors in the name of democracy and trade freedom to buy themselves an English football club, a ticket for State presidency or a seat of prime minister in Ukraine (as did Ms. Yulia Timoshenko).

Russia and the West deserve better than these rash judgments and caricatures of news. So, in early 2014, when the Maidan Square incidents in Ukraine degenerated into a coup and finally into civil war, it had become impossible for me to remain silent and watch without a reaction the new explosion of anti-Russian hysteria that had, once again, taken over the western media. The nauseating explanations by prosecutorial journalism that justified its attacks by allegations of Russian media "propaganda" could not remain unanswered.

Breaching the Wall of Historical Prejudice

So it was with the hope of breaking down or at least lowering somewhat this wall of prejudice that I undertook the writing of this book and delved into the long, complex but fascinating history of the distorted images and biased perceptions Westerners have accumulated on Russia in the course of centuries, and more precisely since Charlemagne broke away from Byzantium.

The insane extent of Russophobia today, the "Russo-madness" that seems to have caught hold of western chancelleries and newsrooms, is not an inevitability, but reflects a conscious choice. This is what the present work intends to demonstrate, a work which, in fact, has but one ambition: convincing readers that there is no need to hate Russia.

Let us specify as well—but isn't it obvious?—that this book in no way proceeds from any anti-Western sentiment. Exposing what drives the hatred of Russia does not imply discarding the values of democracy, freedom and human rights that the West has been promoting ever since the French Revolution, and neither does it mean swooning over President Putin's Russia. Criticizing the West's most dubious attitudes is not exonerating Russia of her faults.

My approach thus has nothing to do with an anti-American or anti-European pamphlet which would reproduce, only topsy-turvy, the binary vision the media loves so much and which would consist a country that is at least as pretty. In a parody mode, a vision thus gradually takes shape, at once ironical and synthetic, of the deeply ambivalent relations binding Europe to Russia and vice versa.

I am very well aware that this is a taboo matter, seldom studied as such in European universities. Several authors quoted in this book actually told me they had to stop their research as their funding was cut off. I am approaching this work in a journalistic manner, not as an academic study led by a history professor holding a prestigious university chair. The aim has been to test new hypotheses and to open new ways of thinking, not to draw up an academic treatise.

I thus accept the risk of being confronted with pitiless criticism from scholars, who will question every point of detail while criticizing "hodgepodge" and unavoidable "generalizations of a too-wide encompassing approach." I will also have to confront ideologues who will try to prove by every possible means that Putin is a noisome tyrant and Russia an expansionist empire, and who are pretending to react to "Russian provocations and propaganda."

But I believe I have answered those objections by avoiding those that I reproach Russophobes for, i.e. selection of facts or opinions that confirm a thesis and discarding or ignoring whatever could invalidate it. Close reading will show that such objections are groundless. Russophobic criticisms are very often disconnected from the effective behavior and actual actions of Russia, which proves that they are anchored very deep in the Western collective subconscious. The long, transnational history of Russophobia actually supports this hypothesis. It was necessary to delve into the past to take apart the Russophobes' subtlest thesis according to which the West was merely reacting to the visceral anti-Western or anti-American orientation of Russian society and power.

Besides, I have compared each of the chosen events to the criticisms or reactions generated by a similar event in a western country. I have also presented the analysis made of it by impartial western experts, an analysis systematically discarded by the media and its Russophobic experts. And finally, in cases where actual accountability is still difficult to establish, as in the case of

Ukraine, I simply show how vexing questions are always asked of Russia but avoided when the West could be implicated. All of this shows that, over the same behavior, Russia is systematically denigrated whereas the West is spared. So this is indeed a form of information warfare, initiated and nurtured by the West, which we have been witnessing for over a thousand years, a hostility naturally prolonged by the vigor of Russian reactions. (There is no war without at least two fighters.)

In fact, Russophobia, contrary to French Anglophobia and Germanophobia, is a phenomenon that, though different of course, resembles anti-Semitism or Islamophobia. Like anti-Semitism and Islamophobia, it is not a transitory phenomenon linked to specific historical events; it exists first in the head of the one who looks, not in the victim's alleged behavior or characteristics. Like anti-Semitism, Russophobia is a way of turning specific pseudo-facts into essential, one-dimensional values, barbarity, despotism and expansionism in the Russian case in order to justify stigmatization and ostracism.

Russophobia also possesses a religious foundation and is not limited in time. It has spread over centuries, reappearing endlessly whenever chance circumstances allow. It passes away here to be reborn there, fades away for generations before being resurgent for some geopolitical reason. And sometimes it disappears entirely to be replaced by unexpected sympathy and admiration. Then, seemingly thanks to a new incident, a misinterpreted intention, a tactless declaration, a new urban legend, or a border conflict, it flares up all over again. In fine, as for anti-Semitism, anti-Islamism and anti-Americanism, Russophobia possesses an undeniable geopolitical component.

Multifaceted, transcultural, protean, multi-ethnic, trans-historical, Russophobia is, however, always linked to the Catholic or Protestant Northern hemisphere. The peoples of Asia, Africa or South America have never been Russophobes. The Chinese and the Japanese have border problems with Russia over which they sometimes went to war, but they are not Russophobic and have never come up with any discourse of this type.

On the other hand, the United States, which has a common border with Russia and has never declared war against her and actually was allied to her during two world wars has developed a phobia of the Russian State that has no equivalent in modern history. We also wanted to explore this phenomenon, one that needs to be developed, elaborated and carried further along, to cut the Gordian knot of tensions that perturb the future of the entirety of Western civilization.

It is impossible for me to thank all those who have helped carry out this work. But I must express my gratitude to my original publisher, Serge de Pahlen, who took the subject very much to heart and provided me with notes and documents, as well as to the authors who have been with me along the way. I am thinking in particular of the pioneers of studies on western "anti-Russianism" who it is no coincidence are almost all American or British. If Anglo-Saxons have pushed Russophobia to heights of sophistication and efficiency, they have also analyzed and denounced it without concession in very rigorous academic works. Tribute must be paid to them.

I thus contracted outstanding debts with Argentinian Ezequiel Adamovski, John Howes Gleason, Troy Paddock, Andrei Tsygankov, Marshall Poe, Stephen Cohen, Felicitas Macgilchrist, Raymond Taras, Iver Neumann and Paul Sanders, who have published fascinating research papers on the various forms of Russophobia.[4]

Closer to me, Slobodan and Marko Despot, Eric Hoesli, Gabriel Galice and Georges Nivat have given me useful advice or pertinent criticism. *Le Monde diplomatique*, too, has been very useful, as have Jacques Sapir's always well-informed blog and Vineyard Saker's more antiauthoritarian website.

Finally, I dedicate this book to all my fellow journalists who, in spite of the difficulties inherent in their trade, keep on working as their conscience demands and as circumstances allow. May the memory of the 110 journalists killed in 2015[5] and of the 17 victims of the *Charlie Hebdo* attacks make us realize that threats against freedom of expression do not always come from an outside enemy but also surge from the murkiest depths of ourselves.

PART I

THE POWER OF PREJUDICE

Neither group was entirely convincing. Neither the Occidentalists, reduced to brownnosing a West that rejects them most of the time, nor the Slavophiles and their Eurasian successors, condemned to hopelessly resurrect the myth of a Slavonic soul untouched by external impurities, can win, for the good reason that they are hemiplegic: Russia is neither Europe nor Asia. Rather, she is *both Europe and Asia.*

If Russia is neither in the West nor in Asia, is it a reason to detest her and present her constantly, as most Western journalists and "experts" do, as a fiend thriving on barbarity, tyranny, reaction, and expansionism? No, of course not, you will say. It is not because Russia is difficult to understand that she must be caricatured and interpreted through the distorting mirror of clichés, biases and propaganda all the more pernicious as it does not want to admit to being such.

And yet, this is what happens, every day, in most embassy chancelleries, newspaper editorial offices and university lecture halls of the Western world.

Why? How to explain this acrimony and why does it target Russia? After all, Westerners, full of themselves though they are, have never dared depict China with so many prejudices. Or even the Islamic Orient that they have much mistreated and caricatured as a hostile "Other."

This is because Russia, unlike China, Mesopotamia or Egypt, is not a civilization thousands of years old that invented writing long before the West. Neither was it the birthplace of the Christ and of the Bible. Ergo Russia, a vast, cold and frozen, barren and wild land, is open to the accusation of barbarity.

Neither Same nor Other

Another common trap: deceptive resemblance. As Mariusz Wilk, a Polish writer who has been living in the Russian Great North for the past twenty-five years, puts it, "nothing is more misleading than this apparent resemblance" with European countries.[3]

It was the scale that wasn't the same, the religious rite a little different, the extravagant State organization ... No people enjoyed such a bad reputation as the Russians, it was observed. For no people looked so alike those Europeans without being of them. No one in the West, neither in the 16th century nor later, ever took the trouble of first understanding Russian reality from the inside.

So it is that the Europeans, for the past five centuries, have but repeated the judgments and representations of the first European travelers in the 15th and 16th centuries, without bothering to revise clichés or correct errors of interpretation.[4] Wilk points out that even a writer-traveler as experienced as his compatriot, Ryszard Kapuscinski, made that mistake.[5] When he recounted his remembrances while at the heart of the Soviet Imperium, from 1939 to 1989, Kapuscinski could not avoid straying into the tourist tale, blowing up some details excessively while ignoring those that did not fit his views.

Let us quote some of those clichés on Russian "barbarity" inherited from tales of those early travelers and still tirelessly recycled by journalists and experts in this, the 21st century, despite the end of communism a quarter century ago.

The Russians, so it goes, are intrinsically violent and brutal because they massacre, deport or torture their ethnic and religious minorities, as they did during the last two Chechnya wars.

It is true that the Russians, indeed like all the other nations, are not soft-hearted when they feel threatened. But if we take into account the wake of devastation across seven formerly sovereign states that has resulted from the actions of the Americans and NATO, the innocent prisoners tortured in Guantánamo and throughout the Middle East, the civilian populations massacred by killer drones and shooting errors in Somalia, Afghanistan, Iraq, Libya and Syria in the last quarter century, won't we come to a total far superior to whatever devastation the Russians might have committed in Grozny—which they then went on to rebuild? Why this deafening silence on the one side and those howling sirens on the other?

Transportation of peoples by Stalin to the arid deserts of Central Asia was an atrocious crime, undoubtedly. But did the deportation of 28 million Africans by the Spaniards, the Portuguese, the French and the English exactly look like pleasure cruises organized by generous tour-operators?[6] What about the dispossession and near eradication of the native populations in the Americas? The West has never bothered to present formal excuses for those crimes against humanity.

Western journalists who keep harping on Russian actions never contextualize them against this sorry record when they denounce the Russians' alleged visceral expansionism. The Russian empire was not conquered with caviar and sweetness, and that's a fact. But did the bullets of Colts and machine guns that made minced meat of the Indians in America, Africans in the Congo and in Sudan, and the aboriginals in Australia sweetly whistle past the ears of those decimated populations? The fate of millions of Russian serfs was not enviable; this rightly generated much indignation. But Tsar Alexander II freed them in 1861 without a bitter civil war that divided the country. Was the fate of Africans deported to America as slaves by the tens of millions until 1865 really any better? Or the racial apartheid (termed segregation) that followed? Didn't it take another century, until Martin Luther King, for legal and systemic racial discrimination to be corrected in the United States, while even now its black population suffers hugely disproportionately rates of incarceration?

In 1991, the disappearance of the Soviet empire, a vestige of Russian colonialism of past centuries, did not take place without pain. But which colonial European power successfully and voluntarily divested itself of its empire? How many Congolese were massacred by the Belgians? How many Malagasy and Algerians by the French? How many Kenyan Mau-Mau and Indian *sepoys* by British troops? And what about the extermination by English colonists of the black aboriginals of Tasmania who were massacred to the last man, woman and child in 1830?[7] Was *gégène* (electroshock) torture by the French army in the Algerian *bled*, twenty years after Stalin's purges, part of the ideals of the French *mission civilisatrice*? In the last five years alone, France has brutally bombed thousands of civilian men, women, and children in the following six countries: Libya, Syria, Chad, Ivory Coast, Mali and Central African Republic.

Forgive and Forget for France and Germany; Not for Russia

And yet, Russia is still ceaselessly reproached for Stalin's crimes while those of the French, past and present, are not mentioned and the Germans have been pardoned for the horrors of Nazism. More significantly, it is willfully forgotten that Russia was the only empire in history to withdraw from her vassal nations without wars leading to their eviction. Within a few months, in 1991, fifteen countries found themselves free and independent. Who has done better?

There has been much indignation over Moscow's will to protect Russian-speaking populations of Transnistria and of the Ossetian and Abkhazian minorities. This has been portrayed as an attempt to revive past grandeur. But who, in Europe, has been concerned about the massacre of Abkhazians and Ossetians by the Georgians and the risk of Transnistria Russians being cut up alive by the Moldovans? Who protected the Armenians in Baku and Nagorno-Karabakh from bloody ethnic cleansing? Helping nations "threatened by the Russians" is viewed as a noble undertaking. But when the very same states in turn massacre their own minorities or maintain them in scandalous discriminatory conditions, as is the case in Baltic countries, do they not also warrant reproof?

The same stance is taken in relation to organized crime, as noted by a French observer:[8]

> Organized crime in Italy causes serious environmental damage with the trafficking of garbage by the Napolitano Camorra, or deaths in Europe with the Calabria N'drangheta. But, we are told, it's the Russian mafia that's the most dangerous! Roberto Saviano, a journalist author

of *Gomorra*, is under a death threat but nobody in his right mind thinks of accusing the Italian government. On the other hand, the assassination of Russian journalists such as Anna Politkovskaya or humanitarians like Natalia Estemirova, killed on July 15, 2009 in Chechnya, is blamed on the Kremlin.

Are we balanced when we talk about Russia?

This is the kind of question we should ask ourselves ceaselessly. Not to excuse the Russians, but to contextualize Russian actions against those of others, which reveals that the Russians are like us, neither better nor worse. We agree with all others that a crime cannot be justified by another crime, but to comprehend and bear in mind one's own misdeeds before criticizing one's neighbor never hurts. It is because the West has always projected its own turpitudes onto Russia without ever acknowledging these or perhaps without even being aware that this is the case, that it has never called its clichés and biased reading of Russia into question. Lacking the will to understand, the West has "measured" Russia by its own scale. Workaday Russophobia has become an analytical grid, a cushion of laziness all the more comfortable in that it ensures those that indulge in it substantial academic or journalistic acceptance, and even advantages. What researcher, what journalist in the West could have made a career of denouncing clichés and painting a more honest picture of Russia?

Putin-Versteher? **Verboten!**

That researcher, that journalist, would have taken an insane risk. In current circumstances, in the wake of a Ukrainian crisis over which the most hysterical defenders of the "West" have lost all common sense, to be taken for a friend of the Russian cause, a *Putin-Versteher* as the Germans phrase it, is enough to disqualify you without any hope of remission. The simple fact of trying to understand what provoked the Russian reaction and listening to the other side *audiatur et altera pars* is deemed an unforgivable fault by most editorialists, intellectuals and politicians who take up the cause against Russia every time they speak.

What about the primary journalistic credo of balance, if not objectivity? As if one could not present the Ukrainean and Russian perspective at one and the same time? As if, in the Middle East crisis, one could not present both pro-Israeli and pro-Palestinian positions? Why should it be compulsory to choose one party against another unless journalism is being replaced by propaganda? Other than when thinking in purely religious terms, the good guys on one side, the wretched of the earth on the other, there is no reason, in those specific cases, to privilege one camp in order to crush the other. We are not, as was the case during the war against Nazism, in a conflict in which one of the parties would deny the humanity of the others and strive for their extermination, or even in a war of ethnic cleansing as was the case in the 1990s in Yugoslavia.

If you think, for example, that the State of Israel has as much right to exist as an independent Palestinian State, why persist in denying Ukrainians in the East and the South the right to choose their future in the same way as West Ukrainians? As soon as their language and existence were called into question, as was the case after the seizure of power that followed the Maidan Square demonstrations, didn't the Ukrainians of the East have the right to demand independence, in the same way as the Slovaks of Czechoslovakia in 1993? Or the Kosovars in 2008?[9]

Navigating the Russophiles

Paradoxically, another difficulty inherent in the study of Russophobia comes from the risk of losing the favor of Russophiles and of the Russians themselves. The Russians, the same as any other people, do not like to learn that they are detested. And Russophiles share the same feeling.

From Voltaire to de Gaulle, via the discoverers of the treasures of Russian literature in the second half of the 19th after supporting the United States in their fight against terrorism after the 9/11 attacks of 2001, Western Russophobes mobilized all the fireworks of their soft power to transform Putin into a new Antichrist. From an ally in the fight against terrorism, the Russian president became persona non grata because he had had the temerity to oppose the invasion of Iraq and the takeover bid on the Russian oil fields that American oil companies were planning to annex by acquiring at bargain price the Yukos Company, that its boss, Mikhail Khodorkovsky, wanted to sell to them.

Russophobia can also be independent of any purported negative behavior of Russia. Waves of hostility greeted the Sochi Games for which Russia made gigantic efforts to welcome her foreign guests, as we will discuss below. Russophobes' tactics consist in turning anything good to negative account, twisting declarations, deforming reality, as was seen during the Ukrainian crisis, during which the mainstream western media kept announcing an invasion of Donbass by the Russian army, which never materialized.

Who are the Russophobes and what are their motivations? First of all, detractors of Russia do not speak with a single voice and are far from representing a united and unanimous nexus that would conspire against Russia and her president morning, noon and night. Here as elsewhere, one must be wary of generalizations. So it would be wrong to think that all Americans are Russophobes and all Russians Russophiles. If the most determined detractors of Russia are to be found in the United States, it is also there that the most skeptical critics of Russophobia such as the esteemed scholar Stephen J. Cohen, former Assistant Treasury Secretary Paul Craig Roberts, and former Congressional representative from Texas and Presidential candidate, Ron Paul, can be found.

"Russophobology" merits becoming a full-fledged science in the United States and in Britain. Indeed, there are practically no serious studies of Russophobia in continental Europe. Yet it must be stressed that there exist in the United States and in Britain soldiers, entrepreneurs, academics and editorialists who are neither anti-Russian nor pro-Russian, but simply realists who take note of the right of Russia to exist and defend her interests, just as their own countries defend theirs, and who consider it perfectly counterproductive if not suicidal to go and wage war in Ukraine, which is clearly not a part of their security zone or even of their zone of influence. In 2016 they were joined by President-elect Donald Trump, which only fanned the anti-Russia hysteria.

Congress Kicks In Against Russia

If the main American newspapers have nine articles out of ten criticizing Russia and open their columns to the apostles of Russia bashing, at least they still have one for those who think differently. Same thing with the think tanks, most of which, but not all, serve the interests of anti-Russian lobbies. And if in the American House of Chamber of Representatives 400 members voted for a bellicose law against Russia, allegedly to defend the new Ukrainian regime, it is also there that ten courageous members found that disposition inept and irresponsible.

Faithful to that high conception of freedom, Texas Republican Representative Ron Paul thus denounced the vote of Resolution H.J. 78 condemning Russia as "one of the worst legislative acts ever voted by Congress" and as an action likely to trigger a war as stupid and bloody as the 2003 war in Iraq. The resolution "accuses Russia of having invaded Ukraine without any proof and reproaches the inhabitants of Donetsk and Luhansk for holding fraudulent and illegal elections in November as if the free determination of peoples was not a recognized human right."

Resolution H.J. 78 demands "the withdrawal of Russian troops from Ukraine though there is no proof that they are there," and accuses the pro-Russian separatist forces of shooting down the Malaysian Airlines plane despite the fact that the "first preliminary report presents no element in favor of the thesis of a surface-to-air missile of that origin." The resolution passed overwhelmingly despite the opposition of ten representatives, five Democrats and five Republicans.[12]

Europe is much more timorous and ambiguous. It takes

disciplinary action while pretending to regret it. It is only very far to the Left and to the Right that dissident voices are found that dare proclaim that Europe erred in encouraging the coup against the legal power in Ukraine and the split within the country between pro-Westerners and pro-Russians.

Contrary to what many people think, there is no American "plot" against Russia. Nor is there a Russian plot against the United States. Plots are secret by definition. With the Americans as with the Russians, everything is occurring in plain view. On both sides, propaganda and official declarations are available. It only takes the will and patience to read them, and to seek out the supporting facts or lack thereof.

Henceforth, conspiracy theses collapse, on both sides. Russophobes have tried often to discredit the Russophiles by branding them as "conspiracy theorists." Let them be warned: I see no anti-Russian plot on the horizon, only a flock of sheep that all bleat at the same time, on a wave of herd behavior that deprives them of their critical faculties.

Self-Hating Russians?

As for the Russians, however paradoxical this may sound, and despite their touchy patriotism, there is also a far from negligible portion of zealous Russophobes who seem to dislike their own country and spend their time denigrating it. They are particularly numerous in the ranks of the Westernizers. But not only. Contrary to western prejudice, there are no fiercer critics of Russia than the Russians themselves. An entire book could be written on Russian Russophobia…

This is so true that the coining of the word 'Russophobia' is traditionally attributed to the Slavophile poet Fyodor Tyutchev, who in 1867 wrote in a letter to his daughter that "it is possible to present an analysis of the modern phenomenon that becomes increasingly pathological. It is the Russophobia of some Russians who are otherwise highly respected." Poor Tyutchev, the very first Russophobes were indeed Russian!

It is obvious from the two quotations heading this chapter that Russian humor vouches for this permanent self-criticism. With their devastating sense of self-derision, the Russians know very well how to express the ambiguous way "the West and they themselves! look at Russia" through very meaningful jokes.

This tendency is found also in the peculiar way Russians vote with their feet: as soon as they have a little money, the Russians massively rush to hotels in Turkey, all expenses paid, or, if they are wealthier, to their yachts on the Azure Coast or St. Barts, as it wouldn't occur to them to go on holiday in Irkutsk or in the Altai Mountains, whose beauty is every bit as striking and exotic as the Rocky Mountains. For a good European, there are loads of places, sceneries and peoples whose very names are invitations to dream—Abakan, Ulan-Ude, Petropavlovsk, Novy Urengoy—when the names of those unknown cities appear on flight monitors at the airport. There are a hundred towns, fifty rivers and twenty provinces in Russia I would like to pace up and down, and to heck with potholes on the pavements![13]

Siberia, along with the Amazon, represents indeed the last frontier of the planet, the last virgin spread of land where imagination and nature can deploy themselves without limit. For the one who experiences it once, Siberia is not a land of exile, but triggers a desire for discovery and symbolic, if not physical, appropriation. But for a Russian from Moscow or Saint Petersburg, this idea is utterly surrealistic, harebrained, as disdain for the province prevails over everything else. Only Moscow and Saint Petersburg find favor in their eyes. The fierce Far West is long dead, buried by the totalitarian marketing of Coca-Cola and Microsoft. It only survives in westerns, whereas the Far East is still very much alive. Too bad the Russians don't know about it!

What is Russophobia, then? "Russophobia is a diverse spectrum of negative feelings, dislikes, fears, aversion, derision and/or prejudice against Russia, Russians and/or Russian culture," says Wikipedia. One can agree with this definition. Russophobia, like all pernicious passions, like anti-Semitism and Islamophobia, creeps into everything. It impregnates the mind to its remotest recesses.

When a Swiss school, in a reputedly democratic and law-abiding State, refuses to hire a Russian teacher to punish her because its "philosophy does not allow it to employ teachers from a country which provokes and fuels civil war and whose president lies and does not respect the law" and "it is in the nature of sanctions that they also affect innocents," the bounds of decency are transgressed.[14] Since when is punishing an innocent an act of justice?

But for Russophobes everything is allowed.

Because Russophobia is not only the manifestation of a feeling. It is first of all the expression of a power balance, of a relation of power. It is not only a passive judgment. It is not just a mass of clichés and prejudices. It is also, and first of all, an active bias, adopted with the intention to harm or at least to reduce the other in relation to one's self. In this sense Russophobia is also a racism: the purpose is to diminish the other with a view to better dominate. And this is what makes Russophobia a phenomenon specific to the West. It proceeds with the same categories Edward Said identified for orientalism: exaggeration of the difference, affirmation of the superiority of the West and recourse to stereotyped analytical grids.[15]

The ultimate strategy of the Russophobic discourse is to provide a full-fledged, infinitely adjustable subject, sufficiently sophisticated for academics in charge of theorizing about Russia yet popular with journalists eager to put that within everyone's reach.

| Chapter Two |

THE PAVLOVIAN RUSSOPHOBIC REFLEX

"Breaking the lie of silence is not an esoteric abstraction but an urgent responsibility that falls to those with the privilege of a platform"
John Pilger, Australian journalist and TV director

To justify their anti-Russian bias, Russophobes put forward an apparently irrefutable principle "no smoke without a fire" then use a tried and tested technique: Russia started it. It is vital to demonstrate that there is a fire and that it was lit by Russia, in order to give the impression that they are *only reacting* to provocations, to an invasion, or to Russian attempts against western rights. Throughout 2014, western leaders and media never stopped hammering home a single thesis: everything that has happened in Ukraine is the fault of the Russians. The corruption of the Yanukovych regime, the refusal to sign the agreement with the European Union, the Maidan violence, the 'annexation' of Crimea, the crash of Flight MH17, the Donbass revolt: all these events were as projected as many fires lit by Moscow. Implicitly: the United States and the European Union had nothing to do with them, and neither had the Ukrainian nationalists, who were merely trying to douse the flames.

It is a clever gambit, consisting simply in taking the effect followed the catastrophe combined all the western stereotypes against the Russians:

> The Russian pilot did not speak good English and for that reason was unable to understand the indications from the flight coordination center. No Russian airplane is reliable. They have no security system and their maintenance is shoddy. For lack of financing, Russian pilots do not attend refresher courses and this casts doubt on their professionalism. With very low salaries, they must moonlight as taxi drivers, therefore arrive at work tired and often drunk. The Bashkirian Airlines Company was practically created for the needs of the Russian mafia.

But what actually happened was the exact opposite: the Russian pilot was very competent and spoke English fluently, the airplane had just been overhauled and was in excellent flying condition, and it was established that the tragedy happened due to a series of mistakes made by the Swiss air control, leaving a single man in charge that night while the Short Term Conflict Alert had been switched off for maintenance. "But the complete arsenal of prejudices on the Russians was presented as something that went without saying: negligence, alcoholism, mafia," noted the lawyer.[5]

By July 5, the revelation of the contents of the black boxes put a definite stop to malicious doubts. The air navigation corporation then turned against their controller. Learning from their mistake, the media redeemed themselves by putting pressure on the Swiss and German authorities to reveal the facts. The drama was to rebound two years later, in 2004, when the desperate husband and father of three of the victims of the accident stabbed to death the flight controller in charge that tragic July night. But the press remained more circumspect and avoided hounding him. Today, ten years after the event, it is accepted that both were the victims of a failing organization and of a fatal chain of events. After this accident, control procedures were modified to avoid contradictions between control tower instructions and those of anti-collision systems onboard airplanes.

But in the meantime, during the two most dramatic days, at a time when families' emotions and public attention were at their height, most media, without any proof and on the basis only of allegations from the Swiss air control and the prevailing anti-Russian prejudice, projected the fault and the opprobrium onto the Russian side, shamelessly brainwashing public opinion with flagrant untruths. Hundreds of dispatches, articles and commentaries were published incriminating the Russians.

It was only progressively, after years of trials and equivocations, that the truth finally was out, when almost everyone had already forgotten the drama, and even then, twelve years after the event, not all procedures had been completed. It took years for the top executives of the Swiss company Skyguide to agree to apologize half-heartedly and for the Russian pilots' honor to be restored.[6]

The only positive outcome of that tragic accident was that the Swiss government, assessing the scale of a tragedy which had struck first innocent children and families, undertook to really mend fences with both the local Bashkortostan authorities and the federal authorities in Moscow. Official Switzerland, which had always been highly suspicious of Russia and held the greatest prejudices about the Russians, finally convinced itself that Russia could become a partner and an ally in many areas. So that, as early as 2005, very regular exchanges started in the form of ministerial, presidential, and economic visits at all levels. These relations of trust were confirmed in August 2008 when, at the end of the brief Russo-Georgian conflict, Switzerland was chosen by both camps to represent their diplomatic interests, and again in 2014 when Switzerland was able to play the part of mediator in the Ukrainian crisis thanks to her opportune presidency of the Organization for Security and Cooperation in Europe.

But such good spiritual dispositions do not last long and are likely to be shattered at the first mishap. Thus it was that the Federal Council saw fit to violate Swiss neutrality and join the European sanctions as early as spring 2014. Then in September 2014 the president of the Swiss National Council, Ruedi Lustenberger, cancelled the visit to Bern of his counterpart in the Duma Sergey Naryshkin for fear of American and European retaliation measures. A month later, a Russian writer living in Switzerland since 1995 felt it necessary to tell the world "what Liar King Putin is scheming for Europe," stating that we "are back to the Soviet times of absolute lie, under which entire generations have grown."[7] Russophobia and its prejudices are ready to resurface at the first opportunity, even under the pen of Russian writers.

In summary, the Überlingen accident revealed great partiality striking in a country like Switzerland which sees itself as dispassionate and neutral. And it is ironic that all it took was a tragic accident to open a small breach in the thick layer of anti-Russian prejudice.

The Beslan Hostage-Taking (2004)

From May to September 2004, attacks multiplied in Russia, each bloodier than the last. On May 9, Chechen president Akhmad Kadyrov was assassinated with a bomb while he attended the military parade commemorating the Second World War victory.

In June, a wave of terrorist attacks struck Nazran, the former capital of Ingushetia. Toll: 95 dead. August 24: destruction in flight by terrorist suicidal actions of two airplanes, Tu-154 and Tu-134, above Tula and Rostov-on-Don: 90 dead. The same day, a bomb attack in the Kashirskoe Shosse metro station in Moscow injures 12. And then on the 31st, a suicide attack by a female terrorist at the Rimskaya metro station kills 10 and injures 50. Responsibility for the attack is claimed twice, first by mysterious "al-Islambuli Brigades" and then by Chechen warlord Shamil Basayev. In five years, starting with the first attacks of 1999 against Moscow buildings, Islamic terrorist attacks killed 1,005 civilians in Russia, one third of the victims of the 9/11 attacks in New York.[8]

September 1, 2004, 9:30 a.m. local time: a group of 32 armed men and women occupy School Number One in Beslan, whose pupils are between seven and eighteen years of age. Most of the assailants wear black balaclavas and some have bomb belts. More than 1,300 persons are held hostage; up to fifty manage to escape in the initial chaos.

Right from the start, the assailants kill some twenty adults to intimidate the security forces. During the following hours, a cordon is established around the school, composed of members of the Russian police and Special Forces while desperate parents of the pupils have gone to fetch their guns to attack the hostage takers.

The terrorists then gather the hostages in the gymnasium and mine the other buildings. To maintain a climate of terror, they threaten to kill 50 hostages for each kidnapper killed by police and 20 hostages for each wounded. They also threaten to blow up the school if the Special Forces make any attempt to intervene. Initially, the Russian government attempts to negotiate and sends over pediatrician Leonid Roshalm who had taken part in the talks during the Dubrovka Theater siege in Moscow in 2002. A special meeting of the United Nations Security Council takes place on September 1 in the evening. It demands "the unconditional release of the Beslan hostages."

The next day, the talks prove fruitless. The terrorists refuse to allow any food or medicine to be brought in, or even that the bodies of the people killed during the assault be carried away. Many hostages, especially children, take off their clothes because of the stifling heat inside the gym. They are thirsty and must drink their own urine, an image that will shock the entire world. In the afternoon, 26 mothers and their children are freed following negotiations with former Ingushetia president Ruslan Auchev. Around 3:30 am, two explosions are heard. It will be learned later that it was two grenades thrown by the terrorists to stop an attempt at infiltration by the security forces.

In the morning of September 3, the abductors authorize medical services to come and evacuate the bodies of the 21 hostages killed as, in the prevailing heat and humidity, they have begun to decompose. The rescue team, composed of FSB[9] men, begins to approach the school but at 1:04 p.m. the terrorists open fire and two big explosions are heard. Two members of the medical team are killed. Some thirty hostages try to flee through the hole created by the explosions, but find themselves in the middle of the crossfire between Russian forces and the hostage takers.

The shootout and series of explosions that follow will be a matter of conjecture later, as to whether they were due to the accidental explosion of a badly secured bomb, whether the arrival of the medical team triggered the spate of shooting, or whether the kamikaze women triggered bombs because of the shooting. Local folks believe that a Special Forces sharpshooter shot down a terrorist sitting on a detonator...

In any case, the explosion is the signal for chaotic fighting between the terrorists and the Special Forces, regular army and troops of the Interior Ministry, with many armed civilians joining in.

Explosive charges are triggered by the terrorists and the gym is entirely destroyed around 3 p.m., but the last skirmishes only end around 11 p.m., when the last house where some terrorists have taken refuge, some forty meters away from the gym, is torched by flame-thrower.

The toll of the attack is horrendous: dead are 331 children and teachers, 11 Special Forces and 8 police officers, 31 of the 32 hostage takers, and at least one civilian who took part in the fighting. On September 17, Shamil Basayev claims responsibility for the attack, which leaves no doubt as to the involvement of Chechen Islamists.[10]

So much for the facts, in all their horror. During the first two days, as during the 9/11 attacks against the twin towers in New York in 2001, there is worldwide anguish at the fate of the hostages and the media remain fairly objective. The extent of the tragedy prevents any dispute. But as soon as the school is taken back, with blood hardly dry on the walls, the Western media will have a field day. Not against the Islamist butchers, which would be only natural, but paradoxically enough against the victims and their liberators! In this case, against the Russian government and law enforcement agencies, under suspicion of manipulation, intimidation, concealment of information, or even being the cause of the massacre!

As early as September 6, the campaign is launched. Radio Free Europe/Radio Liberty titles:

> Troubling Questions Remain About Bloody Beslan Siege ... The exact number of victims, the number of hostage takers and many other details have still not been revealed.

Interviewing a shocked young man in Beslan, the journalist quotes him as saying:

> I had a sister here who died. My other sister is in hospital. What do I feel? Do you hear the people crying? That is how I feel.

And the journalist swiftly goes on:

> But mixed with the tears are increasing questions about what exactly happened in Beslan, when the three-day-old hostage crisis ended in chaos. The idea that Russian forces decided to break the siege at the last minute in reaction to the militants' actions [sic] is a fabrication meant to cover up the disastrous outcome of what he [the young man] believes was a planned assault.

A few paragraphs further down, the article quotes the unavoidable expert, an opposition "military analyst" affiliated with the Jamestown Foundation named Pavel Felgenhauer, who, curiously, speaks in the same terms, word for word, as the young Ossetian.

The idea that Russian forces decided to break

an "Open Letter to Heads of State and Government of the European Union and of NATO"[14] written by PNAC and signed by 115 prominent political and intellectual American and European personalities. The authors of the letter accused the Kremlin of utilizing Beslan "to continue to undermine democracy in Russia and take measures preparing the next step toward a totalitarian regime." Reinforced by the reactions of the radical Russian Atlanticists and in step with the Chechen terrorists' hopes, the lobby utilized the Beslan crisis to lambast Putin as an autocrat unable to negotiate and eager to break the balance of power in the country. In mainstream media, few observers were able to voice their objections to that interpretation of events. The list of countless articles written to revile the Russian government after Beslan is too long to be quoted entirely. Andrei P. Tsygankov provides a sample of it as an endnote to his book. Among the names found there are Robert Coalson, Richard Pipes, Peter Baker, Susan B. Glasser, Michael MacFaul, Khassan Baiev, Mark Brzezinski and Richard Holbrooke, in media as diverse as Radio Free Europe/Radio Liberty, the *Washington Post*, the *Boston Globe*, *The International Herald Tribune* and the *Los Angeles Times*.

In Europe, the same theses are taken up to surfeit by all of the national media close to American and very much anti-Russian networks, such as *Libération*, *FAZ*, *Financial Times Deutschland*, *Neue Zürcher Zeitung* and, of course, *Die Welt*. The titles of their interventions are explicit: "A War on Terrorists or a War on Journalists?" asks Robert Coalson on Radio Free Europe on September 7, 2004. The same day, Ahmed Zakaev publishes in *The Guardian* an article with the eloquent title "Our dead and wounded children." As for President Jimmy Carter's former national security advisor Zbigniew Brzezinski, he did not hesitate to compare Putin to Mussolini in the columns of the *Wall Street Journal* in September 20, 2004.[15]

115 Atlanticists Against Putin

The content and the list of signatories of the Open Letter to the E.U. and NATO are also very significant in relation to the curious utilization of the Beslan drama by Russia's foes in the western media immediately afterward, while families were still crying over their lost relatives. Former Czech president Vaclav Havel, who has remained very much anti-Russian after his denunciation of the Soviet regime, was put in charge of organizing the campaign. Much more diplomatic and careful than American editorialists as the point was to be gentle with the European public, the 115 signatories adopt a tone apparently very factual and express first their compassion for the victims and their families. But this is only to more fiercely attack the Russian authorities, right from the second paragraph:

> …we are deeply concerned that these tragic events are being used to further undermine democracy in Russia. Russia's democratic institutions have always been weak and fragile. Since becoming President in January 2000, Vladimir Putin has made them even weaker. He has systematically undercut the freedom and independence of the press, destroyed the checks and balances in the Russian federal system, arbitrarily imprisoned both real and imagined political rivals, removed legitimate candidates from electoral ballots, harassed and arrested NGO leaders, and weakened Russia's political parties. In the wake of the horrific crime in Beslan, President Putin has announced plans to further centralize power and to push through measures that will take Russia a step closer to being an authoritarian regime. …
>
> These moves are only the latest evidence that the present Russian leadership is breaking away from the core democratic values of the Euro-Atlantic community. All too often in the past, the West has remained silent and restrained its criticism in the belief that President Putin's steps in the wrong direction were temporary

and the hope that Russia would soon return to a democratic and pro-Western path. Western leaders continue to embrace President Putin in the face of growing evidence that the country is moving in the wrong direction and that his strategy for fighting terrorism is producing less and less freedom. We firmly believe dictatorship will not and cannot be the answer to Russia's problems and the very real threats it faces.

The leaders of the West must recognize that our current strategy towards Russia is failing."[16]

Twelve years later, we have to acknowledge that Russia, despite all those accusations, has not become a dictatorship as predicted. Needless to say, neither this PNAC letter nor the raft of media condemnations make any reference to the freedom-restricting measures taken by the United States on the morrow of 9/11 through the Patriot Act, measures at least as destructive of freedom as those taken by the Russians in their fight against their Islamic terrorists. And what about Guantánamo Prison, whose existence was yet unknown at the time, or the systematic phone-tapping practiced by NSA, as would be revealed a few years later thanks to Julian Assange and Edward Snowden, or the CIA torture/rendition Gulag?

Not only did those intellectuals and experts invited by the entire world press engage in virulent criticism against Russia's authoritarian "drift," but they insisted on Russia negotiating with the terrorists and granting their allegedly moderate chief, Aslan Maskhadov and his lieutenant Ilyas Akhmadov, an independent territory in the Caucasus. They cared little about the cooperation Russia had given George Bush after the 9/11 attacks, or about the Russian warnings indicating that the Chechen Islamic rings were the same as those of Al-Qaida and of the Islamic Maghreb who had fought in Bosnia, Algeria and then Afghanistan (before setting foot in Iraq, Yemen, and then Libya and Syria thanks to the Arab rebellions of January 2011) perhaps because these were the very fighters they would go on to support in pursuit of regime change in

Libya and Syria. How they would have shouted with indignation if Russian experts, three weeks after the attacks on the twin towers, had put pen to paper in American newspapers to advise the Washington government to negotiate with Bin Laden and to withdraw American forces from Saudi Arabia as he had requested, when the thousands of victims of Al-Qaida had just been buried!

Half of the 115 signatories were American experts and former diplomats gravitating around conservative Republican senator John McCain and neoconservative Democrat and former chief of the CIA James Woolsey. All of them are convinced advocates of American exceptionalism and of its (and their) vocation to lead the world and establish democracies. (Or at least, the former.) On the European side, we find also intellectuals, experts and former high civil servants of the Right as of the Left, originating mainly from the Nordic countries and from Eastern Europe, united in the same dread of a dictatorial Russia intent on rebuilding her empire. Five Frenchmen signed the appeal: Pascal Bruckner, André Glucksmann, Pierre Hassner, Bernard Kouchner and Jacques Rupnik.

Against this adamant Russophobia, moderate commentators close to conservative lobbies like Anatol Lieven of the Carnegie Endowment for International Peace or Gordon Hahn from the Hoover Institution have distanced themselves from it.[17] But they were promptly swept aside, while a few shy voices called for more moderation in *The New York Times*.[18]

What Really Happened in Beslan

What did really happen in Beslan? Can we really suspect Russian authorities of having manipulated the terrorists in order to provoke a massacre that could justify a Putin dictatorship, as is implicit in western media commentaries, some of whose authors proved to be staunch believers in such a Putin conspiracy theory during the attacks in Moscow in 1999? How to find our way in this thick jungle of propaganda and falsehoods? Ten years after the events and with the facts having been analyzed time and time again, it appears that the most objective report, totally above suspicion of sympathy for Russian authorities, is possibly the one Henry Plater-Zyberk published in November 2004 for the Conflict Studies Research Centre of the British Defense Ministry.[19]

The author produces a detailed synthesis of what actually happened, of the number of hostages killed and injured, of the number and origin of the terrorists, of their armament, of the response of the Russian forces and local and federal authorities, etc. His conclusions are as follows:

> Considering the well planned assault, the nature of the target, the age and the number of hostages, the unrealistic demands of the hostage takers as well as their extreme and consistent brutality, the Russian authorities faced an impossible task. They could have done better mainly by establishing a more distant and more secure perimeter. Only then would one have been able to speculate whether other measures taken by them were adequate. Another area where they failed visibly was in information management. Too many badly briefed officials were allowed to provide speculative or glaringly inaccurate information to the media, both Russian and foreign, undermining the authorities' already shaken credibility even further and provoking speculation.
>
> ...The bad handling of the media by the Russian authorities – something which those working with Russia will have to bear in mind in the future – resulted in unjustifiable accusations of censorship and governmental manipulation. Yet had they been more firm and consistent they would have been accused of dictatorial practices by those who criticised them for lack of firmness and consistency.
> ... The printed media, however, published many

> articles critical of the Russian authorities. There is no evidence that President Putin put pressure on any media organisations, although it appears that some of the media magnates attempted to put pressure on "their" editors in an outburst of unsolicited servility.
>
> …Criticism of the authorities voiced publicly by several liberal democrats was rarely to the point and the solutions they offered correspondingly unrealistic. The western media too frequently repeated their criticism without attempting to examine their content. Those equating anti-terrorist operations in today's Russia with those in Yel'tsin's era were particularly misleading. Their unequivocal criticism of the antiterrorist operation in the Nord-Ost theatre siege presented a distorted picture of the event by suggesting that a well-planned, large scale hijacking might conceivably have a happy ending.

Furthermore, the author gives a pounding to the anti-Kremlin lobby's theories. Like human rights activist Elena Bonner, the widow of dissident academician Sakharov, the lobby called for negotiation with the terrorists along "basic principles" and for a fair trial if they surrendered. He also contradicts journalist Anna Politkovskaya's suggestion that Aslan Maskhadov would have persuaded the pirates to release the children.[20] For Henry Plater-Zyberk, there is no doubt that:

> Basayev had practically condemned the hostage takers to death before he sent them to Beslan, hoping that their operation would end in a bloodbath, triggering an interethnic war in the North Caucasus.

And he concludes his analysis by stating that:

> President Putin will have enormous difficulties

No western journalist or expert has ever written of the repression of Chechen Islamists contextualized against the repression western governments carried out against independence fighters in Ulster, the Basque Country, or Corsica (or indeed, against western support for Chechen separatists, as Russia has claimed).[23] Did the French, Spanish and English press protest and demand compliance with terrorists' demands and the granting of independence to those provinces? Those three cases are nonetheless very similar to that of Chechnya, even though the violence of Basque, Irish and Corsican independence fighters was in no way comparable to the murderous craziness of the Islamists of the Chechen emirate. Did the 115 signatories of the letter to Putin protest against western governments when they were mistreating those poor Basque, Corsican, or Irish fighters?

One last observation: in the wake of the January 2015 attack in Paris, French justice and government filed 54 charges of "apology for terrorism" against humorist Dieudonné and others.

The Second Ossetia War (2008)

August 7, 2008, 11:40 p.m., at the border of South Ossetia and Georgia: Most heads of State were in Beijing for the opening of the Olympic Games and, in the torpor of the summer holidays, the whole world sat in front of TV screens awaiting a show that promised to be grandiose. Little attention was paid to the Caucasus.

After several days of border skirmishes between the South Ossetia separatist militia, supported and trained by Russia, and the Georgian army, hostilities broke out in the night of 7 to 8 August when an assault by Georgian troops left 18 dead in the ranks of the predominantly Russian CIS peacekeeping forces and 162 among the South Ossetians, according to the official toll given by Russian justice by the end of 2008.

Since the arrival of the pro-Western leader in Tbilisi in 2004, South Ossetia had become a political issue between Georgian President Mikheil Saakashvili, who wanted reintegration of those provinces into the Georgian territory, and the pro-independence majority in South Ossetia (whose choice of independence was validated by two referendums, in 1992 and in 2006) who wanted de jure as well as de facto independence. The Russian Federation, which was playing the part of mediator pursuant to an international agreement and which had troops in South Ossetia, was not making any move to resolve the situation.

It is in this climate of high tension that at 11:10 p.m. on August 7, 2008, the Georgian government informed the general commanding the Russian forces of his intention to forcefully restore "constitutional order." Around 11:40 p.m., a grenade killed two Russian soldiers of the peacekeeping force. Several salvos of multiple rocket launchers then destroyed and burned the buildings occupied by the Russians. The Russian soldiers of the peacekeeping force had no tanks but they managed to resist and the Georgians could only take over two-thirds of the town. At 11:56 p.m., the South-Ossetian authorities announced that the assault had begun.

The Russians were aware of important Georgian preparations going on since at least 9 p.m. and the Russian president, Dmitri Medvedev, was informed around 10:43 p.m. He ordered deputy foreign affairs minister Grigory Karasin to contact Mikheil Saakachvili, but he could only reach American diplomat Dan Fried. Fried assured him that the Americans were trying to regain control of the situation. However, as of 2:06 a.m., peace efforts were no longer on the agenda. The Roki Tunnel, neglected by the Georgians, was made secure and fresh Russian troops were on the way, estimated at between 5,500 and 10,000 men stationed in the military district of North Caucasus.[24]

Propaganda from both camps immediately accused the other side of having started the hostilities. The Russians claimed more than 1,500 civilian deaths in the bombing of the South Ossetia capital, whereas the Georgians denounced the Russian troops' use of the Roki Tunnel as part of a deliberate scheme to invade Georgia. Rapidly, both camps accused each other of war crimes and crimes against humanity.

After four days of rapid Russian forces advance and the bombing of several South-Ossetia towns, Medvedev announced that his objectives had been reached and that the Russian troops would remain in the positions defined by the 1992 agreement (which had ended a first war in Georgia against her minorities which had resulted in 3,000 victims).

On August 16, a ceasefire was signed which ended the conflict temporarily without resolving the Ossetia and Abkhazia questions.

On August 26, the Russian Federation officially recognized the independence of South Ossetia and of Abkhazia and declared itself ready "to ensure the security of those two States."

Soon after the conflict, an independent international fact-finding mission on the Georgian conflict was organized by the European Union, led by Swiss diplomat Heidi Tagliavini, who had represented the UN secretary general for Georgia and Abkhazia from 2002 to 2006, and seconded by Uwe Schramm, former German ambassador in Georgia. The report, published September 30, 2009, clearly established that it was Georgia that started the conflict in order to take over South Ossetia.[25]

But in August 2008, who started the war was still not known with certainty. Yet as early as August 8, the press went wild, along the same anti-Russian scenario as for Überlingen and Beslan. Since the Rose Revolution and the arrival to power of Mikheil Saakashvili in 2003, the new regime was viewed as pro-Western. The new president had studied in the United States, at Columbia and George Washington universities, where he established strong ties with the conservative Right and the defenders of American hegemony. He was telegenic, spoke English and French, and was very friendly with presidents Bush and Sarkozy.

As soon as he took on his governmental functions, he expressed his intention to join the European Union and integrate Georgia into NATO. In 2003, he sent a substantial contingent of soldiers set up and trained by the United States to support the anti-Saddam Hussein coalition. The Georgian army multiplied its exercises and collaboration with the American army, as would happen in summer 2008. And during all the years of his presidency, he talked up interventions in the western press in order to look like a good democrat. Eventually, well-versed in communication techniques, he hired an American public relations agency, Aspect Consulting, which also works for ExxonMobil, Kellogg's and Procter & Gamble. Faced with someone who appeared to be a defender of European values and had been craftily presented as a "champion of democracy," the two Russian PR agencies mandated by the Kremlin did not stand a chance, stress the two authors of a study on the media coverage of the conflict.[26]

All American media and many European media were thus accusing wholesale the Russian government of being behind the attack. "Russia Attacks Georgia While the West Watches," claimed a *Washington Post* editorialist, the very Russophobic Anne Appelbaum, in the online magazine *Slate* as early as August 8.[27] The rest of the press followed suit. On August 11, neoconservative spokesman William Kristol led the charge in *The New York Times*, while editorialists everywhere had a field day targeting the "Russian invasion."

No comparison is too far-fetched. Zbigniew Brzezinski stressed that "the Russian invasion of Georgia recalls the attack against Finland" in 1941 (*Huffington Post*). Elsewhere, in the Norwegian press (*Aftonbladet*), the comparison is instead with the invasion of Czechoslovakia by Russian troops in 1968, while still others prefer the Sudetenland in 1938.[28] From Hitler to Stalin, the worst dictators of the past are invoked to demonize prime minister Putin and the Russian intervention in Georgia, in spite of all the facts. The event occurred during the presidency of Medvedev, who claims primary responsibility.[29]

In Western Europe, the tone is the same, if more moderate. In *Le Figaro*, Laure Mandeville, author of a book on "Russian Reconquista" very much hostile to Putin, accused Russia of punishing former republics who were trying to get close to the West. *Le Monde* put forward Russia's desire to regain energy, political and geostrategic interests in the south of the Caucasus, through which oil and gas pipelines

Russians in South Ossetia, Russia recognized the independence of Abkhazia and South Ossetia. A further step today unanimously condemned by western chancelleries which, at the time, didn't even dream of condemning Moscow.[34]

Deliberate disinformation? Ignorance? Or anti-Russian reflex so deeply rooted that, in good faith, things are presented in a way absolutely contrary to even officially established facts? The main western media have a way of twisting reality in the name of the defense of western values which leaves you speechless, so biased do most of them appear. It must be noted in this context that, if most media refused to acknowledge their mistake in the August 2008 war, some to their credit did. In its Newsnight broadcast of 28 October 2008, the BBC made an explicit correction by criticizing the Georgian version of the events.[35] *The New York Times* also modified its position one week later, not without insisting a lot on the "blame given to both camps." As historian Paul Sanders rightly remarks, "None of this changed very much about Russia's image as the aggressor. As media professionals know only too well, all communication is subject to 'threshold dynamics,' where first impressions are critically important. Once media saturation sets in, a potential disclaimer will find it impossible to dislodge the initial images that will have meanwhile solidified into opinions. Cognitive filters will have closed for good."[36]

The Sochi Olympic Games (2014)

This anti-Russian bias reached its height on the eve of the opening of the Sochi Winter Olympic Games on February 6, 2014. This was all the more surprising as it involved a sporting event, civil and pacific. The Georgian conflict had been forgotten for five years, and the demonstrations on Maidan Square in Kiev had yet to degenerate into a bloodbath. Crimea and the Donetsk area were still at peace and lived under the legal Ukrainian regime. In February 2014, there was thus nothing much to criticize Russia about, apart from her offering US$15 billion to bail out the drifting Ukrainian economy and from spending a fortune to make the Games successful.

But such generosity was adjudged unacceptable in the West. Over the ten days preceding the inauguration of the Games, almost all of the radio, television and print media of the western world flooded the waves and pages with negative reports and interviews on Russia and the OG: that Sochi inhabitant who had not been rehoused, that ski tow director who had been dismissed, that too showy town mayor, this Pussy Riot singer haranguing the police to make sure she would be photographed by a western journalist, that Russian homosexual pursued for some negative comment about Putin, those political opponents denouncing the wastage of public money and corruption, this ecologist lamenting the environmental damage and evacuation of used waters, that historian invoking a battle fought long ago close to the ski trails—nothing was spared.

The social networks even had fevered reports of hot-water taps not working in a hotel for journalists while the American site mashable.com counted the "twelve photos of Sochi the Russians probably don't want you to see," one of which showed two toilet bowls for women installed next to each other in a restaurant, as if this was a scoop of planetary importance!

Actually, putting anecdotes aside, Russia-bashing mainly took two directions: the European media stressed above all the waste and corruption linked to the vast expenses undertaken, while the American media, including Channel 4, concentrated their criticisms on the "repression" of Russian homosexuals following the adoption, at the end of 2013 by the Duma, of a law condemning homosexual propaganda involving minors.

Neutral observers promptly pointed out that that measure was similar to a prescription in the French penal code and to a law of the same kind in force in the United States. They further pointed out that several American States, notably Arizona, had just toughened their anti-gay legislation and, by that yardstick, the winter OG in Salt Lake City should have been boycotted, as it is the capital of a State, Utah, that represses homosexuality due to the Mormons' preponderant influence. Even the spokesperson of the Russian LGBT, Nikolay Alekseyev, finally became activated by the excesses of the harassment campaign of the western media and called for a boycott that threatened to deprive millions of Russians of the pleasures of the Games.

This denigration campaign reached an apex during the opening ceremony, a grandiose and very successful show which managed to inflame the antagonism of anchors who knew nothing of Russian culture and history. For their part, political commentators maintained running comments on the risk of attacks threatening the public and the athletes, while climatologists speculated worriedly over the temperature differences between mountain and seacoast, something which had failed to come to their minds during the Vancouver Games.

Contrary to all those somber forecasts and alarmist comments, the Games went on perfectly, with flawless organization, without the least hitch for the competitors, the spectators or the journalists, who found nothing to complain about. Even the trains arrived on time! But none of those virulent critics has ever tried to correct the disparaging comments they had made beforehand. It would be onerous to enumerate in detail the thousands of negative articles and broadcasts on the Sochi OG before the sport took over.

So I will merely quote three informed commentators, starting with the sports editor of the Australian daily *The Sydney Morning Herald*, Andrew Webster, who on February 8 noted that "much of the commentary in the lead-up to the Games has been unfair. Bashing the Sochi Olympics into a bloody pulp has become a new winter sport. ... the frenzy of negativity is turning into a witch hunt." He went on to say how he saw a TV reporter deliberately shoot beams lying in the mud at the Rosa Khutor station to show how badly done the works were, while ignoring the fact that, by the next day, the same place was impeccably laid out and welcomed dozens of smiling Russians eating ice cream![37]

Other media reacted similarly, such as the German magazine *Der Spiegel*, whose Moscow correspondent, Benjamin

Bidder, published a very critical commentary on 11 February on "those people in the West that hold forth on each and every problem linked to the Sochi Games" and stating that "criticism has gone beyond reasonableness." He went on to show how a quote from Sochi mayor Anatoly Pakhomov that went viral on the social networks and media of the planet had in fact been truncated. Just before the Games, the mayor was quoted as saying that "there are no gays here" whereas he had actually said that there were no gay *activists* in his town, his wording confirmed by the fact that only minutes before he had spoken with the manager of a Sochi gay bar.

Bidder reported what happened to Austrian journalist Simon Rosner of *Wiener Zeitung* with his Twitter account. During the storm about the Sochi unfinished works, he took a picture of a dilapidated street in Vienna and posted it with the hashtag #SochiProblems. A CNN web editor then contacted him to use his photo in a gallery of photos on all that was wrong in Sochi. *USA Today*, the biggest American daily, was also interested. His photo was retweeted 350 times. But when he published in the following hours a new tweet to deny the first version and reveal it was in fact a joke and the photo had been taken in a Vienna street, there was no one to retweet that post. Rosner concluded by saying that if the Russians had used buses as old as those that were in circulation in Vancouver during the previous OG, they probably would have been reproached for using "Soviet Union reliquary."[38]

As for Marc Bennetts, he put critics of the Russian anti-LGBT law back in line in *The Guardian*:

> Amid the furore, it's easy to overlook some simple facts. Homosexuality in Russia – unlike more than 40 countries in the Commonwealth and 70 worldwide – is not illegal. To date, over six months since the law came into force, fewer than a dozen people have been fined for "gay propaganda". Not a single person has been jailed. Russian police do not have powers to

How is that for clarity? In such a climate of harassment, it was not surprising that almost all the western leaders boycotted the opening and closing ceremony of the games. No Obama, no Angela Merkel, no François Hollande, no David Cameron. For the first time since 2000, the US has not sent a president, former president, first lady or vice-president to the games. Only Chinese president Xi, Japanese prime minister Shinzo Abe and Turkish president Recep Erdogan accepted to join the event. As if the non-attendance to the official ceremonies were not sufficient, Barack Obama decided to add a supplementary rebuff to Russia by naming two gay athletes to represent the US at the Winter Olympics. The tennis star Billie Jean King and hockey player Caitlin Calhow were tasked to "send a message to the Russian people and the rest of the world that the United States values the civil and human rights of LGBT people."[43]

Two years later, on the eve of the Summer Games in Rio de Janeiro, the anti-Russian bullying focused on a new topic: state-of-the-art governmental doping.[44] The strongest attacks came from the International Federation of Athletics (IAAF) whose newly appointed president, Sebastian Coe, a Briton, succeeded the former Senegalese Lamin Diack on August 31, 2015. The IAAF was suspected of covering-up the doping of hundreds of athletes. In November 2015, the World Antidoping Agency (WADA) released a report accusing the IAAF of corruption, bribery, extortion and doping concealment that especially focused on Russia. The harshest attacks came from Dick Pound, the founder of the WADA in 1999. Initially supported by the International Olympic Committee and based in Montreal, Canada, WADA's three presidents, Dick Pound, John Fahey and the present one, Craig Reedie, came from Britain or Australia as well as the juror appointed to examine the Russian doping case in 2016, the Canadian lawyer Richard McLaren.

Following several TV reports broadcast by the German TV channel ARD in December 2014, August 2015 and March 2016, the WADA published reports which severely pointed to the Russian Federation of Athletism and focused on an "organized doping" plan scheduled at the highest levels of the Russian state.

A massive media campaign followed the declarations of the reports. As a result, nearly one third of the Russian athletes have been banned from the Rio Olympics, leaving the Russian team to Rio dramatically reduced (but likely, as described by Russia's Olympic Committee president Alexander Zhukov, "the cleanest team" at the Games").[45] The Russian Paralympic team was totally excluded. On December 2016, the last part of the McLaren report on Russian doping was released leaving Russian sport as always under international scrutiny. As at this writing, there is even an effort to remove Russia as the venue for the 2018 FIFA World Cup. There are few doubts about Russian doping. But doping remains an issue worldwide in all sports. When the Russian hackers group, the Fancy Bears, released a series of mails from the WADA indicating this organization had provided Therapeutic Use Exemptions to hundreds of prominent western athletes, giving legal status to their doping, almost nobody in the West considered it a scandal. In fact, James Riach of the *Guardian* complained that it was unfair to tarnish all athletes with the same doping brush.[46] Similarly, the WADA considered these revelations as a "bad blow for innocent athletes". The Russian counter-story to State doping accusations is too lengthy for inclusion here. Suffice to say, as Putin did:

> "We need to make sports, just like culture, clean of any politics," Putin said. "Sport is like culture and they must be uniting people and not dividing them." The Russian president said, however, that the problem of doping does exist in Russian sports, just like in any other country.[47]

| Chapter Three |

MEDIA BLINDERS ON UKRAINE

"What paralyzes the western world and leaves it defenseless is that it does not know any longer how to distinguish the true from the false, the indisputable good from the proven bad. 'Always more different ideas,' this centrifugal dispersion triggers entropy of thought. A hundred mules pulling in all directions produce no movement."
Aleksandr Solzhenitsyn[1]

Why? Why, where Russia is concerned, does the Western press lack objectivity to such an extent? How to explain those so Pavlovian reflexes of denigration? Why are the values that have made journalism proud—the search for truth, the desire to understand, the will to know, the acceptance of a confrontation of viewpoints, empathy, respect—why are these thrown overboard as soon as the words Russia and Putin are pronounced?

Of course, not all media do as did that Fox News anchor who, during the Georgian war of summer 2008, seeing that the two women he was interviewing live were praising Russians rather than Georgians and accusing Georgian president Mikheil Saakachvili of having started the hostilities whereas he was expecting Putin to take the full blame, censured his own interview by switching to advertising spots![2]

Or like TF1, which correctly allowed Vladimir Putin to speak on June 4, 2014 on the eve of the ceremonies of the seventieth anniversary of the Normandy landings, but did not broadcast his answers on the events in Crimea or his opinion on the French media.[3] It is as if, for Western media, scholars and politicians, truth no longer depends on facts but on who is talking or on who is talked about.

This feeling is shared by Anatol Lieven, former correspondent of the *Financial Times* and *The Times* and a scholar at the Carnegie Endowment for International Peace and at the New American Foundation. Here is how he assessed the wave of Russophobia that marked the second Chechnya war in 1999-2000:

> The most worrying aspect of Western Russophobia is that it demonstrates the capacity of too many Western journalists and intellectuals to betray their own professed standards and behave like Victorian jingoists or Balkan nationalists when their own national loyalties and hatreds are involved. ... As an antidote, Western journalists and commentators writing on the Chechen wars might read Alistair Horne's *A Savage War of Peace* (about the French war in Algeria), Max Hastings's *Korean War* (especially the passages dealing with the capture of Seoul in 1950 and the U.S. air campaign), any serious book on the U.S. war in Vietnam or French policies in Africa ...
>
> With regard to Russian crimes in Chechnya, they could also read some of the remarks on the inherent cruelty of urban warfare by Western officers in journals like the *Marine Corps Gazette* and *Parameters*. Neither Horne nor Hastings (both patriotic conservatives) were 'soft on communism;' nor are most military writers 'soft on Russia.' They are true professionals with a commitment to present the

facts, however uncomfortable and they have the moral courage to do so. ... when American soldiers became involved in a lethal urban fight in Mogadishu in 1994, the indiscriminate way in which retaliatory firepower was used meant that Somali casualties (the great majority of them civilian) outnumbered U.S. casualties by between twenty-five and fifty to one. In other words, to some extent the degree of carnage in Chechnya reflects not inherent and historical Russian brutality, but the nature of urban warfare."[4]

The Anti-Russian Vulgate

Fifteen years later, nothing has changed, except that the Russophobia of the media has become even more acute with the Ukrainian crisis. Here is how the Vulgate of anti-Russian clichés propagated everywhere in the West runs: Russia is a backward, underdeveloped, expansionist country only dreaming of reestablishing her fallen empire and wallowing in the despotism typical of her national tradition. Russians are narrow-minded, nationalistic, conservative, even reactionary, brutal and drunken beings sometimes given to poetic and artistic creative flashes.

The president of Russia, Vladimir Putin, always presented as a former KGB spy,[5] is anti-democratic, anti-liberal, obsessed by his fight against European and American values. His one and only purpose in life, in the shadow of the high walls of the Kremlin, is to intrigue underhandedly to bind again to the motherland the 25 million Russians scattered in the former Soviet possessions and take back their countries with them.. As a proud heir to czarism and communism, he is an autocrat sticking to 19th century ideas who believes that might is right. Putin is a man of the past and should be treated accordingly.

Let us read, for example, this commentary in the French daily *Libération*, which looks like another pea in the hundred-peas pod that preceded it. On December 18, 2014, the day of President

Putin's much-awaited interview on the fall of the ruble and of oil prices, it noted:

> Putin is paying today the price of his aggressive policy in Ukraine, of the badly disguised invasion of Russian-speaking areas in that country and of the annexation of Crimea. Not to mention the Malaysian Airbus shot down by his henchmen.
>
> Faced with the most serious crisis of his fifteen years of autocracy, the former KGB officer has left for the time being his ministers on the front line while his money collapsed and his economy floundered. In his annual press conference, a routine exercise of histrionics and display of brutal force, the President will have to explain and justify himself. Thanks to his huge popularity based on well-oiled propaganda and shameless exposition of the most chauvinistic themes, Putin may be tempted to play as is his wont on the theme of the international plot threatening Holy Russia...[6]

A few weeks earlier, a fellow journalist in the Swiss *Le Temps* had repeated the same truisms in a slightly more elaborate form:

> The Russian president is the voice of the humiliated, or rather of those that perceive themselves as such, in front of world elites increasingly cut off from their peoples. Putinism is a nationalism exalting a tense identity and the return to lost power. It is the defense of Christendom, affirmation of family, virility, sovereignty. It is a paternalistic, demagogical and protectionist State. It is a thwarted imperialism best defined by what it opposes: anti-Americanism, anti-multiculturalism,

anti-globalization, anti-Islamism, anti-'human-rightism', homophobia, rejection of elites and liberal capitalism. ... Putinism is cousin to Chinese national-communism and enjoys affinities with the American Tea Party.[7]

How to explain that, as soon as they mention Russia, otherwise serious and sensible journalists give up independent thinking to line up anti-Russian commonplaces like nuts on a stick, as we Swiss say, to depict the irrational? Why are they so severe with Vladimir Putin, who governs a country that is altogether much more democratic than China, when they wouldn't allow themselves to take such a liberty with the Chinese president, the American president or the chief of State of their own country?[8]

The most shocking in the attitude of the Western media, which prides itself on being at the forefront of journalistic deontology and is wont to denounce contrary views as "propaganda," is the stupefying lack of questioning, which is basic to their trade. It's settled, they seem to think. The facts are clear, ours is the Gospel truth, move along, folks, nothing else to see.

Is this the case?

For there are dozens of questions which remain unasked. On Ukraine, for example.

No Questions for Victoria Nuland

American Assistant Secretary of State for European and Asian Affairs Victoria Nuland estimated in December 2013 that the United States had invested more than US$5 billion since 1991 to help Ukraine achieve "the future it deserves" by supporting opposition to President Yanukovych. Then it came to light that during the February 2014 crisis, in a phone call to the American ambassador in Ukraine Geoffrey Pyatt, she said "Fuck the EU", asserting that Klitschko (current Kiev mayor) was not needed in the government because cooperation with Yatseniuk (current prime minister) "won't work at this level."[9] Why wasn't the European press indignant as it always is each time Vladimir Putin shocks the West? Despite the crassness of these declarations dismissing any concern for Europe and indicating the extent to which the US is pulling the strings in Ukraine, it merely mentioned them in passing and promptly forgot the matter.

What were those billions of dollars for? To whom were they channeled and why? Why have the main European press outlets never deemed it useful to mention that Victoria Nuland is the wife of Robert Kagan, one of the leaders of the neoconservatives, a fierce ultra-Zionist and anti-Russian, co-founder with former George W. Bush's advisor William Kristol of the Project for a New American Century (PNAC, renamed Foreign Policy Initiative or FPI in 2010), who convinced the United Nations administration to regard the Afghanistan and Iraq wars as legal, and who had been the American kingpin of the Letter of the 115 against Putin in 2004?[10]

European press outlets calmly accepted an American choosing the members of a future Ukrainian government while there was still one legally in office in what would be purported to be a revolution for democracy. Weren't we witnessing instead the live preparation of a putsch? And why did Brussels not protest at being insulted at *"Fuck the EU"* coming from a member of the American government, while it finds it scandalous if the Russian president resorts to a crudity?[11] Western journalists had no time for such questions.

Let us move to the Maidan Square revolt and to the shots into the crowd of civilian demonstrators in mid-February 2014 imputed to the infamous Berkut police officers of the Yanukovych government. With more than 80 people killed, it was the scandal that brought down the government, caused the departure of the legal president and justified the putsch that brought new Ukrainian leaders to power. But then, the more time passes, the more tongues loosen up, and the less obvious do responsibilities appear.

On March 6, 2014, the Estonian Ministry of Foreign Affairs confirmed the authenticity of a leaked phone call its chief, Urmas Paet, had with Catherine Ashton, the European Union's head of external affairs, in which he said that the snipers that had shot down Maidan demonstrators might have acted under orders of the new Ukrainian leaders and not those of the deposed president. Hinting at a possible deeper engagement, he advised that the snipers were firing at both sides.[12]

On October 10, 2014, Reuters published a dispatch revealing that there were serious flaws in the proofs relating to the shots: the Berkut commander who was suspected of the murders had disappeared from his prison and the witness who had recognized him holding a weapon with both hands was confounded because the suspected officer had only one hand, the other one having been blown up in the explosion of a hand grenade a few years earlier.[13]

The news, however crucial for the understanding of the Ukrainian events, was ignored by most of the Western media, because it did not fit anti-Russian prejudice. What are the investigative reporters financed by the Open Society Foundation of the very Russophobic George Soros waiting for to begin investigating?[14] If they had done so, they might have discovered, as Chris Kaspar de Ploeg did, the following:

> In an interview with the *Financial Post* in 2012 Oleh Rybachuk, former deputy prime minister for European integration under Yushchenko, stated that: "We now have 150 NGOs in all the major cities ... The Orange Revolution was a miracle ... We want to do that again and we think we will.' Rybachuk is, amongst other things, the founder and head of Center UA, an umbrella organization linked to various activist projects and NGOs. One of them is the New Citizen campaign which, according to the *Financial Times*, "played a big role in getting the protest up and running". Another example is the Stronger Together Campaign, which aims to "popularize the ideas of European integration and encourage authorities to implement them effectively." Yanukovich felt so threatened that he implemented a series

of draconian laws shortly before his fall, which included obligatory registration of NGOs with foreign funding as foreign agents who would need to pay more taxes and endure extra monitoring. The *Kyivpost* reports that "Center UA received more than $500,000 in 2012, ... 54 percent of which came from Pact Inc., a project funded by the U.S. Agency for International Development. Nearly 36 percent came from Omidyar Network, a foundation established by eBay founder Pierre Omidyar and his wife. Other donors include the International Renaissance Foundation, whose key funder is billionaire George Soros, and the National Endowment for Democracy, funded largely by the U.S. Congress."[15]

Same thing with the massacre at the trade union house in Odessa. On May 2, 2014, forty pro-Russian militants died in the arson of the house where they had taken refuge. Here too, as months went by, tongues untied and the responsibility of an extreme rightwing militia seems increasingly well established. The killings, though half as many victims as on the Maidan, were of no interest to the media, even though they had covered for weeks the demonstrations and violence taking place in Kiev.

Let us quote here the French weekly *Marianne*:

Let us imagine [conversely] that Ukrainian rebels surrounded by partisans of the former regime have taken refuge in the trade union house and that the latter has been torched by hostile forces, under the eyes of an impassive police. Let us imagine that some forty corpses have been found in it. What would have happened? Emotions would have run high in the western capitals. Governments would have screamed bloody mass murder carried out by Yanukovych henchmen. ... BHL [Bernard-Henri

Levy, French philosopher-activist] would already have picked up his media-white shirt. Laurent Fabius [French foreign minister at the time] would be invoking scorned universal values. And what of over there? Nothing or next to nothing.[16]

No further comment.

Crimeans Reaffirm Their 1991 Referendum

Let us consider now the referendum on Crimea accession to Russia organized with the support of Russia on March 16, 2014. The self-righteous media followed the advice of the White House, which had announced a few days earlier that "the proposed referendum on the future of Crimea violates the Ukrainian constitution and international law" and thus would be null and void.[17] The fact that 95% of the Crimeans voted for union with Russia was of no importance whatsoever. Had Western correspondents done their work well, they could however have stressed that this referendum was merely confirming a previous vote, the one the new Ukrainian authorities had organized entirely legally on January 12, 1991: with a turnout of 81.37%, 94.3% of the voters had chosen the restoration of an independent Crimean republic as a member of the new Union Treaty proposed by Gorbachev.

Exactly the same result as on March 16, 2014. But in 1991 as in 2014, the international community, led by the United States, promptly had the vote cancelled: in February 1991, at George Soros's advice, the Ukrainian Parliament reversed its decision and voted in a panic a retroactive law cancelling the Crimeans' vote. The West refused to countenance Ukraine's losing the Sebastopol naval base and offering Russia free access to the Mediterranean Sea. In the chaos of those days, no one paid attention and history was forgotten except by the Crimeans, deprived of their democratic decision.[18] By contrast, in Kosovo in 2008, there was no double referendum and yet the province obtained its independence. Which media brought those contradictory facts to attention?[19]

Malaysian Flight MH17

And finally we come to the most spectacular event, the crash of Flight MH17 of the Malaysian Airlines in the afternoon of July 17, 2014.[20] The mainstream media literally flew into a rage: only minutes after the accident, Russia and Russian-speaking pro-separatists in Ukraine were indicted. Shortly after the accident, President Obama and State Secretary John Kerry also pointed the finger at Russia without any proof. On July 26, when the United States was aiming its second volley of sanctions against Russia, a White House spokesperson again suggested that "Vladimir Putin might be guilty of the plane crash."[21]

For weeks, the entire Western media took up this thesis, multiplied and amplified it at every possible opportunity with concurring quotations by consultants at the innumerable Brussels-based NATO think tanks and in the entourage of the new Ukrainian president, Petro Poroshenko, with the further backing of just as numerous "independent" experts who were prompted to comment on the conflict in the Donbass in a sense always favorable to the new Ukrainian regime. At no time has the Western press, for all its attention to human rights related to Pussy Riot or Russian opponent blogger, Alexei Navalny, pointed out that the bombing of the civilian populations in Donetsk and Luhansk by the Ukrainian army violated the Geneva Convention and came close to being a war crime.

Neither has it pointed out that while it took only a few hours to find debris of the crash of the Air Asia Malaysian plane in the Celebes Sea on December 27, 2014, and 48 hours to read and interpret the data of the black box of the Air Algérie plane that crashed at the end of July in the north of Mali, it has taken more than two years to deliver the first results of the inquiry led by the Dutch Joint Investigation Team.[22] Why has American satellite reconnaissance, able to peruse the shortest of our SMSs and read the plates of our vehicles, reported nothing on this event in Ukraine, in the middle of a territory monitored by AWACs as well as NATO radar stations? And above all, why isn't the press, so unrelenting with questions to Vladimir Putin, questioning Western military authorities, and seeking the release of this information?

Why, when the press is always so ready to express outrage when a pro-Russian separatist mistreats a pro-Ukrainian woman, does it remain silent when the fate of hundreds of victims is at stake?[23] And why does it quote Ukrainian or American sources, even though they are parties to the conflict, while it practically never quotes Russian sources under the pretext that they would be biased?[24] And finally, why consistently and repeatedly report the Ukrainian military's spurious accusations of a Russian invasion of Donbass when such an invasion never took place and seems unlikely to? Over six months, the Swiss newspaper *Le Temps* announced no fewer than 36 times, in bold, small, medium or large characters, a Russian invasion of Donbass.

But let us end here this sorry catalogue and move to elements of explanation that Western press headlines have deliberately withheld on the deep roots of the Ukrainian crisis: NATO expansion to and military buildup on Russia's border.

Alternative Views on NATO Expansion

Republican Jack Matlock Jr., former US ambassador in Moscow from 1987 to 1991, when the Soviet Union ended, and a privileged witness to the arrangements entered upon by George Bush and Mikhail Gorbachev,[25] wrote as follows, "I believe it has been a very big strategic mistake by Russia, by the EU and most of all by the U.S. to convert Ukrainian political and economic reform into an East-West struggle," in his blog of February 8, 2014, in which he points out a few basic facts:

> Ukraine's most serious problems are internal, not external. They must be solved by Ukrainians, not by outsiders. Ukraine will never be free, prosperous and democratic unless it has friendly

Media Blinders on Ukraine 83

relations with Russia. ... The interference of outside powers has exacerbated the regional division rather than healing it.

Concerning the expansion of NATO, Matlock's April 3 blog confirms that while there was no restrictive treaty for the territory of East Germany to remain free of any non-German military presence there was indeed a verbal agreement on the non-extension of NATO in East European countries:

> I am sure that if Bush had been re-elected and Gorbachev had remained as president of the USSR there would have been no NATO expansion during their terms in office.[26]

And he emphasizes the point:

> Imagine the outrage in Washington if China built an impressive military alliance and tried to include Canada and Mexico in it.

Regarding Ms. Nuland and Vice-President Joe Biden's visits to the Maidan demonstrators:

> How would Occupy Wall Street have looked if you had foreigners out there leading them? Do you think that would have helped them get their point across?[27]

Another critical voice is that of political scientist John J. Mearsheimer, former West Point Military Academy graduate and a specialist on nuclear deterrence, author notably of an authoritative book on *The Israel Lobby and U.S. Foreign Policy.*[28]

In a much discussed article published in *Foreign Affairs*, he denounces "the prevailing wisdom in the West," according to which "the Ukraine crisis can be blamed almost entirely on

Russian aggression." He flatly states that the West is responsible for the crisis.[29] At issue: extension of NATO toward the East in two stages: Czech Republic, Hungary and Poland in 1999; Estonia, Latvia, Lithuania, Rumania, Slovakia and Slovenia at the Bucharest summit in 2008. This last extension was then frozen, President Putin having "very transparently hinted" to President Bush that it amounted to a direct threat to Russia and that if Ukraine was admitted into NATO, "it would cease to exist."

In his speech on Europe's overall security held in Munich in 2007, Putin had actually clearly indicated the limits to be respected for peace in Europe. Six years later, during trade negotiations with President Yanukovych, Europe still attempted, once again, to force entry.

> The West's triple package of policies—NATO enlargement, EU expansion, and democracy promotion—added fuel to a fire waiting to ignite.
> ... Putin's actions should be easy to comprehend. A huge expanse of flat land that Napoleonic France, imperial Germany, and Nazi Germany all crossed to strike at Russia itself.

Regarding the misplaced NATO extensions, Mearsheimer quotes the remark of former American diplomat George F. Kennan, father of the Soviet containment doctrine during the Cold War: "I think it is a tragic mistake. There was no reason for this whatsoever. No one was threatening anyone else." He adds that "Given that most Western leaders continue to deny that Putin's behavior might be motivated by legitimate security concerns, it is unsurprising that they have tried to modify it by doubling down on their existing policies and have punished Russia to deter further aggression." Kennan suggested that they "should abandon their plan to westernize Ukraine and instead aim to make it a neutral buffer between NATO and Russia, akin to Austria's position during the Cold War." And this is how, through blindness and with the help of a compliant press, Ukraine has been torn up with guns talking instead of diplomats.

Paul Craig Roberts, former assistant treasury secretary under Reagan and former associate editor of the *Wall Street Journal*, has become a forthright campaigner against American warmongering and hegemonism, which he finds contrary to the pacific and liberal constitution of the United States.

Roberts thinks that "European governments and the Western media have put the world at risk by enabling Washington's propaganda and aggression against Russia. Washington has succeeded in using transparent lies to demonize Russia as a dangerous aggressive country led by a new Hitler or a new Stalin, just as Washington succeeded in demonizing Saddam Hussein in Iraq, the Taliban in Afghanistan, Qaddafi in Libya, Assad in Syria, Chavez in Venezuela, and, of course, Iran."

He denounced the declarations of American chief of staff Martin Dempsey at the Aspen Forum on July 24, 2014, who said that "Putin's aggression in Ukraine is comparable to Stalin's invasion of Poland in 1939" and that "the unproven involvement of Russia in Ukraine [was] the first time since 1939 that country made a conscious decision to use its military force inside another sovereign nation to achieve its objectives."

"Washington has claimed the title from Israel of being 'God's Chosen People'" and "takes for granted that US law prevails in other countries over the countries' own laws," as France experienced in the obligation made in June 2014 to BNP Paribas to pay a US$8.9 billion fine for having served as broker for Iranian oil, and as did Switzerland, whose banks were forced to denounce their clients to the American tax office. "It is a simple matter to establish that Washington organized a coup that overthrew an elected government [and] supports violence against those who object to the coup..." And Roberts mentions a bill European newspapers have never written about, Senate Bill 2277, which "provides for beefing up forces on Russia's borders and for elevating Ukraine's status to 'ally of the US' so that US troops can assist the war against 'terrorists' in Ukraine."[30]

For his part, Irish Martin Sieff, former head of international analysis at UPI news agency, chief analyst of The Globalist website and a contributor to The American Conservative blog, writes that Russia is only applying the old Monroe Doctrine the United States adopted in 1823, according to which no other power can intervene in their immediate sphere of influence. Putin's moves "are truly dangerous in terms of world peace. But one must at least recognize two points, unpalatable though they may be: First, his moves are consistent with Russia's historical fears and legitimate security concerns."

> It was the United States' aggressive NATO expansion, undertaken against earlier commitments, that has created Russia's sense of a need for a determined pushback against the United States' constantly stepping into Russia's sphere of influence. Like it or not, Russia certainly has more justification for intervention in Crimea which was Russian in 1783 (before the time when the United States Constitution was created) and in Ukraine than the United States has for 'its' cases.[31]

One-Track Media Thinking

Stephen F. Cohen worries about the triumph of one-track thinking in American media and policy:[32]

> ...the new cold war may be more perilous because, also unlike its forty-year predecessor, there is no effective American opposition … We opponents of the US policies that have contributed so woefully to the current crisis are few in number, without influential supporters and unorganized. … We have no access to the Obama administration, virtually none to Congress, which is a bipartisan bastion of Cold War politics, and very little to the mainstream media. (Since the

Ukrainian crisis deepened, does anyone recall reading our views on the editorial or op-ed pages of *The New York Times*, the *Washington Post* or the *Wall Street Journal* or seeing them presented on MSNBC or the Fox News Channel, which differ little in their unbalanced blame-Russia broadcasts?) ... In my long lifetime, I do not recall such a failure of American democratic discourse in any comparable time of crisis.[33]

In France too, voices are being raised against this unilateral and biased treatment, which makes events in Ukraine unintelligible because the Russians' motivations are never exposed, with the exception of endless reference to their alleged atavistic expansionism and desire to restore the Soviet Empire— that they themselves terminated. Among them are those of economist Jacques Sapir, former prime minister Dominique de Villepin, former socialist minister Jean-Pierre Chevènement, *Le Monde diplomatique*, the weekly *Marianne*, and, less often, essayist Jacques Attali, French Academy permanent secretary Hélène Carrère d'Encausse, and former minister Hubert Védrine, who present a more nuanced point of view.

"To each his own: for the Brussels institutions, it is only natural for Europe to try to export her liberal norms, ecological standards and 'democratic' values. For Moscow, it is *Drang nach Osten* [Nazi Germany's 'push East' into Slavic lands] under another form. Russia senses NATO behind the EU. The messianism of the one thus nourishes the nationalism and siege mentality of the others," writes Jean-Pierre Chevènement.[34.]

This point of view is shared by Hubert Védrine:

Western policy toward Russia since 1992 has been at once offhand, provocative, firm and weak at the same time, and in the end incoherent. First, bad American advice on the ultraliberal Big Bang (a shock without therapy!) that disintegrated the economic and social system of the Russians and ushered in kleptocracy. Then, promises about Ukraine joining the European Community waived with lack of thought that stood no chance of materializing in the short-term. Vague attempts to extend NATO to Georgia, Moldavia, Ukraine and Azerbaijan launched under Clinton and then under George W. Bush: as many provocations in Moscow's eyes.[35]

Unanswered Questions

Where has our intellectual curiosity gone? Our thirst to understand the world as it is and not as we wish it would be? These questions should ceaselessly haunt intellectuals, teachers, doctors, researchers and all those that profess to think, to understand and to explain. They should obsess the journalists, whose job it is to inform.

But perhaps the first question that we should ask ourselves, like the sensible men and women that we are supposed to be, is this: why don't we, quite simply, dare to ask questions anymore? It's not as if there are none.

What sort of vague terror grabs us at the perspective of passing through the mirror to see what is behind it? What or whom do we fear when we avoid upsetting questions and disturbing hypotheses so much? What if Putin was right after all? What if he is not the lout we are told he is? Isn't this an interrogation as legitimate as the others, would it only be as a heuristic precaution?

Why, in our newspapers, on our radio and television channels, isn't there any questioning of the legality, legitimacy and above all the effectiveness of Western military interventions when we pitilessly denounce the will of countries deemed minor to defend themselves? Effectiveness is proclaimed everywhere as a criterion of excellence, but why isn't it ever invoked when assessing the military operations carried out in the past twenty-five years against Somalia, Afghanistan, Iraq, Libya, Syria, and now bombings against ISIS? Have these been successful? Has this gunboat policy brought about peace or democracy? Do bombs dropped on Afghani Taliban and Mali Islamists cause less suffering and destruction than Russian bombs on Chechen rebels?

Is our vision of the world as impartial as we like to think it is? Are Western acts the fruit of the West's high moral principles or on the contrary largely dictated by material interests the West is averse to divulge? Aren't the moral foundations of Western international policy infinitely variable? Why would the borders of Ukraine be inviolable when those of Serbia were not in 2007 nor those of Czechoslovakia in 1993?

Why should international law be regarded as scorned by the Russians in Crimea but not by the Europeans that endorsed the secession of Kosovo in 2008? Ah, but things were different, we are told. Really? How so? Please explain. The European Union, which protested loudly when Russia favored the return of Crimea to her bosom, kept absolutely silent over the dismemberment of Yugoslavia in 1991. Do the rights of Russian-speaking minorities in Donbass and Crimea weigh less on the human rights scales than those of the peoples of the former Yugoslavia? Do Abkhazians and South Ossetians have fewer rights than the Kosovars, even though they were massacred by the Georgian majority during the 1989 and 1992 pogroms?[36]

Wouldn't the thousands of billion dollars sunk into fragmentation bombs, drones and private mercenary companies have been better invested in eliminating poverty, misery, despair, and the lack of education at the roots of the proliferation of terrorism in those countries? What benefits are we drawing from these armed interventions and occupations? Haven't they triggered chaos everywhere they have taken place? Have the populations "freed" by the magic of Western intervention in Libya, Afghanistan, Iraq, the Central African Republic or Mali achieved peace? Why is this swath of destruction never recalled when Vladimir Putin is criticized for helping the Donbass rebels whose civilian populations are under military attack by the Kiev coup-imposed government?

Why doesn't the media, in its numerous debates that stir up its cozy little world on the freedom of expression, ever examine the conditions related to the production and propagation of information? Why hasn't there been a thorough debate on the book of German journalist Udo Ulfkotte, who worked for seventeen years at *Frankfurter Allgemeine Zeitung* then proved, citing all manner of facts and names, how the section editors of mainstream media worked for NATO under the instigation of politicians and the German secret service? His investigation was immediately denounced as a "conspiracy theory" by the renowned newspapers implicated, but it was not denied. Especially as it was confirmed by another investigation, that of Uwe Krüger, a researcher at the German Institute of Journalism.[37]

Why is it considered good journalism to interview the president of a committee of mothers of Russian soldiers close to anti-governmental NGOs, and not the mothers of Ukrainian soldiers who protested for weeks in Kiev against the sacrifice of their children who were being called on to kill their compatriots in the Donbass? Why are reasons of State, active everywhere, denounced only for the Russians but never shown when they concern Brussels, Washington or Kiev?

If Chinese, Russian, Venezuelan or Iranian journalists are immediately disqualified as suspected of propaganda, then why do we Westerners who enjoy the privilege of working in freedom and democracy never question the actual independence of press agencies, TV channels or newspapers, which to a large extent depend on direct or indirect subventions from the government? In which ways are Radio Free Europe and Fox News more independent and objective than Russia Today,[38] or the big public or private Western press agencies more impartial than the Russian agency Itar-Tass?

Why doesn't the media, which is almost entirely in the hands of a few wealthy families or corporations, ever ask the question of interest linkages and allegiance to the ideology of their owners – at least in relation to competing papers? Is it innocuous for journalists to work in a newspaper with close links to finance, the armament industry or the ministry of foreign affairs? Why wouldn't such proximity contaminate these journalists as much as closeness to the Chinese communist party?

The media have never been independent and journalists know that objectivity only exists in ethics manuals and as slogans seeking to achieve legitimacy and public acceptance. But in the past fifteen years, the crisis of traditional media, following the collapse of advertising revenue and the emergence of social media, has arisen due to its lack of commitment to truth. The subject is taboo among journalists. The fear of losing one's job, of upsetting the announcers and being deprived of support by the authorities has raised an insurmountable barrier to stymie curiosity and instead conform oneself to the presumed expectations of political or economic powers.

Those biases and failings would be more tolerable if the Western press were not so prone to sermonizing. What gives Western media the right to decree that Peking and Moscow journalists are sold to their powers that be and those of Al Jazeera, Cuba and Venezuela practice propaganda instead of providing information?

Those wonderful Western government and media statements on the democracy and freedom aspirations of the oppressed peoples of Ukraine and Georgia are in fine little more than modest fig leaves meant to cover up the pornography of power struggles for control of energy routes, the conquest of new markets, and pursuit of Western (US) hegemony. What about the weapons sales and oil routes that must be secured? Why would reason always, uniformly, systematically, be on the same side? Haven't we been taught to be wary of truths too good to be true and to provide the version of the opposite camp so that the reader, the listener, the viewer forms an opinion?

Why do otherwise serious newspapers for weeks on end reprint the slightest indication of alleged Russian truck convoys at the Ukrainian border and keep repeating that the Russians are arming the separatists while saying not a word on American vice-president Joe Biden's visits to Kiev, or how his son joined the board of directors of Burisma Holdings, Ukraine's largest gas producer, accompanied by David Leiter, the former Senate Chief of staff of John Kerry, the US secretary of state? What about the deliveries of "non-lethal" military hardware to the Ukrainian army? Is the landing of hundreds of military advisers and propaganda experts in Ukraine an innocent measure? Isn't it a "covert invasion" just as much as Russian aid to the Donbass insurgents?

Why are the separatists systematically found responsible for the conflict, as if the Ukrainian army, which has gone to their territory to attack their cities, threw only flowers over the inhabitants of Donetsk and Luhansk? Why doesn't the so-called quality press want or dare to say that the bombing of civilian populations is contrary to the Geneva Convention? Has journalism sunk so low in Western media that it can only parrot NATO communiques without ever giving the point of view of the opposite camp, or else only at the very bottom of a page as if to hide it away? Why are Obama's speeches summarized, analyzed and commented on in abundance whereas those of the Russian president, even the most important ones, are reduced to a few sentences taken out of context, making it impossible to know what he actually said?

Some will say that Russia is a secondary power and her president does not deserve so much attention—though of course Putin is hardly ever out of the headlines. Why this landslide of commentaries, photos and texts on the slightest activities of members of the Russian opposition? Why is the Pussy Riot outrage in Christ The Savior Cathedral in Moscow considered a symbol of democracy and freedom if it occurs in Russia but as a "sad" behavior when the same type of disgusting action by Femen occurs in Paris Notre Dame or in Saint Peter Square in Rome? And why minutely describe Putin's alleged pique during the G20 summit in Brisbane? If he is a secondary character, why focus on his assumed frustrations? And why should we have to learn only through a cultural radio station (France Musique) that actually President Putin's elegance and courtesy were impressive throughout the event, thanking his guests, shaking hands with police officers, and remaining perfectly stoical in front of the Western heads of State, even though they flew into a rage against him, as did, in particular, Australian prime minister Tony Abbott? These are details, but they are very telling of the distorted state of mind of those Western journalists who seem to have renounced their independence of mind and critical duty to turn themselves into servile relays of the official pronouncements of their governments amid a frantic search to publicize whatever might discredit their enemies.

Of course, no one is forced to like Russia and every journalist has the right to criticize her. But why such hatred, such detestation, such systematic denigration, and such pathetic absence of any word of empathy, as if nothing, absolutely nothing positive has ever come out of Russia in the last decades?

Hasn't Russia opened her borders to foreigners as well as to her citizens, as was never the case before? Hasn't she become transparent, so much so that the slightest breach, the slightest infringement of human rights and liberties is the object of a detailed report by NGOs and foreign press correspondents? In 1939, Churchill described Russia as "a riddle wrapped in a mystery inside an enigma." But today the Russian mystery does not exist any longer: everything is accessible to anybody who takes the trouble to look.

Didn't Russia suppress the counter-threat the Soviet Union posed to the West of nuclear missiles and thousands of tanks massed in Eastern Europe? Didn't she withdraw her troops to 2,000 kilometers from Berlin whereas the United States has forwarded theirs to Poland, the Czech Republic and the Baltic countries while maintaining their missiles in Turkey and in Europe and their naval bases everywhere around the world? Haven't U.S. military expenditures exploded in the twenty-five years that the Cold War has been over? Who is threatening, who is arming themselves to the tune of over US$500 billion a year, $582.7 billion for 2017?[39]

By withdrawing peacefully from Europe and Central Asia, by offering a partnership for peace which the West declined, by offering her services to the United States after the 9/11/2001 attacks, hasn't Russia proved she has renounced any kind of military aggression? How can outrageous editorials on the return of Russian expansionism denounce the help provided to the populations of Transnistria, Abkhazia and South Ossetia and even of Donbass, when as a result, for more than twenty years, over millions of square kilometers, a hundred million people have peacefully recovered their independence—at least, from Russia?

Let us take the liberty of going further along these disturbing lines of argument. Despite all that is written in our newspapers and mouthed on our screens, hasn't Russia in some ways been more democratic and more progressive than some Western States? Didn't she abolish de facto the death penalty, which is still practiced on a large scale in the United States? Does she have to be sermonized, when corruption scandals erupt even at the top of the (former) French presidency and for decades have sullied top Japanese leaders' good names without any European media showing concern? And justice, so often decried: isn't Russian justice as transparent as it is elsewhere? Aren't the torture and secret detention of prisoners in Guantánamo more scandalous than the questionable condemnation of an oligarch for tax fraud?

Doesn't NSA's systematic spying on all private conversations of citizens of the world and the relentless hunt carried out against those courageous heroes who have brought to light those serious breaches of democratic freedoms, Julian Assange and Edward Snowden, deserve to be denounced as vigorously as Russia's restrictions on some opposition media? Even if Republicans have condemned NSA surveillance program as "contrary to the right of privacy protected by the fourth amendment of the United States constitution", nothing serious has been done against the mass spying on citizens.[40]

Where is the questioning of the Swedish justice for issuing an arrest warrant for Assange for rape, forcing him to seek asylum in the Ecuadoran embassy for fear of extradition to the United States, then failing to interview him until November 14, 2016, a full six years after a woman in Stockholm accused the WikiLeaks founder of rape? Shouldn't the Nobel Peace Prize be granted to those courageous denunciators of the drift toward global surveillance in our democracies, as much as to the Russian opposition press?

One last point, about the rule of law and legal certainty, which supposedly goes without saying in Western countries and would be faltering in Russia: what can be said about legal certainty in a country, the United States, which rewrites *a posteriori* legal provisions and sues businesses (BNP Paribas for one) for violating Iran embargo rules that did not exist when the incriminating acts took place? Or of tribunals that find in favor of Argentine debt speculators to the detriment of millions of citizens presumed free and sovereign?

The media have specific responsibilities as they are supposed to inform and help shape public opinion. So it is legitimate to ask them a volley of questions as thick as the carpets of bombs that have ruined Iraq, Syria and Libya. Why should the security of the European Union be ensured to the detriment of that of Russia? Why, in the Ukrainian conflict, should West Ukrainians' pro-European opinion prevail over East Ukrainians' pro-Russian opinion? In which way is desire for Europe more legitimate than desire for Russia? Why are deontological rules (critical questioning and need to balance sources) applied only for the Kremlin and not for the Kiev government? If the Western media wishes to be viewed as more than the governmental propaganda bullhorn—as it is increasingly viewed across the entire world—it must try to understand and shed light on the position of the opposite camp, to put itself in others' shoes, at least on the intellectual level, rather than throwing oil on the fire through unilateral commentaries. If there is Russian action against Ukraine, why not contextualize the issue by reminding readers that it started after the overthrow of the corrupt but legitimate Yanukovych government? If elections had been held as specified in the February 22 agreement signed by the European leaders, would Crimea have changed hands and the Donbass war taken place?

With the help of the Ukrainian crisis, detestation of Russia has reached proportions that go beyond rationality and defy imagination. "It's Russia's fault" has become a leitmotiv for American and European editorialists, experts, academics and politicians to explain any internal problem on the European continent. Each sentence, each incident, even the most trivial, is twisted or interpreted in a negative sense. The least pretext is conjured and relayed ad infinitum through feats of delirious imagination.

When, interviewed by a female student at the Seliger Forum on August 29, 2014 on the Ukrainian crisis and its effect on Kazakhstan, which is allied to Russia in the context of the customs union with Byelorussia, President Putin declared that Kazakhstan had never been an independent state but, contrary to Ukraine, had managed to build a solid and stable state structure over the past twenty years, only the first part of his sentence was translated into English by the Western media and the Kazakh nationalist websites, which deliberately ignored the second part to make it sound as if the Russian president was wittingly deprecating Kazakhstan to better dismember it. Deliberate act or the need to be brief on TV?[41]

By mid-September 2014, 75 million Russians were called to elect their local and regional representatives, but no Western newspaper covered those elections. Why did Radio Suisse Romande, after announcing in the morning newscast that an opinion poll had found that 92% of Russians supported Vladimir Putin, spend the entire time allotted to the topic interviewing a female opponent who explained why 8% of the population were unhappy with the government? It is interesting to know why those 8% were angry but we would have been better informed if we had been told why so many Russians support their president.

Yet two days later the Western media had a great time over the house arrest of an oligarch, Vladimir Yevtushenkov, No. 15 on the *Forbes* list of Russia's richest men. Suddenly they had found enough space to relate and widely comment on this event and explain why "the few legal protections Russians still possess are becoming even more limited."[42]

One may also wonder why the fate of the Tartar minority in Crimea garnered so much attention from Western journalists and NGOs while no attention is paid to the massive violations of human rights suffered by the Russian minorities in Estonia and Latvia.

The key problem is of a more global, philosophical order. What has happened to us, heirs to the Enlightenment, that we stop exercising critical judgment when we examine Russian affairs? What has happened to we Westerners, children of Rousseau, Kant, Marx, Kierkegaard, Sartre and Hannah Arendt, that we content ourselves with crass prejudice, hackneyed commonplaces, and clichés repeated ad nauseam whenever the largest of our neighbors is mentioned? That we are happy with silly chatter on freedom, democracy and durable development by the likes of Samuel Huntington, Francis Fukuyama and Bernard-Henri Lévy? What has happened to us that we are repudiating great historians such as Fernand Braudel, Jacques Le Goff, Eric Hobsbawm or Paul Kennedy in favor of self-proclaimed experts for hire to rewrite the past and draw up a future in conformity with most trivial American tastes?

Henry Kissinger shed light on the matter when he said: "For the West, the demonization of Vladimir Putin is not a policy: it is an alibi for the absence of one."[43]

The Unbearable Notion of a Worthy Critical Other

American historian Martin Malia (1924-2004), who taught at Berkeley, tried to explain the cognitive gap and devastating aversion of Westerners regarding their big neighbor in his *Russia Under Western Eyes*.[44] He notes that "Russia has at different times been demonized or divinized by Western opinion less because of her real role in Europe than because of the fears and frustrations, or the hopes and aspirations, generated within European society by its own domestic problems. The prime example of Russia refracted through the prism of Western crises and contradictions is, of course, the combined attraction-repulsion of the Red Specter in the twentieth century."

In other words, Russia upsets the image the West has of itself and of the world. The clash between the West's idealized image of itself and its harsh reality as viewed by Russia clarifies the Western psychological need for demonization of Russia. And vice versa, when the West is in a period of doubt, it tends to idealize Russia. For the West, Russia, with her blue-eyed white population and her own religion and culture, represents one facet of the Same. Hence the bitter disappointment that follows when it realizes that Russia does not have the same conception of democracy, faith, freedom, or capitalism. That Russia is indeed not the same.

The difference claimed by Russia becomes all the more unbearable as it is not visible at first sight.

This thesis reinforces the West's hegemonic agenda that explains both the recurrent Russophobia and determination of media and private research institutes against Russia—because it is your nearest and dearest you hate best, those that are almost like you, those whom you know or think you do. The distant foreigner, the unknown alien, may eventually inspire fear but not hatred. Russians, after all, are white.

The West would not be quite itself without the myth of the Russian bear, of the communist with a hammer and sickle or of revanchist Putin nostalgic of the Soviet Empire. In that perspective, we understand better how the elements of the story the West tells itself each time Russia is involved, have been assembled and perpetuate themselves.

By ceaselessly renewing and remodeling its anti-Russian discourse, the West enhances and reassures itself, strengthens the high opinion it has of itself achieved by belittling the Other. The example mostly comes from the top, from intellectuals and the academic world. Every time there is a crisis, such as that of Ukraine, the media, universities and international relations institutes air the same old clichés all over again and display feats of imagination by inviting the same circle of Polish, Baltic or Anglo-Saxon experts that all sing the same anti-Russian refrain.

Never is a Russian invited to talk, would it only be for the sake of balance. The network seems to operate on a closed-loop cycle.[45]

In 2005, the Switzerland-CIS Joint Chamber of Commerce commissioned a two-way study of the image of Switzerland in Russia and of the image of Russia in Switzerland. The results were perfectly contradictory, in a striking symmetry: roughly three out of four Russians looked at Switzerland with great fondness, as a country that was trustworthy, prosperous and likeable, whereas 75% of the Swiss saw Russians as crypto-communists, spies or Mafiosi. Ten years later, the terms to express that divergence have evolved, other words have appeared to qualify the Russians, but without modifying representations or proportions.

Always the same reflex, which consists in suspecting, criticizing, accusing Russia, is triggered. This conditioning is not random. It has a history, causes, and mechanisms of service and reinforcement. It relies on a psychology and actors that feed it ceaselessly, even if they are not always conscious of it, like journalists, who often content themselves with reproducing a behavior without the will or the time to question it. But then, to borrow again the behaviorist metaphor, this Russophobia is not innate, it has been taught, acquired, and has taken roots in the depths of the West's collective unconscious. Why? How? This is what we are going to examine in the following chapters.

PART II

A SHORT HISTORY OF RUSSOPHOBIA

| Chapter Four |

A WAR OF RELIGION SINCE CHARLEMAGNE

"In Europe, we are seen as Asiatic, parasites and slaves, yet if we go to Asia we will be seen as masters, as Europeans ... Who are they, those Russians? Asians? Tartars? ... What this union of Slavs portends (according to the Europeans) is conquest, plunder, trickery, perfidy, the future destruction of civilization, the united Mongolian horde, the Tartars!"
Fyodor Dostoyevsky, *A Writer's Diary*, 1881

Paradoxical as this may sound, Russophobia began even before Russia entered History. To understand the wall of prejudice that keeps the modern West and the Russian world apart, we must indeed go back to the Great Schism and even further back in time, two centuries earlier, when Charlemagne was crowned emperor and contended with the Byzantine emperor for the succession to the Roman Empire, and modified Christian liturgy to introduce reforms execrated by the Eastern Churches.

Numerous religious, political, economic and cultural factors led to a divorce of the two great entities of medieval Christendom. We shall present only those that were most significant in the birth of the hatred that slowly grew between the

West on the one hand and the Byzantine Empire and the Greek Church of the East on the other, and then including Russia when the latter decided to take over the Byzantine religious and political heritage after the fall of Constantinople.

Already at the time, political rivalries as much as religious divergences exacerbated the conflicts that were slowly surfacing between East and West, until they exploded in a schism that is still not resolved today.

This fracture, which has opposed the two components of Christendom over the past twelve centuries, has conditioned the entire history of the continent and still influences the warped conceptions of both sides, even if in the course of centuries, the religious motives of the quarrel have lost their pertinence and virulence.

If Prince Vladimir had decided in 988 in the Chersonese[1] in Crimea already! to convert to Roman Catholicism rather than to Orthodoxy, the whole history of Europe would have been changed, as no one, either in the West or in the East, would have questioned that Russia was part of Europe. Courted both by Rome, which had just converted the Poles and the Hungarians, and by Byzantium, the first historic ruler of Russia did not, however, hesitate before leaning toward Orthodoxy.

Byzantium, City of Light, Beats Rome in Ruins

For the first rulers of the Russian realm that had taken shape around Kiev, Byzantium offered by far the better choice. The choice of the Greek rite was very rational, especially since the Byzantine emperor had given his sister in marriage to Vladimir in exchange for his military support. It was closer to them in terms of culture, more seductive because of its still very high prestige, and more promising in terms of trade because of the export outlets the harbor of Constantinople offered between the Black Sea and the Mediterranean Sea through the Dardanelles. Byzantium, with its one million inhabitants, easily won over very distant Rome and its tens of thousands of residents struggling to survive in its ruins.

The City of Light, the capital of civilization in the 9th century, was Byzantium, not Rome. The thousand-year Greek presence in Crimea and in the south of present-day Ukraine, added to its regular proclaiming by Byzantine missionaries, decisively tipped the balance in favor of Orthodoxy and the Byzantine Basileus. Furthermore, Byzantium also contributed a writing, Cyrillic, a liturgical language, Church Slavonic, and new arts, such as icon painting, which were to prove prodigiously useful to the young Russian nation.

Before the schism, the choice of one or the other tradition posed no problem in terms of religion. Vladimir's choice even appeared so natural that it was not contested by the king of France a few decades later. At the end of the 1000s, Capetian King Henri I found himself a widower without an heir. Seeking a new queen, he turned toward the prestigious Kiev kingdom, where Vladimir's granddaughter, Princess Ann, daughter of King Yaroslav 1 the Wise, was not married. The king of the Franks sent his best bishop, Roger II of Châlons, to negotiate her hand.

Belonging, as per her faith, to the Eastern Orthodoxy, Anne first married King Henry the First of France in Reims on May 19, 1051. King Henry, for his part, belonged to the Roman Catholic Church, the two churches being still undivided, as this event took place before the 1054 schism. The wedding in Reims was the occasion of great festivities. Anne was to reign until 1061, taking up the regency after her husband's death. She introduced the name 'Philippe' to the court of France, baptizing thus her first born, who would reign under the name of Philippe I. She then married the count of Valois, Raoul de Crépy, one of the great princes of the realm. She died at the end of the 1070s. Cultured and refined, she found the court of the Franks "barbaric," and coarse.[2] Her second marriage is considered one of the first manifestations of courtly love.

Anne of Kiev's story is very revealing of the absence of prejudice and value judgment that reigned in Europe before the schism put its stamp on the vast majority of the accounts of Europeans who were to travel to Russia later. It shows that, before 1054, European rulers had no negative opinion of Russia and that, on the contrary, they had such a positive image of it that they were ready to have their bishops travel over 2,000 kilometers of bad roads to go and fetch a spouse.

It also shows that "civilization" was then flourishing in the East, not in the West, as ulterior historiography would try to accredit. And it underlines that the negative reports penned by European travelers began after the schism and were creations of religious prejudice. They resulted from the anti-Orthodox Catholic propaganda that followed the consummation of the schism. Today as well as yesterday, it is difficult to figure out the respective shares of religion and politics in the birth of the conflict. Did the conflict result simply from religious differences? Or did political ambitions and imperial rivalries take advantage of religious disagreements to vie for supremacy?

Religion as Eighth-Century Soft Power

It is thus worthwhile to go back to the religious and political factors that led to the schism, and to the consequences the latter has had in the history of the West and of Russia. Seen from the 21st century, the reasons for the schism seem futile and groundless. Decades of rationalism, skepticism and agnosticism, as well as the separation of Church and State with the acceptance of secularity in the running of public affairs and education, have made disagreements over the Trinity dogma and unleavened bread during communion obsolete.

And yet, if one agrees that religion was a major stake of soft power during the medieval era, one better understands the dimensions of the conflict that opposed the Christian churches of the East to those of the West and the Byzantine Empire to the Holy Roman Germanic Empire.

Knowing whether or not to add a mention of '*Filioque*' in the Christian Creed of the 8th century today makes us smile, but at the time it had as much importance for the domination of the Mediterranean and European worlds as the ritual invocation of human rights and democratic elections have in the discourse of the European Union and NATO about President Putin's Russia.

So it is useful to review the theological, liturgical and ideological differences that we would now say provoked the schism, how the will to power of Charlemagne and then of the Holy Roman Germanic Empire, the greed of Venetian merchants (the entrepreneurial spirit, in today's parlance) and the popes' desire to impose their absolute power on the Church, all led to the schism with the Eastern Church and the final ruin of the political power linked to it, namely the Byzantine Empire.

We must thus remember that after the fall of Rome in 476, the torch of the Roman Empire was grabbed by Byzantium, which became the sole capital of the new Eastern Roman Empire and took on board Rome's cultural, juridical and, for a large part, religious legacy. While the former imperial capital sank into chaos and anarchy, and Rome itself lost nine-tenths of its inhabitants and fell into ruin, Constantinople's prestige kept growing.

It rapidly became the most populated and most prosperous city in the civilized world (with the exception of Chinese cities), the capital of culture and the arts, and the most important religious center of Christendom. Rome, Antioch and Alexandria were reduced to second rank in spite of the presence of the pope in the first and, in the other two, of patriarchs then equal or superior before the law to the patriarch of the Byzantine Church.

Constantinople, Not Rome, Was Ascendant

The Arab conquest and the progress of Islam as of the 7th century deprived the Byzantine Empire of its Egyptian and North African territories and weakened it considerably, but without really impairing its cultural and political supremacy. It took the Crusades and the conquest of Byzantium by the Latins in 1204 to deal a fatal blow to its prestige. In spite of ceaseless threats of invasion, Byzantium extended the life of the Roman Empire by a thousand years and remained during at least seven centuries the undisputed City of Light of the Mediterranean basin, enclosing within its walls the major part of intellectual life of the era.

From the year 500 to the year 1200, it was in Byzantium

you had to be, what with intellectual debates livelier than anywhere else, top scholars, scientists, and theologians, and blossoming arts. Compared to it, Rome, Aix-la-Chapelle, Paris, or London cut sorry figures or were still small towns of thatched cottages and muddy lanes. At military level, Byzantium was always paramount, at times as a great power, at other times as a middle power, but always respected due to the value of its troops of archers and second-to-none sense of diplomacy, good at dividing its adversaries.[3]

In the religious area, the Byzantine patriarch, thanks to the leading role of his town, often found himself at loggerheads with the bishop of Rome. The early Church recognized the authority of the pope, but as a *primus inter pares*, according to Saint Peter's formula. At that time, the pope had no power to decide on his own but only that of convening and presiding over the ecumenical councils. At the institutional level, the Church was organized into patriarchates, under the aegis of five patriarchs (Jerusalem, Antioch, Alexandria, Constantinople, and Rome) equal under the law and whose declarations of faith had to be approved by the other four before they could exercise their magisterium.

All important decisions had to be taken by consensus during the ecumenical councils gathering all the components of Christendom. This system was thus rather democratic, and the oriental patriarchs, in particular the patriarch of Byzantium, were very attached to this mode of operation.

Thus it was according to usage and the canonical rule then in force that the Council of Nicaea adopted in 381 the Symbol, or Creed, which was originally a public declaration of faith pronounced on Good Friday by candidates to baptism. That version, adopted and recognized by all Christendom, pointed out that the Holy Spirit proceeds from the Father without any mention of the Son. There existed, however, here and there, variations that mentioned that the Holy Spirit proceeded from the Father and the Son (*Filioque*), without this creating any doctrinal difficulty, adoption of "and" being facultative and in keeping with the law.

As of the 6th century, recitation of the Creed became an integral part of the mass and spread in the West, notably in Spain, at Emperor Justinian's instigation, as he saw in it a way to reaffirm his domination over that part of his empire.[4] In 589, a council convened in Toledo at the initiative of Visigoth king Reccared proclaimed that the Creed must henceforth be sung during mass and must mention procession from the Father *and* the Son on pain of anathema. It was probably the Visigoth king's way of affirming his adhesion to the Roman faith and rejection of Arianism (a doctrine contesting the divinity of the Son as equal to the Father's). The version with *Filioque* slowly spread within the Germanic world with at first no one saying anything against it, everyone remaining free to add it or not to the Creed.

The *Filioque* Quarrel Created by Charlemagne

Things began to go wrong early in the 8th century when, after Charles Martel's victory over the Arabs in 732, the Carolingians affirmed themselves as the main power in the European West. At the instigation of Pepin the Short, and then of Charlemagne, they took it into their heads to restore the Western Roman Empire with a view to reinforcing their domination over the newly conquered territories. They decided to firm up their still tottering power by using all the resources of their soft power, i.e. by imposing a liturgical reform, the Gregorian chant, as well as a Credo sung with *Filioque*, throughout their new empire.

Modern Europe owes much to the genius of these two Carolingian rulers. Anxious to anchor their power to solid institutions and give it a legal basis (the notorious Caroline Capitularies), they also knew how to put theology to good political use. Thanks to them, the reformed sacraments of the Church and the new liturgy became the common language and the ideological cement of peoples conquered and reunited under the banner of the new emperor.

To achieve his ambitions, Charlemagne enrolled a first-class lieutenant, high-flying intellectual and propaganda genius, at once minister of the Interior, of Education, and of Information: the English monk, Alcuin. By force as much as by persuasion, relying on the Germanic nations of the empire—Franks, Goths, Saxons, Visigoths—

Alcuin succeeded in convincing the diffident bishops to adopt the new Creed against the will of the pope and the Latin bishops, who held to the old recited version with no mention of *Filioque*, as practiced by the Byzantines and the Eastern Church.

The man western imagination takes pleasure in designating as "the flowery-bearded emperor," as the kind granddad who invented school, was in reality an enlightened but absolute autocrat, a kind of successful Stalin, who reigned as a nitpicker over not just men but also their consciences, to the extent of personally writing to Bishop Amalarius to "ask for information on instructions given to priests as to the administration of baptism as well as a report on ceremonies in use."[5]

As to education, Alcuin reorganized schools and workshops of copyists of ancient texts. He wrote manuals in each subject:

> Come and take a seat now, you whose function it is to transcribe divine law and the sacred monuments of our Fathers' wisdom. Be careful not to let frivolous words into such grave matters; make sure your unthinking hand will make no error. Studiously search for pure texts so that your pen, in its swift flight, follows the right path.[6]

But the most significant event of Charlemagne's reign, which was going to change the fate of the West, was of course his crowning as emperor on Christmas Day in the year 800. This followed tough bargaining with the papacy. A few years earlier, Charlemagne had already been granted the title of defender of the Church by Pope Adrian V. Popes, often unpopular with the Romans and the local clergy, were also at loggerheads with the Lombards, who had invaded the north of Italy.

The king of the Franks lent a helping hand to Pope Leon III, who was "set upon, beaten up, thrown off his mule, stripped of his pontifical vestments" by Roman nobles in 799.[7]

He helped restore the Pope's authority in exchange for the imperial crown, which he obtained on Christmas Day the following year. And to complete his religious authority, Charlemagne had himself ordained as a priest, in order to hold symbolically both temporal and spiritual power, and better compete with the pope for supreme authority over the West.

The Theory of the Two Swords, Papal and Imperial

Alcuin will dress up this maneuver with his doctrinal unction and appease the budding conflict by developing the two-sword theory, whereby the pope defends the faith, and the emperor the Latin Christian world. This union of the swords, in an alliance that later will become the union of the sword and the aspergillum, allowed the Church to revive and the Carolingian power to assert its authority. The thousand trials and tribulations it experienced later did not succeed in breaking it up. As Robert Heath aptly sums it up, it is thanks to the support of the Franks that:

> ...the Roman Church was able to accede to its status as guide at world level. To sum up, the affirmation of universality of the Roman Church and primacy of Rome over the other sees very naturally became the cornerstone of the Frank policy, under the authority of a king who gave himself the role of religious affairs minister and whose policy was conceived by a minister of foreign affairs who controlled the liturgy of the kingdom, namely Alcuin in person."[8]

The aim of this operation was twofold: on the one hand, unify the empire around a new ritual and a new liturgy by forcing the popes to cooperate; on the other, undermine any Byzantine influence in Italy and in Western Europe. Already, after the seventh Nicaea council in 787, the Franks had attacked by insisting on the fact that the Greeks could not be taken seriously since they were governed by a woman, Empress Irene, and the pope had to distance himself from them.

After several years of theological debates, synods and councils convoked at their initiative with theologians in their pay, the Franks achieved their aim. Their beautiful construction resulted in sealing the collaboration between the pope and the emperor and in unifying European Christendom, but to the detriment of the global unity of the Church.

Their policy could not but deeply irritate the Byzantine emperor, who considered Charlemagne's crowning as emperor done without his consent as an act of rebellion, and irritate as well the patriarch of the Eastern Greek Church, for whom the adoption of the Creed, sung and with *Filioque*, without any decision by a properly convened ecumenical council, was an infringement of custom and a disavowal of the Fathers of the Church.

At first, the conflict remained very much local, each side practicing the liturgy and reciting the Creed according to their custom. In exchange for that increase in power, the popes resigned themselves to giving up Roman liturgy and adopted the Frank liturgy in Italy. But initially, they kept reading the Creed and made no mention of *Filioque*. Rather shrewdly, Pope Leon III argued that the two options were possible on a doctrinal level and that one practice did not preclude the other. He accepted the *Filioque* as a truth of faith, but refused to insert it in the Roman liturgy.

Charlemagne having added it to the liturgy of his own court, the pope protested by having the Latin and Greek texts of the original Creed without *Filioque* engraved on metal plaques screwed to the doors of his Roman basilisk.[9] The Byzantines, much more cultured than the Westerners, used to theological controversies and intellectual debates, and practicing for their part an evangelical charity totally alien to the more dogmatic Frank Church, in the end resigned themselves to this semi-solution. The disappearance of the Carolingian Empire a few years after the death of Charlemagne contributed for a while to a lowering of tensions.

The conflict resumed forcibly at the end of the 9th century when Pope Nicolas I (858–867) decided to endorse the Carolingian heritage and decreed that Byzantine emperors, who knew no Latin, did not deserve their titles and that the only true Roman emperor was in the West. The quarrel broke out over the adoption of *Filioque* by the Bulgarian Church, which Rome wanted while under Byzantine tutelage. It degenerated with the deposition of Byzantine patriarch Photius by the pope and, as a retaliatory measure, the excommunication of the pope by the Byzantine Church. Then things quieted down again for a century, until the creation of the Holy Roman Germanic Empire on the ruins of the former Carolingian Empire, and the crowning of Emperor Othon I in Rome on February 2, 962.

The popes were indeed threatened again by the Lombards whose king, Beranger II, had designs on the pontifical States. In 962, Pope John XII—one of the worst popes in the history of the Church according to testimonies of the time that call him debauched and an Antichrist—asked the Germans for help. The latter did not have to be asked twice and like Charlemagne two centuries earlier, used the opportunity to grant use of the pontifical States to the pope and by the same token, to repossess the imperial crown.

German influence was from then on fully brought to bear on the papacy. By 996, the German rulers managed to have German popes elected to the see of Peter who were in favor of *Filioque* and the Frank liturgy, to the detriment of Italian bishops favorable to the Byzantines and the traditions of the original Church.

The Fraudulent Donation of Constantine and the Fight for Papal Supremacy

Marked by the influence of the Frank absolutism, the papacy too was tempted by absolute power. Its search for supremacy was based on a double strategy: reinforcing its temporal power and asserting its eventual supremacy over an undivided and universal Church. To reach its aim and legitimize its pretentions, the papacy was o conveniently able to rely on the alleged Donation of Constantine a forged document fabricated in the 9th century.

This pseudo-donation has two parts, the first (*confessio*) is wrongly dated from the fourth consulate of Constantine in 315 and mentions the faith transmitted to Constantine by Pope Sylvester I. It also describes how the latter cured him of leprosy before he converted.

The second (*donatio*) is an enumeration of the territories and privileges Constantine bestowed on the pope, namely primacy over the Eastern Churches: the basilicas of Latran, Saint-Pierre and Saint-Paul Outside the Walls; possessions in various provinces of the Empire; the Latran palace; the imperial insignia, and the senatorial insignia of the pope's entourage; Rome, Italy and more generally, the West. It concludes with a declaration of the withdrawal of the emperor eastward, thus leaving the West to the sole power of the pope.[10]

The truth of this forged document was only revealed in 1430, five centuries after it had done its work. Now forgotten, it played nonetheless an essential part in the history of the Church and the formation of the West, as it promoted the eviction of the Byzantine Empire from Latin affairs by making it look like a usurper of the Roman Empire and justified the supreme authority of popes over the other patriarchs, in particular the one in Byzantium.

From that time on, the schism became unavoidable, the will of German emperors and of the popes uniting to claim entire temporal and spiritual power over the West, without any reference to the Eastern Roman emperor and the Greco-Byzantine Christian Church, as incarnated by the Basileus and the Constantinople patriarchs. In 1054, according to the tradition maintained by the West, the schism was complete and the two components of Christendom, like the two empires, evolved separately.

In reality, the schism took form only progressively and the relations between the Latin and Greek worlds remained, despite everything, rather tight. As Steven Runciman points out, contemporaries of the year 1000 were not necessarily aware of the schism and, shortly before the fall of their capital in the 15th century, the last Byzantine emperors accepted to submit to the pope.[11] In 1439, when Byzantium had lost all territories and was nothing but a depopulated town under siege by the Ottomans, the council of Florence confirmed the submission of the Church to Rome with the Byzantine emperor's approval. But this last attempt at rapprochement was too late and remained without any practical effect: divergences and resentment had become too strong to ever be wiped off, even in front of the Ottomans' mortal threat.

Westerners Reappraise the Trinity

So much for the political aspects of the religious schism. Let us deal for a moment, though, with the nature of the specifically religious differences, because it is of interest to what divides the West and Russia today.

The quarrel around *Filioque*, "as disproportionate and extravagant as it may appear today,"[12] expresses well the nature of the gap that separated and still separates the Roman-German-Latin West from the Greek-Russian-Orthodox East. On a strictly theological level, oriental theologians, confronted by the Nestorian and Monophysite heresies, supported the principle of a Trinity composed of three Divine Persons with distinctive functions forming a single hypostasis (substance).

The Westerners, for their part, were eager to answer the Arian heresy, and preferred to see the Trinity as a single hypostasis, Father, Son and Holy Spirit alternately. The Easterners gave an important function to the Holy Spirit, omnipresent in all assemblies of the faithful and acts of the Church. For Westerners, "God's unity is absolute and the Persons of the Trinity relative within Him, whereas for the Easterners, the three Persons each have their own competence but are reunited into a single hypostasis."[13]

These two conceptions were on an equal footing in theological terms. The quarrel broke out when the Westerners introduced the mention of "*Filioque*" into the Creed, as this, in Eastern eyes, "broke the fragile equilibrium of functions within the Trinity" and made the Holy Spirit appear to be subordinate to the Son, thus introducing a hierarchy between the divine beings. The proposal of several popes that the wording "the Holy Spirit proceeds from the Father *and* the

Son" be changed to "from the Father *through* the Son" was not accepted by the Franks, who also rejected the pope's suggestion to give up reciting the Creed during mass.

Let us note incidentally that, in religious terms, the conflict also bore on other aspects such as the celibacy of priests (the Eastern Church allowed ordination of already married men) or the distribution of unleavened flatbread during communion in the Western Church, which imposed these practices as early as the 9th century on the Byzantine faithful in Sicily. For the Byzantines, unleavened flatbread (the Host) instead of ordinary leavened bread was a nonsense, given that the body of Christ cannot "elevate us from the Earth to Heaven even as the leaven raises and warms the bread" and given that it is a symbol of joy, whereas flatbread "is lifeless like a stone or baked clay, fit only to symbolize affliction and suffering."[14] This very expressive justification makes us smile now but it illustrates well the cultural gap separating Christians from the East and Christians from the West.

Those questions triggered innumerable debates and virulent polemics during the many synods and councils which were spread over centuries until the Franks and then the German emperors succeeded in imposing their views on the popes, who had meanwhile come under their control, thanks to pressures on the cardinals. The Latins had remained much closer to the Greek and Mediterranean tradition because Byzantium had had possessions in Italy for centuries and regular contacts remained with the other Eastern Churches. By 1014, the Creed and the German liturgy were imposed on the entire Western Church, and Byzantine rites disappeared. Forty years later, in 1054, the schism was complete.

Democratic Easterners versus Absolutist Westerners

But what irritated the Byzantines most was not so much the theological quarrel but rather divergences of opinion about the organization of the Church. Used to ideological debate and much more flexible at the intellectual level, practicing active charity toward minor deviances, they could put up with religious differences so long as they did not put into question the dogma as instituted by the ecumenical councils. But then the Creed without *Filioque* had been specifically approved by the ecumenical councils of Nicaea in 325 and Constantinople in 381.

For the Easterners, only a democratically discussed decision inspired by the Holy Spirit during an ecumenical council gathering all Christian Churches was valid and could in no case be changed by any particular Church without the approval of a new ecumenical council. The decision to add *Filioque* taken on the sly by the local "council" of Toledo in 589, and then imposed in the Creed, which itself had been introduced "fraudulently" into the liturgy of the masses, was perceived as an unacceptable power grab and an attempt not just to bypass but to subject the Eastern Churches to the Western Church.

The conflict was turning into a political rather than theological one. The will of Frank and then of German rulers to reestablish the Western Roman Empire and subdue the Eastern one by putting pressure on the Roman popes to act accordingly at the religious level, was bound to generate a major conflict between the two components of Christendom. At first, the popes resisted German pressures. But the attraction of power, and the German will to assert the supremacy of the See of Peter over the other patriarchs, won the day, especially after the papacy fell into German hands.

For the Eastern Churches and especially the Byzantium Church, this reform was perceived as a betrayal of the spirit of the original Church, of the will of the Apostles and of the Church Fathers. They continued to think that the pope in Rome only enjoyed formal precedence but no particular power, and that all decisions over the dogma or the organization of the Church could only be taken collectively and by consensus. Papal absolutism, and worse still, the pontifical infallibility that was adopted in the 19th century, are notions totally alien to the Orthodox Church.

In the West, this search for supreme power rapidly fueled a lengthy quarrel, with the pope and emperor fighting each other for preeminence. Endless wars between Guelphs, who supported the popes, and Ghibellines, who supported the emperors, tore Italy apart over centuries. But despite their fratricidal fighting, popes and emperors agreed that, no matter what, they were superior to the Easterners, and that the Byzantine emperor as well as the Eastern Churches owed them respect and obedience.

Two Diverted Crusades: 1204 and 2003

Finally, the Greeks and the Christians of the East could not forget the betrayal of the fourth crusade, which was diverted to Constantinople by the Venetians in 1203 and led to the siege and then capture of the town by the crusaders and to the creation of the Eastern Latin Empire in 1204, forcing the Byzantine emperor to withdraw to Nicaea. The civil war between Latins and Byzantines left deep wounds and resulted in much bitterness among the Greeks.

With hindsight, this diversion ironically brings to mind the one the American Right succeeded in imposing in 2003 on President George W. Bush by diverting the crusade against Bin Laden's Islamic terrorism to an invasion of Iraq, for economic reasons very much like those that inspired the Venetians. Though eight hundred years apart, the similitude is striking.

So when two centuries later the fall of Constantinople to the Ottomans became unavoidable, the West did nothing significant to save it and protect the Christians of the East. Aware of the loss the Eastern sinking represented after all for Christendom, the pope did try to mobilize the princes, but to no avail. Constantinople, deserted, was courageously defended by a handful of Italian volunteers and sank into the indifference of the Genoese troops stationed before them, in the Pera citadel, and of the European rulers too busy fighting one another.

In Europe, the fall of Constantinople and the accession of a Muslin emperor to the throne of the Basileus had a considerable impact, comparable, to some extent, to the one following the collapse of the Soviet Union in 1991. The feeling that prevailed in the western courts and leading circles of the time was fairly similar, though inverse, to that expressed at the end of the Cold War by George Bush in his discourse on the State of the Union in January 1992: "They lost. We won." On the other hand, many contemporaries, aware of what they had lost, contented themselves with the prosaic remark, "They lost, too bad for them."

It is at any rate with *Schadenfreude* that the Europeans would have heard of the fall of Byzantium, according to Steven Runciman:

> Western Europe, at the bottom of its ancestral memory, remained envious of Byzantium; her spiritual advisers denounced the Orthodox as schismatic sinners; feeling guilty of having in the end betrayed Byzantium, she opted not to think about it. She found it impossible to forget her debt to the Greeks; but that debt, as she saw it, had to do with the classic age. [For the next generation of Europeans] Byzantium had been only a go-between of superstition, an era that was best forgotten.[15]

For the Greeks and the Eastern Christians, the disappearance of their empire and the victory of the Muslim Ottomans were of course major catastrophes. If they could not really hold the fall of Constantinople against the West, since it resulted primarily from internal divisions and a very long weakening in the face of Arab and Turkish invaders, the schism was something else altogether: it had been entirely provoked by the pretention of Westerners to rule over the temporal as well as spiritual realms.

As lawyer and historian Cyriaque Lampryllos described it very well at the end of the 19th century, the Easterners had the impression that they had been the object of a vast mystification by the Roman Church and the Holy Roman Emperor.[16] Not only had the latter taken that defeat as a pretext to make all that Byzantine Greek civilization had brought to Christian culture, science and the arts disappear while concentrating only on Ancient Greece's contribution, but they had taken advantage of it to rewrite *a posteriori* the history of the schism. The pope and the top Roman administration made some documents disappear and truncated others, in order to blot out Western responsibilities and have the Easterners take the blame for the schism.

A Schism Made in the West

We saw with the fake Donation of Constantine that Roman scribes did not hesitate to make counterfeits when it was a matter of asserting papal supremacy. Thus it appears that Pope Adrian's answer refuting Charlemagne's thesis regarding *Filioque* and Creed, as well as the code containing the letters of "pro-Byzantine" popes from John VIII to Leon IX, simply disappeared, just as the silver plaques bearing the original formula of the Creed put on display in the Saint Peter Basilica by Pope Leon III were removed and then destroyed by the "pro-Germanic" popes.[17] Adding insult to injury, during the following centuries, papal legates, through ignorance or Machiavellianism, accused the Easterners of having themselves truncated the Creed by deliberately suppressing the *Filioque* mention in the original version.

The dust of centuries and the thickness of prejudice had historiographers and the entire West beginning to talk of "the great Eastern schism," when the evidence points to a great Western schism. The mystification was so successful that Roman Catholics and atheistic Westerners are now convinced that it was the Eastern Churches that seceded, whereas what happened was the exact opposite. Even now, the deception still works, and very few western historians, with the exception of Steven Runciman, and even less so the Roman Church, have endeavored to restore the historical truth.

The fact that the Byzantine Empire was weakening while the European kingdoms were in full rise obviously played against the Easterners. Losers do not or no longer have, let alone write, their history. But the schism and distortion of history opened wounds which have yet to heal and which keep poisoning Europe, as roots of the tensions between the West and Russia.

If Western princes cannot be criticized for exploiting their growing power to assert their supremacy over a weakening East and thus take their revenge over the fall of Rome in 476, the revision and falsification of history is inexcusable, if only because of the damage provoked in the construction of contemporary Europe.

The Invention of Caesaropopery and Byzantinism

That damage is of two kinds. First, the virulent polemic opposing Westerners and Easterners over seven centuries, from the 760s to 1450, went beyond a mere theological debate and overflowed into the social sphere. It was during that time that the first Western prejudices and clichés against the East and Orthodoxy appeared.

For centuries, Western theologians have used a whole panoply of rhetorical and semantic arguments to discredit Byzantium, belittling Greek culture because it "ignored Latin," denigrating Byzantine intellectuals' taste for theological debate as "Byzantinism," or systematically reproaching Greek Christians for "their perfidy and hostility."[18]

Later on, Western historians would continue to highlight Byzantium's "Caesaropapism," a disobliging expression which comes up often under the pen of modern anti-Russian intellectuals who elaborated the thesis of Russian oriental despotism, erasing all the differences between Ivan the Terrible and Vladimir Putin. In reality, it is an invention of Western humanistic historiography, engaged in the rehabilitation of antiquity's philosophical values and which, unable to confront the dogmatism of the Roman Catholic Church, attacked instead the presumed Caesaropapism of Byzantium.

Stereotypes on a "complicated, despotic, underdeveloped, cruel and semi-barbaric" Orient have traveled through centuries and are these days applied to Russia under a modernized terminology. Yesterday as today, everything having to do with Byzantium is fraught with a negative connotation in the Western vocabulary and imagination. Even the name "Byzantium" derives from that will to belittle the Easterners, who never called themselves thus. They called themselves the Eastern Roman Empire, called themselves *Romaios*, and called their capital Constantinople, from the name of its founding emperor.[19]

The Arabs, who call the Christians Roms or Rumis, meaning Romans, have actually taken up that moniker. It is the Westerners, for the purpose of belittling, that baptized Constantinople as Byzantium, from the name of the burg of Greek fishermen that Constantine had chosen to make his capital.

Since Hieronymus Wolf (1557), the expressions "history of the Byzantine Empire" and "Byzantine" have been used to designate the Eastern Roman Empire and its inhabitants after 330. They would never have thought of calling themselves thus. That terminology only became prevalent in the 17th century. It is found under the pen of Montesquieu, for example. Unfortunately, this fight had a pernicious effect by giving Byzantium the appearance of a frozen, intolerant, and corrupt empire, while its scientific, philosophical, and literary heritage was in its entirety attributed to the Arabs, as if the Byzantine link had never existed.[20]

The European Crusades against Russian Orthodoxy

Let us now come to the history of the conflict with Russia. As soon as the schism was consummated, Rome forever wanted to take back to Orthodoxy that Russia it had just lost.

Already in 967, the Ravenna Council had proclaimed the need to consolidate Christianity in Eastern Europe. As early as the pontificate of Gregory VII (1073–1085), the conversion of Russia had become a priority, with the help of German feudality. It was at that time that the *Drang nach Osten* began before the term was coined, a push toward the East that was to go on and off over eight centuries, until 1945.

In the middle of the 12th century, in 1149, Krakow bishop Matthew thus wrote a letter to Bernard de Clairvaux, who wished to assess the possibility of sending a mission to the Orthodox Russians, in which he calls for a crusade against Russian barbarians.[21]

In 1200, missionaries entered the Baltic States and by 1220, the Teutonic Knights conquered domains as far away as Livonia, thanks to the Baltic crusades launched by Pope Innocent III to end the scandal of those folks that "disdain Catholic faith." Alexander Nevsky's victory in 1242 put them back where they belonged and left a deep impression in Russian memory.[22] Western historiography does not quite like to recollect the Teutonic Knights' invasions and the Polish and Lithuanian Catholics' attempted armed crusades in the 13th century, as they cast doubt on its version of an aggressive Russia. It would rather forget that in 1240 the Russians had to fight on two fronts, against the German and Polish maneuvers in the west and against the Mongol invaders in the east.

Actually, Alexander Nevsky, prince of Vladimir and Novgorod, was forced to conclude a truce with the Golden Horde to go and save Russia from the Swedes in the battle of the Neva on July 15, 1240, and in the "battle on the ice" of the frozen Peipus Lake against the knights of the Teutonic order, present in the region since 1237, who were trying to convert Russia to the Latin Church. If Western Catholics have forgotten that episode, the Russians for their part have never been able to forgive the Catholic knights for taking advantage of the Mongol attacks to assault them from the rear.

The Holy Roman Germanic Empire, despite a few initial successes, remained for its part weak and divided. It never succeeded in imposing its rule on the whole of Europe. The French, the English, the Hungarians, the Poles and the Slavs of Central Europe and the Balkans succeeded in avoiding its domination. But it was not for lack of trying:

> The aspiration to domination in Europe, the universalist tendencies (in their religious

and imperial variations) are present in some historical and literary works of the 13th and 14th centuries. In *De Ortu Et Fine Romani Imperii*, a work written between 1307 and 1310, German author Engelbert d'Admont defends the need for a single empire and a single head in Europe. He considers the emperor as 'the supreme arbiter in the maintenance of peace.'[23]

The imperial ideology, craftily masked behind the Universalist façade, was already at work.

Seen in retrospect with a pinch of humor, the 2015 European Union, with its plans of expansion eastward, in Ukraine and Georgia, after swallowing the Balkans, Poland and the Baltic States, is in every way reminiscent of the objectives of the German emperors, Charlemagne, Otto I and Henry II, the emperor who founded officially the first Reich in 1014 by sealing the alliance of the Empire and the Church under the egis of Pope Benoit VIII. In 1157, Frederick Barbarossa completed the alliance by proclaiming his empire "holy."

The Czar and the Roman Germanic Emperor

Meanwhile, the Russia of Kiev was soon to disappear under divisions and conquests. By the middle of the 13th century, it fell under the control of the Mongols (Tartars) during vast invasions initiated by Genghis Khan. Russia survived, however, and managed to rebuild a lasting state around Moscow by the 14th century.

So much so that after the fall of Constantinople, the new state was able to take over from the defunct Byzantine Empire. By 1462, the new prince, Ivan III, managed to get rid of Mongol control and assert himself as "Sovereign of all Russia." The title of Czar, contraction of the word "Caesar," marks his claim to a double filiation at once Byzantine and Mongol by its very consonance.[24]

After Europe's multiple invasion attempts and two

centuries of heavy Mongol occupation, it was out of the question for the Russians to accept a new yoke of any provenance. This staunch will for independence and being on a par with the other states has remained intact up until now. Since those dire experiences, the Russians are ready to make enormous sacrifices to preserve their independence, as Polish, Swedish, French and German invaders learned to their cost when they tried to imitate the Teutonic Knights and the Mongols.

> By declaring himself the guardian of the Byzantine heritage—a position comforted by his marriage to the niece of the last Byzantine emperor—Ivan III claims he is holding, in the tradition of the last eastern emperors, power of divine origin. This dimension will be at its height when the Czar of Russia is assigned the direction of Christendom, according to a Universalist schema which refuses the authority of the pope and makes henceforth of Moscow the Third Rome.[25]

In 1520, the monk Philotheus of Pskov will anchor this political decision within the Orthodox tradition, declaring that "all Christian empires have collapsed, only one remains standing and there will not be a fourth one. ... Two Romes have collapsed but the third, Moscow, towers up skyward and there will not be a fourth one. ... All Orthodox countries have been reunited under your scepter, you have become the sole prince of the Christians," thus creating the future basis of Russian nationalism.[26]

Westerners have used this text often to denounce Russian imperialism and apply to the Russians a messianic will to "invade" Europe. This is of course a patent lie, given that Western attempts to convert Orthodox Russians began as early as the 12th century, three hundred years before Philotheus' declaration. In Russian eyes, this declaration only emphasizes the fact that Russia is equal to the other powers and should never submit to a third power, be it from Europe or from Asia. It has exactly the same symbolic value as the story of the Soissons vase or the story of Joan of Arc in French national mythology.

By deciding to take over where Byzantium left off and by posing as champion of Orthodoxy, Ivan III seized the opportunity to have Russia enter a new era. He made of her an actor on the European scene. His role and that of his successor, Vasili III, are thus of capital importance. Through his decision, he placed Russia on an equal footing with the European rulers by claiming the same royal titles and qualities as Western monarchs, as well as by placing himself in line with the same divine legitimacy as the kings and emperors of the West.

And he also opened Russia to European arts, notably by inviting to Moscow Italian and Ticino architects such as the Ticino-born Florentine, Pietro Solari. This explains why the Kremlin walls, built in 1480, look like those of castles in Milano and Bellinzona.

Renaissance European rulers were very much aware of this, and henceforth began to court Russia and send ambassadors and observers to Moscow. In this context, Ivan III's refusal to accept the title of king from Germanic emperor Frederic III, who wanted to ally himself to him, makes sense, as it would have been synonymous with vassalage to the empire and submission to his ambition of European domination.

Ivan III's answer to Frederic is unequivocal:

> By the grace of God, we have been sovereign over our lands since the beginning, since our most distant ancestors. God granted us this right as He had granted it to them. We pray that He forever grant us and our children that sovereignty we enjoy today. In the past, we have never needed any confirmation, from any quarter; we do not wish for any either today.[27]

The Gothic Churches Divide Europe in Two

In the 16th century, Protestantism took on board distrust toward Orthodoxy and changed nothing in relation to the line which was by then dividing Europe into two. For the ensuing five centuries since the reestablishment of Russian power in the 15th and 16th centuries, the religious frontier has remained very much present in people's minds, not only among practitioners, but also at the cultural and political levels.

The demarcation line separating the two Christian versions of Europe duplicates almost perfectly the border between the European and Russian worlds. It starts from Finland and Sweden, through the Baltic States and Poland, and on to Galicia, Western Ukraine, and Moldavia.

On the eastern side, Romanians and Moldovans are partly an exception to the rule: they have been Orthodox but autocephalous and of Latin culture and language since the Roman conquest of Dacia, whereas on the western side, it is the Serbs and to a lesser extent the Bulgarians, who have always oscillated between the two camps since their reluctant conversion to Orthodoxy that has staunchly kept their Orthodox faith and Cyrillic writing. Of all the Slavs of the West, they have remained closest to the Russians.

As French Catholic historian Alain Besançon points out, the borders of Europe coincide with Catholicism and gothic art:

> The eastern border of Europe can be read as a line gathering in the last gothic churches. That line thus flanks Finland, the Baltic countries, Poland, Hungary, Croatia, and Slovenia. It is exactly the border of Europe of the 25 [28 in 2015] ... Beyond it, through a clear rupture, Byzantine art reigns.[28]

In other words, non-European Barbary. And Alain Besançon concludes his communication by blaming this divide on the Russians, who allegedly detest Catholicism:

> Europe ends there, where ... she meets another civilization, another kind of regime and a religion that does not want her.

But as we have seen, in reality since the 11th century, Orthodoxy has remained one of the most powerful factors fermenting European detestation of Russia. Polish Catholics have never stopped fighting Orthodoxy. In 1596, the Polish-Lithuanian kingdom actually compelled the Western Ukraine Orthodox Church to submit to the pope and even invaded Moscow in 1612, with the Protestant kingdom of Sweden trying to do the same further to the north. The conquest of the Ukrainian Uniate Church was their only victory in a thousand years. At the end of the 20th century, Polish-born Pope John-Paul II was still trying to send missionaries to Ukraine to no avail.

During the Crimean War, in 1854, the bishop of Tulle wrote: "There are men called Christians more dangerous for the Church than the pagans themselves." And the archbishop of Paris, Mgr. Sibourg, proclaimed *ex cathedra*: "The real reason of this war is the need to make Photius's heresy lose ground."[29] Let us not forget that one of the reasons that Napoleon III decided to undertake the Crimean War, besides his desire to take revenge for the defeat suffered by his uncle Napoleon I, was to satisfy the demands of the ultramontane Catholic bishops, who supported the Polish Catholics and wished for a new crusade against Russian Orthodoxy.

At the end of the 19th century, Abbot Rohrbacher, in his *Histoire Universelle de l'Église catholique* (Universal history of the Catholic Church), was still insisting that "Rome and all that is tied to the Catholic Church has no enemy more dangerous than the autocrat in Moscow." He recalled also the commentaries in the French press of the 1840s following the publication of Custine's work:

> It is a Papacy which is being founded in Russia. Everywhere, from the Baltic to the mouth of the Danube and the Gulf of Venice, the plan is being

carried out substituting the Russian Church to the Roman Church, the Czar to the Pope, and to express things in the language of today, the despotism of temporal power to the independence of spiritual power.[31]

And here is how, at the beginning of the 20th century, German historian Paul Rohrbach presented Russian backwardness due to Orthodoxy:

> The last root of Russian cultural backwardness rests in the connection to the Byzantine Church, with which the internal effects of contacts with the Western Catholic community, which would have had a positive impact despite the spatial distance and the Mongol yoke, had been excluded right from the start.
> In the 10th century, if Grand-Duke Vladimir had become a Roman Catholic instead of [sticking to] Byzantine Orthodoxy, it would have had the greatest significance for the incorporation of Russia in the cultural and political community of European nations. It would have been as though the Mongols had never conquered Russia and as if the Khan of the Golden Horde had never been the feudal lords of the Grand Duchy of Muscovy.[32]

More recently, Fátima's Prophesy, extremely popular in the Catholic world, had the Virgin Mary appear to three young Portuguese women in July 1917 to announce, among other things, the conversion of Russia to the true faith in order to avoid a new war even more terrible than the First World War that was then raging:

> To prevent this [war], I shall come to ask for the Consecration of Russia to my Immaculate Heart,

and the Communion of reparation on the First Saturdays. If my requests are heeded, Russia will be converted, and there will be peace; if not, she will spread her errors throughout the world, causing wars and persecutions of the Church.[33]

Vision, revelation, superstition, or what-have-you: Russia is designated as the central pivot of the "Axis of Evil" and personification of the Antichrist. The advent of communism shortly thereafter was to give a wide echo to that prophecy.

Let us recall also the support the Church gave to Polish Catholics during Poland's successive partitioning and the 1830 revolt. During the Crimean War in 1853, Polish insurgent regiments fought alongside the French and the British with the blessings of the pope. In 1941-42, the Croat independent State created by the Ustashas with Mussolini and Hitler's approval, besides massacring Serbs, forced almost 200,000 Orthodox to convert to Catholicism with the Vatican's tacit approval.[34]

When the Yugoslavia War erupted in 1991, the Vatican and the German Christian Democrats led by Helmut Kohl hastened to recognize the independence of Catholic Croatia, triggering the dismemberment of Yugoslavia and civil war.

And finally, to link up with our times, we will cite one newspaper article among countless others denouncing the "impious alliance" of the Orthodox Church and Putin:

> Russia's Orthodox Church, despite decades of brutal repression under Soviet rule, is putting its trust in the KGB to ensure that a remarkable religious revival does not fade with the departure of President Vladimir Putin.
>
> In an unusual move, Alexei II, the Church's patriarch, has endorsed deputy prime minister Dmitry Medvedev ahead of next week's presidential election. The influence of his support on Russia's estimated 100 million Orthodox worshippers is immense. It also illustrates the

unholy alliance the Church has forged with the Kremlin since Mr Putin came to power eight years ago.[35]

A Thousand-Year Conflict Still Virulent

The true challenge, which would make it possible to end this centuries-old confrontation nourishing the antipathy of Westerners toward the Orthodox and the Russians in particular, would consist in reestablishing the facts and, as Robert Heath puts it, "in refraining from pointing an accusing finger at the East."[36]

Those prejudices are still very much noxious today. In his last book, *Holy Russia*[37] Alain Besançon begins his first chapter thus: "The art of lying is as old as Russia. Custine and Michelet noted it as a defining feature." At once fascinated and appalled by Orthodoxy, the author seeks to prove that Russia never stops lying to foreigners, by manipulating the language. He insists on the Orthodox messianic expansionism of the supporters of the "Third Rome" and states that the West "in general has left Russia alone in her forests."[38]

Alain Besançon also deplores that Muscovy failed to accept the generous offer of the Council of Florence which, in 1439, had voted in favor of the reunion of the two Churches, and that the czar had had the Metropolitan jailed on his return. He makes no mention of Alexander Nevsky's sacrifice and seems to consider the aggressions by the Swedes and the Teutonic Knights as peaceful strolls in the forest...[39]

Further along, he hints that Uniatism was due to the fact that "bishops from the west of Russia, terrified by the evolution of the Church under Ivan the Terrible, accepted the jurisdiction of the pope in exchange for the conservation of Orthodox customs and liturgy."[40] Ivan the Terrible is depicted in the worst possible light as an amateur of theology "who had a passion for crime" and was "a nightmarish model," whereas Henry VIII, who had tortured all of his wives a century earlier, is mentioned only for his love of the State doctrine.[41]

But we will readily acknowledge that Ivan was no softhearted jackass.

What is even more questionable is to associate Uniatism and this czar and to forget that the separation of the Uniate Church took place twelve years after the death of Ivan, in 1595-96, thanks to the Union of Brest. Poland and Lithuania jointly tried to benefit from the interregnum and dynastic disorder reigning in Russia to take over the country.[42] It was only then that the Ruthenia Metropolitan decided to break off relations with the Constantinople Church to place himself under Roman jurisdiction. Ruthenia was then part of the Two Nations Republic (Poland and Catholic Lithuania).[43] And nothing is said of the persecutions the new Church inflicted on the believers that had remained attached to Orthodoxy.

As to the alleged Orthodox messianism as the foundation of "Russian imperialism, which is from now on the transcendental value proposed to the Russian people,"[44] the remark is truly laughable. Not only because of Catholicism's millenarian war on Orthodoxy since 1054, but also because the Catholic Church, then the Protestant churches after the Reform, have not stopped since Christopher Columbus sending missionaries everywhere in the world, in Latin America, Asia, China, Africa, in order to convert populations often by force of arms. Has anyone seen Orthodox missionaries doing the same thing?[45] Where are the Orthodox Indians, Orthodox Africans, Orthodox Asians, and Orthodox Americans? Except for a few churches meant for Slav migrants, there is almost no major Orthodox presence on those continents. As for "laic," secular imperialism, a look at the maps of Russia and the European Union in 1991 and in 2015 suffices to prove on which side imperialism is.

Historical Ingratitude towards Byzantium and Russia

Lastly, Europe has shown historical ingratitude to Byzantium and medieval Russia. Not only did she never pay her debt, but she compounded it by ceaselessly denigrating those that saved her from Turkish and Mongol invasions. For what would have become of Europe if Byzantium had not for centuries contained Arab and Turkish advances? And what would have become of her if, from the 13th to the 15th century, Russia had not absorbed, broken, and exhausted the aggressiveness of the Mongol Khans and the Golden Horde?

While the southern half of Russia was reduced to slavery by the Mongols and the northern half was wearing them down through guerilla operations mixed with peace negotiations, and while the Byzantines desperately fought the Ottomans, medieval Europe had plenty of time to rebuild herself politically and culturally, build cathedrals, indulge in courtly love and cultivate scholastic refinements. If, like Charles Martel in the Pyrenees, Byzantium and the Russians had not served as ramparts against the Arabs, Mongols and Turks, it is not just Hagia Sophia which would have been converted into a mosque but all the cathedrals of Europe, and what is known as the European civilization would have never entered its golden age.

And on the other hand, if Byzantium had not served as an intermediary between East and West, thanks to the port and trading facilities offered to the Venetians and the Genoese, the treasures of eastern and Arabian culture would have never reached Europe in such large proportions. It was Byzantium, much more than Andalusia—even if the latter's role was far from negligible—which served as the cultural and civilizational bridge between the two worlds. Just as it was Byzantium, a Greek city, that served as a link between Europe and ancient Greek civilization. How many precious manuscripts from Alexandria and Antioch stranded in medieval cloisters and the Vatican libraries transited through Byzantium, heir to both the Roman Empire and ancient Greece?

Not to mention the massive emigration of Byzantine intellectuals to Italy in the 15th century, when the fall of the town became unavoidable. It was indeed those Byzantine intellectuals who took refuge in Italy during the Latin conquest of Constantinople and then, when it fell, initiated the Renaissance. That emigration played the same role for medieval Europe as did Russian emigration after 1917 and 1945, and then Jewish and German emigration after 1933 to the United States. Seen from abroad, the United States had remained a cultural desert (or culturally very poor) after the 1786 Revolution—there were no universal intellectual figures in America before 1920 (even if there was for sure a handful of valuable thinkers)—and was literally seeded by the massive arrival of European intellectuals, artists and scientists as of the 1920s.[46] It is no coincidence at all that the Renaissance took place in Italy after the capture of Constantinople by the Latins and then over two centuries later by the Ottomans.

It is remarkable to note that, as a measure of the extent of Catholic hatred of Orthodoxy after the schism, the West preferred to blot out the contribution of Christian Byzantium and highlight instead the cultural contribution of Muslim Andalusia. The same stupefying omission was duplicated in the 19th century when, after Greek independence in 1830, Greek antiquities and ancient humanities were rediscovered, but the cultural contribution of Christian Greece remained steadfastly ignored. And, as we shall see later on, the same state of mind prevailed during the Great Game opposing England to Russia throughout the 19th century: Great Britain kept supporting Muslim Turkey against Orthodox Russia, even to the extent of going to war in 1853.

It was in its confrontation with the East, notably with Byzantium, that the West forged itself as a temporal and spiritual power. It was in the chancelleries of German emperors and the sacristies of Roman theologians that medieval and then modern Europe formed herself through opposition to Easterners. It is no exaggeration to assert that Byzantium was the matrix and the mirror of European identity.

Charlemagne, who sought an ideological cement common to the heterogeneous and antagonistic peoples that formed his empire, was well aware of what was at stake. By imposing *Filioque* on the popes and on the nations of his empire against Byzantium, he was giving his possessions, and therefore budding Europe, a common creed and religious practice, a new ideology, and therefore a definite identity, different from that of the universal Church of the origins.

The Saxon emperors and popes that succeeded him also understood perfectly the need for it. In this sense, it can be stated that Byzantium, by playing the part of involuntary sparring partner, did a big favor to the West. The latter kept utilizing that tried and tested recipe in its new attempt at unification, next using Russia as a punching bag. The Europe of Charlemagne and of the year 1000 was in need of a foil in the East to rebuild herself, just as the Europe of the 2000s needs Russia to consolidate her union. At a time when European elites are haunted by a feeling of decline, the rehabilitation of Byzantium should be welcome. As studies on the Roman Empire become more frequent and there is plenty of research trying to understand its success and permanence, it would be a good thing to focus on Byzantium which, in fact, prolonged the existence of the Roman Empire by an extra thousand years. An unprecedented performance unequaled in human history. In terms of durability, Byzantium did last a thousand years longer than Rome, and with far fewer means, while being all the time in the vanguard of Barbarian, Persian, Arabian, and Turkish invasions. Byzantium thus had to be a model to follow rather than a despicable foil.

Without Byzantium, no or a reduced Italian Renaissance. Without Byzantium and without Russia, no Christian Europe and no European civilization. Isn't it an enormous debt modern Europe contracted from the Byzantine Greeks and the Russians of Muscovy and Novgorod? To sum up, the Byzantines did an enormous if involuntary favor to the West by helping it to take shape.

Lies Pervade Western Historiography

What is to be concluded from all this? First of all, that religious confrontation has lost nothing of its virulence and continues even now to impregnate the minds with the same anti-Orthodox and anti-Russian prejudices as in 1054, even if they now hide behind other terms and other arguments.

Next, if lie there is, as Alain Besançon claims, it is less often to be found on the Russian side than on the side of a West which has not hesitated to falsify history, to rewrite it after the schism, to project the responsibility for the breakup onto the Eastern Church, and which twists the Philotheus prophecy to better mask the ceaseless invasion attempts of the Poles and the Swedes in Ukraine and Byelorussia. If you add to that the pseudo Constantine Donation designed, among other purposes, to consolidate the supremacy of the pope against the Eastern Churches, evidence has been provided that western historiography is deceptive.

As shown by the mainstream media fake news related to Saddam Hussein's alleged weapons of mass destruction with a view to justifying the invasion of Iraq in 2003 (one of the latest avatars in a long list of casus belli started with the sabotage of *USS Maine* before the 1898 invasion of Cuba and the alleged North-Vietnamese attack on the *USS Maddox* and *USS Turner Joy* in the Bay of Tonkin in 1964 before the landing in Vietnam), the West has little hesitation in lying to achieve its ends.

In truth, it is the entire history of Europe and of Russia that should be revised to reconstruct a healthy, balanced, and more respectful relationship between the two sides of Christendom. It is a necessary condition to reset the political cooperation and build a true partnership.

| Chapter Five |

FRENCH RUSSOPHOBIA AND THE MYTH OF EASTERN DESPOTISM

> *"Europe will find there the true epiphany of modernism, the almost sensual revelation of the saving power of Beauty. And all that had matured in the St-Petersburg of the czars, so long held to be the citadel of barbarity..."*
> Martin Malia, quoting Arthur Lovejoy, 1948, about Russian cultural effervescence at the beginning of the 20th century.

France has made two essential contributions to Russophobia by providing it with two of its major themes: the myth of expansionism and that of oriental despotism. The myth of Russian expansionism was born under Louis XIV with the fabrication of Peter the Great's fake will, written with the aid of Polish aristocrats. The myth of oriental despotism took shape in Enlightenment times, with Montesquieu, the later Diderot, and the liberal intellectuals of Restoration, Guizot and Tocqueville in particular.

The accounts of the first travelers that visited Muscovy between the 15th and the end of the 17th century played an important role in the emergence of these two myths. Strong religious prejudices and distress over the strange Muscovite lifestyle generated misunderstandings and nourished initial distaste for the "barbarity" of customs and "tyranny" of the princes.

These accounts influenced the first philosophers of the Enlightenment who, early in the 18th century, tried to define the best forms of government, attempted to reconcile freedom and monarchic absolutism, and invented the concepts of progress and civilization.

Some philosophers, such as Leibniz and Voltaire, impressed by Peter the Great's daring reforms, praised the Russia of the time: progress could be achieved thanks to the insights of an enlightened prince. But most of them rejected this thesis, pointing out the lacunae of Russian society, in particular the absence of aristocratic or middle-class forces of opposition able to counterbalance the czar's absolute power.

Once the turbulence of the Revolution and of the Napoleonic adventure was over, the debate resumed in earnest and led to the triumph of liberal theses, which succeeded in winning favor among conservatives worried by the new threat incarnated by socialism, of which Russia, beside her congenital despotism, had developed a frightening metastasis under the form of the rural commune.

At the end of the 19th century, France and Great Britain, finding themselves forced to face the German foe, had to consent to make an alliance with the Russian expansionist despot. Anatole Leroy-Beaulieu, the most Russophile of the Russophobic authors, came up then with a masterly synthesis: Russia was despotic, certainly, but she was subject to amendment. Her potential for progress was all the greater as she was backward. Therefore she could be treated as an acceptable ally for the two torchbearers of civilization and liberty Republican France and the constitutional Empire of Her British Majesty. In 1914, war could thus commence between the central empires and the French and the British allied to the Russians.

And this is, in a nutshell, when French Russophobia was born. Let us see in greater detail how it took shape in the debate of ideas and violent political troubles of the 18th and 19th centuries.

Peter the Great's Forged Testament and the Myth of Expansionism

Let us begin with the myth of expansionism.
As described by American historian Martin Malia:

> in the 1760s French diplomats, working with a variety of Ukrainian, Hungarian, and Polish political figures, produced a forged 'Testament of Peter I,' purporting to reveal Russia's 'grand design' to conquer most of Europe. This document was still taken seriously by governments during the Napoleonic wars; and as late as the Cold War President Harry Truman found it helpful in explaining Stalin.[11]

Louis XV's idea, two centuries before George F. Kennan's containment thesis, was to form a union in order to erect an impenetrable barrier between Russia and the rest of Europe—that is, France, Poland, Prussia, and Turkey. Yes, Turkey! In 1756, a first version of the fake testament surfaced, within an account inspired by a travel to Russia by Chevalier d'Éon, a member of Louis XV's black cabinet. Then in 1797 the Directory reworked the document as revised by Polish general Michel Sokolniki in order to make obvious what had to be presented as a catalogue of recipes allegedly concocted by the Russians to achieve European hegemony, which included:

> Hold the state in a system of continual warfare, in order to maintain strict discipline among the soldiers and in order to keep the nation on the move and ready to march at the first signal.[2]

And so on and so forth.
In 1812, as he was about to launch his great army into the Russian campaign, Napoleon ordered from Charles-Louis Lesur a book of propaganda on Russia in which he would warn the West of the dangers of Russian power, "the most

absolute and most unlimited," "more Asiatic than European," and would present to the general public Peter the Great's fake testament.[3]

Cleverly composed, well documented, this work is considered one of the high points of Russophobia literature, given the huge response it received. The fake will covers just two pages of this nearly 500-page-long book, but is in fact its crucial element. It was reprinted time and again both in French and in English until its demystification, and saw the same success as the fake Constantine Donation of the 9th century or the forged Protocols of the Elders of Zion at the end of the 19th century. The fourteen points of the testament would be reviewed and corrected according to the inclinations of various authors but the substance would remain the same.

Here is as an example of how the French bishop Gaume rewrote the epigraph in 1876:

> The founder of the Muscovite Empire, Peter I, drew for his successors the road that must lead them to universal domination. Whatever the authenticity of his famous testament may be, one thing is certain: it is the religious loyalty with which the Czars have made it, point by point, their rules of conduct. To understand the policy of Russia, in the past, in the present, and in the future, one must consider again this solemn document. Here are the main parts: 'In the name of the very holy and indivisible Trinity, we, Peter, Emperor and autocrat of all Russia, to our descendants and successors to the throne and government of the Russian nation.
>
> 'The Great God to whom we owe our existence and our crown, having constantly enlightened us with His lights and provided us with His divine support, allows us, in our views, which we believe to be those of Providence, to consider the Russian people as destined, in the future, for the general domination of Europe.'[4]

The false testament impregnated all Russophobic thoughts of the 19th century, including those of Napoleon's confessor, Abbot Dominique-Georges-Frédéric de Pradt, who wrote numerous books to exhort Europeans to close ranks and their doors to the Russians: "Russia has developed on the despotic and Asiatic model. ... Europe must cooperate to exclude from her affairs any power with no direct interest to her."[5] Custine too was to be very much taken with it a few decades later. It was actually the commentators on the false document who first came up with the idea of a "China Wall," a sanitary cordon between Europe and Russia.[6]

The hoax was only exposed in 1879, but that did not much alter its posterity, insofar as Truman still mentioned it in 1945 in his talks with George Kennan.[7] The fake testament and its successors also inspired Churchill when he pronounced his famous "iron curtain" phrase in 1946.[8] And they still influence Western journalists, politicians and experts in the 21st century: in Chechnya, Moldavia, the Baltic States, Georgia, or Ukraine, whenever a conflict breaks out on the Russian periphery, the alleged Russian messianic designs thesis is repeated ad nauseam and the need to erect a barrier against Russia is invoked.

Meanwhile, the forged testament had started its career in Britain as early as 1815, when the English began to develop quasi-paranoid Russophobia against a Russian Empire they felt threatened their own colonial empire (see next chapter). It was to be subsequently translated into Russian and introduced into the country by nationalist and Slavophile circles, which endorsed it as if it were true. Western propaganda was of course to use that endorsement to advantage. It was easy for it to draw on that use to justify its denunciation of "Russian expansionism".

Throughout the 19th century, this successful manipulation also inspired countless caricatures showing how the Russian bear, symbol of the autocratic and barbaric Asia, was about to devour civilized, democratic, innocent Europe. And, for all the evidence of its falsehood, the meme has kept on wreaking havoc until now.

The forged testament, much more than Nicolas I's authoritarianism, thus anchored in the European imagination, during the first half of the 19th century, an idea which was never to disappear: that of "the barbarian at the door," the bloodthirsty Cossack ready to pounce on European civilization at the slightest opportunity. The age-old fear of the savage coming from the East, tethered in the depths of European collective subconscious since the sweeping invasions that had made the Roman Empire fall, was now resurrected against Russia. Thanks to a forgery and its repeated use.

The First Travelers Launch the Notion of Russian Barbarity

But before going into further detail, let us see on which grounds the thesis of the alleged Russian expansionism germinated. We saw in the previous chapter that it was in opposition to Orthodoxy that the first prejudices against Russia were born. What was the content of these early accounts? How did they emerge and why were they so unanimously negative? To what extent were they pertinent or, on the contrary, unfounded?

It was in the time of Ivan III that visits of western ambassadors, emissaries of the pope and travelers intensified in Russia, spawning a growing number of travel narratives. In 1553, the English created the Muscovy Company, trading wood and furs, which for the next three centuries would be the Nordic equivalent of the notorious East India Company. Muscovy made it onto European maps and chancelleries.

The first European traveler to publish a known account on Russia was a Renaissance-era Venetian diplomat, Ambroglio Contarini. Arrested by the czar during his return to Persia over some compatriot's unpaid debt, he told of his brief time in jail and escape, and made a few rare comments on Muscovy, whose people he found "beautiful but brutal," and on the Patriarch too submissive to the prince. Venetian to the core, he was mainly interested in the commercial potential, notably for the fur trade.

In 1501, a Livonian Catholic, Christian Bomhover, who would later become bishop of Dorpat in Estonia and a peddler of indulgences, worrying about Russian advances, convinced the pope to allow him to preach a crusade against "schismatic" Russians. He described the Russians as pagans whose customs looked like those of the Turks, i.e. barbaric and cruel, and whose master Ivan III was a tyrant who had committed the absolute crime of allying himself with the Tartars and the Turks to destroy true Christendom[9] which was in complete contradiction with the fact that Ivan III had specifically rejected the Tartar yoke at the start of his reign.

In 1514, Polish King Sigismund took up the same thesis with the pope and the emperor to convince them that Poland and Lithuania had to be helped in their fight against barbaric and infidel Russians. Muscovites, he stated, were no Christians, they were cruel and barbaric. They were Asians, not Europeans. They were in league with the Tartars and the Turks against Christendom.

He had the ear of the papal legate, Hungarian Jacob Piso. Entrusted with fostering peace between Poland and Muscovy to together fight the Turks, Piso was pro-Poland and anti-Muscovite. So he nonetheless sided against the Russians. His account of his travel in Poland says among other things that the Great Russian Prince is a tyrant who makes many Muscovites suffer because of their Catholicism and that they "are oppressed by the cruelest laws, they are born in that condition, they grow thus and are all subject to them."[10]

With one or two exceptions, all authors of the time developed the same themes. Including the most important of all, Imperial diplomat Sigismund von Heberstein, author of *Notes on Muscovite Affairs*, published (in Latin) in 1549 but written during his stay in Russia between 1517 and 1527. He too had been sent to the East, but by Emperor Maximilian, to negotiate an alliance against King Sigismund. When the latter had the bright idea to cede Hungary to Maximilian in order to curry favor with him, the emperor asked his envoy to negotiate peace between Poland and Russia. His book is by far the best documented of his time. But due to its influence and countless reprints, it is also considered as the work at the source of the commonplace notions of "Russian tyranny."[11] The czar,

...disposed at his pleasure of their lives and possessions without anyone resisting, and even persuading themselves that he had no other will but that of God ... so that by such great cruelty this nation became fierce and savage, so much so that one simply cannot say whether it is the cruelty of this barbaric people that deserves such tyranny, or if the people are in fact so cruel for being thus tyrannized.

Heberstein cuts up Russian political life into four elements: 1) absolutism: the Great Prince enjoys total control over the various political, administrative and military organs of the realm; 2) despotism: the Great Prince enjoys total control of his subjects' possessions, in particular real estate; 3) slavery: the Great Prince's subjects are his slaves; and 4) quasi-divinity: the Great Prince's subjects adore him as if he were God.[12]

This description would then be taken up by almost all accounts that followed until the 18th century. Some added commentaries of their own, to spice things up, according to their degree of hostility to Russia. By the end of the 16th century, numerous pamphlets were being published in Germany, notably among the Protestants, with plenty of illustrations to revile the Russia of Ivan IV the Terrible, depicted as an atheist, a cruel invader determined to destroy Livonia and Christendom, guilty of unspeakable atrocities against the people of his Court (during the massacre of revolting boyars). A pamphlet published in 1561 in Nuremberg came up with a new accusation which was to thrive in the following centuries, that of the Russians' unprecedented cruelty with women, virgins and infants.[13]

The pamphlet reads like a Spanish priest's account describing the customs of American Indians in order to better justify their sanguinary conquest. Sure of their racial and cultural superiority, the Europeans have been generous with this sort of description in all the countries they visited and conquered, from the Americas to the Indies and to Africa. Russia will not be spared from them either.

As Martin Malia notes, "it was in this situation of high tension between Russia and the outside world that the negative Western image of Muscovy was formed. Stubbornly schismatic in the crucial matter of religious faith, old Russia was deemed to have inherited from her erstwhile Tatar overlords the most slavish political despotism, to which was adjoined the savagery and poverty of the ancient Scythians, a combination of qualities that for Western Christendom denoted Asia."[14] Despotic, barbaric, backward: those three terms, ceaselessly updated with different terminologies, will constitute the gist of the anti-Russian discourse during three centuries, until President Putin.

In his excellent book, Marshall T. Poe presents a very detailed study of the texts and authors that have written on Russia before the Enlightenment philosophers, and tries to explain their tendency to exaggerate the authority of the Russian ruler by a penchant for acute binary oppositions and a profound desire to oppose to "despotic" Russia the antithesis of an idealized European freedom.

Can There Be a Tyranny with Consenting Subjects?

All of these authors ended up with a conceptual paradox, inasmuch as tyranny only exists if the czar constrains his subjects to servitude by force, but not if his subjects are consenting. And this seemed to be the case of the Russians. So, to solve this problem, some authors suggested that the Russians were born slaves and barbarians and thus doomed to despotism by nature. A simplistic explanation which, under today's criteria, is a form of racism or at the very least of crass cultural prejudice.

To explain this widely spread critical bias without denying the Russians' free consent to czarist authority, Marshall Poe offers more convincing arguments. The first one is a matter of terminology: the translation of Russian words into European languages has been subjected to semantic shifts that have reinforced the tyranny-slavery cliché.

In the mouth of a Russian sovereign, "autocratic" means that he is no one's vassal, that he is free regarding any foreign power and owes his power only to God. When Ivan III (the Great) takes the title of czar (Caesar) after the disappearance of the last Byzantine emperor, the Russian Court, which has just ratified the end of subjection to the Tartar Khans, conquered the city-States of the North and gathered "all of Russia," changes its ceremonial and adopts a new label sanctioning this new reality.

This is how the Great Prince, who until then was but some sort of primus inter pares, takes the title of Gospodar or Hospodar (a word derived from the Tatar language meaning lord, master, slave-owner) while, by logical antisymmetry, the subjects adopt the formula *kholop tvoi* (your slave) to greet the prince while bowing their heads with the polite formula *bit'chelom*, which means "with my humble salutation."

The Europeans will do the same at the court of Louis XIV and will keep greeting the king and the nobility, calling themselves "your servant" without, for all that, considering themselves as their slaves. But when transcribing Russian texts, given the distance and religious and cultural prejudices, it was the literal sense that prevailed, when it is obvious that all those formulations have to be taken metaphorically.

A similar evolution will explain the sense the word "despot" took on in European languages: what was originally the translation of the Slavic word for "king" little by little took on the negative meaning of "tyrant," as a Slavic king (despot) could be nothing but a tyrant. In the mouth of a European, the word designates a tyrant who only dreams of reducing his people to slavery. For a Russian, originally at least, it was a word of praise. For a Westerner, it is an insult. The same misreading would happen if the polite *"monsieur"* of the French were interpreted literally as *"mon sieur"* i.e. *"mon seigneur"*: no Frenchman would ever think of his interlocutor as his lord deserving of a low bow.

To those semantic misunderstandings was added a misinterpretation of what the Russians meant by "slavery" and submission to the prince. None of the authors ever saw fit to encompass the whole of that relationship, and specify that if the subjects are the "slaves" of the prince, the prince, for his part, is the "slave" of God, whose mission is to protect his subjects, to ensure their personal safety and that of their possessions, defend them against invaders, who were numerous (Teutonic Knights, Mongol invaders, Catholic missionaries, Polish and Lithuanian aggressors, Swedish invaders) and protect them against themselves, that is to say, against their own divisions and disastrous civil wars.

To Polish magnate Samuel Maskiewicz, who negotiated with the Muscovites before invading Moscow in 1612 and called on the Russians to unite with the Poles to obtain freedom, the Russians answered:

> Your way is freedom, while ours is bondage. You do not have will, but rather simple caprice: the strong plunder the weak; they can seize another's property and very life ... In contrast, among us even an esteemed boyar does not have the authority to offend the least simple person: upon the first complaint, the tsar brings justice and right. If the sovereign proceeds unjustly, it is within his authority. Like God, the tsar punishes and pardons. It is easier for us to suffer offenses from the tsar than from our brother, because he is the ruler of all the world.[15]

This text explains very well how different the concept of authority is between the West and Russia. If the Russians were just brainless slaves, how to explain the revolts they sometimes carried out against their rulers? And conversely, if they were not consenting subjects, why would they have supported for so many centuries that "autocracy" the West considers to be tyranny pure and simple?

It shows also very well that for the West freedom, starting with the Renaissance humanists and under the influence of Protestantism, is a means to achieving perfection of the self, hence eternal salvation (social justice in its secular version), and that it is for that reason that God gave it to man. Whereas for the Russians, freedom is considered as a capricious and discretionary power which plunges man into depravity and takes him further away from salvation. And this is why freedom has been delegated to the prince for him to ensure peace for all.

This delegation is conditional and the prince cannot hoard it for personal use, lest his subjects rebel legitimately. In a word, for the Russians "the Czar's will is God's will."

Reconceptualizing Despotism

Marshall Poe concludes that "despotism" should rather be called "a patrimonial regime," and in fact it has provided Russian elites with a remarkably sparing means of stabilization, unification and mobilization of their subjected peoples and territories strewn over a huge area.

Russian power achieved this by solving the four difficulties common to all modern monarchies: the problems of factions, prosperity, resource mobilization, and resolution of conflicts thus avoiding the countless civil wars that have punctuated the construction of European centralized kingdoms and nation-states, and that in a context of scarcity of resources and enormous geographical dispersal.

The cliché of a tyrannical, barbaric Russia oppressing a people of slaves was thus well anchored in the West when Peter the Great acceded to the throne. His decision to Europeanize Russia and to give it a capital on the Baltic Sea, as well as his victories over Sweden, made of the Russian power one of the five that counted in Europe, alongside Great Britain, France, Austria, and Prussia.

By opening to Europe and adopting spectacular reforms, Peter the Great changed for a while the negative perception of Russia in Europe. The era of "enlightened despotism" began with him. So that in the 1730s, Swedish von Strahlenberg and Russian Vassili Tatichev proposed to fix the limits of Europe to the Urals, a decision confirmed by the Vienna Treaty in 1815, whose protagonists needed to delineate precisely the superficies of the European states in order to be able to attribute or compensate territorial gains and losses to be negotiated after Napoleon's defeat.

With this grand entrance into the very select club of large European empires and kingdoms, Russia won sympathy but also awoke old antipathies, in France in particular.

The image of Russia in the 18th century was indeed very much in contrast, positive at the beginning, thanks to the influence of Leibnitz, Voltaire and early Diderot, before becoming increasingly negative as the Revolution approached and the ideas of Rousseau, d'Alembert, the later Diderot, the astronomer-traveler Chappe d'Auteroche and Abbot Mably asserted themselves.

From the Quarrel of the Ancients and the Moderns to the Notion of Progress

The growing influence of philosophers and the vogue of the Republic of Letters coincided with the emergence of a line of rulers among the most gifted of the century and most enlightened in the history of Russia, from Peter the Great to flamboyant Catherine II, via very reserved Czarina Elisabeth. Russia became the subject of an abundant literature. Some philosophers from the Age of Enlightenment loved to take her as a model, while others used her as a counter-example. For their part, the Russian czars cultivated links with the philosophers to establish themselves as enlightened princes, each side benefitting from this very political mental trade.

The camps at loggerheads were each to generate different visions of Russia, one positive and bearing hope for humanity, the other thoroughly negative and on the contrary portraying Russia as a threat to mankind. These two visions of Russia were to endure for centuries through historic turning points and ideological fights. Liberals and conservatives would privilege the dark side, while romantics and socialists would be more sensitive to its luminous side.

At the beginning of the 18th century, the Russian question thus constituted one of the key elements of the European political debate, thanks notably to two conceptual innovations of the philosophers of the Age of Enlightenment. The concepts of progress and civilization appeared at almost the same time, in the 1740s to the 1760s, and would serve as universal keys to the reading of all political, social or philosophical theories, each and every one having their own idea on how to climb the ladder of progress and civilization and on the respective position of each nation on that ladder.

So they must be examined closely. The idea of progress is a little older and goes back to the Italian Renaissance, during which humanists and scholastics were at loggerheads. The controversy rebounded at the end of the 17th century with the quarrel of the Ancients and the Moderns. The first, led by Boileau, insisted that good literature rested on imitation of ancient classical authors. This thesis was founded on the idea that Greek and Roman Antiquity represented artistic perfection, accomplished and unsurpassable.

The Moderns, under the leadership of Charles Perrault, insisted on the merits of contemporary writers, and maintained on the contrary that ancient classical authors could be bettered and that literary creation consisted in innovating. They thus argued in favor of literature adapted to its time and of new artistic forms.

The concept of progress as belief in the global linear perfectionism of mankind only appeared at the end of the 18th century. It was theorized in 1795 with the publication of Condorcet's *Esquisse d'un tableau historique des progrès de l'esprit humain* (Sketch for a historical picture of the progress of the human mind). With it were born the modern notion of progress and the conviction that society, whilst growing, evolves regularly toward improvement: accumulation of riches, accretion of scientific and technical knowledge, improvement of customs and institutions, development of the human mind.

As for the word "civilization," the first to use it in its modern sense was Victor Riqueti de Mirabeau, Mirabeau's father. In 1758, in *L'Ami des hommes* (Men's friend), he wrote: "Religion is indisputably the first and most useful brake of humanity: it is the first resort of civilization." For Condorcet, the idea of civilization designated the progress accomplished by mankind in a given nation when it was possible to go from the barbaric state to that of citizen, of civilian, or of civilized.[16]

At the time, the neologism had only one of its two modern meanings. It did not designate a particular civilization conceived as a unique body of qualities proper to a given society and did not refer either to an organic community created by History: in the 18th century, the term meant only a high level of material, intellectual and moral development, the apex of the ascent out of the savagery stage (presumed to be still observable in the New World) by going through the barbarity of the Europe of yore, the one still surviving in Asia (and in Russia).[17]

Until the end of the 17th century, the word "policed" was preferred to "civilized," from the idea that it was the State, hence the king, that had the mission of developing civilization, rather than it resulting from the action of society and citizens.

Leibniz and Voltaire as Adepts of Russian Enlightened Despotism

The first great modern philosopher to propose a role for Russia was Gottfried Wilhelm Leibniz at the end of the 17th century. Aware of Peter the Great's efforts to reform the country, build a new capital open to Europe, and modernize its institutions on the Western model, he was the first to come up with the idea that Russia could be a bridge between the two great world civilizations, the European and the Chinese, and that Russia was, in fact, a tabula rasa, a clean slate on which to place the better social order possible according to Reason.[18]

Leibniz recycled the commonplaces on Russian tyranny and barbarity, but in a positive way, suggesting what could happen due to enlightened actions of her ruler guided by Reason (and advised by philosophers, Voltaire was to add, in case the implicit point hadn't registered) to bring Russia out of her barbarity and accede to the boons of a social and political state as good, if not better, than those of European kingdoms still ensconced in their absolutism and medieval traditions.

His encounter with Peter the Great in 1711 flattered the budding builder of the Republic of Letters and ensured the themes of tabula rasa and despotism a prestigious career throughout the 18th century. The Englishman Jeremy Bentham, Physiocrat economist Le Mercier de la Rivière, and young Diderot would become their champions.

But the most brilliant and most influential philosopher of the Age of Enlightenment who was to propose the image of Russia as "space for all sorts of possibilities" was Voltaire.[19] Several of his books (*Histoire de Charles II*, 1731; *Anecdotes sur le czar Pierre le Grand*, 1748; *Histoire de l'empire de Russie sous Pierre le Grand*, 1759–1763) popularized his favorite theses, to wit, "Progress cannot come about without destruction of the past and abolition of unwarranted privileges acquired by the nobility and the clergy" and "happiness on Earth depends on men and their will to transform society according to Reason."

For him, Russia "emerging from nothingness" posed a golden opportunity to demonstrate his theories. He established as close relations with Catherine II, the "Northern Semiramis," as Leibniz's with Peter the Great, convinced as he was that Russia was playing a vanguard role for Reason in Europe and that "truth came from the North." Several authors followed his lead, including Diderot in his early days. The latter actually traveled to Saint Petersburg and Catherine II acquired his library at a hefty price.

This idea of Russia as tabula rasa, a unique land of experiment which might catch up with or even overtake the decadent West, would be taken up again after 1917 by the Bolsheviks, who advocated a new Russia, "at the vanguard of the proletariat and at the forefront of the construction of communism." At the other end of the ideological spectrum, that same tabula rasa idea which was used by the apostles of neoliberal capitalism during the first mandate of President Yeltsin at the beginning of the 1990s to loot the place.

That prospect of unfettered change led by enlightened despotism put Russia, during parts of the 18th and 20th centuries, at the top of the list of vanguard countries, a positive image for many intellectuals. But in the long history of Russophobia, those interludes were mere exceptions confirming the rule. Voltaire's theses did not survive him.

Montesquieu and the Absence of Russian Counter-Powers

In his famous *L'Esprit des lois* (The Spirit of the Laws) published in Geneva in 1748, Montesquieu tried to systematize Aristotle's classification and distinction between democratic, monarchic and aristocratic regimes and their possible warping into tyrannies or oligarchies when they lose the virtues that underpin them.

Like Voltaire, Montesquieu used Russia to prop up his theses, but in the opposite direction: relying on ethnographic accounts by European travelers in centuries past and on their commonplaces on Russian tyranny and barbarity, he made Russia the epitome of the hateful despotic regime, however well-intentioned its rulers. Montesquieu thus distinguished three regimes, monarchy, aristocracy and democracy, able to degenerate into tyrannies when they were corrupted. The best regime was the one able to moderate itself by institutionalizing counter-powers, hence his famous theory of the separation of powers, which is at the root of our modern democracies.

Montesquieu's preference went to an aristocratic or a monarchic regime softened by the existence of a nobility as counterweight to the monarch, despotism being seen as the absolute foil. And, as relevant to his argument, he quoted Muscovite customs as so many characteristics of despotism.

Thus, since in despotic regimes "one is so miserable that one fears death more than one cherishes life, punishment must be more severe," in Muscovy, theft and murder rate the same punishment. And Montesquieu adds:

> Muscovy would like to shake off its despotism but cannot. ... Even trade contradicts its laws. The people are only composed of slaves attached to their lands, and of other slaves called ecclesiastics and gentlemen because they are the lords of those slaves. So there is no one left for the Third State, which much form the workers and traders.[20]

In this way, Montesquieu acted as the father of the anti-Russian bourgeois-liberal cliché, founded on that characteristic failing of Russian society: the absence of an intermediate estate, of a Third Estate, or of a middle class as we would say today. This theory shortly became commonplace, with a rich posterity which was used as the foundation of contemporary American Russophobia, as we shall see later.

Rousseau too utilized Russia as an example of what not to do. Faithful to his exaltation of the state of nature, he criticized Russia and Peter the Great's reforms as unauthentic, artificial and contrary to the true nature of the Russian people and Russian soul. Furthermore, he delighted in wrong-footing his foe Voltaire while flaunting his bias in favor of Poland, which had entrusted him with writing a constitutional draft (*Considérations sur le gouvernement de Pologne*, 1771-1772).

In his opinion, Peter the Great's reforms were superficial because the czar endeavored to make Germans or Englishmen of Russians, instead of trying to make real Russians of them. He also formulated a new thesis, which was to become very popular in anti-Russian circles and would be rehashed at nauseam by editorialists and propagandists, which was that the Russian Empire gave itself the aim of subjugating Europe before being itself subjugated by the Tartars. He thus endorsed the myth of the Russian invader distilled by the first version of Peter the Great's fake testament of 1756.

In the 1770s, Father Mably (*Du Gouvernement et des lois de la Pologne*, 1771–1776) developed Montesquieu's proposition. He advised the Poles to emancipate the peasantry in order to create "that class of precious men known elsewhere under the name of bourgeoisie or Third Estate. Without that 'intermediate class' located between the excess of wealth of the rich and the miserable condition of the poor, and bearer of the 'genius' that these two classes lack there can be no 'industry'" nor progress in trade.[21]

But it was Diderot who made the most accomplished synthesis.[22] Rejecting the return to the state of nature dear to Rousseau's heart, he made the bourgeois-liberal viewpoint of the need for a third estate coincide with the idea of civilizational progress. He can therefore be considered as the founder of the modern theory of civil society as agent of social balance (the affluent acting as counterweight to despotism and tyrannical or oligarchic drifts that an excess of inequality might lead to). He was also the first to formulate the idea that the middle class was the bearer of political and social progress. (Marx would later bestow this function on the proletariat.) This viewpoint projected Russia to the bottom of the civilization ladder.

The American Revolution was to confirm the role given to the middle class as the agent of progress. The French Revolution too, but its radicalism would highlight the rifts excessive equality could engender, generating a conservative reaction which would wear off only slowly. Then came the Napoleonic episode, which reinforced the middle class as a social class but brushed it aside as a political counter-power, and finally the Restoration, which tried to conciliate the aristocracy, middle class and monarchy.

French Clichés versus Japanese Objectivity

It was also at that time that astronomer-abbot Jean Chappe d'Auteroche's *Voyage en Sibérie fait en 1761 (avec la description du Kamtschatka)* (Travel to Siberia in 1761, with description of Kamchatka) was published. D'Auteroche was typical of intellectuals of the Age of Enlightenment. And yet his vision was totally twisted by prejudice. Sent to Tobolsk in Siberia to observe the famous transit of Venus under the disk of the sun, due on June 6, 1761 (the mission was a scientific success) he brought back from his travel an account which was very negative for Russia but which made its mark in France. As one of his critics said, he "often limits himself to copying his predecessors: he talks of things he has not seen and those he observed he did very superficially."[23]

This narrative, full of curious facts and details, is jam-packed with disobliging observations. Everything is negative, in particular Russian social life and the state of abasement of the people, submitted to serfdom. The author gave the impression he only met cases of brutality, drunkenness, whipping, and torture.

The engravings in the 1768 edition could not be more explicit, what with the author a contemporary of de Sade who enthused over the Russian knout as an instrument of torture, seemingly delighting in the Russian forms of torture. Everything was minutely described, with spectators who seemed to take pleasure in the spectacle of naked women being whipped, in a kind of theatrical posturing which "creates a pornography of barbarity."[24] The work was very popular in France and had the honor of being refuted by Russian Empress Catherine II herself, who was furious at its description of her country. In 2003, Hélène Carrère d'Encausse, Honorary Perpetual Secretary of L'Académie française and a native of Georgia, published a book in which she opposed the two points of view (presented the two versions), which she placed on an equal footing at the level of knowledge.[25] This was at least a way of acknowledging that one reality can have two facets.

Auteroche's anti-Russian viewpoint was in no way exceptional, but his book is interesting because it was published at about the same time as the account a Japanese boat captain named Kodayu made of Siberia and Russia under Catherine II.

The Japanese captain did not at all see there the same things as the "enlightened" French scientist had.[26] He recounted how he was shipwrecked on an Aleutian island with his crew before being rescued by the governors of Kamchatka and Yakutsk and sent to Catherine II's court. He lived several months in Saint Petersburg before being finally allowed to return to Japan. He learned Russian and traveled the whole length of Russia twice. His account was collected and transcribed by a scholarly scribe, Katsuragawa Hoshu.

As noted by the French author of the postface, his tale is a "jewel of travel literature." He gives a detailed account of lifestyles, administration, the court, cooking, alcohol, nature, people, political life, and brothels, but without any judgment of value or prejudice. With total lucidity and sincerity devoid of any bias. The Japanese man travelled through the same towns, across the same rivers, witnessed the same punishments, and virtually met the same people as the Frenchman. But they seem to describe two different planets, two opposite worlds, given how dissimilar the impressions taken in and experiences lived are.

For the Japanese, there is no trace of the intolerable despotism, odious serfdom and medieval castigations omnipresent for the Frenchman. Russia is described, with distanced empathy and in a style which evokes a kind of poetic transcript, as an ordinary country, with its oddities and qualities. Contrary to the European traveler, the Japanese captain described what he "saw with his eyes," not what he believed he had seen or what he was told. Reading both books is fascinating as it reveals so plainly the influence and in Kodayu's case the absence of influence of prejudice on the writer's perception, and shows how Westerners are literally obsessed by the need to judge and amplify the civilizational gap existing between their world and the one they are visiting.

The First Liberal Theories and Oriental Despotism

Until 1820, Russia remained attached to enlightened despotism and continued to arouse ambivalent feelings among Europeans. Some were relieved at the role she was going to play to deliver Europe from the Napoleonic yoke. Such was the case with the English and the Germanic monarchies, as well as the opponents to Napoleon such as Germaine de Staël. But the ideologues of reaction, Englishman Edmund Burke and Frenchmen Louis de Bonald and Joseph de Maistre, remained critical: they were suspicious of Russia's enlightened despotism, finding it too modernistic. They wanted a return to the old system and its three orders, and considered that the Catholic religion and the pope were the only factors of order and progress. In their opinion, Alexander's Russia was modernizing too much and was not open enough to the clergy and the nobility.

But in 1815, once the Napoleonic peril had been dealt with, the liberals too began to dislike Russia. Following the revolution and Napoleonic experiences, Montesquieu and Diderot's theses found favor with a new generation of thinkers hostile to Revolution but favorable to liberalism. These helped make of Russia a thorn in the flesh of liberal Europe and the triumphant middle class including the abbot of Pradt already quoted, who, in his *Parallèle de la puissance anglaise et russe relativement à l'Europe* (Comparison of English and Russian powers in relation to Europe), published in 1823, opposed Russia to Europe in terms of barbarity versus civilization, describing the first as a "different universe and an oriental despotism enemy of all European liberties."

For his part, Alphonse Rabbe, in his works on Russian history and geography, decried Voltaire's embellishments and stigmatized, after Rousseau, what he viewed as the awkward and superficial character of Russian civilization, characterized by the absence of an intermediate political body. Let us mention as well the influential MP, journalist and Sorbonne professor, Saint-Marc Girardin, for whom Russia's awkward and despotic civilization was the enemy of the liberal revolution that had emerged out of the French Revolution.[27]

The trend was indeed towards conservatism in Europe, which was in the middle of the Restoration. Russia, having become the guarantor of the Vienna Treaty, turned into "Europe's policeman" and, under the iron rule of a withdrawn czar, Nicolas I, was to take part in the repression of the revolutions in ferment here and there in Europe, seeking to preserve European order as defined in Vienna. It was on this backdrop that the myth of enlightened despotism gave way to that of oriental despotism.

In Paris, three theoreticians were to play a crucial role, for different but complementary reasons: Guizot, Tocqueville and Custine.

Guizot, essayist and historian, and then prime minister of King Louis-Philippe, became famous with his injunction to the French middle class: "Enrich yourselves!" In his hefty *Histoire de la civilisation en Europe* published in 1828-1830, Guizot was the apologist and theoretician of the middle class as the engine of economic development and as foundation of a stable social order. Never mind the political regime, republic or monarchy: what mattered was the social base of the government, the middle ground that would give society its stability and thus ensure its progress. Paradoxically, and in opposition to others, Guizot made no mention of Russia in his *Histoire*, even though in his time Russia was considered as the main power in Europe. In this sense, Guizot was a Russophobe by omission. If he deliberately forgot to mention Russia, it was because her despotic social and political regime contradicted his vision of progress through the bourgeoisie, since Nicolas I's Russia had no intermediate class guaranteeing social progress and political stability. Yet the regime of the czars at the time was a model of stability, which contradicted Guizot's thesis. But his intellectual influence and the role he gave to this intermediate class soon to be called middle would be decisive.[28]

Tocqueville and the Bible of Russophobia according to Custine

It was a little later, in 1835, that Alexis de Tocqueville published his master work, which became the bible of liberalism and of modern liberal democracy, *De la démocratie en Amérique*. As a worthy aristocrat, Tocqueville was mainly preoccupied with tyranny as a byproduct of excessive equality as vaunted by the French Revolution and the destruction of the counter powers the three estates exercised during the Ancien Régime. In his eyes, two countries would play a key role in the future of civilization, the United States and Russia. He had a preference for the United States, which had established a moderate regime whose "progress rests on free personal interest and the strength and reason of individuals," as opposed to Russia's, "which rests on servitude and concentration of powers in the hands of a single man. Their starting point is different and their ways diverge; nonetheless, each seems called on by a secret design of Providence to hold one day in their hands the destiny of half of the world."[29]

Excessive democratic equality might indeed lead to some sort of democratic or bureaucratic despotism (totalitarianism, as we would say today). This drifting must be avoided at all costs, thanks to two essential conditions which the United States managed to produce: the middle class, as its countless crowd of owners made it "the natural enemy of violent commotions" and ensured the stability of the social body; and the associations, as "an association, be it political, industrial, commercial, or even literary or scientific, is a powerful body of educated citizens, and when defending its private interests against power encroachments, it saves the common liberties."

In the eyes of Tocqueville and his liberal friends such as de Beaumont, Russia was actually the country of uniformity, despotically egalitarian with its peasant communes:

> Everything there is so perfectly uniform: ideas, laws, customs, and even the most trivial details of the appearance of things. This seems to me like America but without the enlightenment or the liberty, a sort of democratic society which makes you feel terrified.[30]

The apex of French Russophobia was reached in 1843 with the publication of the travel notes of Baron Astolphe de Custine, *La Russie en 1839*. The work was reprinted dozens of times until the end of the 20th century and translated notably into English, German, Danish, Italian, and Russian.

Contrary to Tocqueville, Custine was no theoretician. He was a conservative aristocrat who went to Russia looking for arguments against representative government. He had read all the anti-Russian literature and its stereotypes and, once confronted by the oddity of Russian customs, came back completely converted to "Constitutions," and so Russophobic that he deemed that there was practically nothing to be saved in Russia.

> Muscovy was formed and has grown at the school of abjection that the terrible Mongol slavery was. Her strength, she only gathered it by becoming a past master in the art of servitude. Even once she

was emancipated, Muscovy has kept on playing her traditional master-slave role. In the end, Peter the Great tied to the political skillfulness of the Mongol slave the proud aspirations of the master to whom Genghis Khan had handed down the task of conquering the world.

He himself was convinced that "only conversion of Russia to Catholicism could implant in the empire of the czars the reality of European civilization," of which, he was convinced, "Russia only possesses the veneer."[31]

The entire book was of the same ilk. His conclusion was a true masterpiece of Russophobia:

> A huge, disorderly ambition, one of those ambitions that can only form in the soul of the oppressed and feed on the misery of an entire nation, is fermenting in the heart of the Russian people. This in essence conquering nation, turned greedy through privations, is expiating in advance at home, through demeaning submission, the hope of exercising tyranny upon others; the glory and wealth she expects distract her of the shame she is suffering and, to wash herself of the impious sacrifice of all public and personal freedom, the kneeling slave is dreaming of dominating the world.[32]

The themes of Russophobia in the 19th, 20th and 21st centuries were thus in place.

Custine's book has been much studied, commented upon and republished. It has been considered in Europe and America for the past 150 years as the greatest Russophobic monument ever erected. It synthesized, indeed with a beautiful pen, the whole of anti-Russian prejudices of the West, on democracy, expansionism, barbarity of lifestyles, drunkenness and corruption. It was chock-full of spicy details and anecdotes on court etiquette, dispatch rider outfits, and the deference of the nobility, the ins and outs of customs, in brief, the thousand and one aspects of Russian life, each interpreted in a negative way. Concrete, colorful, biting without ever being abstract, Custine's book has become the universal bible of the Russophobes, who find in it inexhaustible arguments and images.

Its career has been prodigious. Suffice it to say here that Custine's work again became a bestseller during the Cold War, after being reprinted in the United States with a preface by Walter Bedell Smith. This United States ambassador to Moscow between 1946 and 1948 considered *La Russie en 1839* "a political observation so shrewd and timeless that it could be called the best work ever produced on the Soviet Union." In 1987, in a new reprint, Polish Zbigniew Brzezinski drove the point home by writing on the trailer:

> No Sovietologist has yet improved on de Custine's insights into the Russian character and the Byzantine nature of the Russian political system.[33]

The latest critical edition in French was published in 2015 (Éd. Classiques Garnier).

The Rise of Socialism and the Russian Commune

In the meantime, a much more worrying threat than Russia had appeared for the wealthy and the privileged, be they democratic liberals or monarchist conservatives: socialism. The excess of equality so much feared during the Revolution had come back under the guise of socialism. Fear suddenly reunited conservatives and liberals, formerly at loggerheads, under a common banner.

It was the genius of Guizot, Tocqueville and Custine to oppose to socialism an attractive model, that of American-style liberal, middle-class democracy, while brandishing the best possible scarecrow: Russia, at once despotic by her political regime and collectivist in her organization into egalitarian farmer communes ignoring private property. During the 1840s, Europe was indeed in a ferment. Marx, anarchists, and utopian socialists wrote a lot, and revolution broke out in 1848 all over Europe.

In the second quarter of the 19th century, many socialist and anarchist theoreticians had indeed begun to praise the Russian "commune." Taking the opposite view to bourgeoisie theses, Victor Considerant and Ernest Cœurderoy even praised those Cossack barbarians that came from the North to help European peoples start a revolution, and sang praises to those Russians who would soon be called, Cœurderoy wrote, "the elder brothers of socialism."[34] He did not know just how right he was.

It was German baron August von Haxthausen who—in the wake of Herder and the German romantics who had rediscovered the virtues of Slavs at the beginning of the century—greatly popularized the Russian commune in the three volumes of his influential *Studien über die inneren Zustände, das Volksleben und insbesonderer die landlichen Einrichtungen Russlands*, published between 1847 and 1852. He saw in Russia a kind of utopia: whereas "in all the other parts of Europe, the instigators of social revolution rebel against wealth and property, such a revolution is impossible in Russia as the Utopia of European revolutionaries already exists there, fully incorporated into national life."[35] The rising power of socialism and sympathy of some intellectuals for the Russian Left and agrarian proto-communism had a double effect. The first was to bind together scared conservatives and liberals. In the face of the socialist threat, the conservatives discarded any illusion of finding in Russia a model for return to the Ancien Régime, whereas the liberals placed their hopes in American-style middle-class democracy. Both parties agreed to task the wealthy middle class with the mission to counter the socialist threat on property, society, and the State.

But the sympathy utopists and anarchists felt for the Russian form of agrarian socialism, popularized by Alexander Herzen, exiles to Switzerland and France in the 1840s and 1850s, and authors such as Cyprien Robert, professor of Slav language and literature at Collège de France, also resulted in radicalizing the German Left in an anti-Russian and anti-Slavic direction. Marx and Engels wrote very harsh pages against the Slavs, czarism, and Russian backwardness. With them, the theme of backwardness became one of the leitmotivs of left-wing Russophobia. Marx and Engels gave birth to left-wing Russophobia, which was then adopted by social democracy and European socialist followers after the break with the communist parties and the 1917 Revolution.

That influence, even with the repudiation of Marxism by socialist parties, is still felt today: the social democrats, now campaigning for societal reforms rather than defending the social interests of their electorate, are often among the most virulent contemporary Russophobes, as could be seen during the debates in early 2014 seeking the recognition in Russia of LGBT rights.

With their foremost commitment to combatting anarchists, such as Élisée Reclus, defender of the "Russian commune" as a model farmers association in his *Nouvelle géographie universelle*, and above all Bakunin, who called for the union of Slav peoples to get rid of foreign yokes (Austrian, Ottoman, and German in this instance), Marx and Engels long considered Slavs and Russians in particular as hopeless reactionaries.

> The Germans and Hungarians are not only symbols of progress and revolution, but also the bearers of Enlightenment and civilization to the Slavs.

And Engels went on to say that the creation of a Bohemian-Moravian State (the future Czechoslovakia) would have resulted in the tearing apart of Germany and Austria-Hungary "like a chunk of bread gnawed by rats."

> Where it is a matter of existence, of free development of all the resources of a great nation, any sentimental concern for a number of Slavs dispersed in various places is superfluous.[36]

One would think the editorialists of the European press of the 21st century directly drew their inspiration from Engels' theses when they write about Europe and Russia!

Individual Freedom versus the Russian Commune

But let us go back to the debate on democracy and the introduction of the notion of the opposition between western liberal democracy and Russian despotism-communism.

Throughout the 19th century, the intellectual debate centered on equality: should citizens' equality be total or relative? —and on sovereignty—to whom does ultimate sovereignty belong: to the people, to the king by divine right, or to a fraction of the people ... (the middle class)? Any "excess of equality" must be avoided. Faced with the systemic threat that the majority of the people represent, institutions must be established to counterbalance absolute power (separation of powers neutralizing the executive) and the power of the popular majority (by guaranteeing the rights of numeric minorities). Hence the importance of associations and of civil society to make up for the eventual "tyranny" of the popular majority.

The discovery of a "communist" component in the Russian social organization concomitant with "oriental despotism" was to offer the liberals an opportunity to disqualify Russia at once for her autocratic system and her socializing element. They wished to remove the seduction Russian autocracy exerted on those who were nostalgic for the old order and to put a stop to the praise romantics and non-Marxist socialists showered on Russia, described as "a paradise of equality and autonomy."

Criticism of autocracy was the easiest. The charge was mainly against the Russian commune, presented as generating uniformity, with the State crushing the individual. The excessive power of bureaucracy was emphasized. As Ezequiel Adamovski summarized it well, French liberal thinkers' priority was the individual. Discourse on the middle class took second place in favor of the cult of the individual (the wealthy individual in this case) as bearer of democracy, progress and civilization against powers that sought to crush him (czarist despotism and egalitarianism of the agrarian commune).

At the same time, Russia and her double threat were little by little relegated to a non-European, non-Western space belonging to Eastern Europe and Asia. Construction of the European idea which, in the 18th century, included Russia, by the 1850s proceeded from a concept of western civilization which sought to exclude her. The times coincided actually with the Crimean War and the constitution of a Franco-British coalition against Russia. Napoleon III, who dreamt of taking his revenge on his uncle's humiliating defeat, was no friend of Russia.

Final Synthesis: Amendable Russia and Redeemable Backwardness

It was only from the 1870s that the tone changed in France. After the abdication of vindictive Napoleon III, the humiliation of defeat and the reunification of Germany, and after Russia had abolished serfdom and shown her desire to open herself to industrialization and normal capitalism, France became more conciliating.

The isolation of France and the growing power of Germany were beginning to worry the leaders of the Third Republic, who were looking for new allies. This evolution was particularly obvious among the great Slavophiles and experts on Russia, on the model of the most famous of them, the brothers Paul and Anatole Leroy-Beaulieu. The first was professor of economy at Collège de France, and the second, professor of contemporary history and oriental affairs at Sciences Po from 1880 to 1910. Both knew Russia well and had visited her. Anatole's major work, *L'Empire des tsars et les Russes* (four volumes published between 1881 and 1889), was to be translated into many languages and is authoritative even now.

Although he professed friendship with Russia, Leroy-Beaulieu recycled the usual clichés on the country, "its oriental despotism, its inferiority, its ignorance, its fanaticism, its artificial imitation of western civilization, its dual nature, its abnormality, its incompleteness" and above all "its 'deficient country' side," a country to which something is missing to make it rightfully belong to western civilization.

> The history of Russia differs from that of other European nations more by what it lacks than by what it owns, and to each gap in the past corresponds a gap in the present, which time cannot fill—a gap in her culture, her society, as well as in the Russian spirit itself.
> This void in the history of the country, this absence of national traditions and institutions in a people that has yet to learn how to make those of others their own seems to me to be one of the secret causes of nihilism and "nothingism" in morals as in politics. ... Russian history, compared to that of western nations, appears to be entirely negative.[37]

As we can see, Russophile though he might be, Anatole Leroy-Beaulieu still perpetuated the clichés of the anti-Russian liberal discourse developed during the 19th century. He insisted on what Russian otherness lacked: the absence of feudality that brought the sense of law, of chivalry (sense of honor), of independent institutions such as the Church (to moderate State power), of civil society and associations, of a middle class, of individual initiative, etc. In short, Russia may be sympathetic, but it was still retarded and backward. In this sense, Leroy-Beaulieu appeared to be the perfect representative of Progress as incarnated by Europe and by American democracy. At the apex of colonial expansion, there was nothing surprising about it. In his *Hégémonie de l'Europe*, published in 1894, Élisée Reclus rejoiced over the "Europeanization" of the world and the fact that the West had integrated the East and the rest of the world into civilization.

In a magnificent panorama opposing the chapters of Tocqueville's *De la démocratie en Amérique* and those of Leroy-

Beaulieu's *L'Empire des tsars et les Russes*, Ezequiel Adamovsky shows well the correspondence between the two books, how their structure is similar while their theses conflict, Russia appearing systematically as the antithesis of America.

And that, from the first chapter, dealing in one as in the other with the physical geography of both countries: while the United States enjoys, according to Tocqueville, a variegated climate and a geography favorable to industry and commerce boosted by European immigration, Leroy-Beaulieu's Russia owns a compact and homogeneous territory totally different from Europe, with an inappropriate population, is deprived of European immigrants, and has a climate that favors individual passivity.

Everything else is of the same ilk. Chapter Three addressing the Anglo-American social state stresses the equality of individuals as independent and educated owners, whereas Russia's social hierarchy shows the gap between social classes, farmers' equality crushed under despotism and bureaucracy, as well as collective ownership and the absence of individual initiative.

Another section opposes the people's sovereignty, democracy, and non-violent competition of parties in the United States with Russia confronted by the rise of the revolutionary spirit, of nihilism, of terrorism, and of the risk of a revolution. Leroy-Beaulieu actually quotes Tocqueville on several occasions.

Leroy-Beaulieu wrote at a time when France and Russia, in a complete reversal, got together and signed a series of agreements between 1892 and 1894. In 1907, the two powers— for so long enemies—allied themselves with Great Britain to form the Triple Entente against their new common adversary, the German Empire, and its Austrian ally. While repeating anti-Russian clichés, Leroy-Beaulieu also had to take this context into account. Actually, taken in its entirety, his work achieved a masterful synthesis of contrary propositions. Under his pen, bourgeois democracy as defended by Tocqueville, czarist "despotism," and Russian egalitarian communism were altogether reconciled!

All of this was accomplished without endangering the new alliance or contradicting frontally the virulent Russophobia deployed by French and English intellectuals since 1820, and notably during the Crimean War in the 1850s. In so doing, Leroy-Beaulieu, a renowned professor, naturalized liberal criticism of Russia in the academic sphere and gave it a moral and scientific authority which has endured up to now in European and American universities.

How did he achieve this result?

Through a choice of adequate vocabulary and a very academic sense of nuance, which coated critical speech and made it more palatable, but above all by adding his own stone to the construction of the anti-Russian liberal discourse. Sure, Russia was backward, despotic and riddled with defects, he implied, but she could still mend her ways by letting herself be irrigated by beneficial western values, those of technology, industrial progress, foreign investment, and capitalist development, which would provide her with her institutions, her laws, and her political system.

Russia was definitely not Leibniz's tabula rasa, but her shortages, her gaps, could be filled by positive contributions from western civilization. The great Belgian liberal economist Gustave de Molinari, who was hostile to any state intervention, had already criticized the insufficiency of reforms and maintenance of state socialism as well as the absence of creation of authentic private property and the weakness of the middle class in Russia.

Leroy-Beaulieu took up this analysis, but inverted the perspective and put forward the idea that these backward aspects were as many proofs of Russia's potential. Her backwardness was no longer an incorrigible handicap, a *sui generis* defect; it was only a defect asking to be corrected. Through Witte's reforms and the massive contribution of French and English capital, this correction had even already begun to exercise its magical effects and nothing was opposed any longer to Russia becoming the ally of France and the United Kingdom.

The liberal ideology thus put in place would be deployed throughout the 20th century, at times showing its claws, when Russia fell into communism, at times showing its seductive potentialities, when it was a matter of getting Russia's help to fight Hitler and Nazism or of converting her to economic liberalism after the breakup of the Soviet Union in the early 1990s.

The irony is that it was France, now considered a country of sclerotic socialism, which was then at the forefront of doctrinal reflection on political liberalism and which provided modern Russophobia with some of its theoretical gear, and that she had done since the beginning of the 19th century.

France even largely contributed to the rapprochement between political liberalism and economic liberalism, thanks to the Physiocrats and their theories on beneficial luxury, beneficial wealth, the kind that trickled down to the poor and fed growth, even if that conceptual effort was, at the economic level, first achieved by Adam Smith and David Ricardo.[38]

It is also piquant to note that French liberal ideologues, who could not find words strong enough to lambast despotism, serfdom, and the Russian slavish mentality, had nothing to say about slavery, which was rife in the United States until President Lincoln abolished it in 1865, four years after the end of serfdom in Russia, after an abominable civil war. Let us point out as well that Prussia, Austria and Tibet put an end to serfdom in 1823, 1848, and 1959, respectively.

In this sense, liberal democracy appears truly like a privilege reserved if not for the rich at least for the wealthy of European origins, other men being excluded, Blacks and Asians to begin with. Similarly, while accounts of Russian cruelty, notably during the wars of conquest of the Caucasus in the 1850s against Imam Chamil, were abundantly described by writers and travelers such as Alexandre Dumas, none of the theoreticians of western civilization showed any emotion over the genocide of American Indians then going on before their eyes.

After the 1917 Revolution and then the Second World War, and the swing of the world's intellectual center of gravity from Europe to the United States, liberal "Russophobia" was to become one of the main ingredients of American criticism of Russia and of the anti-totalitarian discourse.

The Theory of the Cultural Gradient

The concepts of progress and civilization as defined by Condorcet at the end of the 18th century engendered both a theory of development and a theory of diffusion. The most common idea was that progress was achieved by stages, gradually, going for instance from slavery to feudality then to bourgeois democracy (and socialism with Marx), or from tyranny to aristocracy, to absolute monarchy, and then to liberal democracy, if we follow Montesquieu and Tocqueville (and to the disappearance of the oppressive State after a short period of dictatorship of the proletariat, according to Marx).

This theory of the progression of progress came with an attempt to explain its diffusion within mankind (a problematic which, after Darwin, was to give birth to the hierarchy of races, some of them being adjudged lower on the scale of progress, or of adaptation according to social Darwinists). In Europe, the promotion of the liberal model by opposition to autocracy, and affirmation of civilization by opposition to Asian barbarity, also gave birth to the theory of the cultural gradient.

Viewed thus, civilization would progress west to east from a central focus located between Paris and London, and then deploy itself eastward, as the peoples of central Europe, and then of Eastern Europe, and finally of Russia would become civilized. This idea was developed during the 19th century, as romantic reaction to the universalism of the Enlightenment had Germany entering progressively great "Kultur" and catching up with the civilization cradles of France in the intellectual domain and of the England of the early industrial revolution in the economic domain.

As the century went along, the theory became consistent. When Alexander II abolished serfdom, it was noticed that the measure came half a century after that of Prussia in 1807. Similarly, the introduction of the parliamentary system in Russia after the aborted revolution of 1905 came several decades after the first election in the Reichstag.

It was English Prime Minister Palmerston who, for the

first time, formulated the "system of the Two and the Three," the two liberal countries or maritime powers (France and United Kingdom) opposing the three monarchies of the North, terrestrial and autocratic (Prussia, Austria, and Russia).

Then the structure of the gradient became still finer, with *Mitteleuropa* formed by Germany and Austria-Hungary appearing as an intermediary stage of civilization between France and the United Kingdom at the apex, and Russia perceived and described as at the very bottom of the civilizational scale, perhaps having yet to reach the first rung.

As Martin Malia remarks, "if the strange Cyrillic characters that amused so much Lewis Carroll are the first sign of Russia and of her difference for the western traveler, let us not forget that at the same time (and until the 1950s) Germanic Mitteleuropa used for its part gothic characters, of a strangeness somewhat 'intermediary' in the eyes of Western Europeans used to Latin characters. The three scripts (Latin, Gothic, and Cyrillic) are a rather useful image of the three rungs of the European west-east gradient."[39]

The theory of cultural gradient is interesting because it allows the integration or exclusion at will of Russia into and out of European civilization, according to circumstances at any one time. When Russia becomes useful as would be the case in 1890s France, 1900s United Kingdom, and again during the Second World War she will be admitted into civilization, by underlining, as Leroy-Beaulieu did, her compatibility with the West. What will then be emphasized as was the case more recently during the Gorbachev period or during the years 2001-2003 after the World Trade Center attacks will be the convergence of Russia toward the ideals of the West, pluralistic democracy and liberal economy.

But when Russia was perceived as a threat after 1815, 1917, and 1945 or after Vladimir Putin took control of the economy in 2003 then the theory of the gradient became useful again in the other direction as it allowed for excluding Russia from among civilized nations and projecting her into barbarity, with the whole range of usual clichés: authoritarianism, atavistic expansionism, state control, retrograde conservatism.

So it is not surprising that the hypothesis of gradual development of civilization according to a west-east or northwest-southeast axis since the French Revolution did not take into account deviant western behaviors. The barbarity of Europeans in their South American, African or Asian colonies, as well as that of the terror imposed in China by the colonial armies after the Boxer Rebellion of 1901, were never mentioned, and neither was the barbarity of Americans against the Indians nor the fact that the suppression of slavery in the United States took place at the same time as that of serfdom in Russia and that, from a strictly human point of view, the United States was not more "civilized" than Russia was at the time.

Let us point out too that the oriental gradient theory does not explain the shift of civilization toward the west, when the economic and cultural center of gravity swung toward the United States after 1945. Nor does it explain its eclipse during the period of recovery under Stalin and the 1960s, when the axis of progress seemed to shift to the east.

During the pre-war years and then until the end of the 1960s, the Soviet Union indeed seemed to be, in the eyes of millions of Westerners and citizens of the new nations of the Third World, a model of progress and modernity against a West tangled up in the defense of outdated colonial privileges.

For a few decades, an ideological battle raged as to in which camp the engine of progress was running. But by the end of the 1960s, the old dichotomy resurfaced yet again, to the exclusive benefit of a West centered again on the United States and transformed into a First World while the Soviet bloc formed the Second.

This second-ranking role given Russia in the world order long constituted the modern form of cultural gradient before being modified after the disappearance of the Soviet Union in order to make room for China.

Actually, from having been explicative at the beginning, the cultural gradient theory rapidly became essentialist: by defining Russia as far behind West European models, this backwardness was reified, hypostasized, to be made into an absolute constitutive and discriminatory element, according to the usual reasoning of racism: the Russian is barbaric as the Jew is miserly, the Black lazy, the Muslim a terrorist. And from there, it is but a short hop to describing Russia as an enemy of civilization, as can be read every day under the pen of contemporary Western editorialists.

In addition to an apparent need to classify, to order, to hierarchize the different human societies, this obsession with taxonomy and ranking serves to dampen that anguish so typical in the West of the top pupil who must ceaselessly verify that he is still ahead of the pack and his pursuers are not gaining on him. Since the Age of Enlightenment, the West keeps needing to reassure itself, to prove to itself that it is still at the forefront of progress and civilization, and that its "values" are truly universal —albeit specific to the West. This is the price that must be paid to ensure the feeling of superiority and justify the will to dominate. And Russia, at once so near and so different, is the ideal yardstick for that purpose.

Georges Sokoloff, in *Le Retard russe*,[40] aptly shows the difficulty the West has always had in classifying Russia, and how its classifications "result too easily in hierarchies which go beyond economy and politics to include culture and lifestyle. Being behind becomes backwardness." In the 1960s, the Russian-born American economist, Alexander Gerschenkron, had already answered W. W. Rostow's simplistic liberal theses on the five stages of economic development and the advent of the consumer society that was to coincide with pluralistic democracy. He had shown that the "late" countries could jump over some stages by taking advantage of the experience acquired by their predecessors, which had been the case of Russia in the 1930s. As to knowing if economic development precedes political development or capitalism engenders democracy or if imperialist imposition can ever assure either, the debate is not over.

"The reader must make the effort to reflect that Russian peasants, even wrapped in sheepskin, are human beings like us," British author Donald Mackenzie Wallace wrote in 1877.[41] One hundred and forty years later, sheepskins have disappeared but not the mentality that presents the Russian like a retard always struggling to climb the scale of liberal economy and pluralistic democracy, which are viewed as the quintessential culminations of advanced western civilization.

| Chapter Six |

ENGLISH RUSSOPHOBIA: THE OBSESSION WITH EMPIRE

"Russia ... a riddle wrapped in a mystery inside an enigma."
Winston Churchill, October 1939

"A Stereotype, Wrapped in a Cliché, Inside a Caricature."
James D. J. Brown, University of Aberdeen, 2010.[1]

The contribution of England to Russophobia too is essential. English Russophobia appeared right after Napoleon's defeat in 1815. Like that of France, the English contribution has been twofold. On the one hand, the English have hoisted Russophobia to the geopolitical level by describing it for the first time as a participant in the rivalries of powers endeavoring to secure "the empire of the world" since the beginning of the industrial revolution. The Great Game, which characterized the shock between Russian and English imperialisms in Asia in the 19th century, was an illustration of this. But through her democratic system England also has introduced Russophobia at the level of the general public. To make good on their imperial ambitions, the

English government and colonialist lobby had to convince voters as well that Russia had become, right after the Vienna Treaty, a power threatening English domination in Asia.

While the French philosophers fought on the battleground of ideas, discussed the merits of democracy, and sharpened their arguments against oriental despotism, the English, for their part, opened new commercial routes and ceaselessly conquered new markets.

English Russophobia had no religious or philosophical character. Allusions to Russian despotism were purely incidental, merely a propaganda argument for opposing the czar. The bottom line was that the English were not at all interested in criticizing despotism; to counter the Russians, they would not hesitate to ally themselves with the Ottoman sultan, the very archetype of the oriental despot.

England, growing demographically in the middle of an industrial revolution, enjoyed at the start of the 19th century an enormous surfeit of power begging to be of use. So she focused on enlarging her empire and clashed with Russia in the Mediterranean Sea and in Central Asia. North America having escaped her, with the exception of her Canadian dominion, powerful England was interested in the southern maritime routes and in the domination of the lands richest in men and resources, namely the thick belt of lands stretching from the Caribbean Islands to China via Africa, the Middle East, India and Australia.

Prussia, occupied by the Russians in 1760 and then beaten by Napoleon, was still only a second-class power. Austria was wholly preoccupied by internal problems and the fight against the nationalist virus introduced by Napoleon infecting the various nationalities composing her empire. France had to recover from her defeat and catch up in industrial terms. As for the Ottoman Empire, gnawed at by the Russian progression in the north and the vague attempts at autonomy of its North-African subjects, it had already been on the decline for a few decades.

In 1815, with the Napoleonic peril out of the way, the United Kingdom found itself without any rivals on sea or on land. Ahead, there was only Russia, the big ally against the French emperor, whom Russia had vanquished in 1812, occupying Paris in 1814. Russia had also dominated the Vienna Congress and by her size and her army was now a European power of prime importance.

Since the first establishment of relations at the beginning of the 16th century and the creation of the Muscovy Company, relations between London and Moscow had always been good. But tensions rapidly replaced those three centuries of cordial exchanges. In less than three decades, they threw the two former allies into war. Having been pro-Russian before 1815, English public opinion and leaders turned to very aggressive Russophobia, even though the two countries had no common border and no concrete motive for a dispute.

Why this unexpected and very radical turnabout?

Suddenly after 1815, Russia Becomes a Threat

A Harvard University researcher asked himself this question at a time when the phenomenon was repeating itself, at the end of the 1940s, while the then-ended Second World War, which had seen the Soviet and Anglo-Saxon coalition beat Nazi Germany, was turning into a new war, the Cold War, between the two erstwhile allies. It was with this preoccupation in mind that John Howes Gleason wrote his remarkable book on the birth of English Russophobia.[2]

The first paragraph of the book reads like this:

> Russophobia is a paradox in the history of Great Britain. Within the United Kingdom there developed early in the nineteenth century an antipathy toward Russia which soon became the most pronounced and enduring element in the national outlook on the world abroad. The contradictory sequel of nearly three centuries of consistently friendly relations, this hostility found expression in the Crimean War. Yet that singularly inconclusive struggle is the sole conflict directly between the two nations; theirs is

a record of peace unique in the bellicose annals of the European great powers. And in the three primary holocausts of modern times, in which among the major powers Great Britain alone escaped defeat, her victory thrice depended on the military collaboration of Russia. Why then did Russophobia become a persistent British sentiment?[3]

Remarkable sentences, at once lucid and premonitory, so much so that they remain relevant sixty-five years after their formulation and perfectly match the American and European Russophobia of this beginning of the 21st century. Why did Russia, which three times had saved the western world, then at a time when she did not or not any longer represent a threat to it, and even now still, generate so much hatred and hostility in Western media, universities and chancelleries?

The first answer that comes to mind to explain British Russophobia is simple: it was the confrontation of the imperial ambitions of two great powers which, far away from each other before 1815, came to direct friction after the self-effacement of France—a situation that can be compared to that of the United States and the Soviet Union after 1945.

For Gleason, this explanation is not sufficient, as it does not explain why two allied countries had to confront one another when their respective colonial ambitions did not clash frontally, one being spread over the "soft underbelly" of Asia, the other much more to the south, in India, China, Egypt and Africa.

Similarly, Gleason adds interestingly, why didn't Great Britain take any account of Russian remarks and protestations when Moscow worried about the provocative policy of Great Britain in the Balkans, the Caucasus, Constantinople, Afghanistan, Syria, and Egypt? It seems history is repeating itself as the oblivious British provocations in the years 1815–1840 are so similar to those of the United States, the European Union and NATO in Eastern Europe and Central Asia in the years 1990 to 2010! And Gleason goes on: "...had the Russians appealed to the criterion of deeds rather than words, which their British contemporaries applied against them, an impartial judge must probably have rendered a verdict in their favor."[4]

Therefore, to explain this eruption of Russophobia in the United Kingdom in the years 1820–1840, Gleason introduces a second hypothesis: "The heart of the matter will be found to lie in the interaction of policy and opinion." More than from the shock of colliding empires, Russophobia flows from the way the battle for domination of public opinion was carried out by English political parties.

In substance, he thinks, the true reason is to be found in Britain's internal political battles. Political parties used fear of Russia either to denounce the too conciliatory policy of the government of the day given the threat the Russian Empire represented for the British Empire, or to justify, on the contrary, operations of military or economic conquest of new territories which had to be acquired before the Russian "barbarians" and "despots" grabbed them.

The observation is interesting as it can be applied in copy-paste mode to the United States situation in 2015: same bipartisan system, same parliamentary blockages and better-than-thou contests, same exploitation of public opinion via the media, and same exacerbation of anti-Russian hysteria for internal political purposes. Between the Great Britain of the Whigs and Tories of 1815 and the United States of the Republicans and Democrats of the 2016 presidential elections, there is little difference. The Democratic Party's projection of supposed Russian hacking of the Party servers during the electoral campaign to obscure the Wikileaks exposures that were very damaging for Hillary Clinton and the Clinton Foundation and revealed the bias used by the Party leaders to eliminate the candidate Bernie Sanders, are typical. After Trump's victory, this hysteria became tremendous, with President Obama himself incriminating Russia with the support of the intelligence agencies.

In both cases, Russia plays the part of a providential scarecrow and is condemned to incarnate the image of The Bad Guy that the parties, in a paralyzed bipartisan system, throw at one another's heads with the hope of winning the favor of public opinion and resulting electoral gains. One can actually wonder if the same phenomenon did not also take place during the 2013-14 winter when the European Union, unable to agree on the policy to follow regarding Russia because of its internal divisions, inconsiderately fanned the flames and put increasing pressure on Russia in the Ukrainian conflict.

According to that thesis, English Russophobia would thus be, initially, less the fact of the government than of opposition parties trying to excite public opinion against alleged Russian imperialism or, reversely, denouncing loudly alleged government concessions in increasingly powerful media. Political leaders and other public figures tend indeed to be influenced and to "listen carefully to the many voices in the public chorus, blatant or surreptitious, known and unidentified."[5]

To complete Gleason's theories, a more anthropological explanation can be invoked, which is that Nature abhors a vacuum, and a power which has become hegemonic, as was Great Britain after the Napoleonic wars, tends to install its hegemony indefinitely and to destroy all dissent as long as it does not meet with an opposition capable of bringing it to its senses.

This explanation can also be connected with Montesquieu and Tocqueville's theses: any power without a counter-power tends to become absolute, be it within its borders or outside when there is no other power or group of powers able to contain it, international law being seldom a sufficient safeguard against distortions.

A candidate dictator will always manage to modify the fundamental rules in his favor when he faces no challenger capable of opposing him, just as a power can always "interpret" or rewrite international law according to its interest when there are no other forces capable of resisting it. The law then only becomes a mask hiding pure powers of domination.

The Evolution of English Russophobia

But let us see instead how Great Britain turned into a

virulent hotbed of Russophobia. The first serious breach in good Anglo-Russian relations happened in 1791 with the Russian conquest of the Ottoman Empire's Ochakov fortress. This fortress, located at the mouths of the Dnieper and Bug rivers, near Odessa, commanded access to the Ukrainian plains. Its fall in 1788 provoked a reaction from the Pitt government, which wanted to launch a naval expedition to force Catherine II to withdraw.

Abandoned by his public opinion and by his members of parliament who couldn't see why this change of masters was of concern to England, Pitt was forced to abandon his project. This first skirmish was left to stand, the two countries later making common cause against the French Revolution and then against Napoleon.

But English political leaders drew the lesson from this incident: for the first time in English democratic history, public opinion had forced the government to back down on an important foreign policy issue. From then on, before venturing abroad, it was understood that public opinion would have to be prepared, press and propaganda campaigns devised, and soft power resources mobilized. In this sense, Gleason is right to insist on England's internal reasons and on the role of English political life in generating British Russophobia.

The next tension flared up during the Vienna Congress. If Castlereagh, Metternich and Alexander I shared the conviction that a return to the Old Order constituted the best guarantee for peace and prosperity in Europe, Castlereagh's opposition to Alexander I's obstinate wish to be crowned king of a Poland united with Russia triggered the reappearance of the antagonism born during the Ochakov crisis. Poland had always been a master card of the English continental policy, as it provided England with a lever against Germany, Austria-Hungary, and Russia. Since the partitions at the end of the 18th century, and up until now actually, Poland has always been able to rely on England, which did not want at any cost to see Russia settle down in the heart of the European continent by controlling Poland.

It was also during that period that the first articles were published insinuating that Napoleon had tried to conclude a secret alliance with Russia and Persia in order to conquer British India. Real or alleged, these declarations seemed to confirm Peter the Great's forged testament,[6] which had just been translated into English. For British nationalists and imperialists, it was a sufficient grievance for Russia to be ostracized. The imperial lobby, increasingly powerful in London, would never thereafter lose sight of Russia and became the most determined adversary of the Russian cause.

The English colonial lobby and economic circles had been traumatized by Napoleon's continental blockade. Deprived of access to European harbors, they could no longer sell their goods abroad—absolute horror for a maritime power that lost all its means when deprived of outlets. The blockade resulted in the English becoming aware that mastery of the seas was a necessary but not sufficient condition for their power: indispensable land relays had to be added without which that power could not be deployed. That did change the perspective: Russia could become a potential obstacle.

By the 1820s, the most fervent admirers of the empire began to launch polemics and broadcast most alarming news in the British press about the czars' thirst for unlimited expansion and the threats they posed to British interests in the Mediterranean, Central Asia, India, and China. This is how the Great Game was born, which throughout the 19th century opposed the English and Russians for control of Central Asia and which led the English to launch two preventive wars in Afghanistan in the name of the protection of their possessions in the Indian subcontinent, today's Pakistan, India, and Bangladesh.

The Whigs, who represented then the "liberal-bourgeois" opposition to the Tory government and the tenets of British free trade imperialism, were the most violent (exactly as are the US Democrats in our days). Here is what *The Morning Chronicle* of October 24, 1817 wrote about an utterly absurd rumor claiming that Spain had allied itself with Russia in order to obtain her help in South Africa in exchange for the cession of possessions in the Mediterranean:

> A very general persuasion has long been entertained by the Russians, that they are destined to be the rulers of the world, and this idea has been more than once stated in publications in the Russian language.[7]

"To do the Russians justice," the editorialist goes on, "their aggrandizement has never for a moment been lost sight of under the various Sovereigns, who, for a century, have filled the throne. The most arbitrary Sovereigns must yield to the prevailing inclinations of their people, and the prevailing inclination of the Russians is territorial aggrandizement."

> With such a feeling, and with the confidence which recent events have given them, to suppose that a colossal Power like Russia will be contented to remain without any other maritime communication than the Northern Ocean and the Baltic, both accessible only at certain seasons of the year, and that she will not endeavor to obtain for by far the most valuable part of her Empire, the command to the situations which secure an entrance to the Mediterranean, does not plead in favor of a great degree of political vision."[8]

Greek Independence and the Polish Revolt

It would be tedious to quote the polemics and detailed crises that fed British aggressiveness toward Russia after the 1815 Entente Cordiale up to the outburst of the Crimean War. For the record, we shall only mention the most outstanding events addressed by Gleason: the proclamation of Greek independence in 1822, the Polish Revolution of 1830, the 1833 crisis, the Vixen affair in 1836-37, the occupation of the Persian island of Karrak, and then the Afghan crisis in 1838, and the Near East crisis of 1839-1841.

Close to the Greeks through Orthodoxy and the Byzantine

heritage, Russia had kept recovering from the Turks the territories conquered by the Tartars and the Ottomans since the Middle Ages. Members of the Greek diaspora did actually govern numerous principalities in Moldavia and Walachia (Romania). They felt close to Russia. The latter, at the end of the 1768-1774 Great War, had snatched away many territories, as well as the title of defender of Orthodoxy, from the Sublime Porte (a metonym for the central Ottoman government).

The Küçük-Kainarca Treaty of 1774 between the Ottomans and Russia had made the czar of Russia the protector of Orthodoxy in the Ottoman Empire, which gave him the legal ability to intervene to support the Greeks whenever they felt in danger. The treaty had been completed in 1779 by a new agreement, and then by a commercial convention in 1783. From then on, the Greeks could sail in the Black Sea and the Mediterranean under Russian flag and sail in them they did.

When the Greek insurgency erupted in 1821, the European powers went on the alert, none of them being willing to let Russia alone take advantage of the situation, while the czar at first hesitated to intervene as he was anxious to keep things as they were according to the terms of the Vienna Treaty.

After countless incidents and various reversals, the conflict had degenerated into civil war. In 1826, the new Russian czar, Nicolas I, decided to take the initiative. He addressed an ultimatum to Mahmud II. The sultan yielded. The Akkerman Convention of October 1826 granted the Russians commercial advantages in the entire Ottoman Empire, and above all the right of protection over Moldavia, Walachia and Serbia. This Russian success triggered a reaction from the United Kingdom, which proposed in July 1827 a British, Russian, and French mediation between Greeks and Turks. The Greeks were no longer in a position to refuse: they controlled only Nafplio and Hydra. But the sultan rejected the offer. The three powers then threatened to intervene militarily. They concentrated their fleets in Navarin, where an incident triggered the destruction of the Turk-Egyptian fleet.

At the same time, a French expeditionary force landed

in Morea[9] and obtained Ibrahim Pacha's departure. Russian troops invaded the Rumanian provinces and took over Erzurum, in eastern Turkey, and Adrianople (Edirne) in western Turkey in August 1829. To prevent a takeover of Constantinople by Russian troops, the United Kingdom obtained a diplomatic settlement. The sultan had already yielded and signed the Adrianople Treaty with Russia (September 14, 1829). This treaty was completed in February 1830 by the London Conference: the independence of Greece was proclaimed and guaranteed by the great powers.[10]

The British Press Enflames Public Opinion

So much for historical facts. Throughout the Greek independence war, the British parties and press were on a war footing, and took at times hysterical positions against Russia. Here is what *The Times* wrote about the Adrianople Treaty:

> The terms of his [Czar Nicolas I's] 'moderation'... are known to everybody. They leave about as much national independence to Turkey as victorious Rome left to her ancient rival Carthage. ... There is no sane mind in Europe that can look with satisfaction at the immense and rapid overgrowth of Russian power.

In 1827, its competitor, *The Herald*, was hardly less conciliating:

> It is evident that it is not the real intention of Russia to make Greece an independent state, but to transfer her dependency from the Turkish yoke to her own. By that means the Autocrat of the North will possess what the Muscovite Cabinet have long been endeavoring to obtain: a naval station in the Mediterranean. ... By such an accession to her power she can, whenever she pleases, with

little comparative difficulty, take possession of Constantinople, and, extending her arms eastward, shake the throne of our Asian Empire.[11]

It was against this background of tensions that the uprising in Poland took place at the end of November 1830. After the partition of 1795 with Prussia and Austria, the Vienna Treaty had granted the Warsaw duchy to Russia. Nicolas I had put his brother, Grand Duke Konstantin, in charge. The grand duke was much disliked by the Poles, who revolted. A war ensued, which ended with the crushing of the Poles in 1831, triggering great emotion in France and in England.

The episode was made famous by the unfortunate declaration of French foreign minister Sébastiani, "order reigns in Warsaw," taken up in Granville's well-known cartoon featuring a Cossack standing up surrounded by Polish corpses. The reconquest of Poland and the repression that followed had a disastrous effect for the image of Russia and played a large part in the reputation as oriental despot of Nicolas, who lost his aura as "liberator" of Greece, a moniker the other powers were eyeing.

This episode naturally boosted the morale of the most exalted supporters of British imperialism. Already in 1828, Colonel George de Lacy Evans had published an incendiary brochure (*On the Designs of Russia*) which warned Europe and notably France against the fact that "possession of the world's strongest strategic position [i.e. Constantinople and the control of the Dardanelles] would enable [Russia,] ipso facto, to dominate the Mediterranean and Central Asia and thus to undermine the trade and power of France and Great Britain. With Constantinople as a base, universal dominion was within Russia's easy grasp."[12]

This scenario was pure fabrication and did not take any account of reality on the ground. But, like Peter the Great's fake testament, it had the advantage of comfirming English opinion that Russia was decidedly an aggressive and dangerous power.

In July 1833, a new crisis burst out between Russia and Great Britain when, against all expectations, Russia made peace with the Ottoman Empire by the Hünkâr İskelesi Treaty. Turkey was indeed confronted by troubles that threatened her possessions in Syria and Egypt as well as by English and French designs on the Nile delta and the Near East. The two empires promised each other mutual assistance in case of an attack by a foreign power. Far from appeasing the British imperial lobby, which worried about each war Russia led against Turkey, the treaty fueled their hostility.

The United Kingdom and France feared that the Turks might give Russia the freedom to send her fleet beyond the Dardanelles. The opposition and the media in England flew into a rage against Russia, concealing entirely the fact that Russia was in reality as worried about the decrepitude of the Ottoman Empire as were the English and the French, and that she feared nothing as much as its deliquescence threatening the whole southern part of her empire.

Arming the Circassians

A few years later, in 1836, a new development took place: the *Vixen* affair. The Adrianople Treaty had given Russia authority over Circassia, a mountainous area located by the Black Sea between Crimea and Sochi, but the Circassians rejected this change of masters. The English chargé in Constantinople, David Urquhart, decided to get round the Russian embargo on English and French weapon deliveries to Circassians by organizing a clandestine delivery with the *Vixen*, a schooner under English flag.

What had to happen happened. Unsurprisingly, the English boat was boarded by the Russian fleet while delivering 8 cannons, 28,000 pounds of powder and all sorts of other weapons. The sequestration of the boat drew the ire of the English press and hypocritical protests from London; such a restraint on trade was intolerable. The Tories tabled a question in Parliament casting doubt on the legality of Russian jurisdiction over Circassia, and Russia was threatened with war.

The latter responded in the same vein.

As London proved unable to find an ally on the continent to declare war on Russia, hostilities were toned down; the English liberal government answered the Tory question by declaring that Russia owned Circassia legally as per the Adrianople Treaty. But war had been quite close.

Hardly had the *Vixen* affair been forgotten when Urquhart and his friends resumed their assaults on the Russians in Circassia. In 1837, James Bell, son of the *Vixen* ship owner, and John Longworth, "occasional contributor to *The Times*," landed with the Circassians with lead and powder to enjoin them to rebel against the Russians. They brought with them "David Urquhart's latest invention, a flag." To maximize its impact, Urquhart presented it as a sacred symbol, or *Sandzak Sheriff*, as dubbed by Constantinople religious leaders. Its fortune has crossed centuries: still now, the flag is the official emblem of the Adygea Republic, one of the autonomous republics of the Federation of Russia.[13] The expedition was left to stand alone. London changed policy and the Circassians finally integrated into the Russian Empire. Even the Crimean War did not succeed in dislodging the Russians from Circassia, nor did it prevent them from defeating Imam Chamil and putting an end to the Chechnya Rebellion, offering Chamil an honorable surrender with respect.

The Great Game and the Struggle for Asia

In the history of Anglo-Russian relations, the 1830s will remain the decade of the launching of the Great Game, as historians call it. This expression was coined by Arthur Conolly, an English officer who tried to make Turkestan tribes revolt against the Russians and ended up beheaded in Bukhara in 1842. The southern confines of the Russian Empire then experienced two serious crises at the end of the decade.

In the fall of 1837, a Persian attack against the then Afghan town of Herat triggered anew the hysteria of the English imperialistic lobby and the newspapers devoted to it. They denounced it as a maneuver of the Russians to conquer India, Russia having an ambassador in Teheran, Count Simonitch. The

English responded by ordering the Indian army to occupy the Persian islet of Karrak in the Persian Gulf.

The conflict then drifted to Afghanistan, the English having decided to invade that country to make the British Raj feel secure. In the summer of 1839, they conquered Kabul and put an emir in their pay in charge. This resulted in an insurgency and the massacre of the English garrison by the Afghan insurgents. Normality was hard to restore in 1842, and peace was more or less maintained until the second Anglo-Afghan War in 1878-1880. But Afghanistan remained unstable, with a third conflict erupting in 1919.

In 1839-1841, a new crisis brought attention back to the Mediterranean. Focused on deploying their policy of contention with Russia, the English, still led by Russophobic Palmerston, had given themselves two objectives in the Mediterranean: maintaining the sultan on his throne and preventing a separate action of Russia in Turkey. But Muhammad Ali's aspirations for Egyptian independence put the sultan and the European powers on red alert.

In 1839, Egypt rebelled against the sultan and defeated the Turkish troops, thus putting everybody on a war footing. As usual the English led the movement. They first tried to convince France of Russia's intent to weaken the Ottoman Empire. Metternich offered his services to help Austrian interests progress in the Balkans. Meanwhile, the British East India Company had the Royal Marines land in Aden, occupy the territory, and stop pirate attacks against the British expedition in India. The conflict ended with a treaty, signed in London in July 1840.

Great Britain, Prussia, Russia, and Austria agreed to curb Muhammad Ali's ambitions. He was given authority over Egypt in a hereditary capacity but remained nominally under the tutelage of the Ottoman Empire. France, which wavered in favor of Muhammad Ali before eventually relenting, was totally sidelined from the agreement, and this unleashed an enormous wave of anger in Paris.

In 1841, an international convention completed the treaty of the previous year by guaranteeing the neutrality of the Dardanelles and interdiction of the Marmara Sea to war vessels. Russia found herself in the same camp as Great Britain. But it was only a respite, as the imperialist lobby was not giving up its antipathy, its followers having multiplied scathing anti-Russian articles in the London and Indian press.

As a result, in the early 1840s, in less than twenty-five years, English public opinion had been completely turned around. From privileged ally, which had entered into war against Napoleon alongside Great Britain out of unwillingness to participate in the anti-English blockade wanted by the French emperor, Russia had become public enemy Number One of the United Kingdom. From great ally of liberal England, the czar had become a barbaric, furiously expansionist despot.

From then on, solidly implanted in public opinion, British Russophobia was rapidly going to translate into open warfare. A mere spark might start it. That was struck by the Orient Issue.

During the 1840s, the problem of the Orient[14] steadily grew in import. The Ottoman Empire, having become "the sick man of Europe," was on everybody's mind. Great Britain was still haunted by the threat an eventual Russian progression toward Constantinople could bring to bear on trade routes linking the Asian and European territories of her empire. France, hankering for international recognition, deplored that the Black Sea had become a "Russian lake" and tried to tear off the Ottoman Empire the status of "protector of Christians" in the Holy Land.

In 1844, Czar Nicolas I went to London with the hope of coming to terms, but the encounter proved fruitless. The press kept up the pressure, prodded by a very Russophobic political class, starting with Lord Palmerston, who had understood how much advantage he could gain from the media. He exploited the traditional anti-Russian vein by presenting the war as "a fight of democracy against tyranny." And with a cheek quite like that of modern American think tanks passing off the Chechnya Islamists of 2004 as "rebels" in Syria, he dared to present the war supporting Muslim Turkey led by its despotic sultan as a war for Christendom!

The Orient Issue as Catalyst for the Crimean War

So, when debate heated up on the Holy Places, with Orthodox and Catholics fighting for preeminence over them, calls for war against Russia were on the rise in Paris. In August 1853, David Urquhart, always on the go, fiercely attacked Russia and those that opposed war in England in the columns of *The Morning Advertiser*.[15] In early October 1853, Turkey declared war on Russia. On November 30, Russian boats crushed the Turkish fleet to pieces in Sinope. Everything had happened according to the rules, but it was too much for the English, who deemed that battle a casus belli and used it to obtain public approval, "just as the Tonkin Gulf incident of 1965, contrived as it may have been, spurred popular support for direct American intervention in South Vietnam."[16]

What followed is well known. The ill-prepared landing of badly led French, English and Sard troops in Crimea resulted in a long, expensive war that was frightful in terms of living conditions for the soldiers, who died more of cholera, cold and privations than in the fighting.

The Crimean War is considered to be the first modern war in history, due to the weaponry used—shotguns with rifled barrels, steamboats, railway, telegraph and the sudden emergence of the role of the media. It was in Crimea that the first war correspondents (William Howard Russell of *The Times*) and war photographers (Roger Fenton of *Illustrated News*) landed. The range of means mobilized and the massive usage of propaganda intent on pacifying public opinion to better hide imperialist ambitions were also firsts in the history of war.

On numerous points, the Crimean War anticipated contemporary wars: it too was made, according to its official motivations, in the name of the right to humanitarian interference (protection of Christians in Palestine) and of the fight against tyranny, with the same contradictions as today, since the Ottoman Empire was anything but a democracy and was submitted to a tyranny far worse than the Russian enemy.

For the first time too, war was no longer declared in the name of dynastic interests, but of stakes under the heading of "the fight of Good against Evil, of civilization against barbarity," as Martin Malia has it, who quotes the prose of a British journalist for whom "Muscovites had no access to ordinary motives of the human family."[17]

In 1855, the fall of the Malakoff bastion led to the desertion of Sebastopol and victory over Russia was achieved, but at a high cost. Peace in 1856 forced humiliated Russia to withdraw momentarily from the territories conquered from the Turks. France recovered her rightful position on the international scene but Britain came out more shaken than expected from her apparent victory.

The Fragility of the British Empire

In the second half of the 19th century, Great Britain was at the apex of her territorial expansion and had reached the pinnacle of her power. Thanks to her military and merchant navies, she had expanded her possessions over all continents, in China, in Central and Southeast Asia, in Australia and New Zealand, in Egypt and in the Middle East, and of course in Africa.

But in Crimea, the prestige of the English army had suffered from the incompetence of its commanders. Florence Nightingale's devotion as she gave succor to wounded soldiers cynically abandoned by their officers had much moved public opinion, and the doggedness of the Russian defense, in spite of all the propaganda on Russia's inanity, corruption and backwardness, had not gone unnoticed either. The British Empire, despite a series of victories since 1815, had shown cracks that were to durably worry its most committed eulogists, such as the writers Rudyard Kipling and Bram Stoker, the author of *Dracula*.

The British Empire was universal, but fragile. In Afghanistan, the first campaign had almost turned into a disaster. In the Sudan, General Gordon's army was defeated. In London, the imperialist camp, from David Urquhart to Cecil Rhodes, fought on the media and ministerial fronts to further the colonial cause. But the germ of doubt persisted nevertheless: if its maritime supremacy was uncontested, the empire remained vulnerable on land. In Crimea, the British army showed weaknesses, and victory was obtained only thanks to the French. In the Sudan, it took all the energy of Kitchener to blot out Gordon's humiliating defeat.

A sea empire without firm outlets on the continent was but half an empire, unstable and insecure. How could a whale beat an elephant, to borrow Bismarck's formula? For such a power, what was more worrisome, more disquieting, more unbearable than that gigantic Russian Empire, whose mass seemed to permanently threaten the rich and populated continent that Great Britain intended to dominate, Eurasia? At a time when geography was the science par excellence and geographical societies were annexes of the foreign and commerce ministries, these doubts and questions would haunt British imperialism supporters until the end of the century. It was only then that the fear of Russia dissipated, for a while, before the fear of Germany.

Meanwhile, the British press kept on serving as a sounding board for the imperial lobby, which the favorable ending of the Crimean War had not at all soothed. English newspapers raised their voices each time Russia so much as blinked. To the slightest hint of a Russian move, in the Dardanelles or in Central Asia, they sounded the alert. In the 1880s, anti-Russian hysteria reached a peak with the publication of several books, in the wake of that of the former British consul in India and Persia, Sir Henry Rawlinson, who had just warned England against "the inexorable advance of Russia in Central Asia" and the war she threatened to start in India.[18]

With the new Russian-Turkish war of 1877-78, which saw Russia again progress southward and get closer to the Dardanelles, British alarm was at its height. Queen Victoria threatened to abdicate if Russia took over Constantinople. "If the Russians reach Constantinople, the Queen would be so humiliated that she thinks she should abdicate," she wrote to Prime Minister Disraeli, who sent the British fleet into the Dardanelles in February 1878 and secretly mobilized the reserves of the British army in India to take over Cyprus, were the threat to materialize.[19]

History would show that that threat had been greatly exaggerated, with Russia merely trying to take her revenge on her defeat in Crimea and having no intention to overthrow an Ottoman power which guaranteed calm on her southern flank. On the other hand, the English did not hesitate to move their pawns in the Mediterranean. During the First World War, they finally succeeded in occupying Cyprus.

They had in any case obtained satisfaction thanks to Bismarck, the great architect of the Berlin Treaty, which, in 1878, ended the Russian-Turkish War by obliging the Russians, once again, to give up their conquests. Anxious to gain the favors of the English and the Austrians after his war against France and the creation of the German Empire in 1870, the Iron Chancellor had decided to switch sides and betray Russia, Prussia's all-time ally. The Kaiser's cousin, Queen Victoria, could breathe a sigh of relief: she had no need to abdicate any longer.

In 1881, Edmund O'Donovan, a *London Daily News* reporter, described the pillage and massacre of Turkmen during the conquest of Merv by the Russians with a luxury of revolting details.[20] A volley of incendiary articles followed, as the Russians had decided to build a trans-Caspian railway and the Turkmen accepted to pay allegiance to the czar, contrary to British hopes. In his book published in 1994, Peter Hopkirk tells in detail all the stages of the Great Game and the intense propaganda that went with it.[21]

English Russophobic literature reached a peak in 1885, with the simultaneous publication of a dozen books by different authors. The most ardent and best known at the time was Hungary-born British Russophobe, Arminius Vambery. A great traveler, Vambery had wandered ceaselessly across Central Asia since the early 1860s, disguised as a Muslim. Like Urquhart fifty years earlier, he flooded the English press with his anti-Russian warnings. In 1885, he published the synthesis of his travels and articles in a book with explicit title and subtitle, *The Coming Struggle for India. Being An Account Of The Encroachments Of Russia In Central Asia, And Of The*

Difficulties Sure To Arise Therefrom To England, which would become a bestseller.[22]

Dracula, an Imperialist and Russophobic Novel

Vambery, like his imperialist colleagues, justified English imperialism in India, Afghanistan, and Persia by "the civilizing mission England alone can carry out, the Russians having proved they were totally inept at that task."[23] Vambery is also interesting for being the one who inspired the author of *Dracula*, Bram Stoker.

Bram Stoker (1847–1912) was born in Dublin and pleaded all his life for the unification of Ireland with the British Crown. A theater buff who greatly admired actor Henry Irving and was to become his closest friend, he became administrator of his theater and wrote several works of fiction and fantastic novels in tune with the British taste of the times, following in the wake of Mary Shelley's *Frankenstein* and Robert Louis Stevenson's *The Strange Case of Dr Jekyll and Mr Hyde*, published in 1886.

He was also a close friend of Rudyard Kipling, the great narrator of English colonial adventures, author of a famous novel, *Kim*, which tells the story of Kimball O'Hara, the orphaned son of an Irish soldier turned spy in the service of the Crown in the Great Game, foiling a Russian plot against British India.

His brother George also had much influence on Bram. A physician, George Stoker served as as volunteer ambulance serviceman in the Ottoman army in Bulgaria and Turkey during the 1877-78 war against Russia. He brought back from it a caricatural book depicting the Turkish allies as heroes whereas the Bulgarians, allied to the Russians, were half-human savages, corrupt, ignorant and vicious, and transforming the Turks themselves "in the eyes of the British public from bloody [Turkish] butchers of Bulgarian Christians into heroic fighters resisting the onslaught of the gruesome Russian bear."[24] George Stoker does not hesitate to jibe at the few English journalists that reported atrocities committed by the Turks. He castigated them for "insults to the prestige of journalism."

It was into this imperialist and Russophobic circle that

Bram Stoker decided to launch his masterwork, the writing of a gothic novel which must summarize all the most secret dreads, anguishes and longings of end-of-century Victorian society through the tale of the ambitions of a Vlach count, Dracula, a frightening, crazy aristocrat who transforms himself into a vampire to suck the blood of his victims to find the energy he needs to conquer virtuous and innocent England.

The countless studies made of Stoker's novel show in effect that the author was largely inspired by the current events and prejudices of the time and stuffed his novel with allusions to the Russians and Russia, and that Vlad the Impaler, the Vlach prince taken as model, was in fact a mere pretext. A synthesis of these studies can be found in Jimmie E. Cain's already quoted book. Countless details, from the choice of the site of the novel and the location of the count's castle to the various ups and downs of the plot that reveal names and anagrams of Russian names, make the text explicit, even though today Romanians have claimed it as their own for touristic purposes.

The character of Dracula does combine the projected features of the evil Russian spirit. His refined cruelty is directly inspired by Ivan the Terrible and he himself claims to be descended from a line of boyars, whereas he has all the attributes of the Russian aristocrat: idle, parasitic (not only does he not work, he does not even make his money grow), sexually depraved (through the female character of Lucy Westenra who, once "vampirized," transforms herself into a sex-craving vamp) and of course jealous of England.

Another researcher, Felix Oinas, has highlighted the relationship between vampires in the Slavonic world. "Belief in vampires is well documented in the tales of the first Russians and the term 'vampire' appears for the first time in 1407 about a Novgorod prince," he states, adding: "The existence of a vampire cult is illustrated by the struggle the clergy led in the encyclicals that condemned the sacrifices they received."[25] According to Oinas, the Slavonic accounts noted that "vampires, whose bodies do not rot, are said to rest in tombs, which they leave at midnight to go into houses to have sexual relations or suck the blood of their dwellers." Which indeed would scare prudish English folks at the end of the 19th century.

These researches are all the more striking as already in the 1850s, in the middle of the Crimean War, the English press was in the habit of caricaturing the czar with vampire wings. Several cartoons in *Punch* in particular prefigure Dracula by showing the winged phantom of the czar prowling around the French and English valiant freedom fighters, a courageous English lion scaring the two eagles and the dreadful Russian vampire off, or Nicolas I with his two bat wings on his back starting to sing the Te Deum.

The end of Stoker's novel is even more explicit: the world is rid of the horrible Nosferatu thanks to the courage of British Crown agent Jonathan Harker.

> Like the Americans Sylvester Stallone in *Rambo* and Chuck Norris in *Missing in Action*, British Harker delivers the world from evil and restores the honor of the Empire.

Another researcher, David Glover, recreated the final scene, Hollywood fashion:

> With its troop armed to the teeth, the campaign against the vampire is played out in truly imperial style with a paramilitary raid, a search and destroy mission in the heart of Transylvania.[26]

After which England can enjoy her so long hankered for bridgehead at the confines of the Balkans and Russia.

Stoker's contribution to the great Russophobia novel did not stop there. In 1904, war between England and Russia almost broke out again when the Russian fleet, on its way to the Far East to support her army surrounded by the Japanese, fired on English ships mistaken for enemy vessels. In his last great novel, *The Lady of the Shroud*, published in 1909, Stoker drove the point home. The action is again in the Balkans, not far from Montenegro. It ends of course to the advantage of the British who, this time, manage to purely and simply install a colony in the heart of the Balkans, to thwart the Germans, the Austrians, and the Turks while watching the Russians closely.

For the times had rapidly changed between 1904 and 1909. The growing power of Germany, which wanted to provide herself with a fleet to compete with England, worried to the utmost the British admiralty and the British colonial lobby. Turkey had its long railway to Baghdad built by Germans, and Austria had just annexed Bosnia and extended her influence in the Balkans. In front of these new threats, England, like France, turned around and moved closer to her old Russian enemy. Britain signed the Entente Cordiale with France in 1904 and in 1907, a convention with Russia to delimit their respective zones of influence in Afghanistan, Persia, and Tibet. Former viceroy of the Indies Lord Curzon and still active Arminius Vambery accused Downing Street of betrayal. But such voices no longer carried weight in Westminster. For a time, Russophobia became less trendy in London.

"An Elephant Does Not Fight with a Whale"

How to interpret this wave of English Russophobia, which appeared suddenly after 1815 and flooded Britain's international policy during the entire 19th century?

Concluding his study, J. H. Gleason comes back to the deepest reasons for this behavior. The argument of the rivalry between the two greatest empires of the time did not convince him.

> As Bismarck later observed, it is not easy for an elephant to battle with a whale. The age was that of the *Pax Britannica* during which the British Isles enjoyed a military security almost without parallel. Thus the rivalry of the two states, and

with it the propaganda of Russophobes was centered on remote, more or less colonial, areas. The competition was of a kind with that between two less Gargantuan powers. Their special stature is not the explanation of their rivalry.[27]

As we shall see with the theoreticians of maritime power, American Mahan and English Mackinder,[28] this judgment seems to us to verge on irenicism. If size is not the determining factor in a conflict, what are the triggering factors? Gleason offers several elements of explanation: the unavoidable war of ideas between liberal West and autocratic East, overestimation of the Russian threat and the provocations, such as the *Vixen* affair, carried out by the imperialist lobby led by David Urquhart, the ruinous effects of anti-Russian agitation carried out by the numerous Polish refugees after 1830, the negative influence of big industry and big commerce eager to enlarge their markets. As a typical Anglo-Saxon, he concludes:

> Ultimately, then, the growth of Anglo-Russian hostility must be attributed to the failure of both Englishmen and Russians to preserve the agreement with regard to major purpose which had existed during the struggle against Napoleon. In the absence of common intent, essentially minor disagreements assumed an intrinsically unmerited importance. Differences with regard to method appeared to reveal divergence of aim. Lack of sympathy induced distrust, suspicion fostered jealousy, alliance was transformed into rivalry. Such was the soil in which well-intentioned patriots, [Russian foreign minister] Nesselrode, and the tsar, Urquhart and Palmerston, planted the seeds from which grew Russophobia. It is the soil of all international relations and its crop is the fate of mankind.[29]

The explanation leaves us dissatisfied, given that this kind of misunderstanding, amplified by antipathies, distaste and unfounded accusations back and forth, exacerbated by media manipulated by lobbies or simply eagerness to outbid the competition, seem to repeat themselves throughout history, as was seen in the sudden acceleration of the Ukrainian crisis and the instant degradation of Western-Russian relations between February and August 2014. The question remains under another form: if the deterioration of relations was due to an accumulation of misunderstandings, why wasn't anything done to dispel them? If they persisted, it must be that there were powerful interests that tried to make them last.

The genesis of English Russophobia between 1815 and 1840 is also interesting for another reason. It shows how a nation allied to Russia against a redoubtable common enemy could transmute within a few years into a Russophobic nation even though neither its direct interests, nor its borders, nor its internal security were under threat. The parallel with the birth of American Russophobia after 1945 is thus more than striking and deserves to be studied carefully. The periods, means mobilized, ideologies, and destructions were different, but the basic causes, unfolding and consequences were similar.

Between 1941 and 1945, the United States and the Soviet Union had fought together against a redoubtable common enemy, Nazi Germany. Once the war was over, the United States was not threatened in its security or in its vital interests. It had the atomic bomb, which the USSR had yet to acquire. It had come out of the war richer than ever, while the Soviet Union had been devastated. And yet, in 1945, it took only a few months for an Anglo-Saxon empire to again launch into a merciless battle against the Russian ally and into a propaganda war which has yet to dry out seventy years later.

The phenomenon is all the more curious as neither in 1815 nor in 1945 had Russia conquered new territories. In both cases, Russia (and the USSR) scrupulously respected the signed agreements, the Treaty of Vienna in 1815 first case, and Conference of Yalta for the second in 1945. In the late 40s', per Stalin's famous "napkin agreement" with Churchill at Yalta, the USSR promoted the emergence of communist regimes in its Eastern European sphere of influence while not protesting as Great Britain supported the royalist troops in order to crush the communist resistance during the Greek civil war 1946-1949. How to explain, then, this exacerbation of anti-Russian sentiment a century and a half apart?

Many hypotheses have been offered: the need to counter communist subversion and expansionism intrinsic to Russia; defense of democracy against Russian despotism and totalitarianism. But these are more justifications than explanations. So it must be believed that, contrary to what J. H. Gleason thought, English and American Russophobia was primarily engendered by the imperial ambitions of these two countries and by their irrepressible drive to dominate the world. These nations have been and still are maritime powers in search of new lands. Both have sought and one of them is still seeking to impose their supremacy on other nations by all means: whether military through gunboat diplomacy, be it B-52s or drones; economic through the imposition of free trade treaties; cultural through mobilization of soft power resources.

In conclusion, it can be asserted that English Russophobia does not reach the doctrinal heights of French Russophobia, but largely compensates for this handicap with overflowing efficiency, imagination, and creativity. Far from being confined to intellectual circles, it has taken hold of the popular press, and of caricature and the novel, two very popular techniques, and is at the forefront of the art of soft power handling. English journalists, draftsmen, and novelists prefigure Hollywood and the mobilization of leisure industry resources that the United States was to utilize in the next century and until now to embed Russophobia.

It must be noted that, while Urquhart, Kipling and Stoker had gone to war against Russian expansionism in their articles and novels between 1815 and 1900, the British Empire grew by twenty times the size of England, the French Empire by almost as much thanks to its expansion in Africa and Indochina, while the Kingdom of Belgium fared even better by taking over the Congo, as did the

United States by conquering the West thanks to the massacre of the Indians and the slavery of the Blacks. In the meantime, Russia, so execrated for her acute "invasion pruritus," increased a mere 25%, by adding to her territory in Bessarabia, the Caucasus, Turkestan, and Manchuria. As Muslim reformist Djamal al-Din al-Afghani (1837–1897) remarked as he observed the English Great Game between London and India, "England is dismantling the Ottoman Empire and absorbing, one by one, all parts at her convenience, exactly as she absorbed the Indies, slowly but surely."[30]

Once Egypt was dominated, it was the turn of Iraq and of Saudi Arabia thanks to the doings of Lawrence of Arabia during the First World War, then of Iran in 1953 thanks to the coup against Mosaddegh.

In 2015, centuries later, we can indeed express wonder at the impressive success of English Russophobic propaganda, craftily taken up and amplified after 1945 by that of the former colony become dominant power, the United States of America. It can even be asserted that this success was total, as noted by Lebanese essayist and former minister Georges Corm.

> That England, situated to the north of Europe, succeeded in dominating the Mediterranean Sea, the Atlantic Ocean and the Indian Ocean poses no problem in most history books, but that czarist or Bolshevik Russia, whose borders are a short distance away from the Mediterranean, has tried to have access to it has always been denounced as a perverse form of Slavic or Bolshevik imperialism.
>
> Today, that the United States, situated fifteen thousand kilometers away from the Middle East, lays down the law there and occupies Iraq has not given rise to any indignation, but that Iraq or Syria, important regional powers, want to have influence and be heard there, is considered a hostile act and puts us to the brink of war.[31]

Georges Corm's text goes back to 2009. Since then, two new wars, dubbed civil but largely fueled by the West and friends of the West, have broken out: in Syria and in Libya. A third went off in Ukraine. The great Western media have taken them calmly, apart from accusing Russia, as usual.

| Chapter Seven |

GERMAN RUSSOPHOBIA: FROM *LEBENSRAUM* TO HISTORICAL AMNESIA

> "Other stereotypes carry a negative social identity, for example when the Russians are depicted as aggressive. Such concepts of the enemy are an important form of propaganda ... The concepts of enemy do not need to be in agreement with reality."
> Hans-Werner Bierhoff, 1989[1]

In the race to Russophobia, the Germans started late, not until the end of the 19th century. But they soon made up for lost time. So much so that, following the humiliation of the 1918 defeat and the economic crisis of the years 1923–1930, they took Russophobia, with the rise of the racist Nazi State, to its most extreme. In the social hierarchy established by the national socialists, the Slavs east of the Dnieper River were just as bad as the Jews and the Blacks. They paid for it as a result. That racial war was worsened by the ideological fight against "Judeo-Bolshevism" incarnated by Stalin's communist Russia. This led to the greatest massacre in human history, as it is estimated that more than 25 million Soviets including 14 million Russians and 7 million Ukrainians, especially Jews and Slavs of the east died because of the Nazis during the Second World War.[2]

These facts are known and need not be lingered over. The Nazi period has been well studied and, after long tergiversations, Germany finally resolved to undertake a remarkable catharsis, and apologized for crimes committed against the various parties. So it can be considered that the Nazi transgressions were exceptional in all respects (which is not the case for Stalin's killings which are readily considered as a typical trait of Asian-Russian despotism). More than its manifestation in the Third Reich, what interests us is the genesis of Russophobia during the Second Reich, and the way it has been perpetuated to the present day in a Germany that has become "normal" again.

With the exception of the Teutonic Knights' crusades during the Middle Ages, relations of the German states with czarist Russia were rather good until German reunification in 1870. Catherine II was German, and the Romanovs had close ties to several German aristocratic families. Nicolas II's spouse, Alexandra Feodorovna, was born in Hesse. Between the end of the Thirty Years' War in 1648 and the 1848 revolutions, Prussia and Russia were allied, except for a short war in 1760.

Similarly, Russia had good relations with Habsburg Austria, whose survival she ensured at various times and whose throne she saved in 1848. The situation changed after 1850, with the Crimean War. The Austro-Hungarians had designs on the Balkans and found themselves in competition with the Russians, who were backing the independence of Slavic peoples, Bulgarians and Serbs, and of the Romanians against the Ottomans. The Austrian Empire, despite its debt to Nicolas I, then took advantage of the opportunity to betray the czar and push its pawns into the Danube Plain and the Balkan Mountains. At first Prussia, wishing to achieve German unity under her lead, remained neutral to avoid upsetting the French and the English.

But as for the King of Prussia wearing the imperial crown, Austria had to forget about that. This was by no means self-evident to the House of Habsburg, which had worn it many times. In 1866, in Sadowa, during a short war, Bismarck defeated the Austrians, of whom he only wanted one thing: that Austria renounce the crown of the Holy Roman Germanic Empire.[3] Four years later, in 1871, Bismarck put the finishing touches to his undertaking by beating Napoleon III's France, and founded the Second Reich by having the King of Prussia, the Kaiser, crowned in Versailles.

From then on, German dynamism was to know no bounds. The new Reich was twice as populated as its neighbors and industrializing at full speed. Toward the end of the century, it was beginning to feel cramped within its borders and, having failed to seek the conquest of overseas colonies in time, was seeking new expansion into the region that appeared to it most accessible and most promising: that of huge Russia.

It was on this fertile ground that, after the defeat of the Russians by the Japanese in 1904 and the 1905 revolution, German Russophobia was to grow. On the one hand, the empire of the czars had shown its vulnerability and, on the other hand, its policy of reunification of the Baltic countries gave Germany the pretext for an intervention. Russia's rapid economic growth in the years 1905 to 1914, following Witte's reforms, was also an aggravating factor, as Germany had to pursue its agenda quickly before Russia became too strong. Russian pan-Slavism, brandished as a specter, was used by pan-Germanists to develop the *Lebensraum* or living space ideology, and to deploy their eastward expansion policy, *Ostforschung* first, and then *Drang nach Osten*.

Let us see more closely how all of this took shape.

The Romantic Vision of Germanity

German Russophobia was born of a very peculiar vision of the German culture, people and nation-state, progressively articulated by the Romantics and then by idealistic philosophers in reaction to the abstract universalism of the French Age of Enlightenment and of the paradoxical philosopher of the French Revolution, Prussian Emmanuel Kant (1724–1804).

This patient maturation thus bore the marks of the geniuses of German Romanticism, Lessing (1729–1781), Herder (1744–1803), and above all Goethe (1748–1832), Schiller (1790–1805), and Hölderlin (1770-1843), as well of idealist philosophers, from Fichte (1762–1814) to Hegel (1770–1831). They were the ones that created *Deutschtum*, the Germanness concept, which was to be used as a catalyzer of German Slavophobic expansionism.

At once contemporary and heir to the Age of Enlightenment, Kant hoisted Reason to as yet unequaled heights by bartering realism or empiricism, then still dominant in the theory of knowledge, for a critical idealism founded on the transcendental categories, that is to say a priori, of experience (time, space, causality) and morals founded on the categorical imperative (Act according to a maxim such as you might at the same time want it to become a universal law). Kant's political thinking was resolutely republican, like Rousseau's whom he professed to follow, as well as internationalist and pacifist as claimed in his 1783 *Idea for a Universal History with a Cosmopolitan Purpose* and 1795 *Perpetual Peace: A Philosophical Sketch*. No doubt, if his thinking had won in Germany at the beginning of the 19th century, the course of European history would have been altogether different.

Contrary to Kant, who died before Napoleon created the Empire, most of the founders of German romanticism, though influenced by the Age of Enlightenment and the French Revolution, were more deeply affected, and in a negative sense, by the Napoleonic wars and the French occupation, which led them to aspire to German unification.

Discovering the virtues of the German language, which owes them its reputation for excellence one century after the French classics, they felt the need to anchor their feelings, their intellectual and spiritual emotions, in the language and forms proper to the German genius, creating the figure of the rebellious hero, through characters like Guillaume Tell for Schiller or, in a less political register, Wilhelm Meister and Faust for Goethe. The romantic movement of *Sturm und Drang* (storm and stress) was born of that aspiration.

By 1795, Schiller had already published a reflection on "German greatness." Pastor Johan Gottfried Herder theorized the movement by inscribing it within human history: as per divine Providence, each people, at a given moment of its development, makes a contribution to the building of universal Progress. After the stage of French *civilisation* comes the great moment for German *Kultur*.

At the turn of the 19th century, this literary ferment coincided in fact with extraordinary creativity. All of the arts were involved, such as music. Beethoven composed his *Heroic Symphony* in 1804 and his *Ninth Symphony*, with its "Hymn to Joy" ending borrowed from Schiller: "*Seid umschlungen Millionen ... Alle Menschen werden Brüder.*"[4]

In Kant's wake, Fichte, Schelling, Feuerbach and above all Hegel were, to take German philosophy, starting from the 1800s, to unprecedented heights. Fichte, like many German romantics, was among those disappointed by the French Revolution and its imperial avatar, Napoleon, whom he called "that man without a name." He was a progressive democrat, but anti-French. In 1807, he pronounced his famed *Addresses to the German Nation*, which excited public opinion against France and which some would consider, wrongly, as the first expression of pan-Germanism.

For Fichte, the Nation is incarnated as the State, which represents and decides "the orientation of all individual forces toward the finality of the species." But his State contributes to progress: it must be democratic, ensuring everyone's freedom, and the possibility for everyone to have a happy and profitable life by ensuring an equitable distribution of riches. Man "must work without anguish, with pleasure and joy, and have enough time leftover to raise his spirit and his eyes to the sky for the contemplation of which he has been created ... That is his right as he is man at last."[5]

Hegel and the Prussian State

But it was Hegel who exercised the greatest influence on the German conception of State and Nation. Boosted by his dialectical vision of the human future, he tried to demonstrate that human reason, thanks to dialectics, was able to achieve perfect consciousness of itself, transcendence, the absolute Idea, and to understand both internal and external worlds.

Transposed from metaphysics to human history, Reason, according to Hegel, was notably going to incarnate itself in the State, and more precisely in the Prussian state, tasked with accomplishing the mission history had conferred on it. Transforming Herder's vision, according to which culture takes roots first in a language and a people, Hegel now associated culture no longer with the people but with the State in this case, the German state of a Prussian persuasion. The logical conclusion that followed was that it was up to the State, to the Prussian state, to realize the romantic ideal of culture borne by the German people.

As Martin Malia remarks, with Hegel, the states have become "the true configurations of Reason." Yet "no Slavic people of Europe (for Russia was excluded) possessed an independent state any longer: the Poles, the Czechs, the Slavs of the Balkans just as their Hungarian neighbors had all lost the game to more rational dynastic empires. So was the specifically German idea born according to which the inferior races of the East were intrinsically incapable of building a state and thus deserved to be governed by others."[6]

Tense debates followed on the respective merits of *Zivilisation*, a French and English idea embracing all universal values but also the materialistic ideas taken from the Age of Enlightenment, and of Kultur, which regroups the values, but also a history, of the traditions, rites, feelings, and emotions proper to a given people, and which grows rich ceaselessly thanks to *Bildung*, formation, of a mind eager to receive spiritual, intellectual and artistic nourishment. Later, sociologists took up this dichotomy in the debate of *Gesellschaft* versus *Gemeinschaft*, in which, to the evolved but atomized society specific to civilization, was opposed a more organic, more fraternal, more "German" human community.

This idealism with initially very high aspirations was then to influence enlightened circles in German society: politicians, historians, scientists, and artists. Wagner would be their most eminent representative after 1850.

After the failure of romantic revolutionary aspirations in 1848, German society fell back on more bourgeois and more pragmatic values. A more or less conscious swap took place: German society somehow bartered its ideal of liberty and democracy for the unification and creation of an imperial nation-state led by Hohenzollern Prussia. This was how the Second Reich was founded in 1870 on the ruins of the defunct Holy Roman Germanic Empire. Bismarck was the inspired architect of this "compromise" between the middle class and the monarchy.

Germanity Takes Root in Geography and History

From the 1850s until the First World War, with the exception of Marx exiled in London, German intellectuals' efforts mainly focused on history, geography, sociology, and the sciences. Lofty reflections on the German state and the German people climbed down from Olympian heights where they had been placed by writers and philosophers in the early part of the century to become subjects of the human sciences and be of service to political ambitions.

In the wake of Otto Ranke, who was to modern history what Kant was to philosophy, a long line of historians and thinkers like Max Weber delved into the past of the German people and fathomed the depths of its soul in hopes of finding the future of the new nation-state. The so-called hard sciences too were subjugated by this cultural imperative, following the publication of Charles Darwin's *On the Origin of Species* in 1859. Many German scientists were impregnated with the quasi-metaphysical dimension of Kultur acquired during their childhood.

This was how ecology was invented in 1866 by Ernst Haeckel. A trained physician and biologist, Haeckel popularized Darwin's theories in Germany and developed a theory of the origin of humans he called "anthropogeny." He contributed much to the diffusion of the theory of evolution. He considered politics as applied biology and is seen as one of the pioneers of eugenics, even though he himself had no eugenic ideas. As a scientist confident in the progress of evolution, he saw it going toward greater development, not toward "degeneration."

For Haeckel, ecology was the science of the distribution of species in a given space. From that to applying the thesis to the human species and its German subset, the German nation, there was only one step, which was soon taken. Germany and her various states, and even Great Germany enlarged to her *Lebensraum*, thus slowly became seen as a privileged biotope on which the German race could—would, pan-Germanists would say —live in symbiosis and organically deploy the three pillars of its power: its culture, its people, and its state.

That application was to be the handiwork of Friedrich Ratzel, a pharmacist turned zoologist and then geographer. In his major work published between 1882 and 1891, *Anthropogeography*, he tied land and man in a systemic vision. For Ratzel, the aim of anthropogeography was to highlight the diversity of human societies, to which corresponded an equal diversity of natural habitats. Ratzel thus became one of the main pioneers of geopolitics. Very much influenced by Darwin and his theory of evolution, he applied his concepts on a more general scale, that of the states, which he compared to biological organisms. Like the latter, states were subject to growth or decline in the course of time.

The state was subjected to the same influences as any form of life. It was born, lived and died as living organisms do. The conditions for extension of human life on earth determined the extension of their states. Borders could only be conceived as expressions of an organic and inorganic movement, and peoples' expansion had to allow them to regain the spaces of less vigorous neighbors, a vision which legitimized German imperialism. Ratzel was thus at the origin of the first concept of *Lebensraum*, which first expressed the idea of space linked to culture, to areas of civilization, and their interaction with the environment.[7] Later, the pan-Germanists and the Nazis would reverse the notion: the living space would no longer be conceived as a means to deploy a civilization, but as an end in itself, a sacred right founded on the alleged historical presence of German tribes in the remote past.

This *Weltanschauung*, this vision of the world, flourished at a time when German demographic and economic dynamism resulting from the political unification reached extraordinary summits, but those great national ambitions were being restrained by the absence of colonial possibilities. This vital dynamism confronted by the impossibility to expand was to generate increasingly intense and noisy frustrations.

Cosmopolitan Russia: The Model to Avoid

It was in this very specific context that German Russophobia blossomed. The conception of a people living in symbiosis with its territory and state left actually no room to other cultures and other peoples within that state. The Russian Empire, of mixed races and multinational, with ill-defined boundaries, and seemingly moving backward, became, at the dawn of the 20th century, the model not to follow for the Germans.

In 2010, Troy R. E. Paddock, who teaches modern European history at Southern Connecticut State University, published a book in which he explains in detail the creation of the "Russian peril" in imperial Germany in the years 1890 to 1914.[8] He shows how, in that Germany with an acute sense of the nation-state, prejudices passed on by schools and a system of education riddled with pan-Germanic ideology, in less than twenty-five years converted German public opinion to Russophobia and prepared it for war. So much so that in August 1914, German newspapers talked of "Russia's war," persuaded that it was a war desired and launched by Russia with the support of France.[9]

This trajectory was illustrated by the hero of Thomas Mann's *The Magic Mountain*, Hans Castorp. Fascinated by beautiful Russian Claudia Chauchat, he is constantly lectured by his Italian preceptor, Ludovico Settembrini, who teaches him how to distinguish good Russians and those bad Russians that are "more or less barbaric and uncivilized."

It is not without significance that the place is full of Muscovite and Mongolian types. These people ... do not put yourself in tune with them, do not be infected with their ideas; rather set yourself against them, oppose your nature, your higher nature against them; cling to everything which to you is by nature and tradition holy, as a son of the godlike West, a son of civilization: and, for example, time. This barbaric lavishness with time is in the Asiatic style; it may be a reason why the children of the East feel so much at home up here. Have you never remarked that when a Russian says four hours, he means what we do when we say one? It is easy to see that the recklessness of these people where time is concerned may have to do with the space conceptions proper to people of such endless territory. Great space, much time they say, in fact, that they are the nation that has time and can wait.[10]

Russian "barbarity" suited the Germans all the more as it comforted their feeling of cultural superiority: the themes of autocracy, inefficient and corrupt bureaucracy, material misery of the countryside, backward economy, and illiteracy were the stock-in-trade of German commentators before 1914. Actually, nothing has changed since then.

Russophobia Indoctrination through Schoolbooks

Following the example of Castorp's preceptor, geography schoolbooks inculcated in pupils the notion that "thanks to its intellectual formation, the German Reich leads the other European nations" and that "despite her mammoth size and mass of people, with her little developed culture and form of government, Russia is comparable to an Asian rather than a West European country."[11]

Another schoolbook described Peter the Great's failed reforms thus:

> With his barbaric customs and violent nature, he gave Russia a new political and cultural orientation, of a power oriented eastward and semi-Oriental with European power status. ... He himself had not understood the current nature of European culture and his world had remained a 'confusion of European form and Asian practice.' Another author is no more lenient with Alexander II's reforms who did not succeed in surmounting 'the old disadvantages of the Russian way of life, the coarseness of the masses, the deceit and corruption of the bureaucratic elite, and the widespread semi-education.'[12]

In its reports and commentaries, the German press, from *Kölnische Zeitung* to Prussian *Kreuzzeitung*, peddled the same clichés. In the dozen influential newspapers studied by the author, what is striking is the absence of direct knowledge of Russia: "The czar and the Cossacks are barbarians" and that's about all, was the way noted sociologist Norbert Elias summarized it, confessing that while he was a student before leaving for the Russian front, he knew "nothing, absolutely nothing" of Russia, apart from the few commonplaces spread by the school and the press.[13]

Actually, the fiercest propagandists of Russophobia in Germany were the historians and essayists of the beginning of the 20th century. Five of them played a particularly prominent role: Theodor Schiemann and Paul Rohrbach, two Baltic emigrants who were at the forefront of the fight against the Russification of the Baltic countries that they had experienced in their youth, and three "liberal imperialists," Max Lenz, Friedrich Meinecke and Hans Delbrück, to whom others, such as Max Weber and Otto Hoetzsch, at times gave a hand. Most were students of Heinrich Gotthard von Treitschke, the father of German nationalist history.

A national liberal M.P. and professor at Berlin University, Treitschke supported Bismarck's policy after publishing in August 1870 a work entitled *What Do We Want from France? Alsace*. His anti-Semitic theses were very successful in Germany, where the Nazis would later take up his famed formula, "The Jews are our plight," printed in 1879 in *Preussische Jahrbücher* (Prussian annals). His political philosophy was articulated around the formula *Der Staat ist Macht* (the state is power), exalting the power policy (*Machtpolitik*) of the state in the international space.

The states, which crystallized the union of peoples into independent powers, were necessary to man's realization and complied with the will of Providence. To exist and show its power, the state needed to confront other states. It was in war that the human being realized himself, making his noblest political nature and values triumph over materialistic preoccupations.[14]

Theodor Schiemann and Paul Rohrbach shared this ambitious vision of Germany's civilizing role. Thanks to her incomparable culture, Germany was in a position to become co-master of the world with England and to accomplish in Eastern Europe what the latter has achieved in the rest of the world. Thanks to their position in the academic world and at the head of influential reviews such as the Prussian annals, they were to exert a predominant influence on German nationalist thinking.

Avowed Russophobe and Ukrainophile Schiemann was close to Kaiser Wilhelm II, who vouched that "Schiemann enjoyed my special trust. An honest man, native to the Baltic provinces, a shrewd politician and brilliant historian and writer, Schiemann was constantly consulted to advise me on historical and political questions. I owe him much good advice, especially on the East."[15]

Friedrich Meinecke and the "Slavs' Bestiality"

But one of the most remarkable contributors to *Deutschtum*, to Germanity, was no doubt Friedrich Meinecke (1862–1954). He was still a modest teacher in Strasburg and the author of a thesis on Marshal Hermann von Boyen when he published in 1908 a work which caused quite a stir in Germany, *Cosmopolitanism & National State*.[16] The title was in itself a program, the book showing the superiority of the unitary nation-state, whose power results from the organic link between Kultur, the people, and the state. Meinecke, who was to have a long academic career, was accused of anti-Semitism, while his "bestiality of the Slavs" formula stuck in people's minds. For him, Russia, with her mixture of races, languages, and religions, was the cosmopolitan empire par excellence.

The growing tensions with France and England further intensified the attacks against Russian pan-Slavism, viewed through the distorting prism of the Russification of Courland (Estonia) and the Baltic countries. German intelligentsia considered Russian nationalism, which it analyzed by the yardstick of its own nationalism, which is to say as a legitimate ambition and the people's inalienable mission, as "an obstacle preventing the achievement of the objective of a European community inspired by German culture."[17]

The German press and German thinkers made of it their favorite hobbyhorse, scrutinizing and inflating to excess "pan-Slavic" declarations they believed they detected under the pens of journalists or in the mouths of Russian politicians. Exaggeration and denunciation of pan-Slavism had indeed a double advantage for German nationalists seeking space in the East: this allowed them to present Russia as the aggressor and to disregard their own by now obsessive pan-Germanism while deflecting nationalists' attention away from the cosmopolitan and multinational nature of their Austro-Hungarian ally. The threat of the "Russian peril" allowed a modest veil to be thrown over German expansionism, which had become very threatening, as well as on the cosmopolitanism of the Austro-Hungarian Empire, which hardly complied with the ideal of Germanity.

"Russian chauvinism demands also domination of the Balkan Peninsula. It demands it in order to complete the control of the Bosporus and Hellespont; it demands it because the inhabitants of the

Balkan Peninsula are for the most part Slavs and *Stammesbrüder* [tribesmen] of the Russians. It demands it because these peoples are members of the same Church as Russia," wrote, for example, Hans Delbrück under the pen name "Vir pacificus," or Pacific Man, in 1896.[18]

It was in the 1900s that pan-Germanism took the shape of an actual doctrine and applied to Eastern Europe the concept of *Lebensraum* formulated by Ratzel. In 1905, Joseph-Ludwig Reimer edited *A Pan-Germanicist Germany*, a 400-page reference book. By reinterpreting history in the interest of pan-Germanism, he tried to prove the superiority of the German race through its cultural and historical contributions, along with neighboring nations such as France, Belgium or the Netherlands. Racial and ethnographic study took pride of place.

In 1911, Otto Richard Tannenberg developed similar theses in a seminal book for that doctrine, *Grand Germany*, taken up later by the Nazis. In 1912, Friedrich von Bernhardi published *Germany and the New War*, in which, for the first time, Eastern Europe was clearly identified as a potential objective for this so passionately wanted expansion.

So it is not surprising that a few months before the war, on March 2, 1914, *Kölnische Zeitung* published an article on "Russia and Germany" written by its correspondent in Saint Petersburg, *Oberleutnant* Ulrich. The journalist announced in substance that Russia, still too backward to be a short-term threat, would attack Germany as soon as she was ready by fall 1917.

> Two years ago there still was a doubt, but now it is publicly stated, including in [Russian] military reviews, that Russia is arming herself with a view to making war against Germany.

The article caused quite a stir and was criticized by *Frankfurter Zeitung* and other newspapers. It provoked heavy losses on the French and Russian stock exchanges, and it said a lot about the state of mind of the German intelligentsia on the eve of war.

A few months earlier, Chancellor Bethmann Hollweg had stated before the Reichstag that Russia, "a monstrous empire endowed with inexhaustible resources," was "operating a surprising economic takeoff, accompanied by an unprecedented reorganization of the army in quantity and quality of armament, organization, and speed in transition from a state of peace to a state of war." [19]

However, all those hypotheses, dangerous though they were, were not racist. In 1914, Germany, which had become very Russophobic (but also very anti-British and anti-French, although in a different way as these two countries were placed on the same cultural level as Germany), still remained a humanistic country. Cultural superiority had not yet mutated into racial superiority. Germany legitimized her ambitions through culture, as France and Great Britain did, justifying theirs by the "civilizing mission" they claimed to be fulfilling in their colonies. In German minds, it was a matter, in the East as in the West, of fighting a short war, clean and "humane," with proper respect for the high values of German culture.

Implementation of *Ostforschung*

The hard life in the trenches, followed by a bitter defeat, were to completely change that state of mind.

In 1918, Germany came out of the war ruined and humiliated. It was on that fertile ground that the *völkish* and national socialist ideology was going to prosper. *Ostforschung* was implemented at that time. This was the name given to the body of research the Weimar Republic was to carry out in the East for the purpose of providing arguments for the revision of the eastern boundaries imposed by the Versailles Treaty in 1919.

In a context marked by the denial of defeat, the occupation of the Rhineland in the west, and Poland's enterprising policy in the east, a new research space was being developed under the influence of historian Hermann Aubin, active in the Rhineland, and geographer Albrecht Penck. Based on Penck's theories, this academic subject created a differentiation between linguistic and cultural borders, which made it possible to claim that some territories had been Germanic since prehistoric times: German colonists would thus have conferred a Germanic character to Central and Eastern Europe, even in the absence of a Germanic language.

Those researches coincided with the concept of *Volks- und Kulturbodenforschung* (research on people and culture's land) forged by the *Stiftung für deutsche Volks- und Kulturbodenforschung* (Foundation for People and Culture's Land Research), a circle created in 1923 at the initiative of the Ministry of the Interior. That concept distinguished three concentric zones: *Reich*, i.e. the territory controlled by the State; *Volksboden*, the "ethnic territory" on which Germanic populations lived; and *Kulturboden*, the "culture zone" where Germanic culture was felt. In 1926, Hans Grimms's *Volk ohne Raum* (A people without space) became a classic, and the book title a slogan of the Nazi party.

At the same time, these ideas directly influenced Karl Haushofer (1869–1946), one of the most important theoreticians of German geopolitics. Influenced by Ratzel's works, Haushofer developed his geopolitical theories and founded in 1924 the review *Zeitschrift für Geopolitik* (geopolitics review), which soon gathered an international readership. Addressing a large public, the review only presented the position of German geopolitics. Hitler met Haushofer on several occasions and by and large adopted his "living space" theory, which he integrated, somewhat distorted, in *Mein Kampf*. Haushofer was never a member of the Nazi party and instead defended the idea of an alliance of Germany and Russia, in order to create a great continental bloc with Japan to counter the Anglo-Saxon "anaconda" strategy that aimed at choking continental powers in the coils of maritime powers.

In *Mein Kampf*, published in 1924, Hitler made the concept of *Lebensraum* evolve by refocusing it only on Europe. Seven hundred years after the Teutonic Knights, he thus launched anew the idea of a "push toward the East" (*Drang nach Osten*) and emphasized the racist elements of *Lebensraum*, explicitly linked to the *Herrenvolk* (race of Masters or superior race) theory designating the "Aryans" or the "Germanic race."

So we National-Socialists cross out deliberately the political orientation of before the war. We begin where it ended six hundred years ago. We stop the Germans' eternal march to the south and to the west of Europe, and we look toward the East.

We shall put a stop to pre-war colonial and commercial policy and will inaugurate the territorial policy of the future. ... But if we speak today of new lands in Europe, we would only think first of Russia and the bordering countries depending on her.

And Hitler goes on:

The fight against Jewish world Bolshevization demands a clear attitude regarding Soviet Russia. The devil cannot be driven out by Beelzebub.[20]

Lebensraum and Racism

This adaptation of the *Lebensraum* concept to the anti-Slavic, racist German state was all the easier since Russia had become communist in 1917. The Junkers and the German monarchist bourgeoisie, who might have had some affinities with the Czarist Empire and Russian aristocracy, had nothing any longer to hold them back, since Bolshevism was also the enemy of liberal democracies and of Anglo-Saxon capitalism. Between the wars, Russophobia coincided with anti-Bolshevism. For Hitler, "the organization of the Russian state was not the result of political aptitudes of Slavism in Russia, but rather a remarkable example of the state-creating abilities of the Germanic element, in the middle of a race of lesser value."[21]

Starting from 1933, these theories were put into practice notably by the Rasse-und Siedlungshauptampt, the Bureau of Race and Population. Hitler considered the inhabitants of the Soviet Union and the Slavs in general as "sub-humans" and thereby gave himself the right to conquer Soviet lands. *Lebensraum* thus acquired, before the Second World War, a new expansion even wider than that entertained by the pan-Germanists.

In 1943, the institutes of geographic research linked to "ethnically Germanic" populations were regrouped in the Central Security Office of the Reich (RSHA linked to the SS). They then took the name of Reich Foundation for Geographic Studies and were put in charge of analyzing the eastern territories by establishing statistics on their population and density. Geographer Walter Christaller took care of the general government of Poland and of the Generalplan Ost (East Plan), while his fellow geographer Emil Meynen ran the Reich Bureau for Studies of the Earth, in charge of planning for territories conquered in the East.[22] On top of the massacres, the East Plan anticipated displacing 30 million persons from the west of Russia toward Siberia.

We know what happened: this mystique of German soil and blood enlarged to non-Germanic territories translated into the biggest massacres of all times and were centered mainly on the "Judeo-Bolsheviks" (meaning the Russians) and on the Slavic sub-humans of Soviet territories, among whom must be included the Jews, the gypsies and the handicapped.[23]

1966: No Change in German Schoolbooks

In 1945, Soviet Russia found herself in the winning camp and occupied the eastern part of the German territory, conditions that obliged Russophobia to be very discreet in Germany. But with the beginning of the Cold War by 1946, and above all in the 1960s with the construction of the Berlin Wall, it became very active again under the guise of anti-communism.

Of course, anti-Sovietism differs from Russophobia on many levels. But it borrows most of its themes from Russophobia, often by simply renewing the terminology, as we shall see in the chapter on American Russophobia. So much so that anti-communism often became an excellent pretext to fight Russia without seeming to be taking aim at Russia, per se. If not, how to explain that once communism disappeared after 1991, Russophobia resumed with renewed vigor in the West? If Russophobia continued after the fall of communism, we are bound to conclude that its source was not linked to anti-communism but to Russia, and the attempts to associate Putin with Stalin and the recovery of Russia of the 2000s with a return to the Stalinist Empire being once again an aberration and an anachronism. Or maybe it was just that merely linking Putin to Stalin, who has already been thoroughly demonized, is simply a convenient smear that doesn't require further explanation or documentation, much like rampant comparisons to Hitler imply no need for further comment.

> In a certain sense, American Troy Paddock notes, the Russian peril remained intact in the German public sphere after the Second World War. The Cold War again put Russia back in the heart of German public consciousness, as de facto leader of East Germany and a threat to the Federal Republic, and by extension to all Europe. ... German schoolbooks have not changed their vision of Russia. Volkmann notes that in 1966-67, 'an opinion poll of fifteen-year-old pupils in Hamburg indicated that the image of Russia had not changed. The Russians were depicted by the pupils as "primitive," simple, very violent, cruel, mean, inhuman, cupid and very stubborn.' The bitter memory of the Eastern Front remaining, the Russians were nonetheless considered as 'the strongest in war but also the most brutal.' And Volkmann concludes by saying that 'the *Völkerstereotyp* was practically identical to, if not worse than, that which used to characterize the prototype of the Russian in the schools of the Third Reich.'"[24]

Nazism = Communism

In any case, after 1945, German Russophobia perpetuated itself, but under other, often more subtle, forms. The most striking example is the historic "revisionist" attempt made in the 1980s by historian Ernst Nolte.

Nolte, born in 1923, and a specialist of fascism and of political movements between the wars, used to teach at the Free University of Berlin. In his first book, *Fascism in its Epoch*, he compared the nationalist movement of Action française with Italian fascism and national socialism. Similarly, he derived these three right-wing trends from anti-communism presented as one of the major causes of the formation of three types of European fascism. Nolte also studied the genesis of the Cold War and wrote several books on Bolshevism, which he compared to Nazism.

In *The European Civil War*, published in 1989, he stated:

> What is most essential in national-socialism is its relation to Marxism, to communism in particular, in the form it took thanks to the Bolsheviks' victory.

His thesis was that fascisms were a double reaction against both the Bolshevik revolution and the democratic system. Fascisms borrowed an important part of their ideology from democracies (the system of union of people and government, the notion of "general will") and from communism (totalitarian system, elimination of opponents, unification of society). He pointed out that Hitler was anti-Marxist before he was anti-Semitic, and that he talked in his youthful writings of a "Judeo-Bolshevik" plot because of the strong presence of "de-Judaized" Jews in communist instances.

Nolte suggested that one point common to fascist regimes and Bolshevism was, in each case, the designation of a minority of implacable enemies of the people, responsible for all the plights of society, which had to be eliminated physically. For this reason, he considered them "civil war" regimes. An adept of the theory of totalitarianism, he also established a causality link between the Gulag and Auschwitz: Nazism was a reaction to the Bolshevik regime. "There is no fascism without the provocation of bolshevism," he wrote.[25]

With reason, Nolte has been reproached for his method and definition of fascism as a "transnational" European phenomenon and, above all, has been accused of minimizing Nazi crimes. Jürgen Habermas and the Frankfurt School in particular have much criticized him. Nolte has defended himself by claiming that his aim was to "make intelligible" the national-socialist episode, which implied no sort of particular indulgence for Nazism, which he accused explicitly of having committed "atrocious crimes to which no other can be compared in the history of the world."

That controversy, known under the name *Historikerstreit* or historians' quarrel began with the publication, in *Frankfurter Allgemeine Zeitung* of June 6, 1986, of an article entitled "A past that won't let go" in which Nolte asked himself whether "the Gulag archipelago is not more primal than Auschwitz" and whether "assassination for reason of class as perpetrated by the Bolsheviks is not the logical and factual precedent to assassination for reason of race as perpetrated by the Nazis."

Nolte has received support from Italy and France, notably from the French historian François Furet. Furet, however, refused to consider Italian fascism and National Socialism as essentially anti-Marxist ideologies aiming to counter Bolshevik totalitarianism.

So much for the general scheme. What creates uneasiness is that, in his *European Civil War*, Nolte gives the impression that he is trying to justify Nazism through its antipathy to communism and, when comparing the two totalitarianisms, to promote the fighting of German soldiers on the Eastern front as "defenders of Europe against Asian hordes."[26] He also gives the impression of passing off the June 1941 Nazi attack as a reaction to Stalin's failure to respect the 1939 Ribbentrop-Molotov Pact and of considering Stalinist crimes as "worse" than those of Nazism.[27] "Tending to total extermination of a world people, [the final solution] differs in essence from all genocides and constitutes the exact reversed image of extermination, also as a trend, of a world class by the Bolsheviks. In this sense, it is the copy of the original, the social character of the latter having been replaced by a biological character," he wrote.[28] And as everybody knows, the copy, by definition, is less reprehensible than the originator, and thus, in this specific case, of lesser gravity...

The undeniable intent of Nolte's thesis was to dilute the ills of Nazism, transforming it into a mere biological repetition of the Bolsheviks' social extermination program, and insidiously deflecting the responsibility for subsequent carnages to Bolshevism, hence to Russia. A particularly contrived form of Russophobia, we must say, destined to enlist behind it Western anti-communists as well as public opinions influenced by decades of Cold War.

In the 1980s, this thesis coincided with the emergence of a new German generation, born after the war, which thus felt less "guilty" of Nazi crimes than their parents. Germany having finally acknowledged her crimes and apologized publicly, and indeed paid reparations to Israel at least, the "punishment" seemed sufficient and the need to pursue contrition elsewhere less imperative.

Lastly, it coincided as well with a new consolidation of the European community and the fact that a disciplined Germany was rejoining the ranks of democracies and taking the place she deserved in the European Union, notably by constituting the "engine" of its construction through her alliance with her former "hereditary" enemy France. Germany's new legitimacy in the West also contributed to making the memory of Nazi horrors less imperative, though they were of course kept alive by Israel, and all who promoted that state's interest. By moving the cursor of responsibilities for global ill-doing further toward the East, toward Russia, which was still communist at the time, many Germans and Europeans were rehabilitated.[29]

And so it was that numerous works putting Hitler on the same footing as Stalin and on communist gulags and crimes followed, with the common point of dismissing the two regimes and discrediting Russia by equating her with Bolshevism. The Soviets, who had contributed most to the war effort, and the Russians, who themselves decided to end the communist regime in 1991, could not but find this revisionism particularly revolting. Needless to say, the positive achievements of the Communist regimes—inter alia, free education, health care, greater social equality—received little play in the West. But the Left, which might have defended these, was dominated by Trotskyists, consumed with their animosity to Stalin.[30]

Pinning Communist Crimes Only on Russia

Maintaining the association between communism and Russia is indeed one of the tried and tested techniques of post-war western Russophobia. All Russian dissidents, not just aristocrats and dispossessed landowners, but also those who, in the West, fought it sincerely during the Cold War, such as Anatol Lieven, Martin Malia or Stephen Cohen, differentiate between Russia and communism.

But they are a minority. Most western commentators and intellectuals prefer to obfuscate the matter, especially since the collapse of the Soviet Union. It was in the best interest of the intelligentsia in newly independent countries, Poland, the Baltic countries and the Czech Republic, to accuse Moscow of all sins and to have it forgotten that they themselves had been communists and had been led by national communists. This subtle segregation could be observed just about everywhere: the crimes and darkest aspects of communism were attributed to the Russians, while the other peoples took the advantageous status of poor victims, thus exonerating themselves of any responsibility.

And yet the facts are a little more complex. The infamous *holodomor* or "genocide" by famine in the years 1931 to 1933, which Ukrainians blame entirely on Stalin, was put into place with the approval and active participation of Ukrainian communists such as Khrushchev. Similarly, Ukrainians tend to forget that Ukrainians participated in the massacre of Volhynia Poles in 1942 and 1943 and that the guardians of Jewish extermination camps of the East, Treblinka, Sobibor or Belzec, were predominantly composed of Ukrainians and Lithuanians, not German SS.

Still in the same register, it is striking to note that Stalin's Georgian origins are never mentioned when it is a matter of attributing to him rightly the worst crimes of communism. He is always mentioned as "master of the Kremlin" or as the "red czar" as if he had been Russian. It seems indeed so logical to attribute the entire communist barbarity to the Russians that one never wonders whether Stalin's Georgian roots had as much of an influence on his behavior as communism.

Are Stalin's crimes attributable to communism and inherent in social change imposed by revolution and the struggle against counter-revolution—in which case there was nothing specifically Russian about the paradigm—or are they attributable to the social and ethnic origin of the communist leaders of the time (Georgian for Stalin and Ordzhonikidze, Moldavian for Frunze, Polish for Dzerzhinsky, Ukrainian for Khrushchev, Hungarian for Rákosi, Jewish for Trotsky, Sverdlov, Zinoviev, and Kamenev or indeed as we saw above, to Germanic antecedents, as Hitler claimed, and so on)? If either should be the case, how can it be claimed that communist crimes are due to the Russians only and no one else? Isn't it a form of anti-Russian racism in all but name, consistent with denouncing as anti-Semitic those who, in Hitler's wake, consider that Bolshevism is "an invention of Jews to dominate the world?"[31] If Nazism and its crimes appear to be a German invention, communism and its misdeeds are clearly not an invention as "Russian" as Russophobes make it out to be. Besides, neither Mao nor Pol Pot were Russian, which proves that their crimes were first and foremost due to the upheavals inherent in communist social-engineering ideology and to anterior colonial or imperial oppression clamoring for vengeance, and not to the ethnic origin of their authors.

Who Defeated the Nazis?

Placing Nazism on the same level as Russian communism is also a way of diminishing the predominantly Soviet contribution to Hitler's defeat. It is particularly unjust and unbearable to the

Russians, who all lost relatives in the "Great Patriotic War." They see in it, quite rightly, an attempt to negate their sacrifice and to despoil them of recognition of their victory. Once the war was over, the West hurriedly forgot the Soviets' major contribution. "It was thanks to our deliveries of weapons and food!" we are wont to stress, that led to the victory over Nazi oppression.[32]

This segregation of memory became increasingly obvious as 1945 receded and the memory of war sufferings faded. We still remember Stalingrad but we have forgotten the decisive tank battle of Kursk in the summer of 1943. And we forget that, if the Allied landing in Normandy on June 6, 1944 succeeded, it was thanks to the sacrifice of tens of thousands of Zhukov's soldiers engaged in an offensive on the Eastern Front (Operation Bagration) to pin down the German troops and prevent the Wehrmacht from transferring its tanks to France.

In 1944, each Ryan soldier who landed in Normandy knew what he owed to the sacrifice of Comrade Ivan in Byelorussia. The Allied press of the time, which celebrated Zhukov and Stalin on its covers, was not mistaken. The two of them made the covers of *Time Magazine* several times in 1944 and 1945. But with the passing of time and the launching of the Cold War, those memories gradually faded to be replaced by the grandiloquent celebrations of the landing in Normandy.

Hollywood and all the resources of cinema have since contributed to celebrating the Landing as the major operation during the war, when the Russians had already done most of the fighting in the East. If we keep going on in this way, students in 2030 will end up learning that the Second World War has been only won by the Americans and the French Resistance,[33] the latter having seen its role inflate so much in the last decades, as the contribution of the Soviet Union and the other Allies shrank away to nothing...[34]

This tendency to rewrite history to deprive Russia of any credit is so strong that on January 27, 2015, as the 70th anniversary of the liberation of the Auschwitz camp was being celebrated, Poland did not even see fit to invite Russian president Vladimir Putin to the commemorations. Polish foreign minister Grzegorz Schetyna even had the cheek to claim that the Auschwitz camp was liberated by "Ukrainian troops."[35] Revisionism has settled at the top of the Polish state, without any of the European heads of state present during the commemorations having anything to say about it.

Minimizing the victory of the USSR thus contributes to putting in place memory obliteration with the aim of excluding Russia from the western sphere and discrediting her by reducing the West-USSR opposition to a democracy vs. communism clash whereas, in actual fact, the USSR and communism, through their huge contribution to victory, saved European democracies from Nazi servitude. Detestation of Soviet communism, as well-founded as it might have been, should not lead to the obscuring of the USSR role in the fall of Nazism.

Those who abhor communism must not fall into the trap of contemporary Russophobia, which promotes the association of Russia with communism, or which, in total contradiction with history, tries to liken Russia to Nazism. The technique of demonization consisting in likening Putin to Stalin or to Hitler, contrary to common sense as some European leaders in Poland and the Baltic countries in particular, and many newspapers during the Chechnya War, the Georgian War, and the 2014 Ukrainian crisis, and more recently Hillary Clinton, have done aims precisely at achieving that objective.

This obliteration of positive memories waged against Russia functions mostly by subtraction—the Russian contribution to the liberation of Europe is cut out or reduced—but also by addition: Russia is held accountable for everything, by accusing, as does Nolte, the 1917 Revolution of being at the origin of Nazism. Or, more subtly, of having provoked the First World War. When a Cambridge University professor as respected as Dominic Lieven asserts that "the First World War was initiated by the fight between the Germanic powers and Russia for domination of Eastern Europe, and ended against all predictions by the defeat of all East-European empires,"[36] he explicitly places the fault of the war on Germany and Russia while exonerating Great Britain and France of their responsibilities.

At the same time as these phenomena, there has been, from the 1980s, a contest over the ranking of the victims of the Second World War. That Jewish organizations have succeeded, after a long battle, in having a reticent West recognize the unique and monstrous character of the Shoah is indeed something to be applauded. It is an important achievement and it must remain so. But at the same time, whilst in all big cities Holocaust museums in the likeness of the best of them, the Yad Vashem Museum in Jerusalem, keep being inaugurated, and whilst just about everywhere in the world ritual ceremonies in memory to the victims of the Holocaust area are continually organized, uneasiness has been growing about the other overlooked victims of the Second World War.

On the one hand, they have had reasons to feel increasingly excluded. Holocaust museums in most cases make no reference to other victims of the war. On the other hand, the feeling has been growing that these commemorations were being twisted or instrumentalized for political purposes by some Zionist movements to support the State of Israel and legitimize its policy of the occupation of Palestine.

Deluging the Memory Market

This movement coincided after 1990 with the arrival on the already much cluttered "market" of victimhood remembrance, of a crowd of proponents of new memories eager to find recognition: Baltic, Polish, Czech, Hungarian memories, and memories of all those ex-members of the Soviet bloc that vengefully sought the overthrow of communism and massively turned against a weakened Russia, now seen as the sole source of their past turpitudes. To take but one example, as early as 1991, the Ukrainian embassy in Paris had an official request referred to the French foreign ministry for a modification of Queen Anne of Kiev's gravestone inscription.[37] Instead of the words "*Anna, reine de France, princesse de Russie,*" the Ukrainians intended to inscribe "*Anne, reine de France, princesse d'Ukraine.*"[38] The Estonian crisis in 2007 over the relocation of the Bronze Soldier, the Soviet World War II memorial in Tallinn, proceeded from the same will to obliterate remembrance.[39]

Estonia justified this relocation by arguing that there was no "difference between denial of the Holocaust and denial of Soviet communist crimes" and that in 1944 it was not the Red Army that had liberated Tallinn from Nazi troops but "a legitimate Estonian government,"[40] neglecting the thousands of Soviets who had died to liberate Estonia and forgetting that before 1945 the Baltic countries were governed by fascistic regimes that sympathized with Germany and had persecuted their Jewish nationals, which was the reason why the Allies had not protested when Stalin occupied the Baltic countries in 1939 and had legalized this state of affairs in Yalta in 1945.

Lithuania has even pushed anti-Russian nationalism so far that her new Museum of Genocide Victims limits the word "genocide" to "what the Russians did to the Balts, and not what the Nazis and their local collaborators did to the Jews," while several Baltic ministers have paid tribute to SS veterans as freedom fighters and encouraged renewal of pro-Hitler feelings.[41] So many such facts are seldom, if ever, commented on by western media and academic circles, or even by Jewish organizations.

Fortunately, there are archives. The Soviets filmed the massacres as early as 1941 and transmitted them to the Allies in 1942 to incite them to open a second front. The images show Red Army cameramen filming mass crimes in Estonia, Crimea, Ukraine, and Poland.[42] But the Allies, eager to keep the Indian and Middle Eastern possessions of the British Empire, and keep communications open between London and New Delhi, preferred to counterattack in North Africa and waited until June 6, 1944 before landing in France.

Even the Germans did the same, with films and books which restored to the Nazis the honorific image of heroic resistance fighters on the Eastern Front. Similarly, historiography and literature began to stigmatize the atrocities committed by the Red Army during its advance and the sufferings of German women raped by Russian soldiers. That it was the Red Army that liberated the death camps and ended the genocide of Jews is being willfully forgotten.

If the declared purpose of those works was not to rehabilitate Nazism, they had in any case the very clear, and involuntary (but not always) effect of belittling as much as possible the extent of the Soviet contribution to the liberation of Europe. At the end of the 1980s and at the beginning of the 1990s, sordid accounting to establish who 'Hitler or Stalin' had liquidated the most people, the scale slanting naturally to the Gulag side rather than that of *Vernichtungslager*, was part of that trend.[43]

The other Europeans did nothing or only protested mildly, with the memory of the fight against fascism fading as veterans passed away, and as the necessity to find room for Germany in the new European construction curbed anti-Nazi ardors.

Conclusion: this struggle to establish a hierarchy of World War II victims, with the Holocaust at the forefront, has concretely resulted in denying the sacrifice of 26.6 million Soviet deaths and of 14 million Russian deaths.[44] Doesn't the truth matter? Is this worthy of a democratic and liberal Europe in the 21st century, which simply would not exist if Hitler had won the war against the Soviet Union?

The Artful Deceptions of History and Historiography

Other examples can be given showing how Second World War history is rewritten in a way advantageous to the West and discrediting to the USSR, and through it, to today's Russia.

Take the example of Poland.[45] How many Europeans remember that Marshal Pilsudski, dictator in Poland until 1935, wanted a "Poland from the Baltic to the Black Sea," thus including Ukraine and Moldavia? And that during the 1921-1922 war, when military operations seemed to turn against the Bolsheviks, he proposed to his western allies to conquer Moscow? And who remembers that in 1938, after the annexation of the Sudetenland by Hitler, Polish foreign minister Beck tried to form an alliance with the Nazis to tear Czechoslovakia apart, and that on October 2, 1938, Polish troops took over Czech Silesia? Or that, until Hitler changed his mind in the spring of 1939, Germans and Poles had had long discussions on how to share Lithuania, Byelorussia, and Ukraine, to be conquered from the Russians by a joint attack against Stalin?[46]

Another example: the Molotov-Ribbentrop Pact is presented in the West as a prelude to, if not a cause of, the Second World War. A maneuver thanks to which the western powers are absolved the easy way for their capitulation in front of Hitler at the Munich Conference in 1938, a cowardly act long thought determining in the outbreak of the war.

It must be remembered that immediately after Hitler's accession to power in 1933, Germany and the USSR ended their economic and military cooperation as decided in the Rapallo Treaty of 1922. Feeling threatened, Russia then grew closer to western democracies and notably France in order to negotiate a security alliance similar to the one prior to 1914. But western democracies did not trust Red Russia. The 1935 treaty of mutual assistance between France and the USSR thus became void of substance. Starting with the re-militarization of the Rhineland in 1936, everybody knew that Germany wished to attack her neighbors east and west. The only question was which would be aggressed first. From then on, the strategy of the great powers bordering Germany—France, Great Britain, and the USSR—consisted in making sure that the first attack would be launched against any country but their own.

It is in this context that the Munich treason must be understood. Daladier and Chamberlain were not stupid. As next-door neighbor and designated target, France sought first to preserve herself. Her interest coincided with the British strategy, which aimed at having Hitler attack the USSR first, the idea being to achieve at last what the Great Game of the 19th century had not allowed her to achieve: mastery of Eurasia. Great Britain bet on the wearing out of German forces in Russia, following which, once the USSR was eliminated, Great Britain and her allies would only have to attack Germany at the right time, in order to recover her conquests as so many ripe fruits while suffering minimal destruction at home. By giving in to Hitler over the Sudetenland and Czechoslovakia, London diverted his attention to the east.

It is also in the light of those strategic schemes that the events in Asia at the end of the 1930s must be interpreted. The United States and Great Britain were attempting to involve Japan in the overthrow of the Russian power, in a pincers maneuver with Germany in the west. By the end of 1937, Japan's war against China had doubled in intensity. The United States and England let Japan fight in exchange for peace in their Southeast Asian colonies. Thus liberated in that sphere, Japan attacked the Soviet Union on the Khalkin Gol River, in the north of Manchuria, in May 1939, with a view to conquering Siberia. Japan's first targets, before the conquest of the Pacific, were China and the USSR. It was only after her defeat against Zhukov that Japan turned toward Southeast Asia and the Pacific, and resolved to attack the United States at Pearl Harbor on December 7, 1941.

The German-Soviet Pact against Munich

Stalin had perfectly understood those maneuvers. Seeing itself isolated and knowing that it could not count on ill-intentioned western allies, the Soviet Union undertook to protect itself by throwing the ball back into its so ambiguous allies' camp: by concluding a pact in August 1939 with Germany, the USSR made sure that Hitler would attack first to the west and that the British could not take advantage of the war to grab Eurasia. It is in that spirit that Hitler's declaration of August 11, 1939 must be recalled—ten days before the signature of the Molotov-Ribbentrop Pact:

> Everything I undertake is directed against Russia. If the West is too stupid and blind to get this, I'll be forced to beat the West first, and then, after its defeat, to turn around against the Soviet Union.[47]

The British strategy failed entirely, Stalin showing himself, in fine, shrewder than expected. What was thus left to be done was to cover up the defeat and make him endorse the responsibility of the German-Soviet pact for the outbreak of the war, as if Munich and the Anschluss had been merely secondary details.

Finally let us mention, anecdotally, one last, extremely subtle form of Russophobia, which shows how it can slip into the most improbable cracks of the western psyche. We mean the fashion of repentance that spread after acknowledgment of the Holocaust. It has already been mentioned that that acknowledgment, achieved after a long fight, was an achievement that needed to be preserved. But what was unexpected was that it would transform into a new secular religion and that its cult would lead to the self-celebration of western superiority over the rest of the world, as is happening now.

Let us quote Georges Corm again:

> As a result, naïve beliefs about the superiority of the 'white man,' of western civilization over the other cultures, religions and value systems become legitimate again. In that vision, indeed, only Westerners have reached a supreme stage of morality, thanks to their repentance after the butcheries of the Second World War, repentance instituted by the permanent denunciation of the Holocaust, but also by the fact of having attained a 'supreme stage' of democracy which has now banned violence between States that used to fight one another so ferociously. Denunciation of racism then tends to shrink to next to nothing, to the sole denunciation of anti-Semitism and anti-Zionism."[48]

Seen from Europe, this misappropriation of the Holocaust for cultural supremacy purposes is not recognized for what it is. But this is how it is perceived outside of the West itself, even if Westerners are not aware of it.

2014: *Lebensraum* in the East

In conclusion, we see that Germany, after having brought Russophobia to an unequaled degree of violence during the Second World War, following a pernicious nationalist evolution inherited from Romanticism, then metamorphosed it into a suave, invisible, impalpable but extremely efficient ostracism. Many western historians of today behave exactly in the same manner as the pope's theologians of a thousand years ago: rewriting history extensively, relying heavily on dubious documents and "forgetting" embarrassing documents to such an extent that they are able to erase Russia from European memory as theologians did six centuries earlier with Byzantium. What then remains to be done is to have Easterners bear the responsibility for the erasure; with the forgetfulness of time and the death of witnesses, the maneuver will, if it has not already, reach the same goal—to evict the memory of Russia as liberator from Nazism and to install in its place the myth of an Atlanticist liberation of Europe. And then have Russia bear responsibility for two world wars as Byzantium was made responsible for the Grand Schism. Indeed all of NATO's provocations on the Russian border seem to have as purpose pinning the responsibility for WWIII on Putin.

For Germany, like Poland of yore, has never given up her territorial ambitions in the East nor her will to dominate Europe, even if she no longer dares express them explicitly since the 1945 defeat put an end to her military imperialism. Let us look at the map of 2015 Europe. Hasn't Germany achieved, seventy years after her second stinging defeat, with admirable genius and subtlety, the entire program of the First Reich in the 13th century, then of the Second and Third Reich, the domination of Slavs in the Balkans, of Central Europe, of the Baltic countries and of Ukraine? Since spring 2014, with the entry of Ukraine into the European orbit, hasn't she reconquered the last territory she was missing, the one Teutonic Knights and then *Lebensraum* supporters absolutely wanted to subdue? Thanks to the Ukrainian crisis, hasn't the European Union's center of gravity shifted to a Berlin-Warsaw axis rather than the traditional Paris-Berlin axis?

A look at the map is enough to see that this has now been done, and that 2014 saw the Kaiser's old dream materialize. Consider what Kurt Riezler, advisor to German chancellor Bethmann Hollweg, wrote on April 15, 1915, during the First World War:

> Yesterday had lunch at length with the Chancellor to present to him my new Europe, that is to say the concealing of our will for power. The Central European Empire of the German nation. The system of imbrications, which is the rule in public limited-liability companies; the German Empire, a PLC with Prussia as main shareholder. ... That's why there must be a confederation of States around the German Empire. ... We don't even need to speak of annexation to the central power. The European idea, if followed up to completion, leads to such a result...[49]

Isn't this, in another language, the program defined by the monk Engelbert d'Admont in the 14th century?[50] Isn't the 2015 European Union a perfect incarnation of that dream, a gigantic public limited company with Germany as main shareholder and Angela Merkel as chair of the board? Aren't the Greeks, the Spaniards, the Italians reduced to the status of employees on fixed-term contracts, the Greeks in particular, whose further maintenance in the monetary union is to be decided by decree?

By dislocating Yugoslavia in 1991, via the recognition of independent Macedonia and Croatia, and then of Bosnia, didn't Helmut Kohl succeed in what the Austrians and then the Ustasha had tried to achieve without success for centuries, after the failure of the annexation of Bosnia in 1908 and that of the Catholic-fascist Ustasha State after 1941? Wasn't bringing Serbia and the Balkan Slavs to heel with the support of Kosovo's independence in 2008 the culmination of the old Germanic dream, 21st century Germany finally fulfilling the Habsburgs' ambitions?

By discreetly and as though reluctantly letting the European Union and NATO move their pawns into the Baltic countries and the countries of the former Soviet bloc (many of which were her allies before and during the war), hasn't 2015 Germany succeeded in creating peacefully that so much coveted *Lebensraum* she tried to conquer by violence and massacres during two world wars? Is it surprising that, in this context, the West has paid so little attention to the role of heirs to pro-Nazi Bandera in Ukraine's Maidan Square uprising in February 2014 and their probable implication in the shots that triggered the fall of the pro-Russian government? Here the same thing happened as in the former Yugoslavia and Kosovo; the truth-tampered photographs and crimes of "pseudo-freedom fighters" was only discovered afterward, once the global western media had engraved the political results in western understanding.[51]

The German genius has been to put on the mantle of softness, and this is laudable, but with the march of NATO to Russia's borders, there is much to fear from the usual iron fist in a velvet glove. The other members of the European Union have been totally snowed. Wisely staying behind, Germans left US-backed NGOs to pursue their agenda in Eastern Europe and Ukraine, after which, Angela Merkel followed the lead of Joe Biden and Victoria Nuland and only had to grab the stake, while positioning herself, with consummate skill, as the arbiter of a conflict between the West and Russia. A masterful performance indeed.

Only Russia, which obstructed her path, lost in the bargain. Let Emmanuel Todd conclude for us:

> Reunified Germany, having [as in 1870] recovered her zone of economic expansion in Eastern Europe (in fact, the Russian domination space has become the German domination space), is no longer of the same dimensions as France. And France fails to admit it. ... That Germany is no longer Adenauer's congenial, peaceful Federal Germany, it is an autonomous country that is enormous.

Q.E.D.

This is how, overnight, Europe wakes up at the German hour, unaware of what has befallen her. This is how, in less than a quarter century, without striking a single blow and under public applause, Germany has just won the First and Second World Wars!

| Chapter Eight |

AMERICAN RUSSOPHOBIA: THE DICTATORSHIP OF FREEDOM

> *"On Iran, Kosovo, the American antimissile defense system, Iraq, the Caucasus, the Caspian Sea basin, Ukraine—the list is not exhaustive—Russia is in conflict with the United States and their allies ... Here is one of the worst models to which the unified West that won the Cold War has been confronted."*
> "Putin institutionalized" in *The Wall Street Journal*, November 9, 2007.

> *"It is not a matter of what is true that counts, but a matter of what is perceived to be true."*
> Henry Kissinger

American Russophobia begins where the French, the English, and the Germans left off. It is a dynamic synthesis of French liberal-democratic Russophobia and English and German imperialist Russophobias. From France, it has borrowed its philosophy and principles: freedom, democracy, and human rights. From the English, it has drawn its objectives:

domination of the seas, and access to the main continental markets, as well as its strategy: military supremacy thanks to a defense budget that surpasses all of the others aggregated, and communications mastery with permanent mobilization of soft power resources. As for the Germans, they gave it its toolbox, the mass propaganda techniques conceived by the Nazis, and its ideological motivation, the fight against an ideal adversary, Soviet Bolshevism.

Historically, American Russophobia only appeared after 1945 and raged on throughout the Cold War, from the brutal McCarthyism of the 1950s to the very sophisticated theses of anti-totalitarianism in the 1980s and their recycling in the anti-Putin fight starting from the 2000s.

The outbreak of American Russophobia looked very much like that of English Russophobia. It appeared in similar circumstances the same alliance with Russia against a common enemy, Napoleon's France, and then Hitler's Germany, turning into repudiation and antipathy as soon as victory was achieved. Like that of Great Britain after 1815, the United States' turnaround against Russia in 1945 was sudden and brutal. The two countries were in the same situation: victorious but flanked with an ally which, because of its mass and power, had overnight appeared so troublesome that it had to be either fought or, at the very least, contained.[1]

Before 1917, the United States had had nothing serious to hold against Russia. The latter had ceded Alaska to them without much hesitation in 1867, and the only reprimand they had addressed to Russia had to do with the 1880–1905 pogroms against the Jews. But at a time when violent anti-Semitism was raging all over Europe, including in Republican France and Victorian England, that was no grounds for a dispute. At the start of the Russian Revolution, the Americans had hoped Russia would follow their model of liberal democracy. Convinced that America could be an example for Russians exasperated by the world war, they were very disappointed to see them turn toward the Bolsheviks and take another route. Let us try to understand why the American-Russian alliance of the early 1940s suddenly turned into open hostility after the war.[2]

At the end of the 1880s, the United States found itself in the same situation as Germany. They had just completed their territorial unification. In the 1840s and 1850s, they had taken over all Mexican territories between Texas and California. Then they had proceeded to the conquest of the West, which was marked by extreme violence. They had first been able to rely on the manpower of enslaved Africans and then had massacred the Indians of the Great Plains and deported the survivors into reserves.[3] Thanks to this ethnic cleansing, the American space found itself rid of Mexicans and Natives, whose cultures did not fit with libertarian individualism or the needs of the triumphant capitalism of the young State.

By the early 1880s, the Americans began to feel a bit cramped in their new frontiers. In 1885, Josiah Strong published a bestseller, *Our Country*, in which he explained that it was the Anglo-Saxons' duty to spread around the globe the beneficial effects of democracy, Protestantism, and free enterprise. In 1890, historian and political theoretician Frederick Jackson Turner reflected well the spirit of the era when he declared that the closing down of the western "frontier" might trigger a recrudescence of strikes and social tensions. Without a safety valve allowing workers to leave town to go and colonize the great open spaces of the West, the texture of the American social fabric would eventually look like the effervescent caldron of European countries.

Similar to the Germans of the same epoch, the United States launched into the conquest of overseas spaces. Central America and the Caribbean were transformed into exclusive preserves. In 1890, it took over Midway Island, then the Hawaiian archipelago, which it incorporated into the Union as a territory in 1898 against the wishes of its inhabitants. In the same year, taking advantage of a war against Spain orchestrated by the imperialist lobby led by William Randolph Hearst and future president Theodore Roosevelt, who was then assistant secretary to the Navy, it conquered Puerto Rico and extended its protectorate to Cuba, the Philippines, and finally Panama, which occupied a vital position for the development of trade with the Pacific zone. With Hawaii and the Philippines, the

United States owned the links of the naval chain indispensable to the growth of its influence and trade in Asia.

The United States as a Maritime Power

But like England, and contrary to Germany, the United States is, in some senses, an island. Rather than an army, it had, like the English, to build a fleet to rule the seas. So it is not surprising that its first great military and strategic thinker was a sailor, Admiral Alfred Mahan. He it was who defined the American maritime doctrine and sealed the imperial destiny of the United States. His *The Influence of Sea Power upon History, 1660–1831*, published in 1890, was the most influential work of its time in matters of military strategy and foreign policy.

Mahan had been struck by the growth of England's power thanks to its navy and he insisted on the need for the United States to develop a powerful war fleet. Indeed, the British had succeeded in having at once a prosperous external trade that enriched them, a flourishing merchant navy to carry out that trade, a powerful war navy to see to the defense of the trade fleet all around the world, a series of maritime bases where the ships could obtain fresh supplies or be repaired, and finally a continental Empire which provided the raw materials needed for manufacturing and constituted a market of consumers for finished products.

These five elements seemed to Mahan both complementary and indispensable to ensure American power and prosperity. Without them, the United States would lag behind in the drive for global ascendancy. The Americans thus had to take a leaf out of the British book.

With the support of Secretary to the Navy Benjamin Tracy, influential senator Henry Cabot Lodge, and Theodore Roosevelt, Mahan succeeded in providing the United States with an impressive war fleet in record time: in 1898, during the Spanish-American War, the US Navy had five battleships; by 1900, it had the third most powerful navy in the world; and by 1908, the second. America had perfectly integrated Mahan's first lesson:

Maritime power relies first and foremost on trade, and trade follows the most advantageous routes; military power has always followed trade to help it progress and protect it.[4]

After the experience of the Great War, which allowed it to accede to the rank of major international power, after its decision to go back to an isolationist policy, and after the 1929 crisis, the United States withdrew from the forefront for about two decades, until the growing strength of an increasingly ambitious Japan awoke its geopolitical interests in Asia, a zone it considered should be under its influence. And that, at a time when Germany had given herself to Hitler and his thirst for revenge.

That was when the United States resumed paying close attention to geopolitics. In the early 1940s, it rediscovered the theses of the great English geopolitician, Halford Mackinder, whose theories have inspired the geopolitical vision of the United States up to now.

Dominating the Heartland (Russia) to Dominate the World

Like his German colleague Haushofer, Mackinder believed in Anglo-Saxon racial superiority and in the importance of its civilizing mission regarding other peoples. Two historical events had contributed to his way of thinking: the Boer War (1899–1902) and the Russian-Japanese war of 1904. It was in that year that he published his seminal article, "The geographic pivot of history," in which he defined his theory of the Heartland.

Imitating Friedrich Ratzel, Mackinder thought that the world had to be viewed from a polar perspective, not a Mercator projection. The planet would thus be observed in its entirety, from which would distinctly be seen emerging a "world island," the Heartland (covering 2/12th of the Earth, and composed of the Eurasian and African continents), "peripheral islands," the Outlying Islands (or 1/12th of the Earth, America and Australia), with a "world ocean" occupying 9/12th of the planet.

To rule the world, one had to control that Heartland, the huge plain stretching from Central Europe to Western Siberia forming a crescent over the Mediterranean Sea, the Middle East, Southern Asia, and China. He illustrated his thesis by evoking the great waves of Mongol invasions of the 13th and 14th centuries led by Genghis Khan and Tamerlane. According to him, the Ukrainian Plain represented at that time the space of mobility par excellence allowing rapid invasions by means of the cavalry.

In fact, Mackinder's formula can be summarized thus:

> Who hold Eastern Europe holds the Heartland, who holds the Heartland dominates the world island, who dominates the world island dominates the world.

He had taken up the motto of the great English navigator Sir Walter Raleigh, who had been the first to say:

> Who holds the sea holds the world trade; who holds the trade holds the wealth; who holds the world's wealth holds the world itself.

In 1940, American Nicholas Spykman, adopting and adapting Mackinder's theses, developed the concept of Rimland:

> Who controls the Rimland governs Eurasia; who governs Eurasia controls the fate of the world.

He exposed his theses in his two books, *American Strategy in World Politics*, published in 1942, and *The Geography of the Peace*, published in 1944, after his death.

According to Spykman, the world can be divided into three parts: the Heartland, a zone enclosing Eastern Europe and Russia, considered as the center of the world; the Rimland (or inner crescent), a region composed of Western Europe, the Near and Middle East, and the Far East; and the offshore continents (the outer crescent), meaning the rest of the world, Great Britain, Japan, Australia, South and North America, and Africa.

Spykman "stamps as obsolescent the idea of an invulnerable Heartland, totally called into question by the growth of the air weapon. Conversely, he asserts the determining role imparted to the Rimland, i.e. to the intermediate region between the Heartland and the riverine regions. It is this Rimland that has become for him the pivot-zone Mackinder identified previously as the Heartland."[5]

Politically, Spykman thought it was impossible to create a world community around the same set of values. That was why peace could only be obtained through application by one country of a foreign policy efficient enough from a security point of view to minimize the risks of aggression by other countries. "Security being first and foremost based on the defensive strength of a country, the latter must maintain its armed forces in times of peace if it wants to be militarily efficient in times of war," he thought.

This vision of geopolitics crystallized the balance of power opposing sea powers and land powers. Mackinder and Spykman were most wary of Russia, as she dominated the Heartland. That concern was to become an obsession. Never, since then, have military hawks lost sight of it.

In this long history, the alliance of the United States with Soviet Russia against Nazi Germany and Japan appears as a decidedly secondary affair. Four years of alliance against seventy-five years of war more or less Cold is nothing much. It was only when it realized that a newly strong Germany could ally herself with Russia and sound the death knell of Anglo-Saxon power that it took fright, like the English and the French before 1914. It then chose the lesser of two evils. From that perspective, the 1941–1945 alliance appears to be a purely opportunistic and temporary interlude in a long-term structural conflict inscribed in history and geography.

This is surely one of the reasons why the United States, once it had become the major world power after the Second World War, turned at once against yesterday's ally. Researchers consider Nicholas Spykman as one of the main sources of the containment policy formulated by the diplomat George F. Kennan.

Soviet Russia's Containment by Military Bases

Kennan was posted in Berlin until the entry of the United States into war against Germany, and then was sent to Moscow in 1945–1946. In June 1947, under the pen name "X," he wrote an article in *Foreign Affairs*, "The Sources of Soviet Conduct," in which he explained Stalin's foreign policy as a combination of Marxist-Leninist ideology advocating the defeat of capitalist forces throughout the world, and his own determination to utilize the notion of "capitalist encirclement" as a pretext to legitimize the regimentation of Soviet society and the consolidation of his power. It was thus necessary for the United States to respond through a policy countering Soviet expansionism, Kennan argued. This was how the famed principle of containment was born.

The publication of that article divided the American political class. Journalist Walter Lippman, favorable to disengagement in Germany, severely criticized that analysis, which obliged the Americans to engage militarily into the Soviet Union's peripheral territories, thus weakening American confidence without improving American security, left the initiative to the Soviets in triggering crises, and surrounded the United States with heteroclite allies that might exploit the containment doctrine to pursue their own ends. In the meantime, the anonymity of the article had been seen through. The fact that it had been written by Kennan, director of political affairs at the State Department, gave it the standing of an official doctrine.

Kennan later claimed that he had never considered defining future policy. All his life, he would repeat that those warnings did not necessarily imply all the measures that were taken later to contain Soviet expansionism:

> My ideas about containment have been twisted by people who understood and executed them solely as a military concept; and I think this is what led us to forty years of the useless, horridly expensive process that the Cold War was.[6]

He stuck to his guns until the end of his life in 2005.

But the harm had been done. By the end of the 1940s, the United States had multiplied its military bases in the Rimland and strung out military pacts and economic exchange treaties in order to encircle the Soviet Union. NATO was created in 1949.

> American pact mania, in the following years, clearly turned against the USSR—American States Alliance, Atlantic Alliance, ANZUS (with Australia and New Zealand), Japanese-American Treaty, SEATO (with Southeast Asia) and CENTO (Bagdad Pact) showed the will to control the periphery of the Asian continental mass in order to thwart alleged USSR ambitions, while Stalin, more interested in establishing an East-European bloc or in limited gains in Iran for example answered more to the classic geopolitics of Russian power than in a global power project for which he knew he did not have the means. The main objective of the USA, in times of peace as of war, must be to prevent the unification of power centers in the Old World into a coalition hostile to their interests.[7]

This American reading of the world was to dominate the entire Cold War. At the same time as that domination of the Rimland countries (which happen to be overflowing with natural gas and oil), the United States entered into an implacable ideological fight against communism inside and outside of its borders. The Red Scare followed the Russian Peril and a witch hunt period began in the wake of the creation of the House Un-American Activities Committee by the House of Representatives in 1938.

Ideological Containment

In 1946, President Harry Truman set up a temporary commission whose mandate was to investigate the loyalty of federal officers. This consisted in identifying and dismissing subversive civil servants, proponents of ideologies or regimes described as "totalitarian." Five months later, Executive Order 9835 made the program permanent. In 1947, a list of "subversive" organizations was published by the Department of Justice while the FBI collected information on suspects. By 1950, Joseph McCarthy was at the forefront of the American political scene and during two years, in 1953 and 1954, the commission he presided over kept busy flushing out presumed communist agents, militants or sympathizers, attacking in particular intellectuals, trade unionists, and artists suspected of Muscovite sympathies.

That was when the ideological framework and the binary opposition—freedom and democracy versus communist oppression and dictatorship—that were going to last throughout the Cold War were put in place. The old vocabulary used against Russia despotism and tyranny was redeployed under the banner of anti-communism. With the United States supporting coups and the implantation of military or conservative dictatorships in most of the territories, it controlled military regimes in Latin America, monarchies in the Gulf and in Iran, other dictatorships in Asia—the descriptor "dictatorship" was progressively banished and replaced by that of "totalitarianism," in order to better distinguish friendly regimes from the antipathetic socialist regimes which were to be fought. This semantic shift, which philosopher Raymond Aron introduced in France in 1965,[8] allowed the development of a communications strategy as effective with public opinion in European democratic nations as with that in the authoritarian regimes of the liege countries of the Rimland.

The Cold War went on throughout the 1950s and 1960s, coinciding with the period of decolonization and multiplication of liberation movements of Marxist inspiration supported by the Soviet Union. But in 1975, when both the Vietnam War and decolonization were about to end, the East-West confrontation had reached stalemate: neither winner nor loser. The Soviet Union kept the bloc acquired in 1945. Communism, even though divided, had turned out to be a powerful additive to decolonization and had conquered vast spaces, in China and in Africa in particular.

For its part, the United States had kept its domination over client dictatorial regimes in Latin America, Asia and South Africa had even extended it to Chili and Argentine thanks to generals Pinochet and Videla's coups, and had established solid bases in the key countries of the Rimland, notably the authoritarian monarchies of the Middle East rich in hydrocarbon, Iran, Saudi Arabia, and the Gulf countries.

The 1975 Helsinki Agreements

Whatever their successes or failures, by the mid-1970s both camps were tired. The Vietnam defeat and the influx of political opponents tortured or expelled by the military regimes of Chili and Argentina had weakened the credibility of the "free world," whereas the Soviet Union was tangled up in economic difficulties and had lost much prestige following the invasion of Czechoslovakia at a time when the decolonization process that was favorable to her was about to end.

With the Cold War becoming less intense, the two major powers accepted to negotiate an agreement in order to improve their relationship. That was how, in July 1975, negotiations began that eventually would translate into a series of agreements signed on August 1, 1975 in Helsinki by 35 states, including the two major ones (the Soviet Union and the United States), Canada and all European states with the exception of Albania and Andorra. That text (which is not a treaty in the juridical sense of the term) marked the end of the first Conference on Security and Cooperation in Europe.

Its Final Act listed ten fields of application: respect of rights inherent to sovereignty; non-recourse to threat or the use of threat; inviolability of frontiers; territorial integrity of states; peaceful resolution of conflicts; non-intervention in internal affairs; respect for human rights and fundamental freedoms; equal rights and self-determination of peoples; cooperation between states; and fulfilment in good faith of obligations assumed under international law.

The seventh item, on human rights and fundamental freedoms, was going to give new impetus to anti-Soviet American propaganda. It was indeed as early as 1976, with the election of President Jimmy Carter, that the newest form of anti-totalitarian onslaught appeared, in the name of the fight for human rights. Through budding NGOs and with the support of growing numbers of Soviet dissidents published in the West in the wake of Alexander Solzhenitsyn, the fight for human rights received an unprecedented response and proved again very effective.

It must be noted that it was after those agreements that the United States created the Helsinki Watch, originally as part of the NGO Human Rights Watch, which has always kept close to American interests, is heavily funded by George Soros, and remains very active in the denunciation of human rights violations in Russia and in the countries that have remained communist after the disappearance of the Soviet Union in 1991.

For the United States, the Helsinki agreements turned out to be a stroke of genius. They gave it a new opportunity to revitalize the discourse on freedom and human rights, thanks in particular to the exalted speeches of Jimmy Carter, undoubtedly the most sincere post-war president. In 1979, however, the United States suffered a setback, losing a key regime, that of the Shah of Iran. It thought it had countered Iranian revolutionaries by having Ayatollah Khomeini repatriated from Paris to Teheran, in the belief that a theocracy would be more favorable to America than a secular leftwing regime. But that calculation proved erroneous.

Luckily for the U.S., at the end of the same year, the Soviet Union made an even more serious blunder: she fell into the Afghan trap set by Jimmy Carter's advisor, Zbigniew Brzezinski.[9] The invasion of Afghanistan by the Red Army definitely compromised the Soviets' positive image in the Third World while sinking their economy deeper into crisis.

In 1980, Jimmy Carter's transgressions in Iran hastened the election of Ronald Reagan, who immediately discarded his predecessor's personal idealistic dreams and human right concerns to go back to a strictly utilitarian and state-controlled conception of freedom, which was promptly recruited for exclusive service in the anti-communist fight. Reagan received powerful help in this task with the providential election of Margaret Thatcher in Britain.

Freedom versus Totalitarianism and the Left

Freedom as understood in the Age of Enlightenment or by Rousseau, that is to say conceived as a way to emancipate both the person and the peoples, was to be progressively emptied of any subversive content and limited to the economic field alone. The craftiness of the neoliberal discourse consisted in actually making economic freedom and the deregulation ideology look like the progress of freedom in the humanistic and universal sense of the term. This restrained freedom was hardly akin to the freedom French philosophers and revolutionaries had brandished against tyranny and monopolization of wealth by the aristocratic class. But it came at the right time to be used as an incentive for anti-Soviet and anti-Left propaganda in Europe.

As a good Hollywood actor familiar with anti-communist circles and used to westerns that had already transformed the bloody conquest of the West and the ethnic cleansing of the Indians into a great libertarian saga, reducing the collective dimension of the massacres to mere individual blunders, Ronald Reagan proved to be the communication genius the United States needed at that point in its history. He popularized a discourse on freedom and human rights in keeping with American tradition, yet acceptable to a large part of European public opinion, even as he made it compatible with the ambitions of the great capitalist entrepreneurs and the touchiness of allied authoritarian regimes. The latter were in fact gradually softened up before being dissolved into liberal democracy after the fall of the Soviet Union. And soon dictatorships from Latin America to Asia, from Chili to the Philippines, disappeared one after the other. Only Middle East countries kept their authoritarian regimes.

Reagan also reformulated the message of freedom by

giving it an eschatological, transcendental dimension, which drew smiles from western secular intellectuals as it camouflaged the classically geopolitical and economic interests of the United States. By reintroducing the sacred and religion into the political discourse, presented as a battle of Good (the Liberal West) against Evil (Russia, Iran, Cuba, and China to a lesser extent), the crusade took on an aura and a strength it would not have had, had it kept the crude imperialist language of the 19th century.

That discourse was all the better perceived as the Soviet Union found itself in difficulty in Afghanistan, and in Poland with Solidarnosc, and domestically because of its economy running out of steam. Despite the extent to which it had always sided with the colonized, the USSR now found itself in the colonizers' camp in the eyes of world public opinion. In less than five years, from 1980 to 1985, the scales had tipped and the West, under American leadership, had made itself into the unchallenged standard bearer in the defense of freedom.

At the end of the 1980s, under the combined effect of its internal contradictions and economic inefficiency, the Soviet Union exploded. During the entire Cold War, that is from 1945 to 1989, the United States, under the banner of anti-communism, had mobilized with success its forces around two axes initiated by English imperialists, the first a military and geopolitical axis, and the second under the standard of the fight for freedom and human rights.

In 1991, for want of a communist foe, one would have thought that the antipathy would stop there and die out. It was actually in that sense that Gorbachev's diplomatic advisor, Georgy Arbatov, had said: "We are going to do you a disservice: we are going to deprive you of an enemy." That did not happen.

Goodbye Anti-Communism: Welcome Back, Russophobia

With the fall of the Soviet Union in 1991, those who had struggled for forty years against what they viewed as communist totalitarianism had indeed very logically thought that their mission was accomplished and that they could let now-democratic

Russia rebuild herself in peace. Let us quote again Martin Malia, a staunch anti-communist with an excellent knowledge of Russia:

> Russia, therefore, is now back at geopolitical square one: a poor power trying to modernize in the real world after the failure of its caricature modernization in the surreal world of Soviet socialism. It is quite unlikely that in the foreseeable future she will have caught up economically with the West or even with China sufficiently to move into any vacuum in Central Europe. Nor would neo-Russian nationalism act as a magnetic mystique abroad any more than tsarism did. Finally, even if by some extraordinary exertions Russia recovered the still poorer republics of the late 'Union,' this would not make her a significant threat.
>
> For at the end of the twentieth century international power rests not on the extent of territory a state controls but on its level of economic and technological development. Politically, economically, and morally the age of territorial empires is over: crossing frontiers with armies is no longer a permissible road to national aggrandizement.[10]

That was how many former anti-communist militants saw the future of Russia in the 1990s.

The most sincere among them were rapidly brought down to earth, because they had forgotten geopolitical rivalries and American hawks' aspirations to world supremacy. During Boris Yeltsin's first mandate, from 1992 to 1996, everything seemed to go according to prognostication. The economic shock therapy prescribed by IMF ideologues such as Jeffrey Sachs imposed the neoliberal version of freedom to a devastated Russia. Privatizations allowed a small gang of looters to get their hands on national riches under the guise of conversion to capitalism, while Western media applauded when Yeltsin had cannons shoot at the elected Parliament.[11]

But everything changed when, aware of the failure of the imported model, Yeltsin had, in January 1996, to open his government to patriots more caring of the country's interests and, a little later, to name foreign minister Yevgeny Primakov prime minister. It was then that American anti-Russian propaganda was back in a snap, with the same themes and the same ideology of freedom, but turned against the new Russia. Ritualistic denunciation of totalitarianism had of course to be discarded, but old criticisms unused since 1917, of Russia's atavistic tendencies toward expansionism and despotism, were soon resurrected. Anti-Russian propaganda started all over again along the same patterns as usual: territorial domination and geopolitical ambitions on one side, discourse on freedom and progress thanks to happy globalization on the other, the second used to conceal the first since the alibi of fighting against communism was gone.

Brzezinski: Recycling Russian Expansionism and Dismembering Russia

One of the first to take aim was Zbigniew Brzezinski, in the most faithful geo-imperialist traditions of Mahan, Mackinder and Spykman, and in total contradiction to the discourses of the eulogists on the end of territorial empires and obsolescence of Western geopolitics. In 1997, he published *The Grand Chessboard: American Primacy and Its Geostrategic Imperatives*, in which he updated his predecessors' concepts by applying them to the new post-Soviet configuration. He further updated the same theme in 2004 (*The Choice: Global Domination or Global Leadership*) before presenting a new model in 2012 taking into account the rise in power of China.[12]

Brzezinski's 1997 book exerted a determining influence on the American vision of Russia during the Clinton and Bush eras. Of Polish origin, Brzezinski is very close to anti-Russian Baltic nationalists. A former Democrat turned Republican before chasing power back again to Obama, he knows the Washington establishment well and possesses very influential networks in all American conservative think tanks, Democrat as well as Republican. He has had the same career as Madeleine Albright, Bill Clinton's secretary of state, who is of Czech origin and who was very much anti-Russian and anti-Serb during the Yugoslavia War. He is also a close friend of very conservative Vice President Joe Biden.

"Eurasia remains the chessboard on which the struggle for global primacy continues to be played," he wrote, before declaring that "the formulation of a comprehensive and integrated Eurasian geostrategy is therefore the purpose of this book."[13]

As Gabriel Galice[14] notes, "hypotheses and reasoning are of a great intellectual rigor. Eurasia is central, America must be present there to dominate the planet, Europe is the bridgehead of democracy in Eurasia, NATO and the European Union must jointly extend their influence over Eurasia, the United States must play simultaneously Germany and France (maps of respective zones of influence provided), faithful allies but in different, rowdy, and capricious ways." The Ukrainian "geopolitical pivot" is the object of lengthy developments:

> By 1994, Washington assigns a high priority to American-Ukrainian relations' ... During the 2005–2010 period, Ukraine could in turn be in a position to start negotiations aimed at joining the EU and NATO.[15]

Twenty years later, we can say that Brzezinski's program has been almost entirely fulfilled. His readers applied it to the letter. Ukraine, with the active help of the Poles and the Baltic countries, has swung over to the western orbit thanks to a color revolution. The only thing was, Brzezinski had not foreseen that the inhabitants of the east of Ukraine would demur and rebel, preferring to rejoin Russia or demand independence rather than embrace the West.

Brzezinski had imposed drastic conditions on Russia:

> ...the choice in favor of Europe and America, in order for it to yield tangible benefits, requires [of Russia] first of all, a clear-cut abjuration of the imperial past and, second, no tergiversation regarding the enlarging Europe's political and security links with America.[16]

In other words, Russia was ordered to go back into her doghouse, stop barking, and tear off her teeth and claws (unilateral disarmament).

But Brzezinski was not happy with just a passive and neutralized Russia. He wanted much more: a Russia dismantled and incapable of reconstituting her power in front of a much stronger Europe in military terms. He explained very well why Europe absolutely had to extend NATO eastward and Russia had to be cut up into pieces.

> A new Europe is still taking shape, and if that new Europe is to remain geopolitically a part of the 'Euro-Atlantic' space, the expansion of NATO is essential. By the same token, a failure to widen NATO, now that the commitment has been made, would shatter the concept of an expanding Europe and demoralize the Central Europeans.[17]

And then he explains why Russia must absolutely be kept out of NATO:[18]

> If a choice has to be made between a larger Euro-Atlantic system and a better relationship with Russia, the former has to rank incomparably higher to America.
> For that reason, any accommodation with Russia on the issue of NATO enlargement should not entail an outcome that has the effect of making Russia a de facto decision-making member of

> the alliance, thereby diluting NATO's special Euro-Atlantic character ... That would create opportunities for Russia to resume not only the effort to regain a sphere of influence in Central Europe but to use its presence within NATO to play on any American-European disagreements in order to reduce the American role in European affairs.

And to think that, with such clear positions, there still exist European politicians and journalists that claim Russia would be the aggressive one and would turn down western overtures for accommodation!

To complete this militarist program, Brzezinski bluntly suggested to cut up Russia into pieces:

> ...a more decentralized Russia would be less susceptible to imperial mobilization. A loosely confederated Russia composed of a European Russia, a Siberian Republic, and a Far Eastern Republic would also find it easier to cultivate closer economic relations with Europe, with the new states of Central Asia, and with the Orient, which would thereby accelerate Russia's own development. Each of the three confederated entities would also be more able to tap local creative potential, stifled for centuries by Moscow's heavy bureaucratic hand.[19]

What would Americans say if it was suggested to them to carve up the United States into three new states, one Atlantic, one Hispanic, and one Pacific, in order to better develop their creative potential? The prophets of the end of classical empires and the theoreticians of immaterial power—economic, political, and cultural—who clamor that the American superpower no longer needs to "control a territory" to dominate it should have a second, close reading of Brzezinski's pronouncements!

They are prompt in pointing out that Russia "is renewing the outdated traditions of imperialism" when she tries to protect Russian minorities maltreated by the new independent states, so they should also ask themselves if the invasion of Afghanistan and Iraq and the bombing of Libya and Syria by NATO forces have really consigned the military conception of power to the scrap heap of history.

Completing his geopolitical and military analysis, Brzezinski then presented the second constituent of the American strategy toward Russia, that of soft power:

> A clear choice by Russia in favor of the European option over the imperial one will be more likely if America successfully pursues the second imperative strand of its strategy toward Russia: namely, reinforcing the prevailing geopolitical pluralism in the post-Soviet space. Such reinforcement will serve to discourage any imperial temptations.[20]

It is thus very logical that, under the cover of promoting democracy, American NGOs and their European subsidiaries tested their concept first in Serbia in 1999 against President Milosevic, then in 2003 in Georgia, Ukraine, and Kirghizstan.

Nye: Soft Power and the "Smart" Anti-Russian Axis

The era was indeed very favorable. With the invention of the World Wide Web in the early 1990s, the development of new information technologies and the relative reluctance of public opinion to see bloody military interventions multiply, the United States developed a striking force without equivalent in terms of soft power, as formalized by Jimmy Carter's former state undersecretary and Bill Clinton's defense undersecretary, Joseph Nye. Now a professor at Harvard University's Kennedy School of Government, Nye is considered one of the most eminent liberal thinkers of American foreign policy, his colleague Samuel P. Huntington occupying the conservative bastion.

Raising objections to declinologues such as Paul Kennedy (*The Rise and Fall of the Great Powers: Economic Change and Military Conflict from 1500 to 2000*), Nye asserts that American power is not "in absolute decline and is bound to remain more powerful than any other State in decades to come" because the concept of power has to be reconsidered.[21] On the one hand, the United States is and will long remain the first military power, and on the other, it has a new comparative advantage which leads it to play a growing role in the future: the capacity to seduce and persuade the other states without having to use force or threat. For Joseph Nye, this is a new form of power in contemporary international political life, which does not work on the coercion mode (carrot and stick) but on that of persuasion, i.e. on the ability to make it so that the other wants the same thing as you do.

Soft power, or the power of persuasion, rests on intangible resources such as the positive image or reputation of a State, its prestige (often its economic or military achievements), its communications capabilities, the degree of openness of its society, the exemplarity of its behavior (of its domestic policies but also of the substance and style of its foreign policy), the attractiveness of its culture, of its ideas (religious, political, economic, philosophical), its scientific and technological influence, but also of its place within international institutions in order to be able to control their agendas, and so decide on what is and what is not legitimate to discuss. In this way, such a State will be able to freeze power relations the moment they are most favorable to it.

Nye distinguishes the power of command, understood as the capacity to change what others do, and which can rely on coercion or incitement (with the promise of a reward), from the power of cooptation, which is the capacity to change what others want. The latter can rely on seduction or on the possibility of defining the hierarchy of political problems in order to prevent others from expressing convincing viewpoints over the priority of the stakes of the moment.

Thanks to its soft power, the United States has in fact

never ceased being the most powerful international actor. Completing the traditional power of constraint (hard power), soft power has become the most important means for exercising power, notably because of the upheavals linked to globalization: opening of borders, lowering communication costs, multiplying transnational problems demanding a global response—terrorism, global warming, drug trafficking, epidemics, etc.

There are three types of resources, according to Nye: 1) military resources, which are the basis of hard power: the United States has the most, much more than any other actor; 2) economic resources: all industrialized countries have them and those of China are progressing fast; and 3) intangible resources everybody has to varying degrees, government, NGOs, businesses, cultural institutions, etc.

In the short term, the United States must rely on international institutions, defend their universal values, and maintain their power of attraction to have their policies accepted and avoid the growth of anti-American sentiment. In the long term, the spreading of new technologies will diminish their intangible resources and will make the world evolve toward a more balanced distribution of power. In summary, to paraphrase Clausewitz, soft power according to Nye is the ideal continuation of war by other means. It is the absolute weapon of American democracy, which does not want or cannot undertake hard wars when its own public opinion is reluctant.

During the 2000s, the theory became more refined and Nye declared that "America must mix hard and soft powers into smart power as it used to do during the Cold War." And this was how, in 2009, Hillary Clinton, then Secretary of State, declared she would rely on smart power to implement the Obama administration's strategy.

Cinema, Think Tanks and NGOs in the Service of Power

The recourse to soft power and the various resources it mobilizes depends on the political sensibilities of American presidents. It allows for unlimited suppleness, by relying at times on force (landing in Somalia, then in Afghanistan, invasion of Iraq), at times on softness (exaltation of the American model, of pluralistic democracy, and of economic liberalism). All administrations use it freely as it has the merit of avoiding bloodshed.

Some, whose hearts are more to the left or who are more humane, like political scientist Benjamin Barber,[22] are offering to trade preventive war with preventive democracy and suggest behaving like owls rather than eagles or hawks, "soft" predation being preferable to brutal force, even if it often consists in simple exportation of "market democracy," meaning the crudest form of capitalism:

> The desire to favor expansion of democracy is one determining component of preventive democracy understood as national security policy. But this support is often confused with the as intense desire to export capitalism and cultivate world markets.[23]

This tight imbrication of military force, "democratic" consolidation and economic interests is an integral part of the West's strategy of conquest in the Russian periphery. As Gabriel Galice puts it, the association agreement proposed in 2013 by the European Union to Ukraine "illustrates to a large extent the will to develop riches (industrial and agricultural stocks, transit of oil and gas flows) through corruption of new elites in the name of free and fair competition, of workers' mobility, of recuperation or repatriation of invested capital as well as of the profits to which it leads."

> The military constituent is not forgotten: *promoting a gradual convergence in terms of foreign policy and defense.* Article 10 of the treaty aims at *increasing Ukraine's participation in civil and military operations of crisis management, as well as in the maneuvers, including in the frame*

of the common policy of defense and security. Mercury, the god of trade, holds hands with Mars, the god of war. The same article 10 evokes the *potential for military-technological cooperation and improvement of military capacities.* Knowing that between 2009 and 2013 Ukraine was the eighth world exporter of weapons, Europeans and Americans are going to modernize her armament industry, killing two birds with one stone. Would that be the Euro-American Empire?[24]

Others, more left-leaning, suggest disconnecting globalization from the American Empire in the narrowest sense. French researcher and politician Sami Naïr proposes an analysis of world mutations "from a more radical vision: even though America's power has never been so great, that isn't what defines the originality of our world, but rather the formation at world level of a vast trade empire, with its own dynamics, which tends to shape everywhere political, cultural, and social systems, as well as legitimation discourses to ensure only the radical transformation it wants: unlimited extension of the power of goods over persons."

> The European construction, the formation of world elites, the tragedy of the Arab-Muslim world, the interminable Israeli-Palestinian conflict, the disintegration of societies in the South, etc.: there is plenty of data to analyze in the violent expansion movement of that universal merchant empire. Will the latter succeed in submitting the diversity of beings and cultures to the sole law of trade equivalence? Or will we witness the renewed rise of nations, of original forms of citizen sovereignty, of solidarity between peoples against the totalitarianism of the market?[25]

Because, whatever the approach, and whatever the form

of power, soft or hard, power remains power, at work in all domains of collective and individual life. And even in a merchant imperialism turned "world system," autonomous and self-fed, national appetites remain.

"Regional empires" such as the United States find themselves, like private-sector multinationals, in competition to enlarge their shares of the market at the expense of the other competitors. And in that merciless competition, Russia is an easy prey.

After literature, as we saw with Rudyard Kipling and Bram Stoker during the era of British imperialism, cinema represents today one of the major vectors of American soft power. But it is far from being the only one. The think tanks, study centers, and experts that keep proliferating through all sorts of foundations with high-flown names provide the raw material feeding the media with commentaries, free analyses and interviews on the hot topics of the moment. Similarly, NGOs have multiplied in numbers and now constitute the bulk of the enrollment of civil society in full conquest of media space and of forums of the UN and other multilateral international organizations such as the Security Council in New York or the Human Rights Council in Geneva.

This civil society, ever since Kofi Annan generously gave it access to the UN, is very aptly named: it is indeed the civilian wing that completes the armed wing of American power, since those organizations are often led by Americans and financed by western governments via an often very opaque network of private foundations, Hungarian-American billionaire George Soros's Open Society Foundation being one of the best known.

The Anti-Russian Lobby

Having dealt with the bases of soft power at work, let us see now how and with whom American Russophobia operates. As Anatol Lieven remarks, "Russophobia today is therefore rooted not in ideological differences but in national hatred of a kind that is sadly too common. In these architectures of hatred, selected or invented historical 'facts' about the 'enemy' nation, its culture, and its racial nature are taken out of context and slotted into prearranged intellectual structures to arraign the unchanging wickedness of the other side. Meanwhile, any counterarguments or memories of the crimes of one's own are suppressed."[26]

Russophobia's origins are diverse, he notes. One of the most important is "the continuing influence of what the political scientist Michael Mandelbaum has called 'residual elites': groups and individuals who rose to prominence during the Cold War and have lacked the flexibility to adapt to a new reality. To these can be added others who have sought to carve out careers by advocating the expansion of U.S. influence into the lands of the former Soviet Union, in direct competition with Russia. Then there are various ethnic lobbies, whose members hate and distrust Russia for historical reasons and whose sole remaining raison d'être is to urge an anti-Russian geopolitical agenda. Finally, there are those individuals who need a great enemy, whether from some collective interest or out of personal psychological need."

The actors of the anti-Russian lobby in the United States are indeed numerous, varied and powerful, whereas the pro-Russian lobby is almost nonexistent in spite of the million Russian emigrants in the United States. Andrei Tsygankov sorts them out into three categories:[27]

1) The military hawks, who want the United States to be the hegemonic power or the world imperial center, and Russia to be downgraded to subject state status. They rally around the *Wall Street Journal*, *The Eurasia Daily Monitor*, the Center for Strategic and International Studies, the Jamestown and Heritage foundations, the Hoover Institution, the Hudson Institute, and the Brookings Institution. They keep denouncing the "imperial ambitions," "energetic blackmail," and "savage brutality" of the Russians.

2) The liberal hawks, for their part, colonize the pages of *The New York Times* and the *Washington Post*. They are as aggressive toward Russia as the former. But, often of Democrat origin, they differ on certain U.S. domestic policy questions. They

are found in the Carnegie Endowment for International Peace, Freedom House, the National Endowment for Democracy, the National Democratic Institute, the Soros Foundation or the German Marshall Fund. Some were even close to the very reactionary Project for a New American Century around Robert Kagan, William Kristol, Senator John McCain and former CIA director James Woolsey. Other personalities such as Madeleine Albright, Richard Holbrooke, Larry Diamond, Stephen Sestanovich, or current vice-president Joe Biden, are better known in Europe. More at ease with words than with weapons, anti-Russian liberal circles have first and foremost mobilized soft power resources against Moscow, notably by financing numerous NGOs created for the purpose and intended to provoke color revolutions as took place successfully in Ukraine in 2004 and 2014, in Georgia in 2003, and in Kirghizstan in 2005.

3) Finally, the clan of East European nationalists, supporting in particular Polish and Baltic nationalisms against Russia. This is how Madeleine Albright came to be seen sitting alongside the Czechs, Paul Goble siding with the Balts, Paula Dobriansky and George Soros with the Western Ukrainians, Zbigniew Brzezinski and Richard Pipes with the Poles, and Stephen Sestanovich against the Serbs. Representatives of this clan initiated the Week of Captive Nations which commemorates each July in Washington the "millions of people chained by communist Russia," and participate also in the elaboration of memory occultation against Russia.[28]

Provided with a very powerful striking force, the anti-Russian American lobby can rely on a very dense network of academic experts everywhere in Europe. In East European countries in particular, numerous researchers have benefitted from scholarships in American universities and have returned home to found institutes and study centers that are as many relays. Fluent in English, they are regularly invited to universities and international conferences and publish in mainstream newspapers thanks to their affiliation to George Soros's Project Syndicate network, which translates and circulates their articles in all European languages.

It was this network that instigated the open letter by 115 Atlanticists published after the Beslan attacks at the end of September 2004.[29] And it was the Central European members of the same network who, in July 2009, published an anti-Russian statement at the initiative of Vaclav Havel and Lech Walesa. This network presented itself as a group of intellectual and former politician friends of the United States "deeply preoccupied by the future quality of United States relations with the countries of Central Europe" after Hillary Clinton and Sergei Lavrov's decision to proceed with "resetting" Russian-American relations.[30]

At every attempt at Russian-American rapprochement, the lobbies of the military hawks and that of the East European nationalists have mobilized to have it fail. It was the case after 2001 as in 2009. Composed of former dissidents and anti-Soviet militants, very popular in the West, the Central and Eastern Europe lobby is indeed a master card in the American Russophobes' game. It is effective with the media and public opinion, which do not trust the hawks, and it serves to put pressure on both American Democrat presidents, often suspected of laxity toward Russia, and on Western European governments, French and German especially, also accused of intending to make a deal with Moscow as soon as they open a dialogue.

The anti-Russian lobby has deployed its attacks in four directions as of the mid-1990s, when it appeared, with Yevgeny Primakov, that Russia was evading the American takeover of her resources via oligarchs and was aspiring to recover full independence and a proper role on the international stage.

Here We Go Again: Despotism and Expansionism

The communist scarecrow having disappeared, the American promoters of the new anti-Russian crusade took out of the dusty closet the old arguments polished during the 19th century and adapted them to the discourses elaborated during the Cold War. We saw how Zbigniew Brzezinski updated the geopolitical vision of an expansionist Russia as a rival to America.

But it was with the second war in Chechnya starting in summer 1999 that American Russophobes found a more popular and less academic cause. For two years preceding the 9/11 terrorist attacks in the US, experts and journalists close to the anti-Russian lobby in Washington denounced without respite Russian "oppression" and the "atrocities" committed by the Russian army in Chechnya. The election to the presidency of Vladimir Putin, billed as a former KGB officer, obviously fueled their arguments.

But when Russia offered her services to President Bush to fight terrorism after 9/11, the attacks against Russia were toned down for a few months, especially as Russia had let the United States and NATO invade Afghanistan in the fall of 2001. But they resumed with a vengeance when, in 2003, Russia refused to let the war against terrorism degenerate into an invasion of Iraq under the fallacious pretext of Saddam Hussein's weapons of massive destruction. The arrest of oligarch Mikhail Khodorkovsky shortly before he was to sell a majority of shares of his Yukos oil company to the Texan ExxonMobil group thoroughly upset the anti-Russian lobby, historically close to American petroleum interests.

American Russophobes' infatuation with the Chechen cause is in reality a wink at history when we remember the passion the English had for the Circassian cause in the 19th century.[31] We find, 150 years apart, the same strategic and energetic support for the Caucasus, with more or less the same actors (Circassians and Chechens are anti-Russian Muslims whereas there are pro-Russian Muslims in the Balkans) and the same methods (logistical support and covert actions, media war, denunciation of Russian barbarity and atrocities).

Like the English with the Circassians in the 19th century, the anti-Russian American lobby defended the independence of Chechnya by supporting former president Aslan Maskhadov who had dissolved parliament and imposed Sharia law while *jihadist* warlord Shamil Basayev invited Al-Qaida representatives to Chechnya to organize the rebel troops and supervise the billeting of hundreds of foreign jihadists.[32] It should be noted that the present Chechen president, Ramzan Kadyrov, has rebuilt Grozny and has applied a sui generis sharia with Moscow approval.

As if by magic, none of the pro-Western experts and journalists who criticized the Kremlin for its policy and the atrocities committed in Chechnya made the link between Chechen Islamists and Al-Qaida after 9/11 or protested against the coalition bombings in Afghanistan or the tortures inflicted on presumed terrorists jailed in Guantánamo, even when some of them were found innocent.[33] The personalities that wrote books on Russian atrocities in Chechnya have never written books on Allied atrocities in Afghanistan and in Iraq. And yet, in both cases, it concerned the same Islamists.

The third angle of attack of the anti-Russian lobby bore on Russia's "congenital authoritarianism," attacks on freedom of the press, and on human rights. As the very Russophobic president of the American Committee for the Extension of NATO, Bruce P. Jackson, wrote, it was not fair to say "that democracy was regressing in Russia;" rather, it "had been assassinated."[34] For her part, *Economist* journalist Anne Appelbaum, author of a book on the new Iron Curtain as well as of a very recent and controversial history of the Gulag, very seriously stated that "Looking back, we may also one day see 2004 as the year when a new iron curtain descended across Europe, dividing the continent not through the center of Germany but along the eastern Polish border."[35]

The thesis of the "authoritarian tyrant" was mostly developed to justify the color revolutions against "neo-despot" Putin. Various pro-West Russians of the former Yeltsin team, or even of Putin's, such as former economic advisor Andrey Illarionov, former chess champion Gary Kasparov, former prime minister Mikhail Kasyanov, former vice-prime minister Boris Nemtsov[36] or the first harbingers of the Ukrainian and Georgian color revolutions Yulya Tymoshenko, Viktor Yushchenko, and Mikheil Saakashvili, helped by Vice-President Dick Cheney, John McCain, Hillary Clinton, and various highly placed members of the Bush Administration, tried to impose that agenda and that avatar of the old tale of the fight between freedom and despotism.

In 2005, John McCain and Hillary Clinton lobbied, albeit unsuccessfully, to have the Nobel Prize for Peace attributed to Mikheil Saakashvili and Viktor Yushchenko. At the same time, Hillary Clinton made inflamed speeches in an effort to convince Congress to adopt an Act permitting the wearing of a Cold War Victory Medal dedicated to honoring the contribution of Americans who served their nation admirably during the Cold War.[37] The International Republican Institute and the National Endowment for Democracy were at the vanguard of that effort to enhance anti-Russian militancy, disseminated by numerous NGOs active in Eastern Europe in the training of executives for the opposition, such as Freedom House, and in human rights in the West, such as Human Rights Watch.

In 2004, and then after Dmitri Medvedev's election in 2008, anti-Putin and anti-Medvedev articles blossomed all over the American press, comparing Putin to Mussolini, Pinochet, Stalin, and even Hitler. On cue, various western leaders have done the same, starting with Hillary Clinton in the spring of 2014. Or, like the *Washington Post*, mocking Medvedev's "Potemkin election," not to mention the "Putin's Mini-Me (or Not?)" of *The New York Times*, though Western media do not dwell on the fact that the Bush family presented a candidate to the presidency of the United States for the third time in twenty-five years and the Clinton family for the second time in fifteen years, with the argument that it was "her turn".

Addressing again Russia's purported atavistic expansionism, Conservative editorialist William Safire was one of the staunchest defenders of the security of the United States threatened by Russian "expansionism" as early as 1994, only three years after Russia relinquished control over 40% of her territories and of her population! He saw in it a "window of opportunity" for the extension of NATO to Eastern Europe, to the Baltic countries, and to Ukraine, because Russia "is authoritarian at heart and expansionist by habit" and "weak and preoccupied with its own revival." The time to act was now, as "such a move would be an insufferable provocation to a superpower."

In 2004 he renewed his prescription before a NATO summit: "NATO must not lose its original purpose: to contain the Russian bear."[38]

In the meantime, indeed, after his having facilitated their lie on Saddam Hussein's non-existent weapons of massive destruction, the hawks had succeeded in getting rid of Secretary of State Colin Powell, the last moderate voice in the Bush Administration. In 2008, influential senator Richard Lugar had a US$10 million credit voted to prepare Georgia to enter NATO.[39]

Regarding armament and development of the armed forces, the hawks are determined to ensure American nuclear and conventional supremacy. In 2005, Victoria Nuland, then American ambassador to NATO and former advisor to Dick Cheney, who later would be seen alongside the Maidan demonstrators in 2014 as Obama's assistant secretary of State for Eurasian Affairs, and taking a leading role in nominating "Yats" as the new Ukrainian head of government, was militating for a new American rapid intervention force able to operate everywhere, from Africa to the Middle East and beyond.[40]

The same actors had already succeeded in convincing the Bush Administration to leave the Anti-Ballistic Missile Treaty in 2001 and they pushed very hard during the 1990s and 2000s for the deployment of the antimissile shield, allegedly directed against Iran, to protect Poland and the various Central European countries.[41] In March 2012, the Republican candidate for the presidency, Mitt Romney, declared that "Russia is our number one geopolitical enemy."

The final theme abundantly developed by American Russophobes during the last decade is Russia's energy blackmail, a theme which became very popular after the arrest of Mikhail Khodorkovsky in October 2003. In the early 2000s, Khodorkovsky became close with the Bush family and the Carlyle group as well as to American petroleum interests: his Yukos group formed alliances with American ExxonMobil and Chevron Texaco, which were supposed to buy the majority of the Yukos shares in 2003.

The sale of Yukos shares to the level of US$20 billion

would have placed one of the major natural resource Russian companies under the control of American investors. Due to the influence of his American friends, oligarch Mikhail Khodorkovsky was rapidly transformed into an icon of freedom of speech who was being attacked by the Russian government. Thousands of articles were written about him during the ten years of his detention.

Defending Oligarchs to Defame Russia

And so it went, too, for Boris Berezovsky, another oligarch who had initially supported the election of Vladimir Putin, believing he could make of him a devoted puppet. Like Mikhail Khodorkovsky's, his trajectory is emblematic of the first-generation oligarchs.

Under pressure from the Russian people, who were very hostile to oligarchs, the new president launched a period of fighting against corruption, which some qualified as anti-corruption populism, or "hunting the rich down." Putin had police and fiscal investigations opened into the dealings of several suspicious self-made billionaires, including Khodorkovsky and Berezovsky. Russian justice accused the latter of large-scale fraud, notably in the controversial privatization of the Russian airline Aeroflot, and of political corruption.

After resigning from his mandate as a member of the Duma in July 2000, Berezovsky exiled himself to London in October 2001; he was to live alternately in the British capital and on his properties at Cap d'Antibes on the Azure Coast. Under Russian government pressure, he sold several of his holdings. In early 2002, he was dispossessed of his shares in the ORT channel and, in May, the Kremlin took over his other television channel, TV6.

In July 2004, *Forbes* American Moscow correspondent Paul Klebnikov, who had written several articles on Berezovsky's alleged criminal activities, was assassinated in the Russian capital. Klebnikov had published a book in 2002, *The Godfather of the Kremlin: Boris Berezovsky and the Looting of Russia*, in which he presented the billionaire as a genuine mafia godfather who had contributed to the pillage of his country. In 2003, thanks to the links created in Chechnya following his investigation of Berezovsky, he had published a second book in Russian, entitled *Conversation with a Barbarian: Interviews with a Chechen Commandant on Crime and Islam*. He was also preparing a series of articles on millionaire mullahs and the links between Islamism and mafias. Those works had little success.

Berezovsky, from his London exile, began to denounce President Putin's "authoritarian drifts" as a way to divert attention from the crimes he was accused of, earning headlines in the Western press, which had nothing to say about his relationship with an emissary of Chechen separatists, Akhmed Zakaiev, who was under a Russian warrant for creation of armed groups and faced 302 charges for murder and kidnapping. Similarly, his links with Alexander Litvinenko, a defector from the Russian secret services, inspired many articles in the Western press.

When Litvinenko died of polonium poisoning in November 2006, the entire press suspected vengeance from the Kremlin, but offered no proof, and ignored the more plausible thesis of a settling of scores among Mafiosi, just as it had remained largely mute about all the charges against Boris Berezovsky and embezzlement in relation to his companies LogoVAZ and Andava. The latter, registered in Lausanne, had "centralized" the earnings of Aeroflot offices around the world and levied hefty commissions. In the 2000s, Berezovsky was also sued by Brazilian and French justice. He committed suicide in 2013.

Berezovsky's history is interesting because it illustrates, like that of Khodorkovsky but in a more fiendish way, the history of Russia and of the 1990s and 2000s oligarchs, and how the attention the West has paid to them is oriented: booming and favorable when they are opposed to the Kremlin, discreet and compliant when the facts established about the crimes they are accused of become embarrassing.

Thus it is remarkable that Klebnikov's assassination did not make headlines in the western press for weeks, contrary to that of Anna Politkovskaya two years later. And yet, by investigating the various Chechen and western mafias at the risk of his life, Klebnikov had had at least as much merit. But it was indeed difficult to accuse the Kremlin of his murder, and his investigations did not fit the dominant anti-Putin prejudices.

The frustration of the American oil lobby after the failure of the Yukos takeover bid immediately triggered an unprecedented mobilization of the anti-Russian lobby in Western media. Polemics followed polemics throughout the decade, every time an oil or gas pipeline project was considered to bypass Ukraine via the Caspian, Turkey, Georgia, and Bulgaria, or the Baltic Sea, or as soon as a conflict broke out about Ukraine's unpaid gas bills, a country where oligarchs were blithely syphoning the gas in transit.

A *Financial Times* article compared the government takeover of Yukos to a "syndication of the Gulag;" Brzezinski described Putin as "the Moscow Mussolini," while Russophobe lobby websites outbid one another in the denunciation of the Russian president's alleged authoritarianism and autocratic propensities. Swedish Anders Aslund, one of the signatories of the Open Letter of the 115 after the Beslan tragedy, close to conservative Carl Bildt, was so virulent he was even forced to leave the Carnegie Foundation where he worked to join another liberal think tank, the Peterson Institute.[42]

Those attempts at pressure had no effect on Russia, which, following the boycott of persons and goods decreed in summer 2014 after the Ukrainian crisis, turned to China and Asia and abandoned the Southstream pipeline project. One might have thought that the terrorist attacks in Paris on January 7, 2015 should make the United States pay more attention to Russian warnings about Islamic terrorism. Russia has been fighting for twenty years against Chechen Islamists, the Al-Qaida networks, and other caliphate projects in the Caucasus. So she knows well the spheres of influence of Islamic terrorism. However insofar as the fact that the West has been covertly assisting jihadists (in the guise of "rebels") against Syria a secret which is now widely known (see Hawaiian Congresswoman Tulsi Gabbard's bill to Stop Funding of Terrorism)[1] the West will henceforth find it more difficult to convince its public opinion that overall, these movements, which belong to the same galaxy of Sunni fundamentalism as ISIS, are innocent pro-independence rebels.

PART III

COGNITIVE MANIPULATION

| Chapter Nine |

SEMANTICS AND ANTI-RUSSIAN NEWSPEAK

"Words can be like tiny doses of arsenic: you swallow them without noticing, they seem to have no effect, and yet after some time, the toxic effect is felt."
Victor Klemperer, *Lingua Tertii Imperii*
(The Third Reich's Language)

"The problem with the 21st century press is that there is much propaganda and few journalists."
Anonymous

How does cognitive manipulation, or rather cognitive distortion, work? The term "manipulation" is not entirely appropriate as it suggests perpetually active malicious intent, some sort of journalistic plot, when in reality journalists equally fall victim to the stereotypes they reproduce. Often they are not conscious of it, just like NGO militants who are persuaded that they are fighting "for freedom and democracy" and the defense "of ethnic minorities and of the Russian people oppressed by their leaders."

Word Choice and Semantic Distortion

Speech analysis is an ancient academic discipline and there are many researches on the analysis of journalistic practices regarding Russia. This is not the place to carry out an exhaustive examination of them, but our purpose is to show, through a few familiar practices, how the anti-Russian discourse is built in the media and academic studies, even though in a more abstruse way in the case of the latter, thanks to the use of muddling jargon.[1]

The simplest technique to disqualify Russia rests on the choice of words. In the coverage of the Ukrainian conflict, quoting "Donbass separatist rebels" does not have the same signification at all as letting the "anti-coup resistance" speak. "Annexation of Crimea by Russia" does not have the same connotation as "Crimeans choose to return to the Russian motherland." Yet they speak to the same men and the same reality. It is not neutral to talk about the "self-proclaimed republic of Donetsk" and the "legitimate government of Kiev," about "Russian-armed terrorists" as opposed to "soldiers of the regular Ukrainian army." Same thing for "President Porochenko" versus "Putin the autocrat." And what of victims that are always "Ukrainian" and of aggressors that are always "Russian" or "pro-Russian," as if, by some sort of surrealistic fiction, all war shells came from the pro-Russian camp and fell on poor Ukrainian victims exclusively?

Word choice is thus crucial, as it aims at either creating agreement if not complicity, as it concerns NATO and US supported regime changes, or on the contrary engendering distrust, as it concerns anti-Russian sentiment in public opinions. Wording, *Sprachregelung*, the controlled use of words, is thus the first step in the elaboration of a truncated and tailored media discourse. It is in principle the prerogative of communications professionals whose first task consists in producing the elements of language and the wordings that will be ceaselessly repeated until they impregnate normal press parlance, as we have seen in the display of stock phrases dominating the journalistic coverage of the Ukrainian conflict.

An analysis of the wording of news since the beginning of the conflict—and this is valid also for all the others—will quickly reveal the moment when communications agencies specializing in the shaping of the discourse got into the act to police the language of the international press and freeze satisfactory turns of phrase. The dozens of communication specialists put by the American government at the disposal of the Ukrainian government right after the outbreak of the conflict have thus very well succeeded in formatting the anti-Russian "newspeak" of the Western media.

Until the referendum on Crimean independence and the Odessa massacre, one can see the journalists groping about, experimenting with formulas, and hesitating still to side with one camp or the other. The Russians were already largely stigmatized and the referendum was criticized, but one perceived the difficulty the press faced in totally discrediting a popular consultation. Similarly in the Odessa drama, the press took up the Ukrainian nationalists' propaganda but still wobbled a bit when learning with certainty that it was the pro-Russians who were burnt alive. However, thanks to learned work on the use of adjectives, initial hesitations were rapidly replaced by a binary, quasi-totalitarian discourse reflecting the themes of "good Ukrainians" vs. "Russian and pro-Russian baddies."

As formulation specialist Alice Krieg-Planque points out, "the media have in the fabrication of formulas a publicizing role, but they appear more frequently as circulation operators than as creators or initiators."[2] Who then is the initiator? Communications organizations and public relation agencies chartered by governments and firms:

> The sound bites, the arguments, the language elements, the question and answer sessions are, as many practices, thought up in political professional communication in the hope of having the same formulations circulate throughout the media.[3]

Liberal philosophers like to talk of the "marketplace of ideas" wherein the consumer-citizen stocks up as in a supermarket. Except that the marketplace of ideas, like most capitalist markets, ignores perfect competition and is in reality deeply plowed, harrowed, restricted and infested by marketing specialists who try to impose very specific "brands" and formulas to the detriment of others. Under the smooth surface of media competition and freedom of expression, the marketplace of ideas is in reality thoroughly circumscribed and distorted, often transforming it into a monologue to the benefit of a dominant entity.

As an example of readymade "language elements" meant for the press produced by communication specialists, let us cite the instructions for dealing with the press or inquiries in general, provided by the "Israel Project 2009. Global Language Dictionary"[4] since it provides an excellent illustration of how this works. The "Dictionary" provides a catalogue of formulas and answers to use in all circumstances when a foreign journalist asks questions on Palestinians, the bombing of Gaza, the colonization of occupied territories, the segregation wall, etc. It even instructs on how to talk to the American Left on campuses or what lessons should be drawn from Obama's language. Also detailed are 25 important rules in terms of political communication. To convince a western audience, it advises, it is essential to show empathy for both camps and to clearly distinguish the Palestinian people from Hamas (today's foe to be brought down).

Thus it is acceptable to say that "everybody makes mistakes, including Israel," and that "we want to build a better future for all, including the Palestinians," but you must never say that "Israel allows the Palestinians to do or not to do this or that." Chapter 4 teaches how to "isolate Hamas supported by Iran and present it as an obstacle to peace." Chapter 6 explains how to show that "in Gaza Israel has only sought to defend her right to legitimate defense and defendable borders."

Readers are advised to never let their interlocutors speak of the "right of Palestinians to return to their lands, but [must] correct them to stigmatize the 'right to confiscation' the Arab countries exercised on the properties of the Jews forced to flee from them after 1948." Regarding the Israeli Palestinians expelled from their homes after 1948, it advises them to explain that "they have the right to live in a State with their people. Yes, they have that right. They have the right to have a State of Palestine. ... The idea is to have a Jewish State for the Jews and a Palestinian State for the Palestinians. But the influx of hundreds of thousands of Palestinians into Israel, into a Jewish State, is totally unacceptable."

In each situation, to each difficult question, the document suggests the words to use, the arguments to develop, and the sentences to never pronounce. This is quite remarkable as an exposeé of press manipulation. And the techniques it recommends are all the more successful as nothing in them is false. The facts are respected, the reality is not negated. But the simple art of verbal dodging and counterattack, the meticulous choice of formulas, make of it a masterful piece of instruction on the art of manipulated communication. To convince, there is no need to lie, but simply line up facts, forward arguments, choose the right words. This is how, little by little, the image of the good guy is elaborated in the international press, and just as surely, the image of the bad guy.

This is exactly how it went for the anti-Russian discourse during the arrest of Khodorkovsky in 2003, the Georgian War in 2008, the Sochi Olympic Games, or the Ukrainian crisis. All Georgian, American, East European, or Ukrainian official pronouncements were submitted to a "language discipline" carefully elaborated to have maximum impact on the media and to favor the Western camp to the detriment of the Russian party. The press communiques, the spokespersons' declarations, the interviews of officials, the "free" opinion pieces abundantly published in the op-ed pages of the international mainstream press under the pen of experts of prestigious institutes, the caricatures of cartoonists—all distilled the same phrases, the same subliminal gospel: Putin is the new Hitler and Russia wants to invade her weak neighbors.

Selection of Sources

Another favored technique of cognitive distortion is the selection of sources. It consists in favoring some sources while ignoring the contradicting views of others, even as presenting the appearance of the greatest objectivity. Indeed, through this process the meaning of any given speech can be inversed and entirely negative texts can be produced reflecting the opposite view or, reversely, uniformly positive responses can be produced for the camp to be privileged. This is the case in the coverage of China: a huge preponderance of Western articles about China talk of nothing but environmental problems and human rights, thus creating the feeling that China is a huge cesspit in which a billion and a half individuals live in constant violation of their fundamental rights. Who notices that Chinese dissidents and NGO representatives denouncing corruption and human rights violations hog the quotes in Western media—while representing maybe 0.001% of the population? Their criticisms no doubt have some truth and deserve to be taken into consideration. But how to measure the culpability of China if we do not know contrary facts such as, for example, the massive Chinese efforts to turn to alternative energy sources?[5]

The phenomenon is even more massive in the case of Russia. Practically all experts quoted on Russia, the Beslan tragedy, the elections, Chechnya, the Ukraine War, the effects of sanctions, are persons that work for American or European think tanks, NGO executives financed by American or European funds, Ukrainian government officials, soldiers affiliated to some NATO organization disguised as "Center for European Democracy and Security," "Institute for Press Freedom and Human Rights," or "Centre d'analyse pour la paix."[6] Those organizations and experts are well established in Moscow, Brussels, Berlin, Paris, London, and Washington, and colonize newspapers that keep asking for their opinions, and feed them with free reports, analysis and commentaries.

When by chance a Russian is quoted, in most cases it

is an individual who works for a western foundation and who consequently provides a very pro-Western vision very critical of the Kremlin. *The Moscow Times*, Moscow's Anglophone daily, specializes in an ultra-selective choice of sources and authors. It has a circulation of 35,000 and is offered for free at venues frequented by English-speaking foreigners.[7] As pointed out by Stephen Cohen, intellectuals close to the Russian government position or simply having an independent vision are mercilessly kept out of the Western media due to their purported propagation of "propaganda," whatever their nationality.[8]

If you read an American or European so-called quality daily, you will notice that practically all sources quoted on the Ukrainian war either come from the Ukrainian government or the Ukrainian army, or are Western military experts close to NATO or Kiev. These experts and commentators, all cut from the same cloth, are quoted at length, whereas the chance Russian denial, when it is mentioned, is summed up in a sentence at the end of the article, by which time it is likely that 90% of the readers have stopped reading. A key activity is headline writing—that alone can do the trick and even deflect the attention of those who go on to read it from the actual content of the article.

The interviews too are largely biased: they systematically approach anti-Russian elements, and the questions asked are sympathetic—meant to allow them to justify their views, without the interference of any critique, or event contextualization which might expose causation. Russian personalities are almost never asked for their views.

True journalistic work would consist in being specific about the choice of sources and transparent about the pedigree of the person quoted. And indeed, as the Israelis always demand, presenting a balancing view that would shine a different light on what is being claimed. It is not an innocuous fact that Victoria Nuland, the American undersecretary of state who supported the Maidan revolt and chose Arseniy Yatsenyuk as prime minister of Ukraine, "Yats" as she calls him, is the spouse of one of the staunchest American Russophobic military hawks, Robert Kagan, leader of the neoconservatives.[9] And yet no mainstream medium ever provides information of this kind.

As an example, let us quote the article John Laughland published in *The Guardian* of September 8, 2004 which provides the kind of information rarely cited by the anti-Russian press. He pointed out that most anti-Russian propaganda at the time of Beslan came from a mysterious American Committee for Peace in Chechnya, since then renamed American Committee for Peace in the Caucasus (ACPC).

> The list of the self-styled 'distinguished Americans' who are its members is a rollcall of the most prominent neoconservatives who so enthusiastically support the 'war on terror'.
> They include Richard Perle, the notorious Pentagon adviser; Elliott Abrams of Iran-Contra fame; Kenneth Adelman, the former US ambassador to the UN who egged on the invasion of Iraq by predicting it would be 'a cakewalk'; Midge Decter, biographer of Donald Rumsfeld and a director of the rightwing Heritage Foundation; Frank Gaffney of the militarist Centre for Security Policy; Bruce Jackson, former US military intelligence officer and one-time vice-president of Lockheed Martin, now president of the US Committee on NATO; Michael Ledeen of the American Enterprise Institute, a former admirer of Italian fascism and now a leading proponent of regime change in Iran; and R. James Woolsey, the former CIA director who is one of the leading cheerleaders behind George Bush's plans to re-model the Muslim world along pro-US lines.[10]

With such an introduction, the fighters for democracy in Russia and for freedom of the Chechen people take on an altogether different coloration. And seem less credible. For all that, it would be the naked truth.

The same manipulative discretion applies to the NGOs. Civil society and the NGOs have been praised so much that it has become taboo to question them on their functioning and their financing. And yet nothing is more antidemocratic and more opaque than an NGO.[11] The media monitor—mercilessly and quite rightly—politicians' money, but NGOs are never questioned about their choice of targets and sources of financing, which might shed light on the former. Most of those that fight for human rights or freedom of expression are financed by private or public Western organizations with very definite interests. Which explains why they so often observe tasteful discretion with "friends" and allies while being so vindictive toward governments deemed hostile, in Venezuela, Russia, China, or Iran.

This is unfortunately the sort of inclination that was noticed for the NGOs that loudly denounced attacks on LGBT rights before the Sochi Games while keeping quiet as it related to Saudi Arabia, for example. Similarly, during the diversionary attack led by the American hawks of the Brookings Institution in early February 2015 advocating the selling of American weapons to Ukraine, there was not a single newspaper that asked who those "experts" were, where their interests lay and why they published their report at such a time, when the Ukrainian offensive against the separatists was turning into a rout after the fall of the Donetsk airport. Was that initiative linked to the publication, a few days earlier, in the international mainstream press of a statement co-signed by George Soros and Bernard-Henri Lévy calling for the rescue of the new Ukraine and for increased financial support from the European Union for the new regime in Kiev, portrayed as pro-European reformers desperately needing financial aid to survive Russian assaults?[12]

Discourse specialist Teun van Dijk has described well the impact arbitrary selection and biased presentation of sources or facts can have on the description of reality. The trick is to slightly alter the facts without distorting them:

1) Highlight our qualities and good actions; 2) highlight their defects and bad actions; 3) mitigate our defects and bad actions; and 4) mitigate their qualities and good actions.[13]

So it is no surprise that a protest by a Russian soldier's mother receives immense attention, with her interview being heard over all radio and television channels in the West, while the mothers of Ukrainian soldiers protesting against the Kiev authorities are never interviewed, as per the strategy of inflating Russian defects and mitigating indeed, omitting those of the parties the West supports. Negative accounts of "separatist rebels" are legion, whereas accounts on the battalions of Ukrainian extreme-rightwing nationalists equipped with the most sophisticated American arsenal are cruelly lacking. When a European daily reporter goes to Crimea, it is not to meet Russian Crimeans who form 90% of the population, but to narrate the misery of "oppressed Tartars." And when he has done the rounds of the demarcation line with one of the two generals in charge of watching over it for the OSCE,[14] it isn't with the Russian that he speaks, but only with the Ukrainian.[15]

The same is true as it concerns the Russian economy, the effect of sanctions, the fall in the price of petroleum, capital flight, the collapse of the ruble, or the failure of a rocket launch in Baikonur. Only personalities who are known to be critical are quoted to make sure that the objective of inflating Russian failures and minimizing their successes be achieved. This is a black mark against journalists and the media who profess to thrive on quality and balance. Because if the choice of discriminatory formulas is often initiated from the outside and aimed at journalists used as channels, the choice of sources, on the other hand, is not at all imposed and is up to the editorial staff.

Let us point out as well that sources can be selected in both senses, to blacken the opposition and to restore one's own camp's image. It is just a matter of choosing the right person and asking adequate questions, as we saw with José Manuel Barroso's interviews.

In that perspective, positive progress is seldom publicized. The radar of the Western press infallibly spots the defects of the Russian system, never its successes.

Framing and Factual Distortion

The third most utilized technique is of unfair reframing of content through the arbitrary selection of facts, of the starting point or causes of an event. This very common bias is much more insidious as it demands of the reader or listener deep knowledge of the situation and of the sequencing of the facts. It also plays very much on readers' incapacity to remember, taken up as they are by the worries of daily life and confused by the ceaseless stream of news.

One of the great ploys consists in dating the start of events in a way that favors one camp rather than the other. The process is usually innocuous as the choice of a starting date is always controversial.

Let us take the case of Ukraine. All those who have followed the course of events will have been struck by how the anti-Russian mainstream media have gotten into the habit of dating the Ukrainian conflict from March 2014, that is, from when the "annexation" of Crimea, as they call it, took place. The Maidan events have almost entirely disappeared from the dating of the crisis for the simple reason that, by having the Crimean and Donbass crisis dated back to February, they would have to point out that the new regime in Kiev resulted from a coup imposed by the street and that the first decision taken by the putsch leaders was to abolish the teaching of the Russian language in Ukraine, even though it is spoken by 45% of the population. Whereas by having the crisis only go back to the annexation of Crimea by Russia, the sole responsibility for the crisis is pinned on Russia.

This form of distortion plays much on the time factor. In most of the events mentioned in this book, like the crash of Flight MH17 over Ukraine, the first to get their views out is the party most likely to determine the future discourse. This is the reason why, the very evening of the crash, a torrent of declarations accusing the Russians without any proof was unleashed at once by Ukrainian and American officials. When there is a crisis, the need for information is such that the media are ready to publish anything that feels more or less of an official nature, whatever the contents. Those who make those declarations are thus sure they will be published. By this means, pro-Western and anti-Russian speech is systematically privileged: all it takes is to speak loudly and to speak first. Timing is crucial, and all communications specialists know it, as it makes it possible to point the press and public opinion in the "right" direction. Once the bad guy has been designated, thanks to a hail of accusations, the general public absorbs the conclusions, and making it change its mind is very difficult.[16]

Communications specialists are past masters at not only formulation but also reaction speed: the communique that arrives first in all likelihood will be quoted and repeated in a continuous loop before an alternative discourse can hope to temper the first version.

This is the reason why announcements of Russian pseudo-invasions of Donbass can be and were repeated at the rhythm of one per week on average. The previous one is already forgotten, and by the time the separatists issue a denial, the harm is done. For the MH17 crash, information was controlled by real pros and the camp of the Donbass insurgents was practically unable to do anything, even though the facts were far from clear. Same thing with the timing of the Maidan events: the results of the Canadian investigation[17] on the origins of the shots, which implicitly implicate extreme-rightwing commandos, were wiped off the media because they came far too late and none of them wanted to go back on their own versions of events that "everybody has forgotten."

The relation to history is also often open to doubt. Reminding that Crimea has been Russian since the end of the 18th century, that is, since the time when Corsica was incorporated into France and fifty years before Belgium became "Belgian," to quote only these two examples, is not included in the explanations given for the reunification of Crimea with Russia in 2014.[18] "Leave history alone," pro-Westerners say, although they do not hesitate to point out that Crimea is Ukrainian because Russia signed an agreement to that effect in 1991.

Another example of manipulative reformatting is that of the eviction of Kosovo from the chain of events. Kosovar separatism, which triggered bloody fighting in the 1990s, was portrayed as a "war of liberation" against Serb oppression and its independence has never been subjected to a democratic vote in Serbia; those events are simply not taken into consideration. Don't mix things up, we are told by those who still insist on Crimea reintegrating in Ukraine so that the inviolability of borders be respected.

Another example of diversion: the extra attention brought on the military situation in Ukraine, the alleged "exactions" of the pro-Russians, and the striking discretion, if executions are at issue, related to President Obama's visit to Saudi Arabia for the King's funeral in January 2015 where the deceased, whom he went to honor, had just had seven persons decapitated—three and a half times as many as the Islamic State during the same period—in the kingdom's public squares during that same month of January. The Western media kept conspicuously silent about that, while the decapitation of two Japanese journalists hogged their headlines for two weeks. In the recurrent crises with Ukraine over gas since the first color revolution in 2004, the story frames are always focused on Russia. It is Russia that allegedly "blackmails" poor Ukraine by "turning off the gas tap." With the exception of Xinhua, which has explicitly evoked Ukraine as the source of the energy blackmail, all the Western media have accused the Kremlin.

> The methods of gangsterism and blackmail now being used by Gazprom are reminiscent of the Soviet era. ... The West has to tell Russia that, plainly and simply its conduct is unacceptable if it wishes to remain part of the club of civilised nations. ... [F]or Russia to use its natural resources as a means

of behaving ruthlessly and unscrupulously with its neighbours is a medieval tactic that cannot be condoned in the modern world.[19]

So, blackmailing Russian into selling gas without being paid for it is considered as a legitimate tactic in the fight for independence and democracy but as an egregious medieval tactic if Russia cuts the gas tap because Ukraine doesn't pay for its purchases! That the Ukrainian oligarchs and governments hostile to Moscow siphon the transiting gas without paying the bill is an issue which is never mentioned in the western press. Ditto for the Khodorkovsky affair; it is always the maneuvering of the corrupt government of the *siloviki* (security forces), who want to monopolize oil profits, that is highlighted, never the fact that what is at stake is preserving a natural resource which was destined to be sold cheaply to the Americans (who, as is well known, redistribute their oil revenues to the poor).

In the 2004 Beslan tragedy, the Western press found itself trapped. It had been accusing the Kremlin of being behind the attacks that destroyed several buildings in Moscow in 1999, and, like Anna Politkovskaya, had supported the demands of Chechen rebels "savagely repressed by the Russian army," but faced great embarrassment when those same rebels took a thousand children as hostages in Beslan and even began to execute them. During the first 48 hours, many newspapers were thus constrained willy-nilly to favor the Russian government and security forces. But that did not last. After two days, almost all had turned against the Russian authorities, accused of brutality, disinformation, and secrecy.[20]

Another form of factual distortion consists in operating cognitive amalgams which are degrading for the opposite camp, in other words fomenting negative stereotypes of persons and their country. For example, let us cite the works of Danish researcher Peter Ulf Moller who has identified eight of them: 1) the Russians are strong and resistant; 2) they are ignorant and backward; 3) they are superstitious and believe superficially; 4) they are coarse and have no manners; 5) they are submissive and live like slaves; 6) they are corrupters and liars; 7) they are dirty and stink; and 8) they have a penchant for immoderate drinking.[21] And indeed, you seldom can read portraits of Russians in which one or more of these qualifications are not present or insert in the discourse the image of "the barbarian at the door of Europe."

It also distorts facts to ceaselessly suggest that Russia started the Georgia war in August 2008, when investigations of the facts have established the contrary and the more honest newspapers have acknowledged it.[22] The idea is to insinuate that Russia is always the aggressor, that she has done the same in Ukraine and in the other conflicts where she was involved in the past, and therefore will do so again in the future. The objective is to imbed in the public mind the notion of Russia as an expansionist aggressor.

The tactic of factual distortion consolidated by repetition is particularly flagrant in the coverage of the Ukrainian crisis by Western mainstream newspapers. It explains why they keep multiply repeating, against common sense, that Russia is "invading" Ukraine. Indeed, if Russia invaded Ukraine last month, why would she invade her all over again? Either she is already there, and there is no need to invade any longer (and indeed, in which case, it would be all up with Ukraine), or she is not there and everything that has been published before is false. But that has not prevented the Western press to continue to announce an "invasion" of Ukraine by Russian armored cars or troops innumerable times in less than a year! At the very least, this means that there was wrong information and proven nonsense in all of the prior times!

On the ravages of anti-Russian autosuggestion on lackadaisical journalists, the Swiss website <arrêtsurinfo.ch> tells the story of a press agency dispatch taken up on the Newsnet platform of Swiss newspapers announcing an upsurge of violence and an umpteenth invasion of Russian tanks in Donetsk. The article was reinforced by the insert title "Renfort de 700 chars russes" (700 Russian tanks reinforcement) and a sentence mentioned confirmation by "several observers." An investigation showed that it was an "error": the observed tanks were not Russian but Ukrainian and it was about maybe—the suppressed question mark having been reinstated—the alleged *presence* of 700 Russian soldiers. Interestingly, announcements of Russian invasions in the Donbass were continuously being made in the media in 2015. If all Russian tanks and soldiers announced since the beginning of the conflict were added, half of the Russian army would ostensibly be found in the Donbass. Confirmation of this might be possible via NATO's satellites and spy planes that watch over the zone, which they surely would have provided had they actually seen anything.[23]

From a Western viewpoint, it is essential to distort facts and denounce nonexistent Russian invasions,[24] to ceaselessly legitimize in the eyes of public opinion certain profoundly illegitimate actions, like the Maidan coup which installed a new government against the Russian-speaking citizens of Ukraine. Indeed, knowing that the Ukrainian crisis is the fruit of a putsch and of treason (non-respect of the February 21 agreement signed by European ministers and ex-president Yanukovych which provided for legal elections within twelve months), the Ukrainian government suffers from a stigma which its subsequent improvised elections did not erase.

Insofar as Western democracies must take domestic and global public opinion into account, they typically seek to prove that they are not the aggressor before launching a war. Or invent false pretexts to justify same, like the so-called mass destruction weapons of Saddam Hussain to justify Iraq invasion in 2003. This means that, again typically, war can only take place when two conditions are fulfilled: proving that one acts to defend oneself and claiming that one acts to promote the good (peace, democracy, people's liberation). This is why any Western war is so much in need of humanitarian benediction before it can be triggered.

Yesterday's monarchs, representatives of God on earth, had to prove that they made war without having countered the will of God, and so they had bishops bless their armies. Today, it is the humanitarians who give their blessings and guarantee that the right to intervene is properly exercised in the name of the sacred duties of promoting peace and democracy. Humanitarian unction has replaced sacerdotal unction, and ritual invocations of human rights; lingering accusations of barbarity have replaced the old sermons on the civilizing mission developed by imperialists in the 19th century.

In this spirit, repeating tirelessly that the Russians are invading Ukraine is meant to convince the public that the aggressor is indeed Russia and to reconfirm the legitimacy of a very fragile Ukrainian government and its very questionable Western support. Without that need to legitimize, how can one to explain such a distortion of the facts? It makes it easy to understand why many editorialists insist so much on claiming and reiterating that Russia started the 2008 Ossetia war. The legitimation chain must not be broken. In emphasis, the Ukrainian government hired as a minister former Georgian, pro-western president Saakashvili, in an effort to ensure that all the pieces of the puzzle held together.[25]

But the Western press does not limit itself to geopolitics or issues of war and peace, in its effort to warp the public image of Russia. Rather, concurrently, it carries on a disparaging discussion of a wide gamut of Russian policies. Not a single aspect of public life escapes the caustic attention of the media: education is necessarily "ethnocentric," immigration "restrictive," religion "discriminating" vis-à-vis the non-Orthodox, corruption "rampant," the condition of homosexuals "appalling," the legal system "inefficient and corrupt."[26]

The tactic of lying also plays an important role in statecraft. All governments lie for reasons of State, and most citizens either don't know or put up with it. But it is important to know which side lies most, or more importantly, which lies are most dangerous for the world. The game of "it ain't me lying, it's Vladimir" is an essential dimension of geopolitics, the most hypocritical being the winner until found out. We could see this game in the Ukraine and Syria events during which Putin is accused of being a liar when denying Russian military support to the Donbass rebellion (as opposed to Russian invasion), or who was complicit in the shooting of Malaysian fight MH17 or the bombing of hospitals in East-Aleppo. But then, on the West side, we have George W. Bush claiming Iraq had weapons of mass destruction, leading to the 2003 invasion which would ultimately destroy Iraq, or Obama who, when denial (lying) fails, seeks to justify NSA global surveillance.[27] How many western newspapers have dared to call President Obama a *wrongdoer* because he excused torture? Or demanded that he return his Nobel Peace Prize for massacring thousands of innocent civilians with drones?

All the art of the court editorialists—for there are court journalists as there used to be court poets in royal times—consists in structuring a *logos* in conformity with the dominant *doxa* by adroitly mixing the various forms of discourse distortion, altering words and facts just enough to make them fit into the mold so that the seams don't show at first glance. This deformation is the greatest danger journalism is exposed to and it explains why, beyond competition from the internet, so many readers are losing interest in the formatted production of the mainstream media.

The "Us" and "Them" Dichotomy

The writing of a press agency dispatch and an audiovisual commentary are not cold exercises devoid of affect. On the contrary, by the tone and words chosen, the images and metaphors used, they try to create a feeling of proximity, human warmth, an affective community, to confirm an identity for "us" as the virtuous, versus "them," all the others, who thus find themselves excluded from the family of the righteous.

In an analysis of a commentary by George Melloan published in the *Wall Street Journal* after Beslan,[28] Felicitas Macgilchrist describes how the Western press aspires to create a subtle gap between "us" and "them," the Russians, while pretending to attack the Islamic terrorists. Macgilchrist distinguishes two major Western metaphorical approaches to Russia: it is useless to talk with Russia, which only understands the language of force. This is the authoritarian model adopted by military hawks. The other attitude, found more often among American and European liberals, stresses good governance and respect of good manners. But the result is the same: in both cases, it is not at all a matter of taking into consideration Russia's desires or demands, except that in the second option, the stress will be on the need to end "corruption," "anti-NGO laws," Chechen "repression," police "brutality" or the alleged "interdiction" of homosexuality, the temptation to "annex" Russian minorities at large (even if they are persecuted by some new states as is the case in the Baltic countries and in Georgia for the Ossetians and the Abkhazians). This amounts to demanding that Russia align herself with the West and renounce all legislative independence. Only the tone and the form of media commentary differ.

In the following extract, it is clearly seen how the composition of the author's sentences in reality castigates the Russian president although the author is to be supposed to be on the side of the victims of the hostage taking:[29]

> 1) Vladimir Putin's *opposition to the invasion of Iraq did not save Russia* from Islamic savagery.
>
> 2) President Putin's *mishandling of Chechen separatism* was but one of a long series of *Russian mistakes in dealing with Muslims* inside the federation and on its borders.
>
> 3) The *brutal Putin response* to separatism and lawlessness in Chechnya four years ago was highly popular with Russian voters.
>
> 4) But by now, *his futile campaign of destruction* has further damaged the already low morale of the Russian army and strengthened the resolve of the Chechen insurgents.
>
> 5) Rather, he [Putin] has seemed *bent on frustrating such a development* [of civil society] by seizing control of TV broadcasting, the most pervasive form of communication in Russia.

6) *The old Soviet habits of secrecy and the manipulation of information* by the state die hard. A vigorous civil society is not likely to develop until there is *greater state tolerance* of free discussion and free institutions.

7) But despite *the misgivings about Mr. Putin's treatment of the Chechens,* the Bush administration will no doubt welcome any offers to support U.S. objectives in the Middle East.

This short text analysis shows very well how a journalist or an editorialist caught between the hammer—the need to condemn an odious terrorist act—and the anvil—the need to continue to criticize Russia no matter what—perfectly attains his aim thanks to learned hierarchizing of the bad guys. At the top you find the terrorists, but Russia is just below, as what must be avoided at all costs is that American readers sympathize with the massacred Russian children.

At the end of the article, the reader is more or less convinced that one is no better than the other, that the party of the victim is hardly better than the party of their butcher, and that none of that would have happened if Mr. Putin had treated well the Chechen Islamists. Their occurrence in relation to Russia may be the only instances in which the Western press seeks to introduce causality as it relates to "Islamic terrorism". It does not address the long Western history of supporting Muslim fighters when that furthers their foreign policy ambitions (Bosnia, Afghanistan, Syria) and the early Taliban against Russia. And yet, as addressed earlier, Putin has effectively resolved the domestic Chechen issue, while it is well known that the West supports the Chechen fighters forming part of the anti-Assad forces.

And the second subliminal impression to draw from reading this article is that "there ain't none of them like us". Between abject terrorism, Russian "savagery" and us, there is no photo finish. "We are the best and life is good in our civilized world" is the primary feeling the reader must retain.

This sort of article is extremely frequent and produced in great quantities each time Russia is a victim of an attack or a catastrophe.

This view and this intensity of criticism are of course likely to evolve according to circumstances and the geopolitical necessities of the moment. Andrei Tsygankov did try to show how the United States' perception swayed between the 9/11 attack in 2001, when Russia was allied to them against terrorism, and after 2003, after she opposed the American invasion of Iraq.[30] The table below is quite telling.

	Following 9/11 (2001-2002)	Post 9/11 (2003-2008)
Historical perception	A new State A strategic partner	Successor to the Soviet system A former colonizer and a defeated power
Chechnya/ terrorism	Muted criticism Emphasis on counterterrorism efforts	Renewed criticism for lack of "political solutions"
Political system	Muted criticism of domestic developments	Broad-ranged criticism for "nondemocratic practices"
Military cooperation	Counterterrorism-based cooperation Proposals to include Russia in NATO	New NATO expansion without considering Russia MDS in close proximity to Russia
Energy cooperation	Growing cooperation in liquid gas	Growing energy competition

Once again it is obvious that Westerners' judgments can change depending considerably on the strategic interests of the moment and rather little on Russia's democratic or other behavior. The same assessment could no doubt be made during the "reset" of Russo-American relations in 2009 by Hillary Clinton and Sergey Lavrov, hardly a year after the Georgia war of summer 2008, and the steep deterioration of relations following Russia's refusal to stop supporting President Assad in 2011 in an effort to avoid chaos in the region leading to the rise of radical Islamists, which became reality in 2014 with the Islamic State takeover.

Andrei Tsygankov then shows how the American anti-Russian lobby succeeded in creating a wedge between "us" and "them" through an ideological conditioning supported by a series of concrete acts:

>1. OBJECTIVE: calling into question Russia's historical identity.
>MESSAGE: Russia is a defeated nation and a revisionist State.
>ACTIVITIES: promotion of Russia's "imperialist instincts"; revitalization of the attitudes and symbolism of the Cold War; promotion of anti-Russian campaigns led by the Baltic countries.
>EXAMPLES: articles on Russian neo-imperialism; attacks against Putin presented as an enemy of the United States; creation of a Medal of the Cold War by Hillary Clinton and John McCain; creation of a memorial to the victims of communism; support of Estonia in the Bronze Soldier affair.[31]
>
>2. OBJECTIVE: calling into question Russia's State identity.
>MESSAGE: Russia is a colonial State which oppresses its minorities (notably in Chechnya).
>ACTIVITIES: promoting the image of barbaric Russia; denying the link between Chechen rebels

and Islamic terrorism; pushing the Kremlin to negotiate with Maskhadov and internationalizing the resolution of the Chechen conflict; opposing the Russian policy of Chechenization.

EXAMPLES: Human Rights Watch reports on atrocities carried out by the Russian side in 2000-2001; theory of a plot implicating the Kremlin in the 1999 Moscow attacks; conference of the American Enterprise Institute on links between Russia and terrorism in 2003; Liechtenstein plan of 2002; Open Letter by the 115 to heads of State after the Beslan hostage taking in 2004; Open Letter to end the "silence on Chechnya" in 2006.

3. OBJECTIVE: calling into question the political system.
MESSAGE: Russia is a neo-Stalinist autocracy.
ACTIVITIES: financing and training orange revolutions; supporting and promoting opposition to the Kremlin; launching media campaigns prior to U.S.-Russia summits; distributing all critical reports on Russia.
EXAMPLES: engagement of the National Endowment for Democracy in Georgia, Ukraine and Kirghizstan; links with the Other Russia; articles by Garry Kasparov in American newspapers; media pressures on Bush before the 2005 Bratislava summit; Russia classified as "non-free" by the anti-Russian think tank Freedom House since 2005; 2005 report of the Council on Foreign Relations on Russia's "bad leadership."

4. OBJECTIVE: calling into question Russia's role in terms of security.
MESSAGE: Russia is a neo-imperialist State.

ACTIVITIES: lobbying for Congress support of NATO extension with testimonies and resolutions; promotion of East European views and governments; opposition to nuclear cooperation with Russia; launch of media campaigns on Russia's military weakness.

EXAMPLES: vote of Congress in favor of the admission of Ukraine and Georgia into NATO in 2008; Senator Lugar's opposition to an invitation of President Putin to the NATO summit in Bucharest in 2008; report of the Project for a New American Century in 2000; article in *Foreign Affairs* on American nuclear supremacy in 2006.

5. OBJECTIVE: stigmatize Russia's energy blackmail

MESSAGE: Russia practices energy blackmail.

ACTIVITIES: opposing the implication of the Kremlin in the energy sector; countering Russian energy deals and price policy in Eurasia; promoting links with alternative energies.

EXAMPLES: public statements in favor of Khodorkovsky and Yukos by Richard Perle and numerous authors starting fall 2003; Senator Lugar's idea in favor of a NATO for energy in 2006; media focus on Nabucco and trans-Caspian pipeline projects.[32]

If Andrei Tsygankov has shown clearly how media campaigns destined to discredit Russia are elaborated, Ezequiel Adamovski, for his part, has listed the elements of language that foment a gap between "us" sophisticated Westerners and advanced democracies, and "them," backward Russians attached to an autocratic tyrant. The following table sums up well the terms of the binary opposition that is used to distinguish the two camps:[33]

The West	Russia or Eastern Europe
Civilization	Barbarity
Modernity, Development, Progress	Traditionalism, Underdevelopment, Stagnation
Freedom	Despotism or Totalitarianism
Democracy	Autocracy
Middle class	Lack of Middle Class
Civil Society or Intermediate Corps	Lack of Civil Society
NGOs and associations	Repression of NGOs
Private property	Collective property
Pluralism and diversity	Homogeneity
Individuals	Masses
Liberalism	Communism
Pluralism	Single Party
Education ('civilization')	Cultural Handicaps
Balance	Contradictions
Normality	Deviance
Rationality	Irrationality
Authenticity and Truth	Artificiality/Imitation (Potemkin effect)
Ability and Efficiency	Incapacity and Inefficiency
Activity	Passivity
Transparence	Opacity and Cult of Secret
Opening	Closure
Human Rights	Violations of Human Rights
Tolerance and Respect	Brutality of Social Relations ('the individual does not count')
Integrity	Corruption
Prosperity	Poverty
Protection (of Minorities)	Annexation (of Minorities)
Security	Cold War
Natural Growth	

This list could go on indefinitely, given that categories are numerous and the vocabulary of differentiation is rich. In most articles that Western media publish about Russia, those dichotomies are at work.

Strategies for a Counter-Discourse

What can be done?

Felicitas Macgilchrist listed a few strategies to pose a counter-discourse to the hegemony of the Russophobic discourse in western media. She found five of them, more or less effective.

The first consists in countering the stereotypes and showing that, e.g., democracy is not in decline in Russia. She cites the example of Peter Lavelle, former correspondent of UPI, Radio Free Europe, and other American media before becoming anchor of Cross Talk broadcast on the Russia Today channel, who in 2005, during the adoption of the law on NGOs, wrote that that law was not as sinister as several media claimed. Indeed, it should be done. But the problem of course, is that not a single mainstream medium printed his dispatch. The media are not interested in news giving a positive image of Russia and contradicting the prejudices they peddle.

Several serious researches have established that democratization of Russian political life has progressed, that advances have been noted in terms of social development, that citizens have become increasingly involved in public life, that there were real signs of improvement of the independence of the judiciary system, as indicated by the fact that 71% of plaintiffs won their trials against authorities. Again, none of these themes have interested journalists and university researchers. Negation is thus not the best strategy.

Parody is another possibility.

If you believed (almost) everything you read or hear about Russia today, your mind's video would run something like this. Vladimir Putin spends his time polishing his KGB medals and lording it over the Kremlin like a diminutive Ivan the Terrible. Having devastated Chechnya and shut down regional democracy, he then ripped the heart out of the independent media. He is bent on establishing a dictatorship.[36]

This is rather funny, but you cannot do it too often for fear of being boring. Or indeed, for fear that it would not be received as parody by a brain-washed public, but straight veritas.

Making things more complex is another way of breaking up the Russophobic discourse. The method consists in contextualizing the events anew and inscribing them in a new, wider perspective, by providing a series of facts and reintegrating what has been left aside. It is the method used in this book. Drawback: it is a herculean task, which does not lend itself to the ceaseless onslaught of the daily press.

Partial or total reformatting may also prove efficient. This is for example what John Laughland did in *The Guardian* on September 8, 2004, after the Beslan hostage taking, when he reframed the picture to focus on the identity of the authors of the anti-Russian discourse and their hidden motives. Having other actors express themselves is also a possibility. You will not have the same feeling of the situation in Donetsk when pro-Ukrainians as when pro-Russians are selected.

We mention these techniques for information only, and without illusion that they can penetrate the Western press. Editorial boards are after images and accounts that tally with the dominant misconceptions. How many reporters on the ground have exhausted themselves explaining to their bosses that reality was a little more complex than they fancied and that it might be necessary to nuance judgments and news presentation? How many have given up doing so for failing to be heard, or simply to survive, because an article or a subject that does not fit the doxa goes straight into the trash can or has you suspected of being a victim of the Stockholm syndrome?

It is thus very difficult to break the anti-Russian discourse, especially when it takes the shape of a story, of a myth. And this is precisely what it has become in the Western imagination, as we shall see in the next chapter.

The New Avatar of Soft Power: The Theory of the Shepherd

Before concluding, let us point out again that, since Barack Obama's election, the use of soft power against Russia has known a new strategic evolution, that of the leader from behind. It is inspired by a phrase from Nelson Mandela, who states in his memoirs that the true leader must behave like a sheepherder. He must stay at the back of the herd, to guide it:

> It is better to lead from behind and to put others in front, especially when you celebrate victory when nice things occur. You take the front line when there is danger. Then people will appreciate your leadership.[37]

The expression was employed in spring 2011 by an advisor to Barack Obama about his successful strategy of bombing in Libya. By letting the Europeans have their way, he obtained the green light from the Security Council without rushing Russia and China, something which neither Clinton nor Bush had achieved during the bombing of Serbia in 1999 and the invasion of Iraq in 2003. This method was harshly criticized by the conservatives who, like Charles Krauthammer and Richard Cohen, presented it as a failure of the United States' natural leadership and as "abdication," for "It is the fate of any assertive superpower to be envied, denounced and blamed for everything under the sun."[38]

It is still too early to assess this new communication strategy, which has the merit of mitigating effects and allowing for operations in the dark. It was practiced with some success against Russia in Ukraine, the noisy interventions of the anti-Russian lobby, led by Vice President Joe Biden, Assistant Secretary of State Victoria Nuland and Senator McCain, alongside the Maidan "democratic" demonstrators, having later masked the February 22 putsch, the accession to power of the United States protégé, Arseni Yatseniuk, and then the military support for the new regime. In Syria, however, it appears to be failing. In early February 2015 the war in Ukraine experienced a new peak with the document published by the Brookings Institution and signed by the flock of military hawks enjoining the United States to give weapons to Ukraine at the level of one billion dollars a year for three years.[39]

NATO has taken on a prominent role as a means of conveyance for American policy. OSCE Secretary General Lamberto Zannier noted at the Vilnius summit in November 2014, that the European Union did not want Ukraine to keep cooperating with her Russian neighbor and had shown itself "inflexible with Ukraine about a cooperation treaty"; and that European commissar Štefan Füle had firmly declared that "the free trade agreement is incompatible with the Russian customs union" and Ukraine had to "choose between the two."[40] And Zannier concluded that "at a time when confrontation policies prevail, a constructive engagement becomes very dificult" and that the viewpoints between the two camps being completely opposed, "promoting reconciliation will be a difficult task which will keep Ukraine and the international community busy for a long time."

In January, American admiral and former commander-in-chief of NATO forces James Stavridis and former German defense minister Karl-Theodor zu Guttenberg signed jointly an article in which they justified the progression of NATO in Europe and projected the blame for the Ukrainian crisis and tensions in Europe onto Russia.[41]

How to sum up Western Russophobia? Contrary to allegations that would make of Putin an adept of military force according to old Cold War patterns and claims that Westerners have gone past that vulgar stage and achieved perfect command of symbols, which is paramount in this digital era, the United States remains addicted to raw military force more than ever. By itself, it spends more on its military than all other states combined. And the invasion of Iraq and the bombing of Libya and of Islamic State fighters in Iraq have shown that they have not given up hard power at all.

Contemporary Russophobia is thus a complex, very sophisticated mixture of hard, soft and smart power, of geopolitical ambitions for world economic, political and military supremacy, and of quasi-religious faith in the sacred values of liberal economics and pluralistic democracy. Is military domination at the service of the liberal idea? Or is it the other way round? The answer depends on the sincerity given to American and European messianism.

Europeans, largely agnostic if not anticlerical lay people under French influence, tend to underestimate the weight of religion in the American discourse, even though it is decisive. Religious references are ubiquitous and so constant they no longer shock. And yet they are hardly less present than in Shiite Iran or Wahhabi Saudi Arabia, even though in America they have been partly secularized and melted into the economic discourse.[42]

This messianism founded on the faith in God and the power of the dollar is at the heart of American soft power and of the unrivalled appeal of the United States. It gives those that propagate it, whether NGO missionaries promoting the democratic gospel or financial apostles preaching the free movement of capital, the force of sincerity. Americans believe what they say and have faith in what they do. So they are habituated to converting the schismatic and burning heretics under napalm, with the same unmovable enthusiasm as Spanish Inquisition monks had in converting Jews, Muslims and Indian pagans during the Spanish Reconquista and the South American Conquista.

The result is the same: unbridled interventionism in the weakest countries, Afghanistan, Libya, Syria, Iraq, and merciless harassment of those that refuse to submit, Venezuela, Cuba, Iran, and North Korea. As for Russia, with her image of perpetual challenger, her military and nuclear power, her enormous natural and scientific resources, her geographic position at the heart of the Eurasian continent, her cultural plasticity and stubborn refusal to submit to American hegemony, she still serves as the enemy to vanquish, peopled as she is with renegades that persist in shying away from both liberal democracy and the virtues of American free enterprise. When you are sure you hold the keys of paradise, it is difficult to admit that the others might prefer what you view as hell…

| Chapter Ten |

THE MYTH OF THE FIERCE BEAR

*"How is the world ruled and led to war?
Diplomats lie to journalists and believe these lies
when they see them in print."*
Karl Kraus, *Epigrams*, 1927.

To convince, manipulating words is not enough. Constant repetition of the same sentences on Russian expansionism and despotism eventually becomes boring. Construction of the discourse is thus a necessary stage, but it is not sufficient. To be effective and widespread, a narrative must also be elaborated, a story narrated that makes sense. An easy myth must be fabricated that will lodge in the collective imagination.

Construction of a Russophobic narrative is thus infinitely complex. More than a narrative, it is a metanarrative, as language analysts call it, that is, a narrative within a narrative, a history within history, which interlocks and gets tangled like Russian nesting dolls. One fact leads to another, one event to a series of events, one opinion to other opinions in other times, other cultures, on other continents. But always those stories are linked to the West, to Europe and the United States.

This agglomeration of tales ends up forming a hyper-fiction and generating a new mythology, that of the fierce Russian bear always ready to charge out of its forests to devour the Little Red Riding Hood of the West. As in every good myth, there must be an ogre, a villain ready to demolish the innocent, which hopefully will come to a bad end. Fabricating a villain—Vladimir Putin in this case—is thus essential to the smooth functioning of the myth.

This myth has a function, anthropologists say. It is to "substitute the truth to better calm apprehensions and provide explanations that bring back tranquility."[1] Literally, a metanarrative is "a narrative on reality whose function is to justify the past and the present." It is a hyper-discourse which "deploys legitimizing functions in politics, functions destined to edify collective values by way of the identity unit." It is

> a unifying discourse able to inscribe innovations in a teleological perspective and to point to criteria for life in common. In a way, the construction of a 'monumental' history that ceaselessly turns the present and the future into the past in order to maintain the (actually dead) political identity. Therefore, the metanarrative places us at the heart of myths and rituals in which and through which politics becomes creed, ceremony and symbolic spread to the detriment of citizens' accountability.[2]

Indeed, by including various myths, the metanarrative tries to transform the current situation. But to do that, the metanarrative must also transform the past. This explains why the dominant Russophobic discourse is so eager to rewrite history. The main mission of memory occultation is to wipe out any traces of the positive historical role of Russia in Europe and thus clear the deck for the postmodern mythology of a united Atlanticist Europe centered around a Warsaw, Berlin-Brussels-Paris-London-Washington axis.

As was done with Byzantium in the days of Charlemagne and the first Roman Germanic emperors backed by the pope's theologians, it is a matter of wiping Russia as European out of the European consciousness. Europe's unity and future demand it, at least so say the modern theologians building the myth of Euro-Atlantic union by opposing to it the myth of the threatening Russian bear.

Seen from that perspective, the systematic interpretation of Russian actions in terms of threats to the West is better understood. In that construction, every detail, every micro-event must be carefully fit into the huge anti-Russian interpretative grid. Putin's briefest statement, the briefest separatist shellfire, the Greek prime minister's meeting with a Russian ambassador, a pro-Western opponent's most insignificant tweet—all of this must be analyzed, taken apart, reformatted and eventually amplified to enhance the huge and moving picture of the horrors that Russia prepares with a view to compromising the glorious edification of a Euro-Atlantic union determined to build "peace, democracy and its peoples' prosperity" for ever and ever.

Plugging Loopholes in the Narrative

This permits us to better understand the West's obsession to erase what it has done to upset the Russian bear, such as thrusting the "borders" of NATO in its very snout. It would not do if an overlooked small contradiction, a tiny grain of sand, or an improbability made the engine seize up.

If NATO were to be viewed as aggressive, rather than Russia, the entire construction of the myth would collapse. If Russia, for the umpteenth time, did not "invade" Ukraine, how to justify support for Poroshenko when he is bombing Donetsk and massacring civilians in his own country, as in the worst moments of the Sarajevo siege in 1992 and 1994? This is why the media and research institutes linked to European construction or engaged in the defense of American supremacy always drink at the same sources, always interview the same persons, always quote the same experts, tirelessly repeat the same refrain: Putin is a villain, Russia wants to invade us.

And this is why, since Charlemagne undertook to build a Latin-Germanic Empire in Europe, Putin's predecessors, Ivan the Terrible, Peter the Great, Nicolas I or Stalin, were consistently portrayed with the vilest features, as maleficent czars bent on crimes and oppression. What is good for the genealogy of good kings is good for that of the bad guys: they must show that the former derive directly from God and the latter from the devil. Filiation is important. Like in *The Lord of the Rings*, the Dark Lord Sauron could not be descended from soft and pacific elves, and neither could a kind hobbit give birth to a killer whale. If the genealogy were reversed, the entire mythology would collapse.

Let us see now how the metanarrative and the myths it carries are articulated. The first myth is that of the evil czar. We have seen that the West had already gifted Russia with a long line of "cruel, despotic czars" obsessed by the restoration of Russian grandeur and imperialist expansion: Ivan IV the Terrible, Nicolas I, Stalin, and today Vladimir Putin fulfil this function. Almost all books and articles about them in the West take it upon themselves to recall the horrors those leaders allegedly committed against humanity and civilization.

Demonizing Putin

Demonization of the enemy and of its leader has been practiced ever since primitive societies used to lampoon the leader of the opposite camp or to devour symbolically his heart before launching into battle. In spite of its flashy modernity and new communication technologies, the West continues to act in exactly the same way.

Let us remember Saddam Hussein, who was praised to the skies when he declared war on Ayatollah Khomeini's Iran, the number one enemy of the United States in the early 1980s, and who abruptly became a target for assassination when he tried, in 1991, to get back Kuwait, an oil emirate created out of thin air by

English colonialism on a territory taken by force from historic Iraq in 1914. He ended up hanged in 2004 after losing a war America launched against Iraq for having weapons of massive destruction that never existed.

Saddam Hussein's case reminds us of Serbian president Slobodan Milosevic, who was also accused of all the evils committed during the Yugoslavia war from 1992 to 1999. His country was bombed by NATO in violation of international law; the U.N. did not approve it. This contempt for the law was nonetheless endorsed by all western countries, who would later voice their adamant insistence on respect for the law related to the peaceful democratic transition in Crimea. As in Iraq, military interventions in Yugoslavia had started with spurious accusations, such as the case of the photograph of Bosnian Fikret Alic standing bare-chested behind barbed wire in July 1992. The English tabloid press published it under the heading "Bergen-Belsen 1992" as if he had been interned by the Serbs in a concentration camp. The photograph had been reframed to show the barbed wire in the foreground. It had been taken by a British private TV team looking for the best angle for a hot shot. They had offered cigarettes to a group of Bosnians yards away to make them come closer to the wire and thus offer a better display. It was hot that day and some of the men were bare-chested.

The same operation was repeated in the winter of 1999 when several newspapers published a photograph of alleged Albanian civilians massacred by Serbs in the Kosovar village of Racak. One of the pictures had been retouched and the wet marks obscured to look like blood flows, while on another one some bodies with military uniforms could be singled out. Those pictures triggered enormous indignation in the press, which immediately accused Milosevic. The NATO bombings began soon after their publication.

Vladimir Putin faces the same technique of villain fabrication. Except that, until now, with remarkable composure, the Russian president has never yielded to provocations and has always kept his calm while constantly referencing and staying within the limits of international legality. Economic sanctions taken by the United States and the European Union have no international legality. As former French president Valéry Giscard d'Estaing noted, the US policy "has violated international law. Who can assume the right to make a list of citizens to whom one applies personal sanctions without examining and questioning them and without them being able to defend themselves and having a counsel. This case marks a worrying turning point."[3] In terms of the rule of law, only sanctions approved by the UN Security Council are legal. All others are considered as unilateral.

To see how the West manufactures "villains," a visit to any bookshop, even the smallest one, will astound you at the extent of the voluminous anti-Putin production. In early February 2015, in a remote valley, the New Titles shelf of the local bookshop in Switzerland had no fewer than five works on Putin, each soliciting more concern than the next.[4] A similar brief visit to English and most other online booksellers produces the same preponderant result.

Respect for copyright forbids us from reproducing the covers of magazines and books that have vilified Vladimir Putin over these last fifteen years. But you can do so yourself: just type "Putin covers" on Google Images and you will face hundreds of sinister magazine covers. The publishing world is bustling with books about, or rather against, Putin. Jack the Ripper and the worst monsters of history were never graced with so numerous and so disobliging biographies. "Dreadful Putin" is an expression often found under the pen of authors and journalists.

Here is an assortment of books that can be found in English and American bookshops: *I, Putin*; *The Strongman and the Fight for Russia*; *Putin's Kleptocracy*; *The War against Putin: What the Government-Media Complex Isn't Telling You About*; *The New Cold War: Putin's Russia and the Threat to the West*; *Red Notice: a True Story of High Finance, Murder, and One Man's Fight for Justice*; *Putin's Wars: The Rise of Russia's New Imperialism*; *Vladimir Putin: The Controversial Life of Russia's President*; *Mr. Putin: Operative in the Kremlin*; *The Putin Mystique*; *Nothing is True and Everything is Possible: The Surreal Heart of the New Russia*; *Sex, Politics and*

Putin: Political Legitimacy in Russia; *Fragile Empire: How Russia Fell In and Out of Love with Vladimir Putin;* *Putin's Russia: Life in a Failing Democracy*; *Petrostate: Putin, Power and the New Russia*; *Putin Redux; Power and Contradiction in Contemporary Russia*; *Putin's Putsches: Ukraine and the Near Abroad Crisis*; *Putin and the Oligarchs: The Khodorkovsky-Yukos Affair*; *The Corporation: Russia and the KGB in the Age of President Putin*; *Putin vs. Putin: Vladimir Putin Viewed from the Right*; *Ruling Russia: Authoritarianism from the Revolution to Putin*; *Kremlin Rising: Vladimir Putin's Russia and the End of Revolution; Putin's Death Grip*; *Putin's Venom*; *The Putin Corporation: The Story of Russia's Takeover*; *Putin and the MH370/MH17*; *Putin's Shoot-Down*; *Putin's New Order in the Middle East*; *A History of Russia and Its Empire: From Mikhail Romanov to Vladimir Putin*; *Putin's Evil Empire*; *Putin: Russia's Choice*; *Putin's Dilemma*; *Putin's New World Order: Russia Out of Control*; *Putin's Game of Shadows: Hybrid War in Ukraine, Propaganda and Fascism* (with a cover showing Putin with Hitler's moustache); *Russia Under Yeltsin and Putin: Neo-Liberal Autocracy*; *After Putin's Russia: Past Imperfect, Future Uncertain*; *Putin's Energy Agenda*; *Kicking the Kremlin: Russia's New Dissidents and the Battle to Topple Putin*; *Putin's Russia Demystified*; *The Search for Modern Russia*; *Russian Populist: the Political Thought of Vladimir Putin*; *Television and Culture in Putin's Russia: Remote Control*; *Putin's Oil*; *Snippets of Vladimir Putin*.[5]

What do all these books say? They tell more or less the same story. Let us quote the review *Le Monde des livres* published on Marie Mendras's work on "the flip side of Russian power":

> Her book demonstrates Putin's *trick* [italics added] of seeking credit for a strengthening of the State and of the law in the last few years compared to the anarchy that reigned during the days of Yeltsin."

On the contrary, Marie Mendras writes, Vladimir Putin's policy has led to "a systematic deconstruction of the institutions of the State and of society." There has been "a public distancing from the values of freedom, democracy, competition."[6] Putin is a spy, his system is corrupt, democracy has been falsified, civil society and the intermediary powers so dear to Tocqueville and to pluralistic liberals have been destroyed.

How is it, then, that the people of Russia have given him an approval rating that is the highest of any leader in the world?[7]

The impact of this mass of books is multiplied as they are publicized by innumerable television broadcasts and radio interviews disseminating the same accusations. The press, in particular magazines, further back up the production of books to spread in the general public the "dreadful Putin" image.[8]

There are hundreds of magazine top stories about Putin that seem to indulge in relentless competition for coming up with the most insulting epithet and the most sordid staging. The titles, the photomontages, the violence of accusations are so excessive that they end up producing the opposite effect: the extremity of the characterization becomes apparent, exposing it as propaganda.

Let us look at the top stories of magazines chosen among the most serious and respected. All represent a threatening, frightening Russian president as a "man who never smiles," evil and at times even lampooned as a Hitler. *Der Spiegel*: "Stop Putin now!" *Newsweek*: "Imperium" in bold letters, "The Pariah. Inside the bullet-proof bubble of the West's public enemy number one," with the Polish edition representing him looking like a straight-jacketed madman; *Time*: "Cold War II. The West is Losing Putin's Dangerous Game," "How to Stop the New Cold War?" *The Economist*: "A web of lies;" "The Putin problem;" and then, dated February 14, 2015, "Putin's war on the West;" *The New Statesman*: "Putin's reign of terror;" *Moneyweek*: "End of game for Putin;" Polish *Historia*: "Vladimir Grozny;" *The Daily Mail*: "Prince Charles: Putin behaves just like Hitler;" *Courrier international*: "La revanche de Poutine," "Poutine, Chavez, de drôles de démocrates," "Back in the USSR," "Poutine Imperator;" *Le Nouvel Observateur*: "La face cachée de Poutine," "Jusqu'où ira Poutine?" *Books*: "Russie. L'État-Mafia;" *The Advocate*: "Person of the Year" (the photograph shows Putin's face looking like Hitler); *L'Express*: "Poutine n'est pas Hitler, mais…"

The list is so long, so pervasive and so repetitive that the purported freedom of the Western press becomes questionable. . . It is interesting to note continuities with the past. The Austrian magazine *News* headlines "Vladimir Putin, Enemy of the World" over a photomontage representing the Russian president as a vampire, with a Dracula-like blood-stained smiling mouth. This is exactly how English caricaturists in the 1850s drew Czar Nicolas I, and the author of *Dracula*, the English imperialist writer Bram Stoker, assimilated Count Dracula to Russian czars.[9] At the time, the czar was lampooned with the same tools of demonization: he was seen flying over Europe with his vampire wings, scythe in hand, or playing piano while flapping his wings to better rejoice in the death of a European personality. Like Vladimir Putin and Stalin at the beginning of the Cold War he was drawn as the great organizer of the Dance of the Vampires, ready to suck the blood of innocent Europe.

It would take too long to analyze the contents of anti-Putin press articles and books. They would fill entire libraries. But they all say more or less the same thing: Putin is a liar, an imposter, a kleptocrat, a manipulator, a dictator, a rapist (of peoples), an oppressor, an invader, a calculating person, a Stalinist, a fascist, a reactionary, a conservative, a Mussolini (Brzezinski), a Hitler (Prince Charles, Hillary Clinton and the Baltic and Polish presidents), a revisionist, a KGB goon, a sex maniac, and nostalgic for the czarist empire and the USSR. "He offers the West to join in the Social Contract of lying."[10] "Putin's gaze is cold, his eyes almost glazed,"[11] with a "mute wax face and a Freudian and pathetic sexual obsession of bulging muscle and Botox." "It is the old czarist tradition of expansion, the will to conquer an empire without borders" that inspires Putin.[12] On the Left as on the Right, never mind contradictions, all comparisons are valid as long as they villify their target.

It is striking to note that most authors seem to be adepts of Marquis de Sade. They allow themselves to be seduced and fascinated by the "monster" they describe, along with his supposed vices. They obsess about what is happening "inside Putin's head." No fewer than ten French-speaking magazines have tried to attract readers with a poster of "inside Putin's head": *Le Point, Le Figaro, TéléObs, L'Express*, the Atlantico website, *ITÉLÉ, La République des Pyrénées, Les Échos*, Tropique FM, and even *Philosophie Magazine*. In early 2015, all of them commented on Michel Eltchaninoff's book *Dans la tête de Vladimir Poutine* (Inside Vladimir Putin's head).[13]

In spite of all these innumerable books and articles, Putin's psychology remains an unfathomable mystery, since the books repeat themselves without any author having been able to see through him. This powerlessness in no way discourages candidates or the most hazardous psychiatric diagnoses. In March 2014, a remark by Angela Merkel amplified by *The New York Times* shook up the media world, the German chancellor having hinted that Putin was irrational and having allegedly told Obama that Putin "lived in another world."[14] Dozens of articles were then published on the improbable mental health of the Russian president rather than noting that this disparity might reflect, e.g., the differing Russian perspective on NATO's arming countries on its borders from that of the West.

In February 2015, a new series of articles was published, indicating that Putin could be a victim of Asperger's syndrome, a form of autism.

> A report of Pentagon military experts is explicit: based on his physical behavior and on videos, they conclude that the neurological development of the Russian president was perturbed in childhood.[15]

The thesis of mental unbalance is thus added to the whole range of vices for which Putin is reproached. Surely any comment is superfluous? We shall merely mention that the Pentagon report, which is said to go back to 2008, was broadcast by *USA Today* before being taken up everywhere in the West. It appeared the same week as the offensive of the American Right to arm Ukraine.

Finally, it is imperative to note that, with only one exception, none of those books is based on Putin's writings, declarations or speeches. In all those portraits, there is no intimation of psychological or political substance. There are extrapolations[16] based on small phrases (always the same, such as the one on the fight against terrorism, even in the shitter). He is ascribed family tropisms, habits as a former spy, sympathy for nationalist philosopher Alexander Dugin's Euro-Asian theses (presented as semi-fascist). But in the end, we still don't know who Vladimir Putin is or what he thinks. Those exercises are so vacuous that even the media are not happy with them and keep asking what is meant to be a troubling question: what does Putin want?

To know that, all it takes is to read his books and the transcription of his public interventions. Everything is there, and totally transparent. Much is available on the internet in English. The 2007 speech during the conference on security in Munich expresses very clearly what Putin wants for Russia, what he is seeking for the security of his country, how he judges the world evolution, and his wish to work with the West.[17]

His latest intervention at Club Valdai in the fall of 2014, made public and translated into many languages, is a brilliant and impeccable analysis of the international situation, with which one is free to disagree but which is perfectly rational and logical for a great sovereign country. And it does not hold any invective against Europe or the United States, apart from a few ironical remarks which are perfectly innocuous when compared to the violent attacks President Obama regularly made against Russia.[18] But there you have it: these sources are public, explicit and understandable by everybody. But to mention them would counter the narrative of Putin, this mysterious and secret demon, this ogre so useful to editorial marketing and Russophobic propaganda.

The point of this exercise in long-term demonization begun as soon as his accession to power at the end of 1999 and kept on ceaselessly since then, with a few reductions in intensity during periods of relative appeasement in 2001-03 and in 2009 is obvious: destroy the credibility of Russia and her president, stigmatize him in public opinion to make him the scapegoat of all world turpitudes. Among other things, he must be held accountable for all that has happened in Ukraine, and public opinion must be prepared, if need be, for a long-term European war of the Yugoslav or Afghan type. When you assimilate Putin to Hitler and put him on the same footing as Milosevic, Saddam Hussein and Bin Laden, everything becomes possible, even the worst.

Let acknowledged expert, American professor John Mearsheimer, answer those fallacies:

> Although Putin no doubt has autocratic tendencies, no evidence supports the charge that he is mentally unbalanced. On the contrary: he is a first-class strategist.

As for the argument according to which Putin would be some sort of Hitler eager to take over Europe and that the odious Munich surrender should not be repeated with him, it "falls apart on close inspection. If Putin were committed to creating a greater Russia, signs of his intentions would almost certainly have arisen before February 22 [2014]."

After the experiences of Vietnam, Afghanistan, Iraq, and Chechnya, "Putin surely understands that trying to subdue Ukraine would be like swallowing a porcupine. His response to events there has been defensive, not offensive."[19]

So much then for the making of the villain and its (brief) refutation. What matters to us here is indeed less refuting allegations than understanding their function in the anti-Russian discourse, where they constantly renew the backdrop myth of the ferocious Russian bear. The making of the evil leader is an indispensable precondition for demonizing the country itself. How to demonize Russia (Iran, Iraq, Venezuela, Cuba, Syria) if her leader has not been demonized first? A country at the heart of the "axis of evil" should not have a friendly, competent and charismatic president.

The battle must thus first be won at the symbolic level before starting at the political and, eventually, at the military level. For Serbia, Iraq and Syria, the maneuver was carried out to the end. Russia is a tougher task. But the first step, the demonization of her president, has been taken. Now, it only requires periodic updates to make sure that public opinion still subscribes to the myth. It is once this stage is over and the loss of legitimacy of the established power[20] is embedded in Western public opinion and, if possible, that of the targeted country, that the second stage can be launched, with the mobilization of all soft power resources (NGOs, think tanks, intellectual and media reserve battalions). Without propitious grounds it is impossible to launch an orange revolution in the targeted country, and the billions injected for the support of local NGOs to destabilize power prove worthless, at least as it relates to regime change.[21]

American Historiography Entrenches Russophobic Memes

In a remarkable article, Paul Sanders, historian and professor at Reims Management School in France, shows how this metanarrative is structured in the academic field. His contribution is entitled "Under Western Eyes: how meta-narrative shapes our perception of Russia—and why it is time for a qualitative shift."[22]

Until now, we have mainly talked about the media discourse and left aside the academic discourse. But universities, historians and political scientists play an essential role in the making of anti-Russian mythology, because of the prestige tied to their status in the chain of production of knowledge, but also thanks to their own contributions, of course. They are the craftsmen of the meta-narrative which then flows into the media in the form of references to specific stories.

Here is how Sanders analyses their contribution in the structuring of the American Russophobic academic discourse of the last three decades. He first distinguishes three types of anti-Russian tales:

1. Blaming Putin for causing bad relations between Russia and the West. Not only is it Putin who forces Russia to oppose the West, but it is also the West which finds itself constrained to oppose Russia because of Putin's antidemocratic manners. Or how to make the

other responsible for everything, including one own misfortune. This is akin to the rapist's pet argument: "Wasn't me! She provoked me."
2. Pointing out the growing gap between Russia and the West, Russia having retrograded in terms of democratic rights and economic freedom since Putin has been in power. This theory is invalidated by sober opinion polls undertaken among Russians by the Levada Center and by academic research, as we have seen in the preceding chapter.
3. Deploying stereotypes, such as "the new Cold War," and the anti-Western bend of Russian authorities and nationalist movements, gathering in Russian society and political life the elements with which to build its discourse. One favorite theme consists in blowing criticisms of the West by Russian intellectual and politicians out of proportion to show to western public opinion that we must not trust Russia. The analyses are sometimes subtle. According to some researchers, western Russophobia would thus be nothing more than an invention by the Russian authorities who keep denouncing it in order to consolidate their power and strengthen their authoritarian tendencies.[23]

Imagine if the United States were only judged by the yardstick of the Tea Party and John McCain, or France by that of the Front national, or England by the UKIP, or Italy by Lega Nord.

It is with those three analytical grids that Westerners have interpreted Russian events since the disappearance of the Soviet Union: the Chechnya war; the attacks in Budyonnovsk, Moscow, Beslan, and the Nord-Ost theater hostage crisis; the dispute over the Bronze Soldier in Tallinn, the Georgia war of 2008… Each time, tragedies, dramas, sometimes comical incidents or satires, occur they are fit into the grand framework, the super-history that confirms what is put forward as the politically correct interpretation of facts—the only one socially acceptable by the West—that of a ferocious and expansionist Russian bear driven by a despotic and cruel master whose mental health is dubious.

Since the 1970s this western super-history has been structured around two concepts defined by American soft power during the Cold War, those of freedom and democracy. Western Liberals and Democrats, in whose camps Russian opponents to Putin have also found a place, find themselves confronted by "nationalists," those "nostalgic for the Empire" and "Stalinist neo-reactionaries" close to the Kremlin supporting Vladimir Putin, who is intend on "muzzling" Russian democracy, the NGOs' freedom of expression, and the independence of neighboring peoples.

This narrative has often been analyzed since the collapse of the Soviet Union, sometimes to introduce nuances or to contest one particular aspect, such as the question of whether there is continuity or rupture between Boris Yeltsin and Vladimir Putin, the members of the Yeltsin clan arguing for the latter and defending Yeltsin as a pro-Western democrat.

Between 2000 and 2010, two schools were competing, that of "failed democratization" and that of "democratic evolutionism." The first, Sanders notes, dominated the western discourse throughout the decade through the "new Cold War" discourse. The second, more favorable to Russia because it supposes a gradual consolidation of democracy interrupted by temporary setbacks, was rapidly dismissed. The refusal to let Texan oil interests grab Yukos in 2003, the gas dispute with Ukraine in 2006, the Georgia war in 2008—all those events helped the supporters of the democratic regression thesis to institutionalize this discourse in most media, universities, research centers and ministerial cabinets in the United States and Europe.

How is it that the framework of the Western anti-Russian meta-narrative was defined in terms of freedom and democracy? To the explanations given in preceding chapters, Sanders adds the one of "European attempts to position the country as its 'Other', a status the country shares with that other classical Orient, Islam and the Arab world," an Orient Edward Said has shown was created by the West to assert the superiority of its civilization over its Muslim neighbors.

In this sense, as Martin Malia says, "the variation in

the oscillating Western appreciation of Russia, especially in the nineteenth century, had less to do with Russian social reality than with the deep mutations that Western society itself was undergoing. Russia served as a foil for European intellectual development, and at the same time as the 'dark double'."[24]

David Foglesong's research on United States-Russia relations since 1914 also shows that this choice was largely inspired by the American "missionary cycle" and the quasi mystical will to interfere with Russian affairs in order to deliver the message of democracy and "people's power."[25] After the failure of that crusade following the triumph of the Bolshevik revolution, the American "missionaries" went back to the United States very much upset and began to develop the theme of the "cultural incompatibility of Russia with democratic western values," a discourse which, as we have seen, deeply inspired American Russophobia during the Cold War and which explains the success of the reprints of Astolphe de Custine's book in the United States.

That failure of American democratic messianism echoes a European vision which, for its part, prefers the metaphor of Russia as an "irregularity" in the development of civilization. Russia is in perpetual transition toward Europeanization and behaves like "a barbarian at the door of Europe," whose civilizational varnish is seldom solid enough to permit its easy passage into the European club. In its better days, Europe has thus at best considered Russia as a dissipated and rebellious trainee never quite able to assimilate European civilization's high virtues of economic freedom and democratic pluralism. And when she goes to a lot of trouble, Russia still merely "copies" the West, imitates it as was the world in the 18th century, but without ever succeeding in reaching her model's perfection.

The common feature of those approaches is that they all discriminate against Russia. They take place in a long-term tradition which endeavors to inscribe the history of Russia in a long continuum of despotism and slavery stretching from Peter the Great to Stalin and, since the year 2000, to Putin. We saw how in Europe, Ernst Nolte and François Furet tried to make of Nazism and Stalinist communism the two faces of the same coin.

In the United States, anti-Russian historiography is incarnated in two schools that merge and criticize each other at times while proposing the same vision: the first is that of the "Muscovite patrimonialism," led by Polish-born Russophobic historian Richard Pipes. It considers that Russian history is that of tyranny: economic and political power is concentrated into the hands of a single man who reigns as a master over a flock of slaves, whether serfs or red proletarians. Under czarism as under communism, individualism and private property do not exist, or very little, in front of the arbitrariness of power. In Pipes' eyes, 1917 was not a break with the past but simply marked the birth of a "second slavery" and the return to the "eternal Russia" of tyranny.

In an article published in 1996 in *Commentary*,[26] Pipes attempts to anchor into the general public the idea that Soviet communism is a uniquely and typically Russian product (even though communist ideology and parties were largely present everywhere in Europe and even in the United States) and that it resulted from a thousand years of Russian history, according to a deeply grounded and immutable pattern of "Russian political culture."[27] From Peter the Great to Lenin, and from Stalin to Putin, nothing has changed and nothing will ever change, he asserts: the "patrimonial" and autocratic conception of power always holds true, as if post-communist democratic Russia was the same as that of the Red Guards, of the big purges, or of Catherine II.

That thesis has been tremendously successful, adopted altogether uncritically by the Western media and political elites who deliberately omit either recognition or crediting of the fact that in 1991 Russia accepted to withdraw from Eastern Europe, pacifically granting independence to fifteen countries which were viewed, under the USSR, as its former satellites.

The other school insists on structural or so-called path dependence preventing Russia from leaving the rails and emancipating herself from a particularly constraining past. By borrowing Byzantium's Orthodox Christianity and Caesaropopery, and then being under the yoke and influence of the Mongols, Russia is deemed to have taken a different, more Asiatic, path which it is proving almost impossible to get out of.

Russian leaders are not necessarily "patrimonial autocrats" reigning over enslaved subjects, but fit in a paternalistic patron-client relationship, merely arbitrating conflicts between clans, parties or party trends, on the model of Mongol clans competing between themselves (like Stalin eliminating his adversaries within the Bolshevik party). Russia would then be an example of "archaic modernization" along a path different from that of the West.[28]

On this backdrop, numerous controversies have been agitating the Russophobic academic backwaters concerning the role of the 1917 Revolution, the continuity between czarism and Stalinism, between Okhrana and Tcheka, and whether the unexpected triumph of the Bolsheviks was due to chance circumstances of the First World War, Lenin having been able to exploit the Russian peoples and soldiers' discontent with the war, or was on the contrary the result of an inevitable and slow evolution due to the progressive crumbling of monarchy and the rise of new social forces.

The fall of the Iron Curtain also is a matter of debate: was 1991 a break with the communist past or was there a continuity? Theses diverge and blend together in a vast hodge-podge, Putin being at times a new czar, a Hitler, a Stalin, Yeltsin's heir or on the contrary an anti-Yeltsin. Never mind the contradictions because what matters is that he properly fulfil his role as "villain" in the imagery carried by the Western discourse.

Another controversial matter: the role to attribute to the First World War. Didn't the true barbarization of the world come from Europe rather than Russia? Wasn't it Europe that followed in the Mongols' path by unleashing a war of total destruction that aimed at the complete annihilation of the enemy? Several Anglo-Saxon historians consider that the Great War was the start of unheard-of excesses that generated Nazi Germany and its moral code of destruction of inferior races, and that it was that war that allowed the excesses, purges and gulags that followed the 1917 Revolution, much more than the nature of communism itself. The old moral code of the soldier demanding respect for the vanquished and for civilians having been shattered under the gases and total warfare of WWI, the failure of civilization might well be regarded as having started in 1914 in the Verdun trenches, not in the jolts that followed the Russian revolution as claimed by anti-communist and anti-Russian historians—a disturbing hypothesis seldom raised in the West.

Historians and economists are at loggerheads as well over the economic transition of the 1990s. Was it necessary to impose shock therapy on Russia to free her from the straightjacket of socialist planning and collective ownership? Wouldn't it have been better on the contrary to proceed more gradually, safeguarding the positive social aspects of communism? The dividing line runs between the neo-liberals, in favor of strong-arm tactics, and the gradualists, such as Economics Nobel Prize Winner Joseph Stiglitz, who was very critical of "market Bolsheviks" who ruined the Russian economy by making it lose 40% of its production between 1992 and 1993. At the same time, others incriminate instead institutional lapses (such as the absence of a law guaranteeing private property).

How to situate Putin in Russian history is also a matter of debate: is he an avatar of the old czarist patrimonialism? An heir to statist and collectivist Stalinism? An ultraliberal bolstering oligarchs and the wildest capitalism? A descendant of "oriental despotism"? Or a sensible reformer making Russian society progress at its own pace without taking into account Western criticism? Is he an expansionist? But then how to explain that he has never claimed any territory since his accession to power and that he even restored to Georgia the territories briefly occupied following the August 2008 counterattack?[29] Objectively, all of these possibilities can be argued, depending on the orientation of the reviewer.

At first glance, the anti-Russian narrative seems contradictory and full of incoherence. But this does not really matter since, as Michel Foucault showed, at one moment or another, for mysterious reasons, some narratives are set aside and others selected as representative of a larger truth. Those representations take place in academic discourses that become institutionalized and are deployed in turn in the practical exercise of political power, Sanders notes.

This is what happens with the various discourses of experts

and the media on Russia and on Putin. At some point, some variants of the discourses become established beliefs, social "truths" that confer to the political powers that wield them a powerful leverage on their adversaries and sometimes are even able to change reality, for example by triggering successful revolutions.

The Weight of Geography

"*Russia delenda est*" (Russia must be destroyed) seems to be the fixation in certain American and Atlanticist circles. But Russia can bend yet does not break. She has never broken, as a matter of fact, neither under the Mongols nor under Napoleon nor even Hitler. She will not break either under western pressure because, by constantly overestimating the determinism of history or of culture, the West underestimates the weight of geography. With Russia, every divergence takes on a geopolitical dimension. The free market and capitalism are not soluble in the long polar night, the permafrost, and three months of $-50°C$ temperatures.

That extravagant geography has another corollary, the weight of the State. Since the triumph of neoliberalism during the Reagan-Thatcher period, the West has only sworn by as little State involvement as possible. The State is the enemy. In Russia, the State has often been and is still often the enemy. But it has mostly been a friend. Without a State, no roads, no Trans-Siberian, no icebreakers. In such a climate, over such distances, through such empty territories, few capitalist investments are profitable. Many capitalist enterprises would have sunk before paying out dividends if they had had to invest on their own. The liberal logic thus comes up against the need for a State, with or without Putin. This is the reason why the Russians are wary of the State, but warier still of foreigners eager to change it. In Russia as in China, the non-existence of the State means anarchy, chaos, famine, civil war, foreign invasions. The non-existence of the State is worse than a prevaricating and torturing State: it would be the end of Russia. For a western liberal, the non-existence of the State is a dream; for a Russian, it is a nightmare.

Similarly, all Western theories trip over typically Russian "black boxes," such as the fact that the Russians, like the Chinese and the majority of the nations formerly colonized by the West, have a different conception of freedom. In the West, it is defined as the liberty to do business without interference and to vote. Elsewhere, freedom is synonymous with State independence and sovereignty.

To be free, for a Russian, a Chinese or an Indian, is to be assured that no foreign power will tell him/her what to do. They do not like to be bullied, in particular by an outside power. The West, which oppresses the rest of the world with its military and economic might, which imposes its cultural superiority, its "values," and its supremacy on the rest of the world in all self-righteousness, obviously cannot understand that interpretation of the term.

Russia also has another kind of relation to property. In a country that stretches over eleven time zones, land registry does not have the same importance as in London, Geneva or New York. And the very tough living conditions make it better to rely on your neighbor than on some title deed to survive. The notion of *krugovaya poruka*, never discussed by Western experts, is nevertheless essential to understanding the social and political workings of Russia.[30] This notion implies joint responsibility between two obligors, the one who receives aid and the one obliged to give it. It is linked to *obshchina*, the ancient Russian commune, and is based on the strength of interpersonal links and informal exchange of goods and services, a principle totally unknown in Western individualistic societies, whose social links are limited to the activity of consumerist atoms.

It is a form of collective insurance guaranteeing support to members of the community and it puts phenomena decried in the West as bureaucracy and corruption under a new more positive light.

All of this shows that Russia is neither Europe nor Asia, and is not reducible to any category of Western philosophy and politics. The West perceives this as an unbearable challenge. It cannot reconcile itself to understanding that this challenge is not imposed by Russia but by itself, because it refuses to admit that its own categories are inoperative and that its narrow conception of freedom and democracy can be considered in another way.

By challenging Russia to convert to its views, the West triggered a war which has extended over a thousand years and which will not end until the West renounces its hegemonic views. And so the myth of the fierce bear is bound to last, even if the Ukrainian crisis were to know a happy ending, because neither the United States nor Europe are ready or willing to throw in the towel.

They are buoyed by the certainty that they are the masters and that Russia is their pupil, and by the noisy demonstrations of support in East European countries. It was Czech writer Milan Kundera, followed by Vaclav Havel and Polish intellectuals, who spoke of a "kidnapped West" to describe East European countries allied to the Soviet Union.[31] As soon as the Iron Curtain fell, the generation that had grown up in opposition to communism was brought to power and rapidly converted to opposition to Russia because of the bad memories of an association too often backed by tanks, but also from the need to find a post-communism identity—to say nothing of the elites who succumbed to the allure and bribery of Europe and America.[32]

After 1991, the representation of Central Europe as opposed to Russia did much to forge an identity for these newly freed countries and allowed them to be rapidly integrated into the European Union and into NATO. With the disappearance of the communist "brother countries" ideology, those nations found themselves devoid of identity. As Slavs, they were neither Latin nor Germanic like the rest of Western Europe. Being Catholic or Protestant, they felt very different from Orthodox countries. This feeling of being hybrids, of belonging to neither side, developed a powerful need to cling to one camp, that of Western Europe in this case. Brandishing the Russian threat has thus been a very effective weapon to accelerate their integration within the European and American orbit, which was eager to regain ground on Russia.

As a result, the newly independent countries facilitated the exclusion of Russia from Europe, providing the bricks that enabled the building of a wall of hostility between her and the West. That gap has generated a still bigger differentiation between "civilized" Europe and an East now more distant and more uncertain. East European borders, which cut Germany into two before 1991, were abruptly displaced 2,000 kilometers to the east. Russia found herself alone, isolated, next to Byelorussia and Ukraine before the latter fell a victim to power grabbing attempts in 2004 and 2014. With the rise of nationalisms in Eastern Europe and in Ukraine, the gap rapidly transformed into violent hostility, as had been the case in Estonia with the case of the Bronze Soldier and in Ukraine, with the Donbass revolt following the February 2014 coup.

Opposing Russia to Accelerate European Integration

Kundera, like Havel, attributed a demonic, malefic power to Russia, accused of having destroyed the secular culture of Mitteleuropa, although it was Hitler who first invaded Central Europe, installed dictatorial regimes, and tore to shreds the old cultural traditions of the Habsburgs' Mitteleuropa. This aggressiveness of the new Central European and Baltic countries against Russia has always served to underline their European identity, hence their legitimacy within the European Union and NATO, Russia having ruled out any interference in their national affairs and having merely protested against the status of quasi-apartheid reserved to Russian minorities which, as in Estonia, find themselves stateless and deprived of political rights.

Central European countries' aggressive quest for identity, when supported by talented writers such as Milan Kundera or Vaclav Havel, is one more element that becomes embedded in the huge backdrop, in the fabric of the anti-Russian meta-narrative woven by the West. That fabric is composed of two main threads, the vertical thread of Muscovite patrimonialism and the horizontal thread of path dependence. Innumerable local and temporary tales come along on top of this left Central European Russophobia, anti-Putin discourse, criticism of autocracy that keeps evolving with time, depending on whether the Russian president is patriotic or pro-Western.

Those tales contradict each other often, claiming on the one hand that Putin is the heir to Stalin or is nostalgic for czarism, or appears to regret that Stalin won the war against Hitler—all of this in an apparent cacophony which gives the impression of a rich debate of ideas and of a plurality of opinions which delights the media. In reality, those divergences are only superficial: seen from above, all those speeches have but one message: Russia is governed by a president "clinging to power" and leading his country against its "true" interests; Russia is a power that wishes to do us harm.

Such is the essence of the anti-Russian myth. Everything else is unimportant.

| Conclusion |

CO-EXISTENCE, MULTIPOLARITY, AND PEACE

"A day will come when, for you too, weapons will slip out of your hands! A day will come when war will seem as absurd and be as impossible between Paris and London, between Petersburg and Berlin, between Vienna and Turin, as it would be impossible and seem absurd today between Rouen and Amiens, between Boston and Philadelphia. A day will come when France, you Russia, you Italy, you England, you Germany, all of you nations of the continent, without losing your distinct qualities and glorious individuality, will merge into a higher unity and found the European brotherhood, absolutely like Normandy, Brittany, Bourgogne, Lorraine, Alsace, all of our provinces, merged into France."
Victor Hugo, "Discours sur l'Europe," Peace Congress in Paris, August 21, 1849.

In a remarkable article, former Australian prime minister Kevin Rudd showed how the Chinese conception of the world was influenced over the very long term by the behavior of Europeans toward China.[1] Not only did the Europeans act as despicable colonialists during the opium wars, and as butchers during the Boxer rebellion in the last hours of the empire, but they so shamefully humiliated the young republic and discredited it so irremediably that it was never able to get over it when faced with communists that were more intransigent toward imperialist powers.

"By 1916," Rudd writes, "the Triple Entente had convinced the infant Chinese Republic, barely five years after its inception, to enter the war against Germany. Back then, in language that sounds very familiar now, they were called upon to behave as a responsible member of the international community and support the allied cause." Hundreds of thousands of Chinese workers were thus sent to the European front to dig trenches and die under bombs and epidemics, an episode totally ignored by our historians, who did not mention it at all during the First World War centenary in 2014.

By way of thanks, China, which belonged in the winners' camp, was prevented from participating in the plenary sessions of the Versailles treaty negotiations and, as the epitome of contempt, the former German colonies in China were transferred to Japan! One can imagine how the Chinese felt. Two years after Versailles, Mao founded the Chinese Communist Party. We know what happened next.

Doesn't this sad episode shed new light on the history of China, Mao's success, the legitimacy of the communist party still leading China, and the deep suspicion the Chinese have for Westerners and their promises? Isn't China's determination, now that it has recovered its strength, to remodel a world order which it finds unjust, understandable? Hasn't it become urgent to "understand China's perspective rather than, high-handedly, as a demander, to simply expect China to buy into the Western canon of values and the order based on it?" It is to the credit of Kevin Rudd that he warned against "the fact that we somehow believe it is self-evident and that it is better than anything else on offer cannot suffice."

What is true for China is even truer for Russia. But, as we have recorded throughout this book, anti-Russian prejudices are so deeply anchored in the Western collective subconscious that it would take ten, a hundred, a thousand Kevin Rudds to successfully eradicate them. The lie has been lasting so long, it has been so often repeated, under so many forms, that it has become official gospel to the extent that no representative in office dares to denounce it. For a European or an American, it will be easier to acknowledge their wrongs toward China than those against Russia. Because Russia is too close. Admitting that Russia might be right, even a little, would be an attack on our deepest identity, on all that has founded our behavior regarding the rest of the world in the past thousand years. Even suggesting that America might work with Russia in a non-confrontational and cooperative manner, as Donald Trump has done, gives rise to an hysterical reaction similar to that to Putin and indeed, the two were soon demonized in tandem.

This is why in Ukraine, Georgia, Syria, and everywhere else, the West is trying so hard to make Putin "see reason," as newspapers are wont to say. It betrays a terrible anguish: if Putin were right, even partially so, it would mean that we are wrong. And being wrong, for Western culture which believes so strongly in the universality of its values and in the superiority of its political and moral order—that is intolerable.

What we see today to the east of Europe is but the repetition of the Great Schism, of the lie and falsification that founded it. To build their empire and establish their supremacy over the other Christian patriarchs, the emperor and the pope had to destroy, or at least subjugate, Byzantium and the Oriental Church. At the cost of a mystification of history designed to have the Orientals bear the responsibility of the separation.

A new chapter of the same history is being written under our eyes right now. The Soviet Union dissolved in peace and Russia has pacifically withdrawn within her borders. That has not been enough. The European Union and NATO are conducting a military buildup in the new independent States, while accusing Russia of wanting to "invade" them. But why would Russia want to invade them when she has just freed them? Never mind the facts. What matters is the discourse, the discourse that helps mask Anglo-American interests behind those of their vassal allies even as they seek to remain blessed with every virtue freedom, democracy, respect of human rights as if we were the only ones to cultivate them.

The myth of the Russian bear and the evil czar only says one thing: Russia is the author of her own misfortunes and of those she inflicts on the rest of the world. Great academic theories on "Muscovite patrimonialism" and "dependence on history and geography" that would explain the atavistic attachment of Russia to autocracy and expansionism, beneath the academic jargon, have no other function than to justify Euro-American imperialism.

At no time do western political leaders, historians, journalists ask themselves the question: do we bear any responsibility for the crises in the world? Are our values really superior to those of the others? Is our unilateral vision of the world in the world's interest? Aren't there wrongs on both sides?

Such questions are brushed aside given the geopolitical stakes and the Western will to dominate the world. The law of the strongest prevails in international relations. But these questions can still impact the discourse, and thereby influence public opinion, to which democratic leaders are sensitive.

It is thus at that level that action must take place if we want to one day end the age-old conflict cutting Europe into two. The discourse must be changed, it must be made to evolve away from long-induced antipathies and move toward negotiation, co-existence, multipolarity and most importantly: peace.

To say the least, this isn't the way things have been shaping up. Since the first publication of this book in French two years ago, the situation has deteriorated further on all fronts.

In Syria, the intervention of the Russian army alongside the Syrian government forces in September 2015 triggered renewed hysteria in the mainstream media. Within a few weeks the Russian air strikes led to a reversal of the situation on the ground and to victories against the Jihadists, whereas the US-led broad coalition that ostensibly was combating the Islamic State had achieved no tangible results after months of bombings. The more victories were notched against the Salafist "rebels", the greater was the rage of Western media against Russia. This Russian-bashing reached its apex in the fall of 2016 when the coalition led by Russia, Iran and the Syrian government launched attacks against the bastions of the Islamic rebellion in East Aleppo. Thanks to a well-orchestrated propaganda campaign, each military operation, each air raid was denounced in the mainstream media as a war crime, a crime against humankind, and an abomination committed against the civilian population. At the same time, the civilian victims of the Jihadists' strikes were systematically unreported, the presence of Al-Nusra/ Al-Sham/Al-Qaida fighters amongst the rebels was denied, as well as the fact that they were holding the civilian population of East Aleppo hostage, preventing everyone from fleeing via the government-announced safe corridors to the government-held area. Probably inspired by former French foreign minister Laurent Fabius, who expressed his admiration for the "good job" done by Al-Qaida in Syria, the complicit mainstream press published reams of reports on the White Helmets, presented as impartial first-aid workers like the members of the international Red Cross, a portrayal soon thoroughly debunked.[2] The tweets and truncated pictures of little Bana al-Abed went viral on social networks with the complicity of the correspondents of the mainstream Western media and press agencies. Even the final fall of East Aleppo and the de-mining operations carried out by Russian soldiers to allow the population to regain their homes did not disarm the mainstream press's propaganda. The presentation of liberated East Aleppo as seen through the goggles of the *Daily Mail* is a marvel of the genre.[3]

In Ukraine, the military situation has been frozen since the signature of the Minsk agreements in September 2014 and February 2015 between the leaders of Ukraine, Russia, France, and Germany. But no concrete progress has been registered. On the contrary, the economic and political situation of the region has steadily deteriorated. Two years after the February 2014 coup, the corruption of the new authorities has become as glaring as that of the previous government, which had triggered the Maidan demonstrations. So much so that all members of the Ukrainian government of foreign origins and supported by the West have resigned, including former Georgian president Mikheil Saakachvili, now governor of Odessa. Similarly, the nomination of extreme right-wingers and neo-Nazis to the highest functions of the state, such as the chief of police, who is a member of the rightwing Svoboda party, has intensified without comment by the Western media, which keep reviling populist parties such as the National Front in France and FPÖ in Austria, for having anything negative to say about it. The sanctions against Russia are routinely extended by the European Union and the United States with the noisy approval of the mainstream media.

Worse than that, aware of the failure of their communications and of the growing responsiveness to Russian media by their publics, the European leaders have tried to create new organizations and to finance centers to combat the dangers of the "propaganda" of the Russian information sites Sputnik News and Russia Today. The success of Russia Today, now more watched than CNN and the main Western news channels, has thrown them into a state of confusion. A center has been opened in Estonia with the help of NATO. And the European Parliament, for all its concern for human rights and freedom of expression, has had nothing better to do than come up with a resolution attempting to censor the Russian media. Forgetting in the process that Western propaganda channels deployed for the edification of Russian-speaking audiences Radio Free Europe/Liberty, Deutsche Welle, France 24 enjoy budgets far superior to those of Sputnik and RT.

But it is in the United States that anti-Russian hysteria has achieved delirious proportions in the last two years, and especially during the last months of the presidential electoral campaign pitting Hillary Clinton against Donald Trump. If, as revealed by WikiLeaks, Hillary Clinton's candidacy was immediately approved by the Democrat establishment, which did everything to eliminate the more critical candidate, Bernie Sanders, on the Republican side it was Donald Trump who won the primaries, to the stupefaction of the party leaders and of the Neo-conservatives, who saw their dominance called into question by an outsider deemed unpredictable as he is beyond their control.

Right from the start of his campaign, Trump, who besides having transgressed by turning away from the traditional media to favor social networks and communicating by tweets in order to get his views out without media adulteration, committed the mortal sin of affirming his sympathy for Putin, whom he deemed "more of a leader" than President Obama.[4]

At the end of July, the Republican candidate had indeed worsened his case by declaring during a press conference: "Russia, I hope you will be able to find back the thirty thousand emails which are lacking in the private mailbox Hillary Clinton used when she was Secretary of State. I think our media will be very grateful." This statement was immediately considered "beyond the pale" and an anti-American act of treason by the entire Washington establishment, Republicans as well as Democrats.[5]

Between the end of summer and the November 8 election, the Democrats' campaign was literally obsessed with Russia and Putin, with candidate Clinton ceaselessly denouncing her opponent's allegiance to Moscow. WikiLeaks' wave after wave publication of the emails of Hillary Clinton's campaign manager, John Podesta, revealed how the Democrat Party had maneuvered to eliminate Bernie Sanders. Hillary Clinton's secret mails, which showed her doublespeak during her plum conferences for Wall Street bankers and her speeches to Democrat electors, as well as the Clinton Foundation's shady deals, did much to inflame the situation. Russia was immediately accused of being the source of those revelations and of having organized the hacking of the Democratic Party's servers. Almost all the media, rallying behind Hillary Clinton, relayed the information and blew it up out of proportion, spoon-fed by anonymous intelligence sources with alleged new revelations passing as proofs of Russian interference. And also, happily, thereby avoiding having to address the actual content of the damning leaked material.

The story could have ended then, had Hillary Clinton been elected. But to the astonishment of the entire American political and media establishment, the unthinkable happened and Donald Trump trumped her. In the wake of stupefaction came disappointment, soon followed by the spirit of revenge. If the major media, which had all failed in their prognostics and confused their role of providing information with their mission of propagandizing in favor of Hillary Clinton, did acknowledge their mistake, they soon recovered their old reflexes: if Hillary had failed and if they themselves had betrayed their mission, it wasn't their fault, but that of the Russians! Prodded by the soon-to-fold Obama Administration, humiliated by the defeat, and in despair over having to relinquish power to a new competing elite over which it has no hold, the establishment had found the ideal scapegoat: Putin and the pack of hackers at his beck and call.

This was how "Russian hacking" became the main occupation of the Obama Administration in the two months preceding its exit. All of the country's intelligence agencies were commanded to provide proofs, which were published in a report made public in early January 2017. Nothing really tangible, just a load of circumstantial evidence of all kinds amalgamated to take the place of "proof"—mere presumptions which no worthy tribunal would retain to condemn a guilty party.[6]

This Russian hacking affair which is purported to have influenced American electors in favor of Donald Trump is rather droll when you remember that, between 1846 and 2000, the United States was the source of more than a hundred electoral manipulations in foreign countries, according to a Carnegie-Mellon University study. As for the Russians, they haven't forgotten the manipulation operation of their 1996 presidential election carried out by Bill Clinton's services. That year, Clinton's teams did indeed torpedo the Russian elections in favor of their favored candidate, Boris Yeltsin, against the Russian people's favorite, Communist Zyuganov. In his excellent investigation published on July 15, 1996, *Time* Moscow correspondent, Michael Kramer, abundantly documented how the Democratic president's services manipulated the polls and the targeted groups, created splinter candidates, took advantage of the main media and television channels then in the hands of oligarchs close to them, bribed parties, and utilized all possible techniques of influence to impose a candidate who to that point had been rejected by a large majority of Russian electors. No doubt that in Moscow and perhaps in the Obama Administration's

Democratic Party circles, this sad episode was remembered when it was time to invent the fable of Russian hackers falsifying the American election.[7]

And finally how can such hysteria over Russian hacking be justified when the United States has initiated a comprehensive, worldwide spying enterprise, as is known from the revelations of Edward Snowden, the most important whistleblower of all times? And how can whistleblowers be encouraged when they serve the interests of the government and criminalized when they denounce its drifts?[8] Isn't there a contradiction? Should not the Nobel Prize for Peace have gone to Edgar Snowden rather than to President Obama?

On January 20, 2017, President-elect Donald Trump took office. Will he know how to, will he still want to, or will he simply give up on trying to turn the tide and bring back civility in the relations between the West and Russia? Is a respite in what is turning out to be a new Cold War at all possible? We certainly wish so.

After all, if the task is almost superhuman, as no one will doubt after reading this book, it just may not be altogether impossible.

BIBLIOGRAPHY

Adamovski Ezequiel, *Euro-Orientalism. Liberal ideology and the Image of Russia in France (c. 1740-1880)*, Oxford/ Bern, Peter Lang, 2006.

Akhvlediani Magdalena, "The fatal flaw: the media and the Russian invasion of Georgia," *Small Wars & Insurgencies*, Vol. 20, No 2, June 2009.

Alexievitch Svetlana, *La fin de l'homme rouge ou le temps du désenchantement*, Arles, Actes Sud, 2013.

Armeyskov Sergey, "Russophobia, the discreet charm of cultural racism & the legacy of hate," on the blog Russian Universe. Understanding Russia with a Russian.

Barber Benjamin, *Jihad versus MacWorld*, Paris, Desclée de Brouwer, 1996.

Barber Benjamin, *Comment le capitalisme nous infantilise*, Paris, Fayard, 2007.

Besançon Alain, *Sainte Russie*, Paris, Éditions de Fallois, 2012.

Bierhoff Hans-Werner, *Person Perception and Attribution*, Berlin, Springer, 1989.

Blanc Simone, "Histoire d'une phobie : le testament de Pierre le Grand," *Cahiers du monde russe et soviétique*, Vol. 9, 1968.

Brown James D. J., "A Stereotype, Wrapped in a Cliché, Inside a Caricature: Russian Foreign Policy and Orientalism," *Politics*, Vol. 30/3, 2010.

Bzrezinski Zbigniew, *Le grand échiquier*, Librairie Arthème Fayard/Pluriel, 2010.

Bzrezinski Zbigniew, *Strategic Vision: America and the Crisis of Global Power*, Basic Books, 2013.

Cadot Michel, *L'image de la Russie dans la vie intellectuelle française, 1839-1856*, Paris, Fayard, 1967.

Cain Jimmie E. Jr., *Bram Stoker and Russophobia. Evidence of the British Fear of Russia in* Dracula *and* The Lady of the Shroud, Jefferson, McFarland & Company, 2006.

Carrère d'Encausse Hélène, *L'Impératrice et l'abbé : un duel littéraire inédit entre Catherine II et l'abbé Chappe d'Auteroche*, Paris, Fayard, 2003.

Cattori Sylvia, "Dick Marty : ce que j'ai découvert m'a profondément choqué," arretsurinfo.ch, January 7, 2015.

Chevènement Jean-Pierre, "Ukraine : il est temps qu'une parole raisonnable se fasse entendre," *Marianne*, May 22, 2014.

Cohen Stephen F., "Hérétiques contre faucons," *Le Monde diplomatique*, October 2014 (from *The Nation*, September 15, 2014).

Conesa Pierre, "La fabrication de l'ennemi : le cas russe," *Libération*, December 31, 2009.

Corm Georges, "Les causes des guerres à venir," *Cahier du GIPRI*, No 7, Geneva, 2009.

Van Dijk Teun, "Opinions and Ideologies in the press," in Allan Bell & Peter Garrett, *Approaches to Media Discourse*, Oxford Blackwell, 1998. Also, *Ideology: A Multidisciplinary Approach*, London, Sage, 1998.

Foglesong David, *The American Mission and the Evil Empire*, Cambridge, Cambridge University Press, 2007.

Galice Gabriel, *Du peuple nation*, Lyon, Mario Mella Éditions, 2002.

Gauseth Daniel, *Framing the Russia–Georgian War. An analysis of the Norwegian print-press coverage in August 2008*, Department of History and Classical Studies, NTNU, Trondheim, 2012.

Gleason J. H., *The Genesis of Russophobia in Great Britain. A Study of the Interaction of Policy and Opinion*, Cambridge, Harvard University Press, 1950.

Haar John M., "The Russian Menace: Baltic German Publicists and Russophobia in World War I Germany," Thesis, Ann Arbor Michigan, University Microfilms, 1986.

Heath Robert G., *Le Schisme occidental de 1054. Les Francs imposent leur Credo à l'Église romaine*, Lyon, Éditions du Cosmogone, 2012.

Heinrich Hans-Georg and Tanaev Kirill, "Georgia & Russia: Contradictory Media Coverage of the August War," in *Caucasian Review of International Affairs*, Vol. 3, summer 2009.

Hoesli Eric, *À la conquête du Caucase. Épopée géopolitique et guerres d'influences*, Paris, Éditions des Syrtes, 2006.

Hopkirk Peter, *The Great Game: The Struggle for Empire in Central Asia*, New York, Kodansha International, 1990.

Jazec Olivier, "L'obsession antirusse," *Le Monde diplomatique*, No 721, April 2014.

Kapuscinski Ryszard, *Imperium*, Paris, 10/18, 1999.

Krieger Uwe, *Meinungsmacht. Der Einfluss von Eliten auf Leitmedien und Alpha-Journalisten – eine kritische Analyse*, Köln, Herbert von Halem Verlag, 2013.

Lampryllos Cyriaque, *La mystification fatale. Étude orthodoxe sur le Filioque*, Lausanne, L'Age d'Homme, 1987.

Leclercq Arnaud, *La Russie, puissance d'Eurasie. Histoire géopolitique des origines à Poutine*, Paris, Ellipses Edition, 2012.

Leroy-Beaulieu Anatole, *L'Empire des tsars et les Russes*, Paris, Robert Laffont, 1990.

Lesur Charles-Ferdinand, *Des progrès de la puissance russe depuis son origine jusqu'au XIXe siècle*, Paris, 1812.

Lieven Anatol, "Against Russophobia," *World Policy Journal*, January 1, 2001.

Luostarinnen Heikki and Ottosen Rune, "The Changing Role of the Media in Conflicts. From Cold War to the Net Age," in *Journalism and the New World Order*, Vol. 2.

Luttwak Edward N., *La grande stratégie de l'Empire byzantin*, Paris, Odile Jacob, 2010.

Macgilchrist Felicitas, *Journalism and the Political. Discursive tensions in news coverage of Russia*, Amsterdam/Philadelphia, John Benjamins Publishing Company, 2011.

MacKenzie Wallace Donald, *Russia. Its History and Condition to 1877*, Boston/Tokyo, J.B. Millet Company, 1877.

McNally Raymond T., "The Origins of Russophobia in France 1812-1830," in *American Slavic and East European Review*, 17 April 1958.

Malia Martin, *L'Occident et l'énigme russe. Du Cavalier de bronze au mausolée de Lénine*, Paris, Seuil, 2003.

Matlock Jack, *Reagan and Gorbatchev: How the Cold War Ended*, as well as his blog, Ukraine and the United States, JackMatlock.com, February 8, 2014.

Mearsheimer John J., "La responsabilité de l'Occident dans la crise en Ukraine," in *Horizons et Débats*, September 17, 2014. Original text in *Foreign Affairs*, September/October 2014.

Moller Peter Ulf, "Russian Identity as an East-West Controversy Outlining a Concept," in *Slavica Lundensia*, No 19, 1999.

Narochnitskaïa Natalia, *Que reste-t-il de notre victoire ? Russie-Occident : le malentendu*, Paris, Éditions des Syrtes, 2008.

Neumann Iver B., "Uses of the Other. The East in European Identity Formation," Minneapolis, University of Minnesota Press, *Borderlines*, Vol. 9, 1999.

Niedermaier A. K., *Countdown to War in Georgia : Russia's Foreign Policy and Media Coverage of the Conflict in South Ossetia and Abkhazia*, United States, Minneapolis, East View Press, 2008.

Nye Joseph S., *Soft Power: The Means to Success in World Politics*, Basic Books, 1990.

Paddock Troy. R. E., *Creating the Russian Peril. Education, the Public Sphere, and National Identity in Imperial Germany, 1890-1914*, Rochester, NY, Camden House, 2010.

Perret Ariane, *Collision en plein ciel. La tragédie des enfants russes*, Paris, Éditions des Syrtes, 2006.

Plater-Zyberk Henry, "Beslan – Lessons Learned?" Conflict Studies Research Centre, Russian Series 04/34, Defence Academy of the United Kingdom, November 2004.

Poe Marshall T., *A People Born to Slavery. Russia in Early Modern European Ethnography 1476-1748*, Ithaca, Cornell University, 2000.

Rey Marie-Pierre, *Le dilemme russe. La Russie d'Ivan le Terrible à Boris Eltsine*, Paris, Flammarion, 2002.

Roberts Paul Craig, "L'insouciance occidentale nous condamne," *Le Courrier*, August 7, 2014 (translated from "The World Is Doomed by Western Insouciance," paulcraigroberts.org).

Runciman Steven, *Le schisme d'Orient. La papauté et les Églises d'Orient aux XIe et XIIe siècles*, Paris, Les Belles Lettres, 2005.

Runciman Steven, *La Chute de Constantinople 1453*, Paris, Tallandier, 2007.

Saffrain Ghislaine, "Russie : les 'zones d'ombre' du massacre de Beslan," in *Au nom du 11 septembre. Les démocraties à l'épreuve de l'antiterrorisme*, by Didier Bigo, Laurent Bonelli and Thomas Deltombe (dir.), La Découverte, 2008.

Said Edward, *L'Orientalisme. L'Orient créé par l'Occident*, Paris, Seuil, 1980.

Sanders Paul, "Under Western Eyes. How meta-narrative shapes our perception of Russia – and why it is time for a qualitative shift," Vienna, Institute for Human Science.

Sapir Jacques, "Un scandale," a blog on russeurope.hypotheses.org.

Siary Gérard, *Naufrage & tribulations d'un Japonais dans la Russie de Catherine II (1782-1792)*, introduction, translation and notes by Gérard Siary, postface by Jacques Proust, Paris, Chandeigne, 2004.

Sieff Martin, "Quand la Russie applique sa recette de la doctrine Monroe," in *L'Hebdo*, May 1, 2014 (adapted from *The Globalist*).

Sokoloff Georges, *Le retard russe*, Paris, Fayard, 2014.

Steingart Gabor, "Face à la Russie, l'Europe fait fausse route," in *Le Temps*, August 25, 2014 (from an English version published in *Handelsblatt* on August 8, 2014).

Taras Raymond, *Russia's Identity in International Relations. Images, Perceptions, Misperceptions*, London/New York, Routledge, 2013.

Tchoubarian Alexandre, *La Russie et l'idée européenne*, Paris, Éditions des Syrtes, 2009.

Temkin Gabriel, *My Just War: The Memoirs of a Jewish Red Army Soldier in World War II*, Presidio Press, 1997.

Trifković Srdja, "Understanding Western Russophobia," *Liberty*, Official Publication of the Serbian National Defense Council of America, June 2014.

Tsygankov Andrei P., *Russophobia. Anti-Russian Lobby and American Foreign Policy*, New York, Palgrave Macmillan, 2009.

Ulfkotte Udo, *Gekaufte Journalisten. Wie Politiker, Geheimdienste und Hochfinanz Deutschlands Massenmedien lenken*, Rottenburg, Kopp Verlag, 2014.

Vambery Arminius, *The Coming Struggle for India*, London, Cassell, 1885.

Védrine Hubert, "Ukraine, comment s'en sortir," *Le Figaro Magazine*, May 2, 2014.

Wilk Mariusz, *La Maison au bord de l'Oniégo*, Éditions Noir sur Blanc, Lausanne, 2006.

Wolff Larry, *Inventing Eastern Europe. The Map of Civilization on the Mind of the Enlightenment*, Stanford, Stanford University Press, 1994.

Zaricki Tomasz, "The embarrassing Russian connection. Selective memory of the Russian heritage in contemporary Poland," in *Russia's Identity in International Relations. Images, Perceptions, Misperceptions*. Edited by Raymond Taras, Routledge Series, 2012.

Internet sites:

arretsurinfo.ch; fr.sputniknews.com; dedefensa;

m.alterinfo.net; thevineyardsaker.fr; theglobalist; mondialisation.ca; the russian universe; russiatoday; russeurope.

ENDNOTES

Foreword

1   Alexandre Soljenitsyne, *Nos Pluralistes*, translated by Nikita Struve, Éditions L'Age d'Homme, 1983, p. 12. The English version (Alexander Solzhenitsyn, *Our Pluralists, Survey*, a Journal of East & West Studies, Vol. 29, No 2 (25), New York, 1985) is unobtainable.

2   On this topic, cf. Anne L. Clunan, *The Social Construction of Russia's Resurgence: Aspirations, Identity and Security Interests*, Baltimore, The Johns Hopkins University Press, 2009. And Didier Chaudet, Florent Parmentier, Benoît Pélopidas, *L'empire au miroir : stratégies de puissance aux États-Unis et en Russie*, Genève, Droz, 2007. See also the criticism of Andrei Tsygankov's book by Florent Parmentier, "Andrei P. Tsygankov: Anti-Russian Lobby and American Foreign Policy," *Critique internationale*, 3/2010, No 48.

3   The references are to be found in the various chapters of the book. One Finnish author on Finnish Russophobia should be singled out, however: Heikki Luostarinen, "Finnish Russophobia: The Story of an Enemy Image," *Journal of Peace Research*, 26/2, Sage Publications, Oslo, 1989.

4   Raymond Taras prefers to use the term "hypopsia" to qualify the generalized fear, mistrust, and suspicion of the West regarding Russia. Cf. *"Scapegoating Strangers": Contemporary politics of fear and hypopsia in Europe*, School of Social and Political Science, University of Edinburgh, April 2015. The term "Russophobia" is more readily understandable.

5   Source: Reporters Without Borders, en.rsf.org.

Chapter One

1   Sergey Armeyskov, "Russophobia. The discreet charm of cultural racism & the legacy of hate," on the blog Russian Universe. Understanding Russia with a Russian.

2   See Edward Said's theses and his book on orientalism and the fabrication of the East by the West, *Orientalism*, United Kingdom, Routledge

       & Kegan Paul, 1978.

3   Mariusz Wilk recounts his experience of the Russian world in several books translated into French: *Le Journal d'un loup* (1999), *La Maison au bord de l'Oniégo* (2006), *Dans les pas du renne* (2009), *Portage* (2010) and *Dans le sillage des oies sauvages* (2012), all published by Éditions Noir sur Blanc, Lausanne. The first one has also been translated into English as *The Journals of a White Sea Wolf* (Random House UK, 2003).

4   See Chapter 5.

5   Ryszard Kapuscinski, *Imperium*, US, A.A. Knopf, 1994.

6   terangaweb.com/quel-est-le-bilan-humain-de-la-traite-negriere.

7   http://katehon.com/article/short-analysis-utter-savagery-nice-france-vous-etes-une-grande-hypocrite and afro04.skyrock.com/417289355-l-extermination-des-aborigenes-de-tasmanie.html. The article reports, among other things, the end of the last aboriginal woman in 1876, whose sister had been kidnapped, whose husband had drowned, and who herself had been raped, and whose body, after being exhumed, was for a long time exhibited in the Tasmania Museum. http://vuesdumonde.forumactif.com/t2017-l-extermination-des-aborigenes-de-tasmanie

8   Pierre Conesa, "La fabrication de l'ennemi : le cas russe" (Fabricating the ennemy : the Russian case), *Libération*, December 31, 2009. See also his *La mécanique du chaos : bushisme, prolifération et terrorisme*, Paris, Éditions de l'Aube, 2007.

9   On February 17, Kosovo's parliament declared Kosovo's independence from Serbia. Following that declaration, the U.S. and several European states officially recognized the independence of Kosovo. https://www.asil.org/insights/volume/12/issue/2/kosovos-declaration-independence-self-determination-secession-and

10   Cf. Stephen F. Cohen, "Patriotic Heresy vs. the New Cold War," *The Nation*, August 27, 2014. thenation.com/article/patriotic-heresy-vs-new-cold-war.

11   See PEW Research Center's polls on the image of Russia in the world. For example, that of July 2014: "Russia's Global Image Negative amid Crisis in Ukraine." Europe and the United States gather more than 70% unfavorable opinions. The Middle East is stable at 68% whereas in Asia, Latin America and Africa the rate of favorable opinions is higher than that of unfavorable ones.

12   On December 4, 2014. "Text of H. Res. 78: Strongly condemning the actions of the Russian Federation,"govtrack.us.congress, as well as "Ron Paul Warns Reckless Congress Just Declared War on Russia," zerohedge.com.

13 See Inna Doulkina, "Se souvenir de la Russie" (Remembering Russia) and Alexei Ivanov, "La diversité intérieure de la Russie est infinie" (Russia's domestic diversity is infinite) in *Le Courrier de Russie* No 268, November 7, 2014.

14 "On m'a refoulée à cause de Vladimir Poutine" (I was turned away because of Vladimir Putin), *20 Minutes*, May 5, 2014 in 20min.ch/ro/news/vaud/story...21545813.

15 See James D. J. Brown, "A Stereotype, Wrapped in a Cliché, Inside a Caricature: Russian Foreign Policy and Orientalism," *Politics*, Vol. 30/3, 2010.

Chapter Two

1 See explanations and references further along.

2 See, inter alia, Chris Kaspar de Ploeg, *Ukraine in the Crossfire*, 2017, Paul Craig Roberts, *The Neoconservative Threat to World Order*, 2015, and Stephen Lendman, *Flashpoint in Ukraine*, 2014, all published by Clarity Press, Inc., Atlanta.

3 Cf. Olivier Jazec, "L'obsession antirusse" (The anti-Russian obsession) *Le Monde diplomatique*, No 721, April 2014.

4 nytimes.com/2002/71-die-when-two-jets-collide-high-above-southern-germany.

5 "L'image internationale de la Russie s'améliorera quand les Russes arrêteront de l'améliorer. Sputnik News 16.07.2012" in https://fr.sputniknews.com/opinion/20120716195366075/

6 See Ariane Perret's thorough investigation, *Collision en plein ciel. La tragédie des enfants russes* (Midair collision: the Russian children's tragedy), Paris, Éditions des Syrtes, 2006.

7 Mikhail Shishkin, "Ce que Poutine, roi du mensonge, prépare à l'Europe," *Le Temps*, October 25, 2014.

8 *Vremya Novosti*, September 2, 2004.

9 FSB: Russian acronym of the Russian Federal Security Service.

10 For a complete and fairly neutral narration of the event, see en.wikipedia.org/wiki/Beslan_school_siege.

11 Jeremy Bransien, "Russia: Troubling Questions Remain About Bloody Beslan Siege," rferl.org/articleprintview/1054690.html.

12 Anna Politkovskaya, "Poisoned by Putin," in *The Guardian*, Thursday September 9, 2004. theguardian.com/world/2004/sep/09/russia.media. Anna Politkovskaya will be assassinated two years later, on October 7, 2006, by Chechen henchmen condemned in 2012 without the identity of whoever ordered the killing being established beyond doubt. Born in New York and holding Russian and American nationalities,

Anna Politkovskaya violently criticized Vladimir Putin's regime and supported the Islamists demanding the independence of Chechnya with the help of sundry American NGOs such as PNAC (Project for a New American Century). This earned her the hatred of hundreds of Chechen and Russian families decimated by the terrorists and this also explains why the majority of Russians detested her.

13   Andrei P. Tsygankov, *Russophobia. Anti-Russian Lobby and American Foreign Policy*, New York, Palgrave Macmillan, 2009, p. 90.

14   "An Open Letter to Heads of State and Government of the European Union and NATO" in "Cessons d'embrasser Poutine" (Let's stop hugging Putin), voltairenet.org/article15120.html. For the German and English editions, cf. "Offener Brief rückt Putin in die Nähe eines Diktators" by Wolfgang Proissl, *Financial Times Deutschland*, September 29, 2004, and "Foreign Policy Experts Protest Putin's Action," by Colum Lynch, *The Washington Post*, September 29, 2004 (washingtonpost.com/wp-dyn/articles/A58044-2004Sep28.html?sub=AR).

15   Andrei Tsygankov, *ibid.* pp. 201 and 202.

16   "An Open Letter to the Heads of State and Government of the European Union and NATO" in *Free Republic*, freerepublic.com/focus/f-news/1237222/posts.

17   See next chapter.

18   Fiona Hill, "Stop Blaming Putin and Start Helping Him," September 10, 2004, quoted by Andrei Tsygankov, *ibid.* p. 202.

19   Henry Plater-Zyberk, "Beslan – Lessons Learned?" Conflict Studies Research Centre, Russian Series 04/34, Defence Academy of the United Kingdom, November 2004.

20   Andrei Tsygankov, *ibid.* p. 14. See also Ekho Moskvy, September 3, 2004, BBC MS and bbc.co.ik/hi/russian/russia/newsid_3646000/3646384.stm. An objective analysis of the impact of antiterrorist fighting on democratic regimes can be found in the collective work *Au Nom du 11 septembre. Les démocraties à l'épreuve de l'antiterrorisme*, by Didier Bigo, Laurent Bonelli and Thomas Deltombe (ed.), La Découverte, 2008. On Russia after Beslan, see Ghislaine Saffrain's contribution, "Russie : les 'zones d'ombre' du massacre de Beslan" (Russia : the dark areas of the Beslan massacre).

21   See the article "Deuxième guerre d'Ossétie du Sud" (Second war of South Ossetia) on fr.wikipedia.org. And also Charles King, "The Five Day War," in *Foreign Affairs*, November-December 2008.

22   In point of fact, there was little mention, speaking of asylum, of Britain's giving asylum to Chechen leaders Akhmad Zakayev (December 2003) and the USA welcoming Ilyas Akhmadov (August 2004) See http://tarpley.net/2007/09/14/russians-blast-us-uk-sponsorship-of-chechen-

terror/.
23 Ibid.
24 Hans-Georg Heinrich and Kirill Tanaev, "Georgia & Russia: Contradictory Media Coverage of the August War," in *Caucasian Review of International Affairs*, Vol. 3, summer 2009. cria-online.org/8_2.html.
25 echr.coe.int/Documents/HUDOC_38263_08_Annexes_ENG.pdf
26 Daniel Gauseth, "Framing the Russia-Georgian War. An analysis of the Norwegian print-press coverage in August 2008," thesis, Department of History and Classical Studies, NTNU, Trondheim, 2012. See also Margarita Akhvlediani, "The fatal flaw: the media and the Russian invasion of Georgia," *Small Wars & Insurgencies*, Vol. 20, N° 2, June 2009, 363. A.K. Niedermaier, *Countdown to War in Georgia: Russia's Foreign Policy and Media Coverage of the Conflict in South Ossetia and Abkhazia*, United States, Minneapolis, East View Press, 2008. Artur Jugaste, "Communicating Georgia. Georgia's Information Campaign in the 2008 War with Russia," thesis, Stockholm University, 2011. ut.ee/ABVKeskus/sisu/.../2011/.../Jugaste_MAp. For a wider vision of media coverage of conflicts, see Heikki Luostarinnen and Rune Ottosen, "The Changing Role of the Media in Conflicts. From Cold War to the Net Age," in *Journalism and the New World Order*, Vol. 2.
27 slate.com/articles/news_and_politics/foreigners/2008/08/world_inaction.html
28 economist.com/node/14560958,andnytimes.com/2009/10/01world/.../01russia.html.
29 Fred Weir, "Was Putin in Charge During Georgia War? Medvedev Begs to Differ," Christian Science Monitor, August 10, 2012. <http://www.csmonitor.com/World/Europe/2012/0810/Was-Putin-in-charge-during-Georgia-war-Medvedev-begs-to-differ>
30 "Refaire l'empire" (Rebuilding the empire), *Le Monde*, August 27, 2008.
31 "Georgia War Report Set to Blame Both Moscow and Tbilisi," Marc Champion, *Wall Street Journal*, September 28, 2009. wsj.com/articles/SB125409588027045015.
32 C. J. Chivers and E. Barry, "Georgia Claims on Russia War Called Into Question," *The New York Times*, November 6, 2008. nytimes.com/2008711/07/world/europe/07georgia/.html?pagewanted=all.
33 "Addendum au rapport sur le fonctionnement des institutions démocratiques en Géorgie." Document 13558, Parliamentary Assembly of the Council of Europe, September 30, 2014.
34 Véronika Dormann, "La stratégie des conflits gelés" (The strategy of

frozen conflicts), *Libération*, December 18, 2014, p. 4.
35 "Ossetian Crisis: Who Started It?" BBC News, August 19, 2008, news. bbc.co.uk/2/hi/europe7571096.stmp. And "What Really Happened in South Ossetia," BBC Newsnight.
36 Paul Sanders, "Under Western Eyes. How meta-narrative shapes our perception of Russia – and why it is time for a qualitative shift," iwm. at/transit/transit-online/under-western-eyes/
37 smh.com.au/sport/winter-olympics/despite-the-knockers-sochi-2014-was-a-success-20140222-338wg.html.
38 Benjamin Bidder, "Sochi Schadenfreude: Ha Ha, The Russians Screwed It Up Again," *Spiegelonline International*, February 11, 2014. See also www.spiegel.de>Englishsite>World>Russia; Simon Rosner, "Als CNN ein Foto aus Sotchi von mir wollte," *Wiener Zeitung Online*, 2.7.2014.
39 Marc Bennetts, "Russia's anti-gay law is wrong – but so is some of the criticism from the west," *The Guardian*, February 5, 2014.
40 "World unites in Russia-bashing for Sochi Olympics," *GBTimes*, February 10, 2014, gbtimes.com/world-unites-russia-bashing-sochi. See also Thom Wheeler, "Why a Media-Bashing Hasn't Stopped Russia Being the Olympics' Biggest Winner," in *Sabotage Times*, February 25, 2014 (sabotagetimes.com).
41 "Distorting Russia," thenation.com/article/178344/distorting-russia, February 12, 2014.
42 See also *Newsweek*, March 10/April 22, 2014. Interview of Stephen F. Cohen by Zoe Slander, "The American Who Dared Make Putin's Case."
43 http://www.csmonitor.com/World/Olympics/2014/0207/Western-leaders-stay-away-from-Sochi-Olympics.-Snub-to-Russiaern leaders. Include ? Also US then : https://www.theguardian.com/sport/2013/dec/18/obama-names-gay-delegates-sochi-olympics
44 For this question please see «Dopage en Russie. Chronologie du scandale – Jeux Olympiques» by AFP on Sport24.lefigaro.fr, 9.12.2016. "Sebastian Coe could be recalled to parliament for Russian doping questions", Press association Friday 17 June 2016 on www. theguardian.com and James Riach "The Fancy Bears leaks shouldn't tar all athletes with the same doping brush", http://www.the guardian. com, September 21, 2016.
45 http://www.bbc.com/sport/olympics/36970627
46 James Riach, "The Fancy Bears shouldn't tar all athletes with the same doping brush," September 21, 2016. https://www.theguardian.com/commentisfree/2016/sep/21/fancy-bears-leaks-athletes-doping-russia-cyber-hackers>
47 http://tass.com/sport/921750

Chapter Three

1 See note 1.
2 Told by Daniel Gauseth as an introduction to his thesis. The full but hard to understand video interview is also available on YouTube: Nikolai Orlov, "Fox News – Cover Up – Georgia Russia War", youtube.com/ watch?v=dKASUchWf_U.
3 Let us note however that the complete interview (41 minutes of which only 24 were broadcast) is on the TF1 website. videos.tf1.fr/.../l-integralite-de-l-interview-de-vladimir-poutine-843075.html.
4 Anatol Lieven, "Against Russophobia," *World Policy Journal*, January 1, 2001.
5 According to his real biography, Putin only served as an intel agent in eastern Germany in his early career years from 1985 to 1990 http://eng.putin.kremlin.ru/bio.
6 François Sergent, "Chauvin," *Libération*, December 18, 2014.
7 Frédéric Koller, "Le tsar des réacs," *Le Temps*, November 2014. This editorial was preceded by many others in the same vein, notably "La tentation autoritaire," April 12-13, 2014; "Dangereux Poutine," April 15, 2014; "Le réembarquement de la Russie," May 9, 2014; "Succès européen, échec russe," June 28, 2014…
8 On media biases, see Mathias Reymond's "Une couverture manichéenne, des clivages inattendus. Médias français en campagne ukrainienne" (Manichean coverage, unexpected divisions : the French media's Ukrainian campaign), *Le Monde diplomatique*, August 2014.
9 "Victoria Nuland Admits: US Has Invested $ 5 Billion in the Development of Ukrainian 'Democratic Institutions'," informationclearinghouse.info/article37599.htm. And "Que l'UE aille se faire foutre," huffingtonpost.fr/2014/02/06/victoria-nuland-ukraine-union-europeenne_n_4740136.html, 6 February 2014.
10 Cf. Andrei Tsygankov, *op. cit.* Robert Kagan is now working for the most committed and most often quoted anti-Russian American think tanks, Carnegie Endowment for International Peace, and the German Marshall Fund. See also Chapter 8.
11 "Ukraine crisis: Transcript of leaked Nuland-Pyatt call", BBC News www.bbc.com/news/world-europe ".... to help glue this thing and to have the UN help glue it and, you know, Fuck the EU." The Brussels reaction has been incredibly discreet. But every Putin declaration is abundantly commented on as grotesque or dreadful. For instance his famous sentence on Chechen terrorists, when he said that he was ready to waste them in the outhouse. The full statement reads: "We are going to pursue terrorists everywhere. If they are in the airport, we will

pursue them in the airport. And if we capture them in the toilet, then we will waste them in the outhouse. ....". https://www.rt.com/politics/putin-honesty-president-magnitogorsk/

12   John Hall, "Estonian Foreign Ministry confirm authenticity of leaked phone call discussion how Kiev snipers who shot protesters were possibly hired by Ukraine's new leaders," dailymail.co.uk/.../Estonian-Foreign-Ministry-co.

13   Steve Tecklow and Oleksandr Akymenko, "Special Report: Flaws found in Ukraine's probe of Maidan massacre," reuters.com/.../us-ukraine-killings-probe-special.

14   For a very detailed scholarly study of the Maidan massacre and of the respective responsibilities of "anti-" and "pro-Maidan" snipers, see Ivan Katchanovski's "The Snipers' Massacre on the Maidan in Ukraine," School of Political Studies & Department of Communication, University of Ottawa, paper presented to the chair of Ukrainian Studies Seminar at the University of Ottawa, October 1, 2014. The Ottawa University report concludes that the massacre was a false flag operation, which was rationally planned and carried out with a goal of the overthrow of the government and the seizure of the power. Full report is available on www.academia.edu. The report by the German ARD TV channel "Zweifel an Berichten zu Maidan-Scharfschützen" is on tagesschau.de/multimedia/video/video1386106.html. http://www.spiegel.de/politik/ausland/ukraine-tote-am-maidan-nicht-nur-durch-scharfschuetzen-laut-monitor-a-963582.html

15   Chris Kaspar de Ploeg, *Ukraine in the Crossfire*, Clarity Press, Inc., 2017.

16   Jack Dion, "Pourquoi le massacre d'Odessa a-t-il si peu d'écho dans les médias ?" (Why has the Odessa massacre so little echo in the media?), marianne.net, May 6, 2014.

17   Céline Lussato, Ukraine. "Pourquoi le référendum en Crimée est illégitime" (Why the Crimean referendum is illegal), tempsreel.nouvelobs.com, March 10, 2014.

18   See the detailed juridical and historical explanation provided by Arnaud Dotezac, "L'inepsie des sanctions économiques" (The inanity of economic sanctions), *Market Magazine*, N° 118, September/October 2014.

19   See *Le Monde diplomatique* N° 721, April 2014. "On February 17, 2008, nine years after a military operation decided without UN endorsement, the Kosovar Parliament voted the independence of the Kosovo autonomous province, against the will of Belgrade, with the support of France and the United States. Russia as well as Spain refused, and still refuse, to recognize this deviation from international

20 law—as does Ukraine."
On this subject, see the very informative interview of American media analyst Edward S. Herman, "Mainstream News Coverage of Ukraine, Malaysia Airlines Flight MH17 Shows Western Propaganda Machine at Work," by Dan Falcon, on the Truthout website, October 10, 2014, truth-out.org.

21 Cf. "Crash du MH17 : de lourdes sanctions sont prises contre la Russie" (MH17 crash : heavy sanctions taken against Russia), RTS Info, Radiotélévision suisse, July 26, 2014. "Crash du MH17 : le système de missile venait de Russie, assure Kerry" (MH17 crash : the missile system came from Russia, Kerry asserts), tempsreel.nouvelobs.com, July 20, 2014.

22 For a pretty fair report of the investigation, see « Malaysia Airlines Flight 17 Most Likely Hit baby Russian-made Missile, Inquiry says, by Nicola Clark and Andrew E. Kramer, on mobile.nytimes.com, October 13, 2015. The criminal investigation team report has been released one year later, on October 2016, and has been strongly contested by russian authorities as "politically motivated" and because of a lack of impartiality of the te am, composed only by dutch, australian, belgian, malaysian and ukrainian experts. See MH17 Investigation : Moscow denounces « biased » investigation as prosecutors say missile came from Russia », by Roland Oliphant and Senay Boztas, on www.telegraph.co.uk, 28 September 2016.

23 "'I was tortured by Russian-sponsored militants,' Ukrainian woman tells UN," blog.unwatch.org, September 17, 2014. The article reports the testimony of Irina Dovgan to the Human Rights Council in Geneva about the violence she suffered at the hands of separatist militants. But the massacre of Donetsk inhabitants by the Ukrainian artillery and the tortures inflicted to separatists by the Ukrainian extreme rightwing battalions are never publicized.

24 Counterproofs put forward by the Russians are surely more credible than the vague clichés gleaned on the internet by the Americans and the Ukrainians. Russians have proposed many times to provide their surveillance radar tracking.

25 In his book *Reagan and Gorbachev: How the Cold War Ended* and his column in *The Washington Post*, "Ukraine and the United States," jackmatlock.com, February 8, 2014.

26 jackmatlock.com, "NATO Expansion: Was there a Promise?" April 3, 2014.

27 "Former US Ambassador: Behind Crimea Crisis, Russia Responding to Years of 'Hostile' US Policy," democracynow.org/2014/3/20/fmr-us-ambassador.

28	John Mearsheimer and Stephen Walt, *The Israeli Lobby and U.S. Foreign Policy*, Farrar, Straus and Giroux, 2006.
29	"Why the Ukraine Crisis Is the West's Fault," in *Foreign Affairs*, September/October 2014 Issue.
30	"The World Is Doomed by Western Insouciance", July 16, 2014, paulcraigroberts.org. In the same article, he exposes the Wolfowitz Doctrine (from the name of George W. Bush's assistant secretary of defense) against hostile powers, that is to say "any country that is not a Washington vassal." Roberts doesn't hesitate to qualify as "presstitutes" western media that relay this warmongering doctrine.
31	Martin Sieff, "Obama's Whitewashed History," April 3, 2014, The Globalist.
32	See also his commentary on the coverage of the Sochi Olympic Games in the previous chapter.
33	Stephen F. Cohen, "Patriotic Heresy..." *op. cit.*
34	"Ukraine : il est temps qu'une parole raisonnable se fasse entendre" (Ukraine: now is the time for sensible voices to be heard), Jean-Pierre Chevènement's column, *Marianne*, May 22, 2014.
35	"Ukraine, comment s'en sortir" (Ukraine, how to get out), Hubert Védrine interview, *Le Figaro Magazine*, May 2, 2014.
36	See the account made by Ukrainian writer Svetlana Alexievich, for all her positioning herself as hostile to Putin, in her book *La Fin de l'homme rouge ou le temps du désenchantement*, Arles, Actes Sud, 2013.
37	Udo Ulfkotte, *Gekaufte Journalisten. Wie Politiker, Geheimdienste und Hochfinanz Deutschlands Massenmedien lenken*, Rottenburg, Kopp Verlag, 2014. And Uwe Krüger, *Meinungsmacht. Der Einfluss von Eliten auf Leitmedien und Alpha-Journalisten – eine kritische Analyse*, Köln, Herbert von Halem Verlag, 2013.
38	Russian information channel abroad, complementary to the Sputniknews information website.
39	http://www.defense.gov/News/News-Releases/News-Release-View/Article/652687/department-of-defense-dod-releases-fiscal-year-2017-presidents-budget-proposal
40	https://www.theguardian.com/world/2014/jan/24/nsa-domestic-surveillance-condemned-republican-resoultion https://www.theguardian.com/world/2013/dec/10/surveillance-theft-worlds-leading-authors http://harvardnsj.org/2013/07/the-nsa-surveillance-controversy-how-the-ratchet-effect-can-impact-anti-terrorism-laws/
41	"Moscow and Astana remain partners despite their leaders' reservations. A seemingly innocuous statement by Vladimir Putin was

used by the Kazakhstani and foreign media to generate a controversy between Russia and Kazakhstan," by Stanislav Pritchin, September 8, 2014. in.rbth.com/world/2014/09/08/moscow_and_astana_remain_ partners_despite_their_leaders_reservations_38125.html.

42   Maxim Trudolyubov, "Russia's halfway house," *International New York Times*, October 25-26, 2014.

43   washingtonpost.com/opinions/henry-kissinger-to-settle-the-ukraine-crisis-start-at-the-end/2014/03/05/46dad868-a496-11e3-8466-d34c451760b9_story.html?utm_term=.831000dbeb86. After being staunchly anti-Russian for a long time, he also stated that "we should want reconciliation, not domination.

44   Martin Malia, *Russia under Western Eyes. From the Bronze Horseman to the Lenin Mausoleum*, Harvard University Press, 2000.

45   Two Swiss examples to illustrate this academic bias: the conferences on Ukraine of two of the 115 signatories of the September 2004 Appeal against Russia (see previous chapter), Bulgarian Ivan Krastev and former German minister Joshka Fischer, given in the fall of 2014 at the Graduate Institute in Geneva, as well as Professor Tomas Janeliunas' conference "Crisis in Ukraine and the New Expansionism of Russia: the Baltic Perspective," Global Studies, Geneva University, October 27, 2014.

Chapter Four

1   According to the tradition of *The Tale of Bygone Years*, however, Prince Vladimir was baptized a Christian in Crimea in 988 and his people the following year on a bank of the Dnieper. Cf. en.wikipedia.org/wiki/Vladimir_the_Great. See also Alain Besançon, *Sainte Russie*, Paris, Éditions de Fallois, 2012, p. 38, which states that Vladimir's conversion to the Byzantine rite of Christianity was due to the splendor of Greek liturgy, so beautiful that "we no longer knew whether we were on earth or in the sky," according to the chronicle.

2   As a matter of interest, Anne of Kiev spoke Russian, Greek, and Latin before she learned her husband's language. She signed her marriage contract in two languages, whereas illiterate Henri I flourished it with a cross.

3   See Edward N. Luttwak, *The Grand Strategy of the Byzantine Empire*, Cambridge, Massachusetts, 2009.

4   Robert G. Heath, *Le Schisme occidental de 1054. Les Francs imposent leur Credo à l'Église romaine*, Lyon, Éditions du Cosmogone, 2012.

5   *Ibid.* p.29.

6   fr.wikipedia.org/wiki/Alcuin.

7	fr.wikipedia.org/wiki/Léon_III_pape.
8	Robert G. Heath, *op. cit.*, p. 30.
9	Steven Runciman, *The Eastern Schism: A Study of the Papacy and the Eastern Churches during the XIth and XIIth Centuries*, 1955, published in French as *Le Schisme d'Orient. La papauté et les Églises d'Orient. XIe – XIIe siècles*, Paris, Les Belles Lettres, 2005. See also, Cyriaque Lampryllos, *La mystification fatale. Étude orthodoxe sur le Filioque*, Lausanne, L'Age d'Homme, 1987.
10	en.wikipedia.org/wiki/Donation_of_Constantine.
11	Steven Runciman, *op. cit.*
12	*Ibid.*
13	*Ibid.*
14	Cardinal Hergenröther, quoted in en.wikipedia.org/wiki/Azymite.
15	Steven Runciman, *op. cit.*
16	Cyriaque Lampryllos, *op.cit.*
17	*Ibid.*
18	Cf. Alexandra Merle, Le miroir ottoman. Paris, Presse de l'Université Paris-Sorbonne, 2003, p. 21. These negative cliches against Greek people are very common after the schism. And are based on very old representations inherited from the roman era.
19	en.wikipedia.org/wiki/Byzantium.
20	Cyriaque Lampryllos, *op. cit.* p. 70.
21	Natalia Narochnitskaya, *Que reste-t-il de notre victoire ? Russie-Occident : le malentendu*, Paris, Éditions des Syrtes, 2008, p. 166, and Marian Pleza, "Les relations littéraires entre la France et la Pologne au XIIe siècle," in *Bulletin de l'Association Guillaume Budé*, Vol. 1, No 1, 1983, p. 72.
22	Alexandre Tchoubarian, *La Russie et l'idée européenne*, Paris, Éditions des Syrtes, 2009, p. 49.
23	*Ibid.* p. 47.
24	See next chapter. And also Marie-Pierre Rey, *Le Dilemme russe. La Russie d'Ivan le Terrible à Boris Eltsine*, Paris, Flammarion, 2002, p. 23.
25	Ian Grey, in *Ivan III and the Unification of Russia*, New York, Collier Books, 1967, p. 39. Quoted in Marie-Pierre Rey, *op. cit.*, p. 24.
26	*Ibid.* p. 25.
27	Marie-Pierre Rey, p. 28, about L. Surius, *Histoire ou commentaire des choses mémorables advenues depuis 70 ans en ça par toutes les parties du monde*, Fr. trans. 1571. Quoted by Marie-Louise Pelus, "Un des aspects de la naissance d'une conscience européenne : la Russie vue d'Europe occidentale au XVIe siècle," in *La Conscience européenne aux XVe et XVIe siècles*, Actes du Colloque de septembre-

28 octobre 1980, ENSJF Collection, Paris, 1982.
28 Alain Besançon, "Les frontières de l'Europe," Académie des sciences morales et politiques, January 19, 2004. amsp.fr/travaux/communications/2004/besancon.htm.
29 "Orthodoxie et Occident," eglise-orthodoxe-de-france-fr.
30 Quoted by Simone Blanc, "Histoire d'une phobie : le testament de Pierre le Grand" (History of a phobia: Peter the Great's testament), *Cahiers du monde russe et soviétique*, 1968, Vol. 9, pp. 289-290.
31 René-François Rohrbacher, *Histoire universelle de l'Église catholique poursuivie jusqu'à nos jours*, Paris, 1900. The first tomes published in 1842–1849 were repeatedly reprinted and completed until the year 1900.
32 Paul Rohrbach, *Deutschland unter den Weltvölkern: Materialen zur auswärtigen Politik, 1899-1918*, quoted by Troy R. E. Paddock, *Creating the Russian Peril*, Rochester, Camden House, 2010, p. 65.
33 en.wikipedia.org/wiki/Three_Secrets_of_Fátima.
34 en.wikipedia.org/wiki/World_War_II_persecution_of_Serbs.
35 Adrian Blomfield, "Orthodox Church unholy alliance with Putin," *Daily Telegraph*, Feb. 23, 2008. telegraph.co.uk/news/worldnews/1579638/Orthodox-Church-unholy-alliance-with-Putin.html.
36 Robert G. Heath, *Le Schisme occidental de 1054*, p. 53.
37 Alain Besançon, *op. cit.* p. 13.
38 *Ibid.* p. 49.
39 Sergei Eisenstein's masterpiece, *Alexander Nevsky*, which narrates that war albeit being filmed in 1938 right in the middle of the communist era (and Nevsky by then had become an Orthodox saint), shows to what extent that traumatism has marked Russian history.
40 Alain Besançon, *op. cit.*, p. 54.
41 It is actually striking to note that Ivan the Terrible is still described as one of the most abominable rulers humankind has engendered in western chronicles because he decimated the boyars, but Cromwell, who decapitated half of the English aristocracy a century later, is presented by historians as a father of British democracy. And Louis XIV, who will do the same with his own aristocracy during the Frond, has become "the Sun King."
42 Which it managed to do briefly in 1612.
43 en.wikipedia.org/wiki/Eastern_Catholic_Churches.
44 Alain Besançon, *op. cit.* p. 63.
45 Religious violence obviously existed in Russia, but the Orthodox Church has known no Inquisition. Neither has it converted by force the peoples integrated into the Empire, who have kept on practicing their religions. As for the violence during Raskol, it targeted other

46 Orthodox, somewhat in the manner of the European religious wars. See Hannah Arendt's theses on the intellectual sterility of the American Revolution. Aside from Benjamin Franklin, there were no notable American intellectuals before the 1920s. Only literature generated world-class writers, while at the end of the 19th century, a few scientists such as Thomas Edison were beginning to distinguish themselves. Even the cinema, an eminently American product, owed much to directors and comedians issued from the 1920s-1930s emigration.

Chapter Five

1 Martin Malia, *op. cit.*
2 Raymond T. McNally, "The Origins of Russophobia in France, 1812–1830," in *American Slavic and East European Review*, April 17, 1958, quoted by Iver B. Neumann in *Uses of the Other. The East in European Identity Formation*, Minneapolis, University of Minnesota Press, Borderlines, Vol. 9, 1999, pp. 89-90.
3 For the original text, see C. L. Lesur, *Des progrès de la puissance russe depuis son origine jusqu'au XIXe siècle*, Paris, 1812, pp. 177-179, 383. In archive.org/details/desprogresdelapuissancerusse.
4 Mgr Gaume, *Le testament de Pierre le Grand ou la clef de l'avenir*, 1876. In catholicapedia.net/Documents/cahier-saint-charlemagne/documents/C347_Mgr-Gaume_Testament-de-Pierre-le-Grand_20p.pdf.
5 Cited by Iver B. Neumann, *op. cit.* p. 91.
6 Cf. Michel Cadot, *L'image de la Russie dans la vie intellectuelle française, 1839-1856*, Paris, Fayard, 1967.
7 Simone Blanc, "Histoire d'une phobie : le testament de Pierre le Grand" (History of a phobia: Peter the Great's testament), *Cahiers du monde russe et soviétique*, 1968, Vol. 9, pp. 265-293, retraces the unbelievable story of this document and shows the influence it exerted on Catholics and anti-Russian English imperialists such as David Urquhart (see the chapter on English Russophobia). persee.fr/web/revues/home/prescript/article/bude_0004-552. See also Raymond T. McNally, *op. cit.*
8 Larry Wolff, *Inventing Eastern Europe. The Map of Civilization on the Mind of the Enlightment*, Stanford, Stanford University Press, 1994, p. 365.
9 Marshall T. Poe, *A People Born to Slavery. Russia in Early Modern European Ethnography 1476-1748*, Ithaca, Cornell University, 2000, p. 19.
10 *Ibid.* p. 21.

11	*Ibid.* p. 117. See also Marie-Pierre Rey, *Le dilemme russe. La Russie et l'Europe occidentale d'Ivan le Terrible à Boris Eltsine*, Paris, Flammarion, 2002, pp. 26-27.
12	Marshall T. Poe, pp. 139-140.
13	*Ibid.* p. 129, in Konstantin Höhlbaum, *Zeitungen über Livland*, p. 121.
14	Martin Malia, *op. cit.*
15	Marshall T. Poe, *op. cit.*
16	fr.wikipedia.org/wiki/Progrès and http://fr.wikipedia.org/wiki/Civilisation.
17	Martin Malia, *op. cit.*
18	Ezequiel Adamovsky, *Euro-Orientalism. Liberal Ideology and the Image of Russia in France (c. 1740-1880)*, Oxford/Berne, Peter Lang, 2006, p. 32.
19	*Ibid.* p. 37.
20	*The Spirit of the Laws* cited by Nicolas Baverez, "Parier sur la Russie au-delà du despotisme" (Betting on Russia beyond despotism), *Le Point*, January 16, 2014. lepoint.fr>Editos.
21	Ezequiel Adamovsky, *op. cit.* p. 45.
22	Diderot was initially very favorable to Russia. He corresponded with Catherine II and met her in Saint Petersburg. The empress financed the *Encyclopédie* and acquired his library. But he changed his mind later, taking up a more "bourgeois" line.
23	Jean-Ferdinand Hoefer, *Nouvelle biographie générale*, Paris, Didot, 1851-1866.
24	Larry Wolff, *Inventing Eastern Europe*, Stanford University Press, 1994, pp. 76 and 77.
25	Hélène Carrère d'Encausse, *L'Impératrice et l'abbé : un duel littéraire inédit entre Catherine II et l'abbé Chappe d'Auteroche*, Paris, Fayard, 2003.
26	*Naufrage & tribulations d'un Japonais dans la Russie de Catherine II (1782–1792)*, introduction, translation and notes by Gérard Siary, postface by Jacques Proust, Paris, Chandeigne, 2004.
27	Ezequiel Adamovsky, *op. cit.* pp. 96-98.
28	*Ibid.* pp. 108-115.
29	Alexis de Tocqueville, *De la démocratie en Amérique*, Paris, Pagnerre, 1850.
30	Alexis de Tocqueville, *Œuvres et correspondance inédites*, Paris, Michel Lévy, 1861, pp. 237 and 245.
31	Simone Blanc, op. cit. p. 289.
32	Adolphe de Custine, *La Russie en 1839*, quoted by Martin Malia, pp. 123-124.
33	Larry Wolff, *op. cit.* p. 365.

34 E. Coeurderoy, *Hurrah !!! ou la révolution par les Cosaques*, 1852.
35 Ezequiel Adamovski, *op. cit.* p. 142.
36 K. Marx, F. Engels, *OEuvres*, Moscow, GPIL, 1957, Vol. 6, pp. 289-306, quoted by Nataliya Narotchnitskaya, *op. cit.* pp. 48-49.
37 Anatole Leroy-Beaulieu, *L'Empire des tsars et les Russes*, Paris,Robert Laffont, 1990. Quoted by E. Adamovski, *op.cit.* p. 198.
38 Adam Smith's *An Inquiry into the Nature and Causes of the Wealth of Nations* was published in 1776, and *On the Principles of Political Economy and Taxation* came out in 1817.
39 Martin Malia, *op. cit.*
40 Georges Sokoloff, *Le Retard russe*, Paris, Fayard, 2014.
41 Donald MacKenzie Wallace, *Russia. Its History and Condition to 1877*, Boston-Tokyo, J. B. Millet Company, 1877.

Chapter Six

1 Churchill's famous formula was made following the invasion of Poland by Germany and the start of the Second World War. The second quotation is from the title of an article on Russophobia written by James D. J. Brown, "A Stereotype, Wrapped in a Cliché, Inside a Caricature: Russian Foreign Policy and Orientalism," *Politics*, Vol. 30/3, 2010.
2 *The Genesis of Russophobia in Great Britain. A Study of the Interaction of Policy and Opinion*, Cambridge, Harvard University Press, 1950.
3 J. H. Gleason, *op. cit.* p. 4.
4 *Ibid.* p. 3.
5 *Ibid.* p. 5.
6 See previous chapter.
7 Obvious allusion to Peter the Great's forged testament, popularized by Napoleonic propaganda and Lesur's book in 1812.
8 Quoted by J. H. Gleason, *op. cit.* p. 43.
9 Name of the Peloponnese from the Middle Ages to the 19th century.
10 en.wikipedia.org/wiki/Greek_War_of_Independence.
11 *The Times*, October 16, 1829, and *The Herald*, October 24, 1827, quoted by J. H. Gleason, pp. 82, 83, 86 and 87.
12 *Ibid.* p. 101.
13 Eric Hoesli, *À la conquête du Caucase. Épopée géopolitique et guerres d'influences*, Paris, Éditions des Syrtes, 2006.
14 Meaning our Near East. For a detailed analysis, see Jacques Frémeaux, *La Question d'Orient*, Paris, Fayard, 2014. He shows how the confrontation of English, Russian, French, and then German and Austrian imperialisms produced, during the 19th century, "the Balkans time

	bomb," the endless wars of the Near East and the Indo-Pakistani-Afghan instability zone, in a space which stretches from Vienna to New Delhi.
15	Jimmie E. Cain, Jr. *Bram Stoker and Russophobia. Evidence of the British Fear of Russia in* Dracula *and* The Lady of the Shroud, Jefferson, McFarland & Company, 2006, p.32.
16	*Ibid.* p. 39.
17	Martin Malia, *op. cit.*
18	Henry Rawlinson, *England and Russia: A Series of Papers on the Political and Geographical Condition of Central Asia*, New York, Praeger, 1875.
19	Jimmie E. Cain, *op. cit.* pp. 70 and 178.
20	Edmund O'Donovan, *The Merv Oasis: Travels and Adventures East of the Caspian*, New York, G. P. Putnam's Sons, 1883, 2 vol.
21	Peter Hopkirk, *The Great Game: The Struggle for Empire in Central Asia*, New York, Kodansha International, 1990.
22	Arminius Vambery, *The Coming Struggle for India*, London, Cassell, 1885.
23	Jimmie E. Cain, *op. cit.* p. 82.
24	*Op. cit.* pp. 103-105. George Stoker's account is entitled *With the "Unspeakables." Or Two Years' Campaigning in European and Asiatic Turkey*, London, Chapman & Hall, 1878.
25	Felix Oinas, "East European Vampires & Dracula," *Journal of Popular Culture*, No 16, Summer 1982, quoted by Jimmie E. Cain, *op. cit.* p. 123.
26	David Glover, "Bram Stoker and the Crisis of the Liberal Subject," *New Literary History*, No 23, Autumn 1992, and Jimmie E. Cain, *op. cit.* p. 143.
27	J. H. Gleason, *op. cit.* p. 289.
28	See the next two chapters.
29	*Ibid.* p. 290.
30	See Jacques Frémeaux, *op. cit.*
31	Georges Corm, "Les causes des guerres à venir," Geneva, *Cahier du GIPRI*, No 7, 2009, p. 21.

Chapter Seven

1	Hans-Werner Bierhoff, *Person Perception and Attribution*, Berlin, Springer, 1989.
2	fr.wikipedia.org/wiki/Pertes_humaines_pendant_la_Seconde_Guerre_mondiale. Those figures, which include civilians, soldiers, and victims of the Shoah, are still contested by historians who, in

the West, are wont to point out that more than one million Soviets were reportedly victims of Stalin during the war. By comparison, total American losses on the Europe-Atlantic and Pacific fronts did not exceed 300,000 killed.
3   The First Reich, the Holy Roman Germanic Empire, created in 962 as seen in Chapter 1, was liquidated by Napoleon in 1806.
4   "You millions, I embrace you ... All people become brothers." Martin Malia, *op. cit.*
5   Johann Gottlieb Fichte, *L'État commercial fermé*, translated by D. Schulthess, Lausanne, L'Age d'Homme, 1980.
6   Martin Malia, *op. cit.*
7   wikipedia.org/wiki/Friedrich_Ratzel.
8   Troy. R. E. Paddock, *Creating the Russian Peril. Education, the Public Sphere, and National Identity in Imperial Germany, 1890-1914*, Rochester, NY, Camden House, 2010. See also on the same subject John M. Haar, "The Russian Menace: Baltic German Publicists and Russophobia in World War I Germany," Thesis, Ann Arbor Michigan, University Microfilms, 1986.
9   *Op. cit.* pp. 3-5.
10 Thomas Mann, *The Magic Mountain*, New York, Vintage International, 1992. fiction2.com/magic-mountain-online-thomas-mann?page=0,143.
11 Troy Paddock, *op. cit.* p. 28, quoting a schoolbook by Fischer, Geistbeck and Geistbeck, *Erdkunde für höhere Schulen.*
12 See Egelhaaf, *Gründzüge der Geschichte* and Frohnmeyer, *Lehrbuch der Geschichte*, quoted by Troy Paddock, pp. 41 and 45.
13 Cf. Vejas Gabriel Liulevicius, *Land War on the Eastern Front: Culture, National Identity and German Occupation in World War I*, Cambridge, Cambridge University Press, 2002.
14 fr.wikipedia.org/wiki/Heinrich_von_Treitschke.
15 Kaiser Wilhelm II, *My Memoirs, 1878-1918*, New York, Cassell, 1922, cited by Troy Paddock, p. 90.
16 Published under the title *Weltbürgerschaft und Nationalstaat*. Cf. Friedriech Meinecke, *Cosmopolitanism & National State*, translated by Robert B. Kimber.
17 Troy Paddock, *op. cit.* p. 74.
18 Vir pacificus (Hans Delbrück), "Politische Träumereien," *Preussische Jahrbücher*, 83 : 1, 1896, quoted by Troy Paddock, *op. cit.* p. 67.
19 Quoted in *Frankfurter Zeitung* of March 6, 1914.
20 Adolf Hitler, *Mein Kampf – Mon combat*, Paris, Nouvelles Éditions Latines, 1979, Tome 2, pp. 658-663 in particular.
21 Hitler was so racist that he could not even acknowledge that the

	Russians could have built their state on their own but only through the help of Germans. He makes reference to German immigrants and aristocrats who, from Teutonic Knights to Empress Catherine The Great, came from Germany to build and rule the Russian State.
22	Wikipedia provides, mostly in German and in English, fairly detailed notices on pan-Germanism, Karl Haushofer, Lebensraum, and Ostforschung.
23	It must be recalled here that the first mass massacres were committed against Russian soldiers. The first gas vans were tested on Russian prisoners before being used for the Jews. As German historian Ernst Nolte and French historian Léon Poliakov note, "in 1941 already, Himmler had said in a discourse pronounced in Wewelsburg Castle that thirty million persons had to disappear in the East." Cf. Ernst Nolte, *supra* p. 544, and Léon Poliakov, *Bréviaire de la haine. Le IIIe Reich et les Juifs*, Paris, Calmann-Lévy, 1951, p. 398. Nolte, who had little sympathy for Russia as we shall see later, admits in the same paragraph that, regarding "the death of millions of Russian prisoners during the 1941-1942 winter … the essential reason remained however Hitler's determination to weaken biologically the Russian people, a determination which had no equivalent on Stalin's side."
24	Hans-Erich Volkmann, "Das Russlandbild in der Schule des Dritten Reich," in *Das Russlandbild im Dritten Reich*, Köln, Böhlau, 1994. The author remarks that most German schoolbooks after 1945 changed nothing to their content but merely modified the borders of the two new states. Just as they did not change much either between the Second Reich and the Third.
25	Ernst Nolte, *Les Mouvements fascistes. L'Europe de 1919 à 1945*, Paris, Calmann-Lévy, 1991, p. 15.
26	Troy Paddock, *op. cit.* p. 230.
27	Ernst Nolte, *La Guerre civile européenne*, pp. 497-509.
28	*Ibid.* p. 558.
29	This is to say nothing of the fact that the US, immediately after the war, via Operation Paper Clip, took to its bosom a raft of Nazi scientists. https://en.wikipedia.org/wiki/Operation_Paperclip
30	Whatever one might think about bolshevism, the positives of this period must be admitted – indeed, many, likely a sizable proportion of Russians, look back to this period favorably, having tasted western-style capitalism. See inter alia : http://in.rbth.com/society/2016/11/07/over-50-percent-of-russians-miss-the-soviet-union_645715
31	The question of the Jewishness of the first Bolshevik leaders remains taboo. It was partly because it touched on this theme, among others, that Soviet dissident Igor Shafarevich's book was banned in France

	(Igor Chafarévitch, *La Russophobie*, Genève, Éditions Chapitre Douze, 1993).
32	On this issue, Natalia Narochnitskaya's *Que reste-t-il de notre victoire? Russie-Occident : le malentendu*, Paris, Éditions des Syrtes, 2008, is of particular interest. For an alternative relation of the liberation of Eastern Europe by the Red Army, of interest too is the account of a Polish Jewish soldier who volunteered into the Red Army and bore witness to the atrocities committed against Jews and the sufferings endured by Russian soldiers in their fight against the Nazis: Gabriel Temkin, *My Just War: The Memoirs of a Jewish Red Army Soldier in World War II*, Presidio Press, 1997.
33	Three percent of the French population.
34	Abundant manifestations of these historical "black holes" regarding Russia and her contribution to the liberation of Europe from Napoleon and Hitler's dictatorships are to be found in Mark Mazover, "War and Peace: The Fact-Check", *New York Times*, June 20, 2010, nytimes.com/2010/06/20/books/review/Mazower and D. Glanz, "American Perspectives on Eastern Front Operations in World War," Foreign Military Studies Office, 1987, fmso.leavenworth.army.mil/documents/e-front.htm. According to Paul Sanders, even serious works such as those of John Erickson (*The Road to Stalingrad* and *The Road to Berlin*), Richard Overy (*Russia's War*), Alan Clark (*Barbarossa. The Russian German Conflict*), Antony Beevor (*Stalingrad*), and Dominic Lieven (*Russia Against Napoleon: the True Story of the Campaigns of War and Peace*) make that mistake.
35	Jacques Sapir, "Un scandale," blog on russeurope.hypotheses.org/3352.
36	"The European Tragedy of 1914 and the Multipolar World of 2014: Lessons Learned," *Horizon*, No 1, fall 2014, p. 77. Dominic Lieven has somewhat moderated this abrupt affirmation in a book which puts Russia back in the history of the First World War, *La Fin de l'empire des tsars. Vers la Première Guerre mondiale et la Révolution*, Éditions des Syrtes, 2015.
37	See Chapter 4.
38	See Chapter 2 as well as Victor Youchtchenko inaugurera la statue d'Anne de Kiev le 22 juin" on www.leparisien.fr . And "Hommage franco-ukrainien pour la reine Anne de Kiev. Le Parisien, 13 mai 2013."
39	en.wikipedia.org/wiki/Bronze_Soldier_of_Tallinn
40	See the article of former Estonian prime minister Mart Laar, "Imperially Deluded," *Wall Street Journal*, May 3, 2007.
41	"Estonian SS Veterans Say They Were 'Democracy Fighters,'" Inter-

fax, July 28, 2007, and "Estonia PM Honors 'Defenders of Republic' From 'Communist Occupation,'" Itar-Tass, May 8, 2007, about those who fought alongside the Nazis. Quoted by A. Tsygankov.

42 Cf. "Filmer la guerre. Les Soviétiques face à la Shoah 1941–1946," Shoah Memorial, Paris. filmer-la-guerre. memorialdelashoah.org/sovietques/documenter/introduction.html

43 Le Livre noir du communisme (Robert Laffont, 1997) is one example. This collective work for instance takes no account of the part played by famines caused by the blockade of the USSR by western powers in the onset of the famine that decimated Ukrainian farmers in the early 1930s. Cf. Georges Corm, op. cit., p. 22. Similarly, this boycott is never taken into account in Stalin's decision to proclaim "socialism in a single country" and to radicalize revolution in order to ensure its survival, rather than trying to come to some arrangement by carrying on with NEP and betting on exchanges with western countries. The beginning of the great purges was, however, triggered by internal resistance to this program, supported by the Soviet communist party's grassroots at the time (those purges will not be denied or underestimated here). Those who are in favor of "sanctions" against Russia today because of Ukraine would do well to remember the deplorable political effects sanctions can have on the radicalization of the regime targeted. Let us remember as well Iran in the 1980s or Cuba after 1960.

44 These numbers include all military and civil deaths. USA lost 0.32% of its population but USSR 16.1 %. For the military only, the Red Army suffered 53 % of all the war casualties, the Wehrmacht 31% while Great Britain, France and USA only 1.8%, 1.4% and 1.3%. For the detailed finaldeath toll, see https://en.wikipedia.org/wiki/World_War_II_casualties

45 Poland, wishing to expand eastward for centuries, developed very intense Russophobia, first on religious and then on political grounds. Poland first dominated the Russian space, at the apex of the Polish-Lithuanian kingdom, and even briefly occupied Moscow between 1610 and 1612. Then at the end of the 18th century until 1917, the balance of power went the other way and Poland was occupied by Prussia, Austria and Russia, the latter administering the Warsaw duchy after 1815. The crushing of the nationalist revolt by Nicolas I in 1830, and the blockade of expansionist ambitions after 1920, stimulated Russophobia, which has remained fierce up until now. But contrary to the Baltic countries, the Poles are currently carrying out deep historical research which "rehabilitates" the Russian period in the 19th century and even the 1945–1990 communist period. "It is often overlooked today that Russian economic, political, and cultural achievements

were duly recognized by the Poles at the turn of the century. I would go further to suggest that much of the Polish elite recognized Russian cultural and economic superiority," writes researcher Tomasz Zaricki ("The embarrassing Russian connection. Selective memory of the Russia heritage in contemporary Poland" in *Russia's Identity in International Relations. Images, Perceptions, Misperceptions*, ed. Ray Taras, Routledge Series, 2012.) "Young scientists, notably in Poland, are also studying the accommodation of society during the communist period, a phenomenon much more widespread than resistance and oppression," writes Graduate Institute of Geneva professor André Liebich in his criticism of Anne Applebaum's latest book (*Le Temps*, January 10, 2015), quoting also American historian Padraic Kenney's works.

46 Natalia Narochnitskaya, *op. cit.* pp. 104-115.
47 *Ibid. op. cit.* p. 119.
48 Georges Corm, *La question religieuse au XXIe siècle*, Paris, La Découverte, 2006, p. 130.
49 Quoted by Gabriel Galice, *Du Peuple Nation*, Lyon, Mario Mella Éditions, 2002, p. 144.
50 See Chapter 4, "A war of religion ever since Charlemagne."
51 This is how the crimes committed by the Kosovo Liberation Army (organ trafficking in particular), though long denounced by former International Criminal Court prosecutor Carla del Ponte and Swiss investigator Dick Marty, were recognized by the international community only after Kosovo became "independent." They could not be recognized before then, since justification of Kosovo independence was sought through Serbian "crimes." Against "evil" Serbs, Kosovars absolutely had to be projected to be the good guys. Now that the independence of Kosovo is a fait accompli and the Westerners who supported it are no longer in power, the truth can be expressed.
52 On this topic, see Emmanuel Todd's gripping interview, "Ne sous-estimons pas cette formidable puissance," in *La fin du modèle allemand*, in *Books*, No 60, December 2014.

Chapter Eight

1 See Chapter 6.
2 This alliance during the Second World War proves once again that the fight against communism was not the cause but indeed a consequence of the Cold War. Or else why have made an alliance with it beforehand? Stalin was still in power and if he had changed, it was rather for the better after the sinister 1930s. Communism was thus the pretext rather

than the motive for the Cold War. Another element in that direction is that the Cold War resumed with a vengeance against Putin even though communism had been gone ten years. Lastly, the very ambiguous attitude of the United States toward China is also a contrary argument. Despites ritual denunciation of human rights violations and the reception of the Dalai Lama at the White House, the United States is putting up very well with communist China, with which it does business on a large scale. The fight against communism and the defense of freedom against autocracy, vigorous as they might have been, are thus not the determining elements of U.S. foreign policy.

3 It must be remembered that the first concentration camps were born at the initiative of the English during the Boer War in South Africa, and that the mass deportations of the modern era were initiated in the United States against the Indians in the first half of the 19th century. The indigenous peoples of Florida, Georgia, and Mississippi, such as the Seminoles, the Cherokees or the Choctaws, were deported to the dry reserves of the Great Plains where they large numbers died of famine. Same thing for Geronimo and the Apaches some time later. Hitler and the Nazis on several occasions admitted that they were inspired by those models and by the Armenian genocide, the first in modern history, to create the concentration camps and undertake the great deportation of Jews to the east that was to lead to the Final Solution. If the history of the Holocaust is now documented and known thanks to research such as that of Raul Hilberg and the books of Primo Levi, that is not the case for the history of the origins of the Armenian genocide, much more disturbing for the Anglo-Saxons.

The deportation of some peoples of the Caucasus and of Crimea Tartars by Stalin to the deserts of Kazakhstan in 1944-45 was actually very much like that of the American Indians a century before. But the first keeps being noisily mentioned by historians while the second is downplayed. Similarly, the fate of the Tartar minority in Crimea is under constant watch by Western NGOs always ready to denounce the least violation of human rights—which is a good thing—while the fate of Indian militants condemned after the Wounded Knee revolt in 1973 leaves them completely indifferent—one wonders why. Not all minorities are of equal value, it seems. The same double standard is found in the United States' massive support for the Chechnya rebellion, while the independence demands of the indigenous movement of Hawaii is ignored by the media and the NGOs. American activist Leonard Peltier's calls for liberation do not carry the same weight as those of Mikhail Khodorkovsky, Pussy Riot or Yulya Timoshenko.

4 fr.wikipedia.org/wiki/Alfred_Mahan.

5	Arnaud Leclercq, *La Russie, puissance d'Eurasie. Histoire géopolitique des origines à Poutine*, Paris, Ellipses Éditions, 2012.
6	An interview with George Kennan : Kennan on the Cold War, April 1 2009, retrieved July 30, 2009. Mentioned in the article George F. Kennan on https://en.wikipedia.org/wiki/George_F._Kennan. On Kennan's critics to Nato expansion in the 90s, see also Thomas Friedman, "Russia; Other Points of View: George Kennan's Prediction", *New York Times*, May 2, 1998.
7	*Ibid.* p. 174.
8	Cf. his book *Démocratie et totalitarisme* published that year.
9	Cf. Operation Cyclone, by which Washington supported Afghan mujahidin as early as July 1979. Brzezinski wrote a note to indicate that that American help would, in his opinion, provoke the invasion of Afghanistan by the USSR, which did happen in December. Two decades later, pleased with himself that the Soviets had exhausted themselves in the "Afghan trap," he answered the accusation of having provoked the Soviet intervention with: "We didn't push the Russians to intervene, but we knowingly increased the probability that they would." See dgibbs.faculty.arizona.edu/brzezinski_interview.
10	Martin Malia, *op. cit.*
11	See Chapter 3.
12	*The Grand Chessboard: American Primacy and its Geostrategic Imperatives*, Basic Books, 1997.
13	*Ibid.* p. xiv.
14	"La crise ukrainienne dans une perspective états-unienne et la problématique de l'empire," Note d'analyse n° 2, Geneva, GIPRI, May 25, 2014.
15	Galice, *op. cit.* p. 1 and Brzezinski, *op. cit.* p. 104.
16	Brzezinski, *op. cit.* p. 119.
17	Brzezinski, *op. cit.* p. 200.
18	At that time, some countries and experts were recommending that, with the communist threat gone, Russia integrate into NATO or achieve a tight partnership through cooperation agreements.
19	*Op. cit.* p. 202.
20	*Op. cit.* pp. 202-203.
21	Joseph S. Nye has presented his theses in several books, notably in *Soft Power: The Means to Success in World Politics*, Basic Books, 1990. He answered criticism of his soft power by launching his new concept of smart power, in *The Future of Power*, prefaced by Madeleine Albright, Public Affairs, 2011.
22	Author notably of *Jihad versus MacWorld*, Paris, Desclée de Brouwer, 1996, and *Comment le capitalisme nous infantilise*, Fayard, 2007.

23 Benjamin Barber, *Fear's Empire*, W. W. Norton, 2004.
24 Gabriel Galice, *op. cit.*, p. 3. His italics.
25 From the note of presentation of *L'Empire face à la diversité*, Paris, Hachette Littératures, 2003.
26 Anatol Lieven, "Against Russophobia," carnegieendowment.org/2000/12/31/against-russophobia-pub-626.
27 Andrei P. Tsygankov, *op. cit.* pp. 21-45 and 62-63. Most anti-Russian American think tanks have opened antennae in Brussels or finance European expertise centers linked to NATO, such as the International Crisis Group, which, under the pretext of analyzing crises, has for example supported NATO intervention in Afghanistan and unilaterally sides with Ukraine against Russia.
28 On this topic, see the preceding chapter on German Russophobia.
29 See Chapter 2. The complete list and curriculum of each of them can be found on reseauvoltaire.net: 115 personnalités atlantistes. Annuaire des signataires de la lettre ouverte "Cessons d'embrasser Poutine." Let us cite as an example the case of Ivan Krastev, a Bulgarian who used to cooperate with the Open Society Institute, the Woodrow Wilson Institute, the German Marshall Fund, and St Anthony's College in Oxford. He is a member of the Atlantic Club of Bulgaria, an advisor to the East-West Institute (New York), and the International Commission on the Balkans, and president of the Center for Liberal Strategies (Sofia). His medal collection includes the main anti-Russian think tanks in Washington. He regularly tours European universities to give conferences. His articles are also found in numerous journals affiliated to the Project Syndicate.
30 An Open Letter To The Obama Administration From Central And Eastern Europe, Radio Free Europe, July 16, 2009. It was signed by Valdas Adamkus, Martin Butora, Emil Constantinescu, Pavol Demes, Lubos Dobrovsky, Matyas Eorsi, Istvan Gyarmati, Vaclav Havel, Rastislav Kacer, Sandra Kalniete, Karel Schwarzenberg, Michal Kovac, Ivan Krastev, Alexander Kwasniewski, Mart Laar, Kadri Liik, Janos Martonyi, Janusz Onyszkiewicz, Adam Rotfeld, Vaira Vike-Freiberga, Alexandr Vondra, and Lech Walesa.
31 See preceding chapters, in particular Chapter 6 on English Russophobia.
32 See Gordon M. Hahn, *Russia's Islamist Threat*, New Haven, Yale University Press, 2007.
33 They did exactly the same in Syria's proxy war with the so-called moderate rebels, trying to portray the Al-Qaida jihadists and other Salafist warriors as freedom and democracy fighters against Assad the "butcher".
34 Bruce P. Jackson, "Democracy in Russia," *The Weekly Standard*, Feb-

ruary 18, 2005.
35 Anne Appelbaum, "The New Iron Curtain," *The Washington Post*, November 24, 2004. *Gulag: A History,* Doubleday, 2003.
36 His assassination in Moscow on February 27, 2015 immediately triggered yet again the usual thesis of an operation ordered by the Kremlin. Cf. Jacques Sapir's "Assassinat à Moscou" (Murder in Moscow) published on March 1, 2015 on his blog RussEurope (russeurope.hypotheses.org/3509).
37 Senator Clinton Introduces Legislation to Honor Cold War Veterans with a Military Service Medal By: Hillary Clinton Date: June 20, 2005 Location: Washington, DC.. As Americans get ready to celebrate Independence Day, Senator Hillary Rodham Clinton introduced the Cold War Medal Act of 2005 today to honor those veterans who fought for our freedom. Senator Clinton's legislation establishes a Military Service Medal to honor the contribution of Americans who served their nation admirably during the Cold War.
38 William Safire, "Strategic Dilemma," *The New York Times*, December 1, 1994, and "Putin's Creeping Coup," February 9, 2004.
39 By 2017, Georgia hadn't yet succeeded in joining NATO despite strong US support. But the membership procedure to admit Georgia is still underway. On September 7, 2016, Jens Stoltenberg, NATO secretary general, estimated that Georgia had improved its democratic institutions in a way that had helped Georgia to get closer to NATO. Laurenta Lagnea "La Géorgie 'se rapproche' d'une possible adhésion à l'OTAN,» www.opex360.com, Sept, 8, 2016. Montenegro joined NATO in 2016. Ukraine is still knocking at the door.
40 Daniel Dombey, "US chooses awkward time to transform NATO," *Financial Times*, January 24, 2005. See also *The Quadrennial Defense Review*, United States Department of Defense, February 6, 2006. On Victoria Nuland, see also Chapter 3.
41 Finally, at the end of its mandate, the Obama Administration decided to deploy a USD 800milion missile shield in Romania on May 12, 2016. A similar base is planned in Poland, provoking an angry response from Russia. In the meantime, the greatest NATO military exercise in Europe since the end of the Cold War, Operation Anaconda, took place in Poland and Baltic countries. See Robin Emmott, "US activates Romanian missile defense site, angering Russia", May 12, 2016, mobile.reuters.com.
42 See for example Robert F. Amsterdam, *Financial Times*, May 1, 2006; Edward Lucas, *The Times*, February 5, 2008; Leon Aron, american. com, January 8, 2007; Anders Aslund, *The Moscow Times*, July 5, 2003; Michael McFaul, *Weekly Standard*, November 7, 2003; Zbig-

niew Brzezinski, *Wall Street Journal*, May 20, 2004; wsj.com/articles/SB109563224382121790.

43   See https://gabbard.house.gov/news/press-releases/video-rep-tulsi-gabbard-introduces-legislation-stop-arming-terrorists

Chapter Nine

Readers who wish to go into this at greater depth can refer to Felicitas Macgilchrists' bibliography, *Journalism and the Political: Discursive tensions in news coverage of Russia*, Amsterdam/Philadelphia, John Benjamins Publishing Company, 2011.

2   Quoted by Thierry Herman, "Aucun mot n'est innocent," Edito/Klartext, *Journal des journalistes suisses*, No 5, 2014.

3   *Ibid.*

4   Cf. "The Israel Project for security, freedom and peace." The document specifies that it is the property of The Israel Project and is not for distribution or publication.

5   In 2015 China became the world's largest producer of photovoltaic power, at 43 GW installed capacity.[1][2] China also led the world in the production and use of wind power and smart grid technologies, generating almost as much water, wind, and solar energy as all of France and Germany's power plants combined. https://en.wikipedia.org/wiki/Renewable_energy_in_China

6   Fictitious names, given as exemplars.

7   https://en.wikipedia.org/wiki/The_Moscow_Times

8   See chapters 2 and 3.

9   See Chapter 2.

10   theguardian.com/world/2004/sep/08/usa.russia.

11   Let us state here that there are numerous transparent NGOs with ethics beyond reproach, such as Paul Watson's Sea Shepherd.

12   Bernard-Henri Lévy and George Soros, "Save the New Ukraine," *International New York Times*, January 28, 2015. The coincidence may be fortuitous but it is striking. It did not escape observers who remarked in the following days that it was very clever to want to have American weapon deliveries to Ukraine paid for by the Europeans. Angela Merkel and François Hollande's determination to propose a "last chance" peace plan to Russia may not be without bearing on that maneuver, the European Union no longer being able to drop Ukraine even if it had to be armed at a price by the United States. As for the American hawks, they would have killed three birds with one stone: selling weapons, having them paid for by others, and maintaining in the heart of Europe a durable conflict, on the Afghan or Iraqi model, which would result in a tightening of

ranks within NATO under exclusive American command. The United States' supervision of Europe would come out reinforced for years.

13 See in particular Teun van Dijk, "Opinions and Ideologies in the Press," in Allan Bell & Peter Garrett, *Approaches to Media Discourse*, Oxford Blackwell, 1998. And also *Ideology: A Multidisciplinary Approach*, London, Sage, 1998.

14 OSCE: Organization for Security and Co-Operation in Europe.

15 Reports in *Le Temps*, February 9, 2015. Ten days later, the same correspondent drew a very sympathetic portrait of Nadiya Savchenko, "a Ukrainian heroine interned in a Russian asylum" waiting to be judged for complicity in the murder of two Russian journalists. You have to read half of the article to learn that the woman is in reality a former helicopter pilot in Afghanistan, who volunteered into the extreme-rightwing Aidar Battalion, and that her mission was to adjust Ukrainian artillery shots at the Donbass population.

16 At this stage, the fact that these accusations may be groundless does not matter. The thirst for information is such that no one has time to check. It is only at a later stage, when the soufflé falls flat, that accusations must be backed up with real or fabricated "proofs," blurred satellite "photographs," anonymous videos, or assumed trajectory patterns.

17 See Chapter 3.

18 Not to mention the fact that 90% of Crimeans are ethnic Russians, not Ukrainians.

19 *The Daily Telegraph*, January 3, 2006, quoted by Felicitas Macgilchrist, *Journalism and the Political. Discursive tensions in news coverage of Russia*, p. 46.

20 See Chapter 3.

21 Peter Ulf Moller, "Russian Identity as an East-West Controversy Outlining a Concept," *Slavica Lundensia*, No 19, 1999.

22 See Chapter 2.

23 Jean-Christophe Emmenegger, "'Chars russes' en Ukraine : un exemple de désinformation jusque dans la presse suisse" ('Russian tanks' in Ukraine: an example of disinformation even in the Swiss press) on the Swiss website arretsurinfo.ch, February 1, 2015

24 We do mean invasion. We do not dispute the fact that there is Russian aid to separatists, in sundry hardware and in volunteers, just as there is massive western military support (in terms of military and political advisors and non-lethal equipment). Ukraine seething with weapons and being the eighth weapon producer in the world, weapon deliveries are secondary. The only question is to know if American military aid, carefully ignored by the western press, is more legitimate than Russian aid.

25 On February 17, 2014 on a French-speaking radio, a former Georgian minister of the Saakashvili government commented on the war in Ukraine, as if he was a neutral and disinterested expert. Yet another example of politically-orientated selection of sources.
26 Srdja Trifković, "Understanding Western Russophobia," *Liberty*, Official Publication of the Serbian National Defense Council of America, June 2014.
27 See https://en.wikipedia.org/wiki/Barack_Obama_on_mass_surveillance.
28 "Descriptions of two kinds of other" in *The Wall Street Journal*, September 7, 2004. In Felicitas Macgilchrist, *Journalism and the Political. Discursive tensions in news coverage of Russia*, pp. 147 and 152.
29 Macgilchrist, ibid.
30 Andrei Tsygankov, *op. cit.* p. 9.
31 See in particular Zbigniew Brzezinski's articles, already cited, and Edward Lucas's book, *The New Cold War. The Future of Russia and the Threat to the West*, published in 2008, or that of Janusz Bugajski, *Cold Peace: Russia's New imperialism*, published in 2004.
32 Tsygankov, op. cit.. pp. 179-181.
33 It consists of a list completed with examples given by Ezequiel Adamovsky, *op. cit.* pp. 265 and 266.
34 Felicitas Macgilchrist, *op. cit.* p. 214.
35 Two of the researchers contacted for this book confirmed to me that they had to abandon their research after failing to obtain financing for a thesis subject outside of prevailing trends.
36 *The Independent*, February 15, 2006, *ibid.* p. 187, quoting Dejevsky.
37 Nelson Mandela, *Long Walk to Freedom*, Hachette Digital, London, 1994.
38 washingtonpost.com/opinions/the-obama-doctrine-leading-from-behind/2011/04/28/AFBCy18E_story.html?utm_term=.08de43ed79c5
39 "Preserving Ukraine's Independence, Resisting Russian Aggression: What the United States and NATO Must Do," by S. Pifer, S. Talbott, Ambassador I. Daalder, M. Yurnoy, Ambassador J. Herbst, J. Lodal, Admiral J. Stavridis, and General C. Wald, brookings.edu/research/reports/2015/02/ ukraine-independence-russian-aggression.
40 Lamberto Zannier, "Ukraine and the Crisis of European Security," *Horizons*, No 2, winter 2015, pp. 44-58.
41 James Stavridis and Karl-Theodor zu Guttenberg, "Who is to Blame?" *Horizons*, No 2, winter 2015, pp. 60-72. Their names are also in the list of 115 Atlanticists already mentioned.
42 In this context, let us mention a talk with the former president of

Benin, Mathieu Kérékou. In 2001, on the occasion of an audience in his presidential palace in Cotonou, he made, before our dumbfounded delegation, a long sermon on the Dollar God, showing how America, by printing "In God we trust" and the eye of God on the one-dollar banknote, had divinized its currency and achieved the fusion of God and Mammon, imposing its cult to the entire earth.

43 China and North Korea are in that list, but for different reasons. North Korea is at the heart of the axis of evil, whereas China looks more like the partner-adversary to be handled with kid gloves.

Chapter Ten

1 Cf. Christian Ruby, "Des mythologies quotidiennes aux métarécits: mythologies du XXIe siècle" (From daily mythologies to metanarratives: mythologies of the 21st century), a conference of the Association française pour l'information scientifique, May 10, 2001, pseudosciences.or.Articles. See also Raison Présente, "Mythologies du XXIe siècle," Paris, École Polytechnique, No 136, 2001.

2 *Ibid.*

3 Interview with Isabelel Lasserre, *Le Figaro*, quoted by www.lescrises. fr under the title "Avec leurs sanctions contre la Russie, les Etats-Unis ont enfreint le droit international" (With their sanctions against Russia, the USA has violated international law)

4 The exceptions were books such as Christine Ockrent's *Les Oligarques*, whose wraparound band heralded *Le système Poutine* (The Putin system), published by Robert Laffont; a reprint of Tania Rakhmanova's *Au Cœur du pouvoir russe. Enquête sur l'Empire Poutine*, La Découverte; editor Hélène Blanc's *Goodbye Poutine. Union européenne-Russie-Ukraine*, Gingko; and Michel Eltchaninov's *Dans la tête de Vladimir Poutine*, Solin/Actes Sud. All four portray Putin in the darkest terms. The only work that is neutral and factual is that of a military expert, Frédéric Pons, soberly entitled *Poutine* and published by Calmann-Lévy. Unlike the others, it does not show either photomontage blackening the character or excessively dramatize his supposedly threatening side.

5 As an example, here is a short list of contemporary French editorial production: *La Russie selon Poutine* ; *Poutine, l'itinéraire secret*; *Poutine et l'Eurasie* ; *La mystérieuse ascension de Poutine. Des rangs du KGB au naufrage du Koursk* ; *Vladimir Bonaparte Poutine*; *Prisonnier de Poutine* ; *Les Espions russes de Staline à Poutine* ; *Vladimir Poutine et le poutinisme* ; *Monsieur Poutine, vous permettez? La mystérieuse ascension de Vladimir Poutine* ; *Le KGB au pouvoir.*

6   *Le système Poutine* ; *Poutine échec et mat !* *De Raspoutine à Poutine*. *Les hommes de l'ombre* ; *Poutine, l'homme sans visage* ; *Le fantôme de Staline* ; *Le labyrinthe de Poutine*. *La face sombre du président russe* ; *L'antisémitisme en Russie de Catherine II à Poutine* ; *Poutine, le parrain de toutes les Russies* ; *Russie de Staline à Poutine* ; *Poutine et le Caucase* ; *L'empire sans limites*. Marie Mendras, *Russie, l'envers du pouvoir*, Paris, Odile Jacob, 2008, in *Le Monde* of December 11, 2008.

7   See https://en.wikipedia.org/wiki/Public_image_of_Vladimir_Putin. For further debunking of standard mainstream media on Russia, see off-Guardian, and in particular https://off-guardian.org/2015/07/26/damned-lies-and-statistics-the-guardian-view-on-putins-mysterious-popularity/

8   Meanwhile, the operation of polishing the image of the new Ukrainian regime has begun. Books glorifying it are published (Alain Guillemoles, *Ukraine : le réveil d'une nation*, Les Petits Matins, 2015). At the same time, discreetly, the first cracks in the new regime, which seems to be as corrupt as the old one, are beginning to show. Cf. "La justice suisse enquête contre un proche du Président Porochenko" (Swiss justice is investigating a close friend of President Porochenko's), *Le Matin Dimanche*, March 22, 2015.

9   As shown in Chapter 6.

10   Mikhail Chichkine, "Ce que Poutine, roi du mensonge, prépare à l'Europe" (What Liar King Putin is cooking up for Europe), *Le Temps*, October 15, 2014.

11   Guy Sorman, "Poutine le Terrible" (Putin the Terrible), *L'Hebdo*, December 4, 2014, and Christophe Passer, "L'internationale poutinienne," *L'Hebdo*, July 24, 2014.

12   Guy Sorman, "Poutine et l'invasion barbare" (Putin and the barbarian invasion), *L'Hebdo*, August 7, 2014.

13   *Op. cit.* It is by scrutinizing Putin's brain that the author claims to find "the imperialist strategy of the Russian president."

14   John J. Mearsheimer, "Why the Ukraine Crisis Is the West's Fault," *Foreign Affairs*, September/October 2014. foreignaffairs.com/articles/russia-fsu/2014-08-18/why-ukraine-crisis-west-s-fault.

15   Anne Prigent, "Poutine et Asperger : un diagnostic peu vraisemblable," in sante.lefigaro.fr, February 6, 2015. The news is all over the European and American press sites, with often less caution than in *Le Figaro*'s title.

16   That of Frédéric Pons, *op. cit.*, who mentions official documents at the end of the book.

17   See http://en.kremlin.ru/events/president/transcripts/24034

18	"Discours de Poutine en 2007 à Munich" (Putin's speech in 2007 in Munich), arretsurinfo.ch; cf. Barack Obama's "Russia is a country that produces nothing. For an insight, read "Obama contre Poutine: les mots tuent" (Obama versus Putin: words kill), on alterinfo.net.
19	John Mearsheimer, *op. cit.* For a more empathic portrait of the man Putin, an interesting testimony is that of an American woman who lived for decades in Saint Petersburg: Sharon Tennison, "Poutine raconté par Sharon Tennison," *The French Saker*, September 19, 2014. Thevineyardsaker.fr.
20	In this context, one of the most effective and most often used techniques of denying Putin legitimacy consists in accusing the Russian president of trying to foment war abroad in order to keep his power or reinforce it further. For this purpose, it is enough to call on complacent ideologues generally attached to some American "laboratory of ideas" in Moscow. Emmanuel Grynszpan, *Le Temps* correspondent in Moscow, mentions, for example, two of them in his February 11, 2015 article about "Vladimir Putin's strategy in Ukraine." This is no doubt a factor to evaluate. But the idea that George Bush invaded Iraq for domestic political reasons and oil interests, that Barack Obama is attacking Russia to calm the Republicans and promote the election of a Democrat in the next presidential elections, or that François Hollande is sending troops to Africa to consolidate his flagging authority in France, is never evoked. This tactic has the double advantage of discrediting the targeted head of State by presenting him as a selfish person concerned only with his own interests and trying to divide the country through promoting a divergence between public opinion and government.
21	Cf. Chapter2, Victoria Nuland's impatience because of the US$5 billion earmarked by the United States for the destabilization of Ukraine remaining without effect until the coup in February 2014. In an interview granted to the Swiss newspaper *Le Temps* (February 11, 2015), John Mearsheimer confirms that "there are proofs of the implication of the United States in the removal from office of Ukrainian president Victor Yanukovich in February 2014."

The role of American or American-supported NGOs, such as the CANVAS organization derived from the Otpor movement in Serbia, in the launching of the orange revolutions has been well documented. To avoid any polemics, let us mention an article by Véronique Soulé in the very Russophobic *Libération* entitled "L'ombre de Washington sur la révolution orange à Kiev" (Washington's shadow over the orange revolution in Kiev), June 22, 2005. Also Sara Flounders, "Des milliers d'ONG financées par les USA à l'assaut de la Russie" (Thousands of US-financed NGOs storming Russia), cairn.info; "Euromaidan : le rôle des Américains et des Européens" (Euromaidan: Americans and Europeans' role), arretsurinfo.ch; Andrew Wilson, "Ukraine's Orange Revolution, NGOs and the Role of the West," *The Cambridge Review of International Affairs*, Vol. 19, No 1, 2006; Gerald Sussman and Sascha Krader, "Template Revolutions: Marketing US Regime Change in Eastern Europe," Westminster Papers in Communication and Culture, Vol. 5, No 3, pp. 91-112.

22 iwm.at/read-listen-watch/transit-online/under-western-eyes.

23 Valentina Feklyunina, "Constructing Russophobia." Raymond Taras, *Russia's Identity in International Relations. Images, Perceptions, Misperceptions*, London/New York, Routledge, 2013, pp. 91-109.

24 Martin Malia, *op. cit.*

25 David Foglesong, *The American Mission and the Evil Empire*, Cambridge, Cambridge University Press, 2007.

26 Richard Pipes, "Russia's Past, Russia's Future," *Commentary*, June 1996, as well as "A Nation with One Foot Stuck in the Past," *London Sunday Times*, October 20, 1996. On Richard Pipes and his influence on historiography and the making of the anti-Russian myth, see also Chapter 10.

27 Anatol Lieven, *op. cit.*

28 Geoffrey Hosking, *Russia and the Russians. A History from Rus to the Russian Federation*, London, Allen Lane, 2001.

29 Putin has always said he would defend Russian minorities mistreated in neighboring countries but he has never conquered territories. The problems of Transnistria, Abkhazia and South Ossetia existed before his time. Ditto for Chechnya. We saw that the Georgian war was triggered by the Saakashvili government, according to the official reports of OSCE and of the Council of Europe. As for Crimea, we also saw that the organization of a referendum on independence followed the February 22 coup d'état in Kiev and the new Kiev regime's decision to forbid the use of the Russian language. And that that consultation followed a referendum on the same subject organized by independent Ukraine in January 1991 before being invalidated under American pressure.

30 See the works of Alena Ledeneva, *How Russia really works. The Informal Practices That Shaped Post-Soviet Politics and Business*, Ithaca, Cornel University Press, 2006. And "The Genealogy of *krugovaya poruka*: force trust as a feature of Russia political culture," in I. Markova, *Trust and Democratic Transition in Post-Communist Europe*, Oxford University Press, 2004.

31 Iver B. Neumann, *Uses of the Other: The East in European Identity*

> *Formation*, Minneapolis, University of Minnesota Press, p. 103.
32 See the excellent works of Iver B. Neumann, *op. cit.*, and Larry Wolff, *Inventing Eastern Europe. The Map of Civilization on the Mind of Enlightenment*, Stanford University Press, 1994.

Conclusion

1 Kevin Rudd, "China's Long View: European Imperialism in Asia," *The Globalist*, January 30, 2015.
2 See http://www.alternet.org/grayzone-project/how-white-helmets-became-international-heroes-while-pushing-us-military
3 http://russia-insider.com/en/despicable-russian-sappers-are-vandalizing-aleppo-clear mines-graffitti/ri18395. For Laurent Fabius' declarations in 2012 about the "good job" done by Al-Nusra, see "Des Syriens demandent réparation à Fabius", www.lefigaro.fr, December 10, 2014.
4 Stephen Lee Myers, "Trump's Love for Putin: a Presidential Role Model", September 8, 2016, on www.mobile.nytimes.com.
5 Ashley Parker and David E. Sanger, "Donald Trump Calls on Russia to Find Hillary Clinton's Missing Mails", July 27, 2016. Mobile.nytimes.com
6 Kelvin Poulsen,"How the US Hobbled its Hacking Case Against Russia and Enabled Truthers", Jan. 6, 2017. ww.thedailybeast.com.
7 "Partisan electoral interventions by the great powers : Introducing the PEIG Dataset", by Dov. H. Levin, Carnegie-Mellon University, USA, in *Conflict Management and Peace Science*, 1-19, 2016. http://content.time.com/time/subscriber/article/0.3309.984833-1.00.html
8 The whistleblower and former employee of swiss bank UBS Bradley Birkenfeld has been awarded a 104 millions USD grant by the IRS for denouncing the fiscal fraud of his employer. But Edgar Snowden is still exiled in Russia and is facing a trial for treason. See their personal notices on wikipedia.

INDEX

A

Abe, Shinzo, 70
Abbott, Tony, 93
Abkhazia, Abkhazians, 29, 60, 63, 89, 297
Adamovski, Ezequiel, 22, 139-175, 302
Admont, Adalbert, 124, 238
Adrianople Treaty, 186-189
Afghanistan, 13, 179, 183, 189, 190, 252, 254, 260, 270, 198, 308, 321
Africa, 40, 177
Albright, Madeleine, 257, 267
Alcuin, 109-110
Alexander I, 157
Alexander II, 28, 171, 182, 215
Algeria Algerians, 28
Al-Jazeera, 57, 91
Al-Qaida, 52, 53, 270
Amalarius, Bishop, 110
American Conservative Blog, 86
American Enterprise Institute, 286, 301
American Revolution, 155
Ancient and Moderns, Quarrel, 149-151
Ann, Princess of Russia/Kiev, 105-106, 231
Anna, Kofi, 265
Anti-Communism, 245-254
Anti-Americanism, 75
Anti-Multiculturalism, 75
Anti-Semitism, 21, 37, 236, 242

Applebaum, Anne, 270
Argentina, 251
Armenia, Armenians, 29
Armeyskov, Sergey, 25
Aryans, 220
Ashton, Catherine, 78
Assad, Bachar, 85
Assange, Julian, 52, 94
Associated Press, 41
Attali, Jacques, 87
Autocracy, 172, 332, 337

B

Bad Guy, 180
Balkans, 124, 179, 198-200, 206, 217, 237
Baltic States, 123, 127, 141, 237, 275, 318
Barbarity, 138, 174, 191, 214, 216, 228, 298, 300, 303
Barber, Benjamin, 263
Barroso, Jose Manuel, 288
Basayev, Shamil, 44, 46, 55, 191
Bashkortostan, Bashkirians, 42, 43
Basileus, 118
BBC, 64
Beethoven, 209
Bedell Smith, Walter, 162
Belgium, 290
Bennetts, Marc, 67
Bentham, Jeremy, 152
Berezovsky, Boris, 273, 274
Berlin, 13
Bernhardi, Friedrich von, 218

Besançon, Alain, 127, 131
Beslan, 44, 47, 49, 50, 53, 57, 292
Bethmann Hollweg,Chancellor, 219
Bidder, Benjamin, 67
Biden, Joe, 83, 92, 239, 267, 307
Bierhoff, Hans-Werner, 205
Bildt, Carl, 275
Bin Laden, Usama, 53, 57, 118, 321
Bismarck, Otto von, 194, 200, 211
BNP Paribas, 95
Bolshevism, Bolsheviks, 242
Bomhover, Christian, 142
Bonald, Louis de, 157
Bonner, Elena, 55
Bronze Soldier, 231-232, 300, 323, 332
Brzezinski, Mark, 50
Brzezinski, Zbigniew, 50, 61, 252, 256-260, 267, 268, 275, 318
Britain, Great, British Empire, 32, 40, 54, 134, 138, 141, 169, 172, 176-204, 234
Brookings Institution, 266, 287
Brown, James DJ, 176
Burke, Edmund, 157
Bush, George H.W., 18, 68
Bush, George, W, 33, 56, 57, 77, 82, 84, 88, 118, 271, 296, 306
Byzantium, Byzantine Empire 17, 19, 103-135, 184, 187, 237, 270, 312, 326, 336
Byzantinism, 121, 122

C

Cabot Lodge, Henry, 244
Caesaropopery, 121, 326
Cain, Jimmie E., 195-199
Capitalism, 263-265
Carrère d'Encausse, Hélène, 87, 156
Carter, Jimmy, 252, 260
Catherine II, 32, 149, 152, 156, 206, 326
Catholicism, 127, 132, 143, 161
Carnegie Endowment for International Peace, 53, 266, 275

Carolingians, 111, 112
Castlereagh, Robert Stewart, Count, 182
Caucasus, 52, 55, 59, 61, 179, 203, 286
Central African Republic, 29, 89
Central Asia, 183-205, 259
Central Europe, 13, 255, 268, 272, 331, 332
Chad, 29
Chappe d'Auteroche, Jean, 155
Charlemagne, 17, 19, 103, 109-125, 312, 313
Charlie Hebdo, 22, 57
Chechnya, 13, 16, 27, 30, 44, 46, 49, 52, 56, 58, 73, 89, 191, 270, 275, 286, 297, 301, 321
Cheney, Dick, 272
Chevènement, Jean-Pierre, 87
Chili, 251, 253
China, 76, 173, 177, 183, 193, 334, 335, 336
Chinese Communist Party, 91
Christaller, Walter, 222
Christendom, 75, 103, 117, 136, 144
Churchill, Winston, 93, 141, 176, 202
CIA, 52
Circassia, Circassians, 188-190
Clinton, Bill, 88, 257
Clinton, Hillary, 180, 262, 268, 270, 271, 271, 300, 306, 318, 339, 340
Coeurderoy, Ernest, 163
Cohen, Stephen, J., 22, 34, 68, 86, 227
Cohen, Richard, 306
Cold War, 68, 84, 86, 93, 248, 251, 254, 262, 271, 303, 307, 318
Colonialism, 183, 314
Condorcet, 150
Connolly, Arthur, 189
Considérant, Victor, 163
Constantine Donation, 113-116, 120, 140
Constantinople, See Byzantium

Corm, Georges, 203-204, 236
Cossacks, 142, 215
Crimea, 14, 3940, 64, 79, 89, 96, 130, 232, 280, 289, 290, 291
Crimean War, 166, 184, 192-196
Crusades, 121, 143, 254
Cuba, 91, 308, 321
Cultural Gradient, Theory, 171-175
Curzon, George, Lord, 199
Custine, Astolphe de, 131, 158-162, 325
Cyprus, 194, 195
Czar, Cesar, 124, 129, 140, 143, 148, 177
Czechoslovakia, 31, 61, 89, 164, 233, 235
Czech Republic, 93

D

Daily Mail, 338
Darwin, Charles, 211
Democrats, 35, 53, 180, 256, 268, 339, 341
Demonization, 313-320
Despotism, Russian, 139-175, 250, 268-270, 325
Dictatorship, 253-255
Diderot, Denis, 149, 152, 154, 157
Dirk, Teun van, 287
Donbass, Donetsk, 34, 40, 64, 81, 82, 89, 92, 94, 96, 305, 332
Doping, 70-71
Dostoyevsky, Fyodor, 103
Dracula, 193, 196-199, 318
Drang nach Osten, 122, 207, 220
Dugin, Alexander, 320

E

Eckstein, Karl, 41
Economist, The, 63, 270, 317
Egypt, 190
Elias, Norbert, 215
Eltchaninoff, Michel, 319
Erdogan, Recep Tayip, 70

Estonia, 97, 142, 217, 232
European Union, 13, 18,39, 50, 62, 76, 77, 82, 88, 89, 179, 180, 226, 39, 258, 287, 310, 315, 331
Expansionism, 139, 141, 191, 268-270, 337
ExxonMobil, 272

F

Fabius, Laurent, 80
Fatima Prophecy, 129-130
FAZ, 90, 218, 225
Felgenbauer, Pavel, 47
Fichte, Johann Gottlieb, 208, 209
FIFA,71
Figaro, Le, 61
Filioque, 106, 108-125
Financial Times, 73, 78
Finland, 61, 63, 127
Fischer, Joshka, 62
Foglesong, David, 325
Forbes, 273
Foreign Affairs, 248, 302
Foucault, Michel, 328
Fox News, 72, 90
France, French, 40, 137-175, 176, 200, 241, 290, 308, 323
Frankenstein, 196
Franks, 109-112
Freedom House, 267, 271, 301
Fukuyama, Francis, 97
Fule, Stefan, 307
Furet, François, 325

G

Gabbard, Tulsi, 275
Galice, Gabriel, 257, 263
de Gaulle, Charles, 17, 31
Gaume, Jean-Joseph, Bishop, 140
Geneva, 11, 12, 265
Georgia, Georgians, 13, 58, 59, 60, 62, 63, 72, 88, 89, 91, 124, 141, 228, 260, 267, 281, 293, 297, 301, 323, 324, 328, 336

German Marshall Fund, 267
Germany Germans, 30, 40, 83, 90, 114, 133, 144, 171, 200, 205-240, 241, 243
Gershenkron, Alexander, 174
Ghibellines, 118
Giscard d'Estaing, Valéry, 315
Gleason, John H., 22, 178-182, 199, 202
Glover, David, 198
Goethe, Johann Wolfgang, 208
Golden Horde, 129, 133
Gorbachev, Mikhail, 80, 82, 84, 254
Great Game, 176-204, 234
Greece, 184, 185
Greek Church, 104-125
Grimm, Hans, 220
Grozny, 27
Guantanamo, 27, 52, 270
Guardian, The, 47, 67, 71, 286, 305
Guelphs, 118
Guizot, François, 137, 158, 159
Guttenberg, Karl-Theodor von, 307
G20, 92

H

Hacking, Russian, 341, 342
Haeckel, Ernst, 211, 212
Harvard University, 178, 260
Hastings, Max, 73
Haushofer, Karl, 220, 245
Havel, Vaclav, 268, 331, 332
Haxthausen, August von, 163
Hearst, William Randolph, 243
Heath, Robert, 111
Heberstein, Sigismond von, 143, 144
Hegel, Georg Wilhelm Friedrich, 209-210
Helsinki Agreement, 251-253
Henry the First, 105
Herder, Johann Gottfried, 207, 208
Heritage Foundation, 286
Herzen, Alexander, 163
Historiker Streit, 225-229
Hitler, Adolf, 61, 63, 84, 170, 220, 221, 228, 234, 235, 242, 271, 327
Hohenzollern, 211
Hölderlin, Friedrich, 208
Holbrooke, Richard, 50, 267
Hollande, François, 57, 70
Hollywood, 229, 253
Holocaust, 236
Holy Spirit, 108, 115
Hoover Institution, 53, 266
Hopkirk, Peter, 195
Horejsova, Alistair, 73
Hudson Institute, 266
Huffington Post, 61
Hugo, Victor, 334
Hungary, Hungarians, 104, 127, 143
Huntington, Samuel, 97, 260
Hussein, Saddam, 60, 84, 136, 294, 313, 314

I

IMF, 33
Imperialism, 183, 212, 337
Ingushetia, 44, 45, 47
Iran, 252, 321
Iraq, 299, 308, 321
Islamism, Islamists 14, 46, 89, 270
Islamic State, 56
Islamophobia, 37
Israel, 31, 83, 85, 231, 264, 281, 282
Ivan III, 124-126, 142, 146
Ivan IV The Terrible, 131, 144, 313
Ivory Coast, 29
Izetbegovic, Alija, 14

J

Jackson, Bruce P., 270
Jamestown Foundation, 47
Japan, Japanese, 155-157, 207, 235, 247
Jews, 205, 224, 281, 308
Justinian, Emperor, 109

K

Kadyrov, Ramona, 270
Kagan, Robert, 77, 267, 285
Kant, Emmanuel, 207, 208, 211
Kapuscinski, Ryszard, 27
Kaspar de Ploeg, Chris, 78
Kasparov, Garry, 301
Kazakhstan, 96
Kennan, George F., 84, 139, 141, 247-249
Kennedy, Paul, 261
Kerry, John, 81
KGB, 74, 130, 305
Khodorkovsky, Mikhail, 34, 272, 273, 274, 281, 292, 302
Khrushchev, 227, 228
Kiev, 79, 90, 124
King, Martin Luther, 28
Kipling, Rudyard, 193, 202, 265
Kissinger, Henry, 97, 241
Klebnikov, Paul, 273, 274
Klemperer, Victor, 279
Kohl, Helmut, 130
Korean War, 73
Kosovo, Kosovars, 31, 80, 89, 238
Kramer, Michael, 341
Kraus, Karl, 310
Krauthammer, Charles, 306
Kremlin, 30, 55, 61, 63
Krieg-Planque, Alice, 281
Kristol, William, 61, 267
Kundera, Milan, 331, 332

L

Lacy Evans, Colonel George de, 187
Lamprillos, Cyriaque, 119
Latvia, 97
Laughland, John, 305
Lavelle, Peter, 303
Lavrov, Sergey, 300
Lawrence of Arabia, 203
Lebensraum, 207-240
Leibniz, Gottfried Wilhelm, 138, 149, 151-153, 169
Leroy-Beaulieu, Paul and Anatole, 166-175
Lesur, Charles-Louis, 139
Lessing, Gotthold Ephraim, 207
Lévy, Bernard-Henri, 80, 287
LGBT, 65, 67, 164, 287
Libération, 63, 74
Libya, 204, 306, 308
Lieven, Anatol, 53, 73, 227, 265
Lippmann, Walter, 248
Lithuania, 123, 147
Litvinenko, Alexander, 274
Lord of the Rings, 313
Louis XIV, 137, 146
Louis XV, 139
Lugar, Richard, 272, 302
Lustenberger, Ruedi, 44
Libya, 29, 52, 89

M

Mably, Gabriel, Abbot, 149, 154
McCain, John, 53, 267, 270, 271, 307, 323
McCarthyism, 241, 249, 250
Macedonia, 13
Macgilchrist, Felicitas, 22, 296, 303
Mackinder, Halford, 200, 245-248, 256
Mahan, Alfred, 200, 244, 256
Maidan Square, 17, 64, 78, 79, 83, 307, 338
Malaysian Airlines, MH 17, 40, 75, 81, 289, 290
Mali, 29, 89
Malia, Martin, 97-99, 137, 140, 145, 172, 193, 210, 227, 255, 324
Mandeville, Laure, 61
Mann, Thomas, 213, 214
Mao Tse Tung, 335
Marianne, 79
Markiewicz, Samuel, 47
Marx, Karl, Marxism, 155, 163, 164, 211, 250
Maskhadov, Aslan, 52, 55

Matlock, Jack, 82
Maximilian, German Emperor, 143
Mearsheimer, John, J., 83, 84, 321
Medvedev, Dmitri, 61, 130, 271
Mein Kampf, 220
Meinecke, Friedrich, 215-217
Mendras, Marie, 316
Merkel, Angela, 70, 239, 319
Metternich, Klemens Wendell von, 182, 190
Meynen, Emil, 222
Michelet, Edmond, 131
Milosevic, Slobodan, 314
Mirabeau, Count Honoré Riqueti, 150
Moldavia, Moldova, Moldovans, 29, 88, 127, 185
Müller, Peter Ulf, 292
Monde, Le, 61, 316
Monde diplomatique, Le, 22, 87
Mongols, 125, 132, 147, 161
Monroe Doctrine, 86
Montesquieu, 153-157
Moscow, Muscovy, 48, 53, 56, 125, 137, 142, 147, 153, 161, 177
Moscow Times, The, 285
Mussolini, Benito, 50, 275

N

Nagorno-Karabakh, 29
Naïr, Samir, 263
Napoleon I, 148, 177, 182, 200, 241
Napoleon III, 166
Naryshkin, Sergey, 44
Nation, The, 68
National Endowment for democracy, 79, 267, 271, 301
National Democratic Institute, 267
NATO, 13, 27, 50, 60, 81-87, 92, 179, 237, 239, 249, 257, 258, 271, 272, 280, 294, 299, 307, 312, 314, 336
Navalny, Alexey, 81
Nazism, Nazis, 29, 40, 84, 87, 170, 205, 212, 221, 228-232, 247, 325, 327
Nemtsov, Boris, 270
Neumann, Iver, 22
Nevski, Alexander, 123, 131
New York, 46
New York Times, 41, 50, 53, 61, 63, 64, 68, 69, 87, 266, 271, 319
Newsweek, 317
Nicaea, 108, 111, 117
Nicolas I, Tsar, 141, 158, 185, 187, 191, 205, 313, 318
Nicolas II, Tsar, 206
Nolte, Ernst, 224-227, 325
NSA, 94
Nuland, Victoria, 76-80, 83, 239, 307
Nye, Joseph S., 260-263

O

Obama, Barack, 33, 159, 180, 262, 282, 291, 296, 306, 340
Odessa, 182
O'Donovan, Edmund, 195
Oinas, Felix, 197
Open Society, 78, 265
Orange Revolution, 78
Orthodoxy, 104-135, 142, 184, 326
OSCE, 43, 251-253, 288, 307
Ossetia, Ossetians, 29, 58, 59, 60, 63, 89, 94, 295, 297
Ostforschung, 207, 219-221
Ottomans, 115, 119, 185, 191

P

Paddock, Troy R.E., 22, 213, 223
Palmerston, Henry John Temple, Lord, 171, 200
Papacy, Pope, 110, 112, 120, 128
Paet, Urmas, 78
Patriot Act, 52
Paul, Ron, 34, 35
Pavlovian reflex, 39-71, 72
Pence, Albrecht, 219
Perle, Richard, 286, 302
Peter the Great, 32, 137, 139-141,

148, 151, 154, 183, 187, 215, 313, 326
Philippines, 243
Philotheus of Pskov, 125, 136
Photius, Patriarch, 113, 128
Pilger, John, 39
Pilsudski, Josef, Marshal, 233
Pinochet, Augusto, 12
Pipo, Jacob, 143
Pipes, Richard, 267, 326
Pitt, William, 182
Plater-Zyberk, Henry, 54
PNAC, 50, 52, 77, 267, 302
Poe, Marshall, T., 22, 145
Poland, Poles, 104, 127, 128, 130, 132, 133, 143, 147, 182, 227, 232, 233, 318
Politkovskaya, Anna, 30, 48, 55
Pradt, Dominique-Georges-Frédéric de, 141, 158
Pravy Sektor, 40
Primakov, Yevgeny, 268
Protocols of Elders of Zion, 140
Prussia, 177, 190, 209,
Pussy Riots, 65, 71, 91
Putin, Vladimir, 19, 33, 50, 53, 55, 61, 69, 72, 74, 75, 76, 81, 84, 88, 92, 93, 98, 106, 131, 145, 223, 271, 273, 280, 297, 298, 313-320
Pratt, Geoffrey, 76

Q

Qaddafi, Muammar, 85

R

Radio Free Europe/Radio Liberty, 47, 50, 90, 303, 339
Rabbe, Alphonse, 158
Raleigh, Sir Walter, 246
Ranke, Otto, 211
Ratzel, Friedrich, 212, 218, 220, 245
Rawlingson, Henry, 194
Reclus, Elisée, 167

Red Army, 12, 232, 252
Red Specter, 98
Reagan, Ronald, 12, 252, 253
Reich, First, Second, Third, 103-136, 207-240
Reimer, Joseph-Ludwig, 218
Renaissance, 133, 134, 147
Representatives, House of, 35
Republicans, 35, 53, 256
Reuters, 78
Rhodes, Cecil, 193
Ricardo, David, 170
Ribbentrop-Molotov Pact, 225, 234, 235
Riezler, Kurt, 238
Robert, Cyprien, 163
Roberts, Paul Craig, 34, 85
Rohrbach,Paul, 129, 215, 216
Rohrbacher, René François, Abbot, 128
Romaios, 122
Roman Catholic Church, 105-1 35
Roman Empire, 19, 103, 142
Roman Germanic Empire, Holy, 106-119, 123, 124, 207, 211, 312
Rome, 104, 108, 121, 125
Romney, Mitt, 272
Roosevelt, Theodore, 243
Rossier, Simon, 67
Rostow, W.W., 174
Rousseau, Jean-Jacques, 154
Rudd, Kevin, 334, 335
Rumsfeld, Donald, 286
Runciman, Steven, 114
Russia Today, 57, 90
Russian Commune, 165-167

S

Saakashvili, Mikheil, 58, 59, 60, 72, 270, 271, 295, 338
Sachs, Jeffrey, 255
Safire, William, 271
Said, Edward, 38, 324
Salt Lake City, 65

Sanctions, Economic, 43
Sanders, Bernie, 339
Sanders, Paul, 22, 322, 323
Sapir, Jacques, 87
Saudi Arabia, 53, 203
Saviano, Roberto, 29
Saudi Arabia, 291, 308
Schelling, Friedrich Wilhelm Joseph von, 209
Schiemann, Theodor, 215, 216
Schiller, Friedrich von, 208
Schism, Great, 103-135, 144, 336
Sebastopol, 80
Serbia, Serbs, 13-15, 185, 260, 291
Serfdom, 170, 171
Siegfried, Martin, 86
Slavery, 144, 170
Slovakia, Slovaks, 31
Smith, Adam, 170
Snow White, 19
Snowden, Edward, 52
Sochi Olympic Games, 64-69, 283, 287
Soft Power, 106, 260-26, 306-308
Sokolniki, Michel, 139
Sokoloff, Georges, 174
Solari, Pietro, 126
Solzhenitsyn, 11, 15, 16, 72, 252
Soros, George, 78, 79, 252, 265, 267, 287
Soviet Union, 119, 173, 201, 233, 234, 235, 245-249, 250, 254, 336
Spiegel, der, 62, 66, 317
Spykman, Nicholas, 246-248, 256
Srebrenica, 14
Stalin, Joseph, 32, 61, 63, 84, 139, 173, 201, 205, 223, 227, 229, 235, 271, 325, 328
Stallone, Sylvester, 198
Stiglitz, Joseph, 328
Stockholm, 95
Stoker, Bram, 193, 196-199, 202, 265, 318
Strahlenberg, Philip Johan von, 148
Strong, Josiah, 243

Sweden, 147
Switzerland, 41, 43, 85, 99
Sydney Morning Herald, 66
Syria, 29, 52, 89, 188, 204, 275, 295, 298, 308, 321

T

Tagliavini, Heidi, 60, 62, 63
Tannenberg, Richard, 218
Taras, Raymond, 22
Tasmania, 28
Tatitchev, Vassili, 148
Tea Party, 76, 323
Temps, Le, 75, 81
Testament of Peter The Great, Forged), 139-141,
Teutonic Knights, 123, 131, 147, 237
Texas, 34
Third Rome, 125, 131
Time Magazine, 229, 317
Times, The, 73
Timoshenko, Yulia, 16
Tocqueville, Baron Alexis, 137, 158, 159, 168
Todd, Emmanuel, 239
Totalitarianism, 253-256
Tracy, Benjamin, 244
Transnistria, 63, 94
Treitschke, Gotthard von, 215, 216
Trinity Holy, 115
Truman, Harry, 139, 141, 249
Trump, Donald, 35, 180, 339-340
Tsygankov, Andrei P., 22, 49, 266-279, 299-305
Turkey, Turks, 93, 134, 139, 185, 188-200
Turner, Frederick Jackson, 243
Tyutchev, Fyodor, 36

U

Uberlingen crash, 19, 41, 44
UK, See Britain
Ukraine, 11, 14, 16, 21, 31, 39, 40, 63, 72-99, 124, 201, 204, 227,

390 | CREATING RUSSOPHOBIA

237, 257, 260, 264, 267, 271, 280, 287, 293, 294, 295, 301, 312, 321, 336, 338
Ulfkotte, Udo, 90
United Nations, UNO, 45
United States, 18, 32, 36, 57, 60, 82, 86, 93, 94, 133, 134, 159, 170, 179, 180, 201, 202, 203, 235, 241-276, 280, 308, 310, 331
Urquhardt, David, 189-205
USA Today, 319

V

Vambery, Arminius, 195, 200
Védrine, Hubert 87
Venezuela, 91
Vermont, 15
Victoria, Queen, 194, 195
Vienna Treaty, 185
Vladimir, Prince, 104, 129
Voltaire, 31, 138, 149, 151-153

W

WADA, 70-71
Wagner, 210
Walesa, Lech, 268
Wall Street Journal, The, 63, 87, 241, 266, 296
Wallace, Donald Mackenzie, 174, 175
Washington Post, 50, 61, 68, 69, 85, 87, 90, 266, 271
Weber, Max, 211, 215
Webster, Andrew, 66
White Helmets, 337
Wiener Zeitung, 67
Wikileaks, 180, 339, 340
Will, Mariusz, 26
Wolf, Hieronymus, 122
Woolsey, James, 53, 267, 286
World Anticommunist League, 11
World Bank, 33
WWI, 211, 240, 327
WWII, 32, 44, 170, 205, 229, 231, 233, 240, 247

X

XI, Jinping, 70
Xinhua, 291

Y

Yad Vashem, 231
Yalta, 201, 202, 232
Yatsenyuk, Arseniy, 285
Yeltsin, Boris, 15, 16, 55, 152, 255, 270, 327, 341
Yanukovych, Viktor, 39, 76, 78, 79, 84, 95
Yevtushenko, Vladimir, 96
Yugoslavia, 13, 89, 130, 238
Yushchenko, Viktor, 78

Z

Zannier, Lambert, 307
Zhukov, Marshall, 229, 235
Zurich, 41